3/04

BLIND MEMORY

Blind memory

Visual representations of
slavery in England and America
1780–1865

MARCUS WOOD

ROUTLEDGE

First published in the United States in 2000 *by*
Routledge Inc
29 West 35th Street,
New York, NY 10001–2299, USA
www.routledge-ny.com

Routledge edition published by special arrangement with
Manchester University Press, Oxford Road,
Manchester M13 9NR, UK

ISBN   0–415–92697–1   *cloth*
        0–415–92698–x   *paperback*

Library of Congress Cataloging-in-Publication Data
Wood, Marcus
   Blind memory : visual representations of slavery in England and America / Marcus Wood.
      p. cm.
   Previously published: Manchester, UK;
      Includes bibliographical references and index.
   ISBN 0–415–92697–1 (cloth) - - ISBN 0–415–92698–X (pbk.)
      1. Slavery in art. 2. Art, English. 3. Art, Modern—18th century—England. 4. Art,
Modern—19th century—England. 5. Art, Modern—18th century—North America. 6. Art,
Modern—19th century—North America. I. Title.

N8243.S576 w66 2000
704.9´49326–dc21   00–020839

Printed in Great Britain

TO ROSE AND MIRANDA

Contents

List of illustrations   *page* ix

Acknowledgements   xix

1 Introduction   1

2 The irrecoverable: representing the 'middle passage'   14

3 Rhetoric and the runaway: the iconography
   of slave escape in England and America   78

4 Beyond the cover: *Uncle Tom's Cabin*
   and slavery as global entertainment   143

5 Representing pain and describing torture: slavery,
   punishment and martyrology   215

6 Conclusion   292

   Bibliography   309

   Index   333

List of illustrations

Figures

1.1 Thomas Clarkson del., 'Abolition Map' (1808). From
*The History of the Rise, Progress and Accomplishment of the
Abolition of the African Slave-Trade by the British Parliament.*
Library Company of Philadelphia   *page* 2

2.1 P. P. Burdett del., E. Rooker sculpt., *A View of the Custom House*
(1750). National Museums and Galleries on Merseyside,
Transatlantic Slavery Gallery, Liverpool   17

2.2 Society for the Abolition of the Slave Trade, London Committee,
Description of a Slave Ship (April 1789). Kingston Upon Hull,
City Museums and Art Galleries, Wilberforce House   18

2.3 Society for the Abolition of the Slave Trade, Plymouth Committee,
*Plan of an African Ship's Lower Deck with Negroes in the proportion
of only One to a Ton* (January 1789). Bristol Record Office   20

2.4 Thomas Stothard, 'The Voyage of the Sable Venus, from Angola
to the West Indies' (1793). From Bryan Edwards, *History Civil
and Commercial, of the British Colonies in the West Indies.*
Bodleian Library, Oxford   22

2.5 Society for the Abolition of the Slave Trade, London Committee,
made by Josiah Wedgwood, abolition seal, 'Am I not a man and a
brother?' (1788). British Museum, Department of Ceramics   22

2.6 Anon., after Sir J. Noel Paton, *Capture of a Slave Ship* (1915).
Private Collection   24

2.7 Anon., model of the slave ship *Brookes* (1790). Kingston Upon
Hull, City Museums and Art Galleries, Wilberforce House   28

2.8 Anon., 'Plan of Noah's Ark' (1668). From John Wilkins, *An essay
towards a real character, and a philosophical language.* Bodleian
Library, Oxford   30

2.9 Anon., 'Arche de Noé' (1776). From *Supplement À L'Encyclopédie,
ou Dictionaire Raisoné des Sciences, des Artes et des Métiers.*
Bodleian Library, Oxford   31

2.10 Anon., 'Plan of Slave Ship' (*c.* 1800). From Isaac Taylor, *Scenes
in Africa for the Amusement and Instruction of Little Tarry at
Home Travellers.* Library Company of Philadelphia   33

2.11 Anon., 'Dhow with Slaves' (1875). From G. L. Sulivan, *Dhow
Chasing in Zanzibar Waters.* Library Company of Philadelphia   34

2.12 Anon., 'African Resistance Continues' (1995). From
S. E. Anderson, *The Black Holocaust for Beginners* (New York,
Writers and Readers Publishing, 1995)   35

2.13 Sista Phyllis M. Bowdwin, 'Who Deserves It More Than You?' (1995). Advertisement back page, *The Black Holocaust for Beginners* (New York, Writers and Readers Publishing, 1995)   35

2.14 Anon., dust jacket for Barry Unsworth, *Sacred Hunger* (London, Penguin, 1992)   36

2.15 John Raphael Smith, *The Slave Trade* (1789). After George Morland, *The Execrable Human Traffic (1788)*. British Museum, Department of Prints and Drawings   37

2.16 Anon., 'United States Slave Trade 1830' (1830). From Benjamin Lundy, *Genius of Universal Emancipation*. Private Collection   37

2.17 William Blake, 'A Negro hung alive by the Ribs to a Gallows' (1798). From John Stedman, *Narrative of a Five Years' Expedition Against the Revolted Negroes of Surinam*. Bodleian Library, Oxford   39

2.18 Anon., after Auguste Biard (1860). Front cover to Richard Drake, *Revelations of a Slave Smuggler*. Library Company of Philadelphia   44

2.19 Anon., after Auguste Biard, 'Scene on the African Coast' (1860). From Richard Drake, *Revelations of a Slave Smuggler*. Library Company of Philadelphia   46

2.20 J. M. W. Turner, *Slaver Throwing Overboard the Dead and Dying, Typhon Coming On*, detail (1840). Museum of Fine Arts, Boston   47

2.21 Peter Brueghel, *Landscape with Fall of Icarus* (1567). Musées Royaux des Beaux-Arts de Belgique, Brussels   48

2.22 Theodore Gericault, *Severed Limbs* (1818). Musée Fabre, Monpellier   50

2.23 Anon., 'Deluge' (1675). From Athanasius Kircher, *Arca Noe*. Bodleian Library, Oxford   54

2.24 Benjamin Robert Haydon, *The Anti-Slavery Society Convention* (1840). National Portrait Gallery, London   61

3.1 Anon., 'runaway' male (*c.* 1840). From L. Johnson and Co., *Type Specimen Book*. American Antiquarian Society, Worcester, Massachusetts   81

3.2 Anon., 'runaway' female (*c.* 1840). From L. Johnson and Co., *Type Specimen Book*. Newberry Library, Chicago   81

3.3 Hamatt Billings, 'Spitting on a runaway advertisement' (1853). From *Uncle Tom's Cabin* (Sampson Low). Bodleian Library, Oxford   86

3.4 Anon., 'runaway' advertisement (1842). From the *Anti-Slavery Almanac*. American Antiquarian Society, Worcester, Massachusetts   88

3.5 Anon., 'runaway' advertisement (1838). Private Collection   88

3.6 Anon., advertisement for male runaway servant (January 1818). From the *New York Gazette*. Reproduced from Clarence P. Hornung and Fridolf Johnson, 220 *Years of American Graphic Art* (New York, George Brazillier, 1976)   89

3.7 Anon., advertisement for female runaway servant (January 1818). From the *New York Gazette*. Reproduced from Clarence P. Hornung and Fridolf Johnson, 220 *Years of American Graphic Art* (New York, George Brazillier, 1976)   89

3.8   Anon., specimen page (1840). From L. Johnson, *Specimens of Printing Types*. Newberry Library, Chicago   90

3.9   Anon., specimen page (1840). From L. Johnson, *Specimens of Printing Types*. Newberry Library, Chicago   91

3.10 Anon., 'Carrying the War into Africa' (*c.* 1850). Library of Congress, Washington, D.C.   93

3.11 Anon., 'The Fugitive Slave' (July 1837). From *The Anti-Slavery Record*. American Antiquarian Society, Worcester, Massachusetts   93

3.12 Richard Ansdell, *Hunted Slaves* (1861). National Museums and Galleries on Merseyside, Walker Art Gallery   96

3.13 Anon., 'F is for Fugitives' (1864). From Iron Gray, *The Gospel of Slavery*. American Antiquarian Society, Worcester, Massachusetts   98

3.14 Anon., 'Letting the Oppressed Go Free' (April 1857). From *The Legion of Liberty*. American Antiquarian Society, Worcester, Massachusetts   98

3.15 Anon., 'The Fugitive Slave' (April 1833). From *The Slave's Friend*. American Antiquarian Society, Worcester, Massachusetts   98

3.16 Anon., 'The Slave Paul' (April 1838). From *The American Anti-Slavery Almanac*. American Antiquarian Society, Worcester, Massachusetts   98

3.17 Anon., *The Fugitive's Song* (1845). American Antiquarian Society, Worcester, Massachusetts   103

3.18 Anon., *The Resurrection of Henry Box Brown at Philadelphia* (1850). American Antiquarian Society, Worcester, Massachusetts   104

3.19 Anon., 'Song sung by Mr. Brown on being removed from box' (1849). American Antiquarian Society, Worcester, Massachusetts   109

3.20 Anon., *Noah in the Ark* (*c.* 200). Bodleian Library, Oxford   111

3.21 Anon., *Effects of the Fugitive-Slave-Law* (1850). American Antiquarian Society, Worcester, Massachusetts   111

3.22 Anon., 'On Receiving the Box' (1851). From *The Liberty Almanac*. American Antiquarian Society, Worcester, Massachusetts   112

3.23 After William Hogarth , *The Four Stages of Cruelty* (1751), plate 1, 'The First Stage of Cruelty' (1843). From *The Legion of Liberty*. American Antiquarian Society, Worcester, Massachusetts   114

3.24 Anon., 'Howard and His Squirrel' (1849). From *Cousin Ann's Stories for Children*. American Antiquarian Society, Worcester, Massachusetts   115

3.25 Anon., 'Henry Box Brown' (1849). From *Cousin Ann's Stories for Children*. American Antiquarian Society, Worcester, Massachusetts   115

3.26 Anon., double portrait of Henry Bibb (1849). From *Narrative of the Life and Adventures of Henry Bibb,* frontispiece. Author's Collection   119

3.27 Anon. (1849). From *Narrative of the Life and Adventures of Henry Bibb*. Author's Collection   121

3.28 Anon., 'For Liberia' (1839). From the *Boston Anti-Slavery Almanac*. American Antiquarian Society, Worcester, Massachusetts   121

3.29 Anon., 'Squire's Office' (1843). From *Narrative of the Life and Adventures of Henry Bibb*. Author's Collection   123

3.30 Anon., 'The First Scene of British Emancipation' (1843). From *The Legion of Liberty*. American Antiquarian Society, Worcester, Massachusetts   123

3.31 Anon. (1843). From *Narrative of the Life and Adventures of Henry Bibb*. Author's Collection   125

3.32 Anon., 'The Flogging of Females' (1835). From *The Anti-Slavery Record*. Author's Collection   125

3.33 Anon., 'Scenes in the City Prison of New York. Stephen Downing' (1835). From *The Anti-Slavery Record*. Author's Collection   125

3.34 Anon., 'Bibb and Malinda Escaping' (1843). From *Narrative of the Life and Adventures of Henry Bibb*. Author's Collection   128

3.35 Anon., 'The Bloodhound Business' (1857). From *The Suppressed Book About Slavery*. American Antiquarian Society, Worcester, Massachusetts   128

3.36 Anon., 'Bibb and Malinda Captured' (1843). From *Narrative of the Life and Adventures of Henry Bibb*. Author's Collection   129

3.37 Anon., 'Running Away' (1857). From *The Suppressed Book About Slavery*. American Antiquarian Society, Worcester, Massachusetts   129

3.38 Anon., portrait of Olaudah Equiano (1789). From *The Interesting Narrative of Olaudah Equiano*   131

3.39 Anon., double portrait of Henry Bibb (1849). From *Narrative of the Life and Adventures of Henry Bibb*, frontispiece, detail. Author's Collection   132

4.1 V. S. W. Parkhurst, card game *Justice* (1852). Strong Museum, Rochester, New York   147

4.2 Anon., 'Little Scipio: a favourite plaything' (1834). From *The Oasis*. American Antiquarian Society, Worcester, Massachusetts   154

4.3 James Gillray, *Barbarities in the West Indies* (1791). British Museum, Department of Prints and Drawings   155

4.4 James Gillray, *Philanthropic Consolations on the Loss of the Slave Bill* (1796). British Museum, Department of Prints and Drawings   156

4.5 James Gillray, *Cymon and Iphigenia* (1796). British Museum, Department of Prints and Drawings   157

4.6 Richard Newton, *The Slave Trade* (1788). British Museum, Department of Prints and Drawings   157

4.7 Richard Newton, *A Real San Culotte* (1792). British Museum, Department of Prints and Drawings   158

4.8 Richard Newton, *The Full Moon in Eclipse* (1797). Andrew Edmunds Collection, London   158

4.9 Richard Newton, *The First Interview* (1797). Andrew Edmunds Collection, London   159

4.10 Isaac Cruikshank, *The Abolition of the Slave Trade* (1792). British Museum, Department of Prints and Drawings   160

4.11 Anon., *The Rabbits* (1792). British Museum, Department of Prints and Drawings   162

4.12 George Cruikshank, *I was barn in St. Kitts* (c. 1805). Victoria and Albert Museum, London   162

4.13 George Cruikshank, *Puzzled Which to Choose!! or the King of Timbuctoo offering one of his Daughters* (1818). British Museum, Department of Prints and Drawings   163

4.14 George Cruikshank, *Probable Effects of Over Female Emigration* (1844). Author's Collection   164

4.15 George Cruikshank, *The Court at Brighton* (1819). British Museum, Department of Prints and Drawings   164

4.16 William Heath, *A Pair of Broad Bottoms* (1810). British Museum, Department of Prints and Drawings   165

4.17 George Cruikshank, *The New Union Club of 1819* (1819). British Museum, Department of Prints and Drawings   165

4.18 William Hogarth, *Election Entertainment* (1755). British Museum, Department of Prints and Drawings   166

4.19 James Gillray, *Union Club* (1801). British Museum, Department of Prints and Drawings   167

4.20 George Cruikshank, *The New Union Club of 1819,* detail (1819). British Museum, Department of Prints and Drawings   168

4.21 James Gillray, *The Apotheosis of Hoche* (1798). British Museum, Department of Prints and Drawings   168

4.22 George Cruikshank, *The New Union Club of 1819*, detail (1819). British Museum, Department of Prints and Drawings   170

4.23 George Cruikshank, *The New Union Club of 1819*, detail (1819). British Museum, Department of Prints and Drawings   170

4.24 George Cruikshank and William Hone, *Peterloo Medal* (1819). Bodleian Library, Oxford   172

4.25 George Cruikshank, *Plantation Scene* (1829). Rhodes House Library, Bodleian Museum, Oxford   172

4.26 George Cruikshank, 'De Black Dollibus' (1847). From *The Comic Almanack*. Author's Collection   173

4.27 George Cruikshank, 'The Banquet of the Black Dolls' (1847). From *The Comic Almanack*. Author's Collection   173

4.28 George Cruikshank, 'The Country Here is Swarmin' with the Most Alarmin' Kind o Varmin' (1846). From *The Comic Almanack*. Author's Collection   174

4.29 George Cruikshank, advertising broadside for Cassell's edition of *Uncle Tom's Cabin* (1852). Victoria and Albert Museum, London   175

4.30 George Cruikshank, 'Mose and Pete foil Shelby' (1852). From *Uncle Tom's Cabin* (Cassell). Bodleian Library, Oxford   176

4.31 George Cruikshank, mock advertisement for *A Slap at Slop* (1821). Bodleian Library, Oxford   177

4.32 George Cruikshank, 'Lucy's Suicide' (1852). From *Uncle Tom's Cabin* (Cassell). Bodleian Library, Oxford   178

4.33 George Cruikshank, 'The poor girl, homeless, friendless, deserted and gin-mad' (1848). From *The Drunkard's Children*. Bodleian Library, Oxford   179

4.34 Anon., 'Slave mother suicide' (1817). From Jessey Torrey, *A Portraiture of Domestic Slavery in the United States*. Library Company of Philadelphia   181

4.35 Hamatt Billings, plagiarisms, 'What's this Dinah?' and 'I had to put it away in a kind of garret, and it cried itself to death' (1867). From *Uncle Tom's Cabin*, (Ward Locke and Co.). Author's Collection   184

4.36 Anon., 'What now! Why these folks have whipped Prue to death' (1867). From *Uncle Tom's Cabin* (Ward Locke and Co.). Bodleian Library, Oxford   184

4.37 Anon., 'Oh Uncle Tom! What funny things you *are* making there' (1852). From *Uncle Tom's Cabin* (Clarke and Co.). Bodleian Library, Oxford   187

4.38 Anon., *A Black Lecture on Language* (1827). Yale University Library, Lewis Walpole Library, Farmington, Connecticut   187

4.39 Anon., 'Eva Teaching the Alphabet' (*c.* 1855). From *Little Eva the Flower of the South*. American Antiquarian Society, Worcester, Massachusetts   189

4.40 George Cruikshank, 'There sat Tom' (1852). From *Uncle Tom's Cabin* (Cassell). Bodleian Library, Oxford   189

4.41 Anon., 'Obeah' (*c.* 1860). From the *Illustrated Police News*. British Library, Periodicals Division, Colindale, London   191

4.42 George Thomas, 'Topsy' (1853). From *Uncle Tom's Cabin* (Cooke and Milford). Author's Collection   193

4.43 George Thomas, 'Topsy's Conversion' (1853). From *Uncle Tom's Cabin* (Cooke and Milford). Author's Collection   194

4.44 Anon., 'Topsy Takes a Lesson' (*c.* 1860). From *Topsy's Frolics or Always in Mischief*. Opie Collection, Bodleian Library, Oxford   195

4.45 'Uncle Tom's Cabin', interior with model figures (photograph, 1996). Photographed by author, The Uncle Tom's Cabin Museum, Ontario   198

4.46 Anon., *Strong's Dime Caricatures. – No. 3 South Carolina Topsey* [*sic*] *in a Fix* (1861). American Antiquarian Society, Worcester, Massachusetts   199

4.47 Anon., *Strong's Dime Caricatures. – No. 3 South Carolina Topsey* [*sic*] *in a Fix*, detail (1861). American Antiquarian Society, Worcester, Massachusetts   199

4.48 Anon., *The Contraband Schottishe* (1853). Library of Congress, Washington, D.C.   200

4.49 Anon., 'Haley Confounded' (1853). From *Uncle Tom's Cabin* (Cooke and Milford). Author's Collection   201

4.50 C. R. Milne, *A Dream Caused by a perusal of Mrs. H. Beecher Stowe's popular work Uncle Tom's Cabin* (1853). Library of Congress, Washington, D.C.   202

4.51 Jacques Callot, *The Temptation of St Anthony*, second version (1635). British Museum, Department of Prints and Drawings   203

5.1 Anon., 'Our Peculiar Domestic Institutions' (1840). From *The Anti-Slavery Almanac*. American Antiquarian Society, Worcester, Massachusetts   218

5.2 Anon., punishment collar (*c.* 1750). National Galleries and Museums on Merseyside, Transatlantic Slavery Gallery   220

5.3   Anon., punishment collar, displayed with perspex cut-out
      representation of slave head. National Galleries and Museums on
      Merseyside, Transatlantic Slavery Gallery   220
5.4   Anon., 'Another Mode of Punishment' (1837). From *Narrative of
      the Adventures and Escape of Moses Roper*. Library Company of
      Philadelphia   221
5.5   Anon., 'A woman with iron horns and bells on' (1838). From
      Narrative of the Adventures and Escape of Moses Roper. Bodleian
      Library, Oxford   221
5.6   Arms of Sir John Hawkins (*c.* 1888). From Mary W. S. Hawkins,
      Plymouth Armada Heroes: The Hawkins Family. Bodleian Library,
      Oxford   222
5.7   Wooden slave yoke, Livingstone Collection. Reproduced in
      David Livingstone and the Victorian Encounter with Africa
      (London, National Portrait Gallery Publications, 1996).
      Photograph Colin Mills   223
5.8   Alexander Anderson, *Injured Humanity* (1805). American
      Antiquarian Society, Worcester, Massachusetts   224
5.9   Alexander Anderson, *Injured Humanity*, detail 'Enlarged View'.
      American Antiquarian Society, Worcester, Massachusetts   225
5.10 Alexander Anderson, *Injured Humanity*, detail 'Mouth piece'.
      American Antiquarian Society, Worcester, Massachusetts   225
5.11 Anastasia (*c.* 1990). Photograph by the author   226
5.12 Shrine to Anastasia, Church of the Rosary of Our Lady of the
      Black People, Salvador, Bahia (1994). Photograph by the author   227
5.13 Shrine to Anastasia, Church of the Rosary of Our Lady of the
      Black People, Salvador, Bahia (1994). Photograph by the author   227
5.14 Anon., 'Items used in the slave trade' (1808). From Thomas
      Clarkson, *The History of the Rise, Progress and Accomplishment
      of the Abolition of the African Slave-Trade by the British
      Parliament*. Library Company of Philadelphia   228
5.15 William Blake, 'Death of Neptune' (1796). From John Stedman,
      *Narrative of a Five Years' Expedition Against the Revolted Negroes
      of Surinam*. Bodleian Library, Oxford   235
5.16 William Blake, 'Whipping of a Samboe Girl' (1796). From John
      Stedman, *Narrative of a Five Years' Expedition Against the
      Revolted Negroes of Surinam*. Bodleian Library, Oxford   237
5.17 [Isaac Robert Cruikshank], 'Whipping of a Samboe Girl' (*c.* 1810).
      Frontispiece to *Curious Adventures of Captain Stedman*. British
      Library   238
5.18 [William Blake] plagiarisms of plates to Stedman, *Narrative*
      (1799). From *L'Amérique Décrite par le Docteur Jules Ferrario. II
      Parte Amérique Meridionale*. Library Company of Philadelphia   239
5.19 Anon., 'Scene from a Jamaica House of Correction' (1834). From
      James Williams, *Narrative of Events*. Rhodes House Library,
      Bodleian Library, Oxford   240
5.20 Alexander Anderson, *Parallel Between Intemperance and the
      Slave Trade* (1828). American Antiquarian Society, Worcester,
      Massachusetts   244

5.21 William Hogarth, *Gin Lane*, detail (1751). British Museum, Department of Prints and Drawings 244

5.22 Anon., *The Branded Hand* (*c.* 1845). Newberry Library, Chicago 247

5.23 Anon., *Walker's Branded Hand* (*c.* 1845). Massachusetts Historical Society, Boston 248

5.24 Anon., *Boston Massacre ... Protest Against Dred Scott Decision* (1858). American Antiquarian Society, Worcester, Massachusetts 252

5.25 Anon., *Martyrdom of Crispus Attucks* (1862). American Antiquarian Society, Worcester, Massachusetts 252

5.26 Paul Revere, *The Bloody Massacre perpetrated in King Street Boston March 5th 1770* (1770). American Antiquarian Society, Worcester, Massachusetts 253

5.27 Francisco Goya, *The 3rd of May: Execution of the Insurgents* (1814). Museo Nacional del Prado, Madrid 254

5.28 Anon., *Ninetieth Anniversary of the Boston Massacre* (1860). American Antiquarian Society, Worcester, Massachusetts 255

5.29 William Woollett, after Benjamin West, *Death of General Wolf* 1776). British Museum, Department of Prints and Drawings 256

5.30 Anon., 'Cotton screw' (1838). From *Narrative of the Adventures and Escape of Moses Roper*. American Antiquarian Society, Worcester, Massachusetts 257

5.31 Richard Newton, *Forcible Appeal for the Abolition of the Slave Trade* (1792). Andrew Edmunds Collection, London 261

5.32 Marcel Verdier, *The Punishment of the Four Stakes in the Colonies* (1843). Menil Foundation, Houston, Texas 262

5.33 Francisco Xavier Chagas, *Flagellated Christ* (*c.* 1750). Convent of the Venerable Third Order of the Carmelites, Salvador, Bahia. Photographed by the author 264

5.34 Francisco Xavier Chagas, *Virgin and Child* (*c.* 1750). Convent of the Venerable Third Order of the Carmelites, Salvador, Bahia. Photographed by the author 264

5.35 Francisco Xavier Chagas, *Flagellated Christ*, detail of back (*c.* 1750). Convent of the Venerable Third Order of the Carmelites, Salvador, Bahia. Photographed by the author 265

5.36 Anon., *Gordon* (1863). Library Company of Philadelphia 267

5.37 Anon., 'Gordon' (1863). From *Harper's Weekly*. Library Company of Philadelphia 267

5.38 C. J. Grant, *The Late Bloody and Brutal Exhibition of Horrid Military Torture, or, Aristocratic Bastards in their Glory* (*c.* 1835). British Museum, Department of Prints and Drawings 270

5.39 Anon., *Gordon* (1864). Raymond English Slavery Collection, John Rylands University Library, Manchester 270

5.40 Isaac Robert Cruikshank, 'English Factory Slaves' (*c.* 1830). Plate 3 from *The Condition of the West India Slave contrasted with that of The Infant Slave in our English Factories*. Library Company of Philadelphia 273

5.41 Anon., 'Sambo and the Lamb' (*c.* 1850). From *Large Pictures with Little Stories*. Opie Collection, Bodleian Library, Oxford 275

5.42 David Claypoole Johnston, *The House that Jeff Built* (1863).
      American Antiquarian Society, Worcester, Massachusetts   277

5.43 David Claypoole Johnston, *The House that Jeff Built*, detail (1863).
      American Antiquarian Society, Worcester, Massachusetts   279

5.44 Anon., 'O man, the blood of thy brother' (1834). From *The Oasis*.
      American Antiquarian Society, Worcester, Massachusetts   281

5.45 Anon., 'The Whip' (1833). From *The Slave's Friend*. American
      Antiquarian Society, Worcester, Massachusetts   282

5.46 Anon., 'Shackles' (1833). From *The Slave's Friend*. American
      Antiquarian Society, Worcester, Massachusetts   282

6.1   Phone Box, Modello Market, Salvador, Bahia (1995). Photograph
      by the author   293

6.2   Capoeira, Rio underpass (1993). Photograph by the author   293

6.3   Portrait, William Wilberforce (1994). Kingston upon Hull, City
      Museums and Art Galleries, Wilberforce House   295

6.4   Life-sized section of a slave deck, Wilberforce House (1994).
      Kingston upon Hull, City Museums and Art Galleries, Wilberforce
      House   296

6.5   Recreation of the slave deck of a slave ship (1995). National
      Museums and Galleries on Merseyside, Transatlantic Slavery
      Gallery, Liverpool. Photograph by author   298

6.6   Scale model of a slave ship, in cross-section (1995). National
      Museums and Galleries on Merseyside, Transatlantic Slavery
      Gallery, Liverpool. Photograph by author   299

6.7   Anon., *The Celebrated Piratical Slaver l'Antonio* (c. 1860).
      National Museums and Galleries on Merseyside, Transatlantic
      Slavery Gallery, Liverpool   303

Plates

1 Lieutenant Francis Meynell, *View of the Deck of the Slave Ship
   Albanoz* (1846). National Maritime Museum, Picture Library, Greenwich

2 Bob Marley, *Survival* (LP Album cover, 1979). Photograph Colin Mills
                                                      between pp. 26 & 27

3 Henri Fuseli, *The Negro's Revenge* (1806). Elke Walford, Fotowedstatt,
   Hamburger Kunsthalle, Hamburg

4 J. M. W. Turner, *Slavers Throwing Overboard the Dead and Dying, Typhon
   Coming On* (1840). Museum of Fine Arts, Boston

5 Auguste Biard, *Scene on the African Coast* (c. 1833). Kingston
   upon Hull, City Museums and Art Galleries, Wilberforce House
                                                      between pp. 58 & 59

6 Thomas Moran, *The Slave Hunt* (1862). The Philbrook Museum of Art,
   Tulsa

7 Giotto, Flagellation of Christ (1303–6). Scrovegni Chapel, Padua
                                                      between pp. 90 & 91

Acknowledgements

Blind Memory brings together writings and visual art produced over a long time in two different continents. The research for it went on in slave ports, universities and archives in England, North America, the Caribbean and Brazil over a period of ten years. It is not possible to list everyone who helped me. Many people changed my preconceptions and opened my eyes. Sometimes it took me several years to see what they had been offering me.

The following list could be seen as a shorthand for the genesis and development of this project. I thank John Adams, Bob White, Gaynor Wood, Jo Carter, Jeanette Winterson, Robert Winder, John Santos, James Derderian, Michael Gearin Tosh, John Bayley, Christian Patterson, Linda Patterson, David Patterson, Nancy Waltman, Teal Derrer, Eathan Johnson, Alice Flaherty, Andrea Rausch, Annie Toup, Henrietta Hendriksen, Peter de Francia, Paulo Herkenhopf, Marcello Araujo, Flavia Ribeiro, Eisabeth de Matos Rodrigues, Dillwyn Smith, Julius Tabaček, Rachel Bud, Don Mackenzie, Asa Briggs, Stan Unsworth, Michael Winship, Michael Dash, Mervyn Morris, Dale Thurston Graden, Ethel Goreham, Doré Ashton, Rufus Wood, Benjamin Ross, Maria Whelan, Katherine Quinsey, Suzanne Matheson, Moira Ferguson, Alex Mackay, Gloria Grant Roberson, Sandra Gunning, Heather Neff, David Alexander, Kate Wood, Emma Wood, Cecille Fabre, Dwight Middleton, Helen Weston, Jean-Claude Vatin, Robin Blackburn, Colin Mills, Jane Pomeroy, James Raven, Emily Hahn, David Landau, Andrew Edmunds, Roger Malbert, Dick Brown, Arlen Harris, David Dabydeen, Jonathan Bate, Michael Schmidt, Paul Holland, Isabelle Cockayne, Greville Lindop, Penny Jones, Jon Mee, Brian Maidment, Diana Donald, Robert Patten, Helen Thomas, Françoise Vergés, Beatrice Wood.

My new colleagues at the University of Sussex have been a continual source of encouragement and my Doctoral students deserve a special mention. Working closely with Juliette Myers, Anita Ruprecht, Chris Abuk and Iman Hamam, on their very different projects, has frequently caused me to rethink my own work.

Several awards and fellowships from specific institutions enabled the basic research for this book to happen. I first started looking at American abolition materials as a Henry Fellow at Harvard, and would like to thank Ken Carpenter, of the Harvard Library Bulletin, for his long-standing interest in my work. The American Antiquarian Society, where I spent

ACKNOWLEDGEMENTS several months as a Peterson Fellow, introduced me to many of the raw materials for the American sections of this book. Joanne Chaison, Georgia Barnhill and Caroline Sloat have been particularly kind in giving time and advice over a long period. John Hench was a great support while I was working there. The Newberry Library awarded me a fellowship which allowed me to complete my research on the populist graphics generated by American abolition. A visiting fellowship to the Library Company of Philadelphia was significant. Jim Green and the whole staff were wonderfully open to the project. I must single out Phil Lapsansky as a figure who had a late but vital impact on the content of this book. I have done my best to acknowledge his individual corrections and contributions but my debt to Phil goes beyond such minutiae.

The Wingate Foundation provided me with a generous award to travel around Rio, São Paulo, and most significantly for this volume, Salvador Bahia. The trip was made originally to gather materials on the iconography of Brazilian abolition but ended up becoming something much bigger. My friendships with Brazilian artists, academics and writers, although manifested only in a few specific images in *Blind Memory*, changed, and continue to change, how I think about slavery. The Brazilian approach to the cultural inheritance of slavery is essentially creative, even celebratory, and often confounds me as an Englishman. Professor Bom Meheny offered valuable insights at an early stage. Consuelo Pondé de Sena allowed me to share her remarkable knowledge of the history and archives of Salvador. Anna Martinez Santos, Fabio Lopez, Christina Soto Martinez allowed me to share their intimate insights into São Paulo's history and culture. Jac Leirner and José Rosendé made my understanding of the iconography of slavery in Rio possible. The practical support of all these Brazilian friends, not only as hosts but as cultural negotiators in some very tricky situations, is something I will never forget.

Countless English institutions offered me their expertise in putting together the images in this book. Anti-slavery International, and Rose McAusland and Jonathan Blagbrough in particular, invited me to advise on exhibitions and to contribute to lecture series. In doing so they helped me to think about how best to represent slavery within contemporary cultures. Anthony Griffiths, Chantal Serhan and Frances Carey of the British Museum Department of Prints and Drawings have my thanks for their continued support in the face of my unending demands. I also owe a big debt to Oxford's research Libraries and to the staff of Rhodes House in particular.

Throughout the writing of *Blind Memory* the Ruskin School of Drawing and Fine Art in Oxford enabled me to experiment continually with the interpretation of the visual art in this book. Stephen Farthing provided me with studio space and with the chance to try out my ideas on race and slavery in the visual arts on lively undergraduate painters and lecture audiences. Jean Lodge provided me with the unique opportunity to talk through my ideas with someone deeply versed in European graphic traditions and with Latin American culture. The Ruskin also offered me continual encounters with visiting artists. Stephen Farthing's impromptu symposia introduced me to Indian and Brazilian artists who inflected the ways in which I looked at the construction of race in the visual arts. Malu Fatorelli was particularly valuable to me in this context.

Liverpool and Bristol, Britain's most significant slave ports outside London, inevitably had a big impact on my book. Both Tony Tibbles and Gary Taylor talked to me at length about the construction and function of the Transatlantic Slavery Gallery in the National Museums and Galleries on Merseyside, and pointed out many dodgy assumptions in my initial reaction to the project. The people at the Liverpool Anti Racist Community Arts Association, and Ibrahim B. Thompson, Abdul Salam Gayle and James Heranandez in particular took a lot of time and trouble to talk to me about Liverpool's current relation to its slave history and to race. Eric Lynch shared with me his special knowledge of the way slavery is encoded within the Liverpool docks and buildings. Bristol recently staged a conference around its challenging slavery exhibition at the Bristol City Galleries. The whole event and the exhibition allowed me to rethink certain aspects of the representation of the middle passage. Madge Dresser was at the centre of my experience in Bristol.

This book would certainly not have been conceived, written or published without the help of the British Academy. It was as a British Academy Postdoctoral Fellow at Worcester College Oxford that I first became convinced of the necessity for writing *Blind Memory*. The British Academy has offered support throughout the ensuing years in the form of further travel grants and awards. At the last hurdle this came in the form of two substantial awards which covered all permissions and hard copy costs for the illustrations. I am deeply grateful to the British Academy, and in the later stages to the Arts and Humanities Research Board, for their prolonged commitment to the project.

I also want to acknowledge my debt to Joseph and Ruth Bromberg who, from the time I first met them, when I became Michael Bromberg fellow at Worcester College Oxford, have been invaluable friends and supporters. I have discussed my work with them throughout its genesis, and their deep humanity and sensitivity to visual cultures have constantly fed into my ideas.

Matthew Frost, my editor at MUP, must be mentioned as a publisher unlike any other publisher. He has been a constant source of humour, common sense and surprise.

Then there are the people who have read this book, or parts of it, in various forms at various stages. My debt to them goes beyond anything that can be expressed in a formal acknowledgment. Their names are Adam Ashforth, James Walvin, Iain McCalman, Benita Parry, John Golding and Sarah Wood.

Introduction

There is a limit at which the practice of any art becomes an affront to affliction. Let us not forget this … What have you done to gain knowledge of the
disaster? (Maurice Blanchot, *The Writing of the Disaster*)

Slavery broke the world in half, it broke it in every way. It broke Europe. It
made them into something else, it made them slave masters, it made them
crazy. You can't do that for hundreds of years and it not take a toll. They had
to dehumanise, not just the slaves but themselves. They have had to reconstruct everything in order to make that system appear true.
(Toni Morrison, quoted in Paul Gilroy, *Small Acts*)

There seems something more speakingly incomprehensible in the powers,
the failures, the inequalities of memory, than in any other of our intelli-
gences. The memory is sometimes so retentive, so serviceable, so obedient:
at others, so bewildered and so weak; and at others again, so tyrannic, so
beyond control! We are, to be sure, a miracle every way – but our powers of
recollecting and of forgetting do seem peculiarly past finding out.
(Jane Austen, *Mansfield Park*)

Recovery and representation: the case of Thomas Clarkson's abolition map

One year after the passage of the 1807 bill abolishing the British slave trade,
Thomas Clarkson published his monumental *History of the Rise, Progress,
and Accomplishment of the Abolition of the African Slave-Trade by the British
Parliament*. The two volumes, totalling nearly twelve hundred pages, are
dedicated to the nine (out of twelve) government ministers who finally voted
the bill through Parliament. The slaves are not mentioned in the dedication.[1]

The first image in Clarkson's book, now, ironically, the first image in
this book, was a large fold-out engraving which was intended to provide a
record of Western abolition in the form of a map [**1.1**]. This map is an extraordinary thing which upends E. C. Bentley's happy little aphorism that
'geography is about maps and biography is about chaps'. The first volume
of Clarkson's vast *History* opens with a detailed overview of the lives and
activities of the founding fathers of British and North American abolition,
and this is then summed up in a cartographic fantasy which presents abolition as a series of tributary streams and rivers, each with the name of a
supposed abolitionist attached. The waterways unite to form two mighty

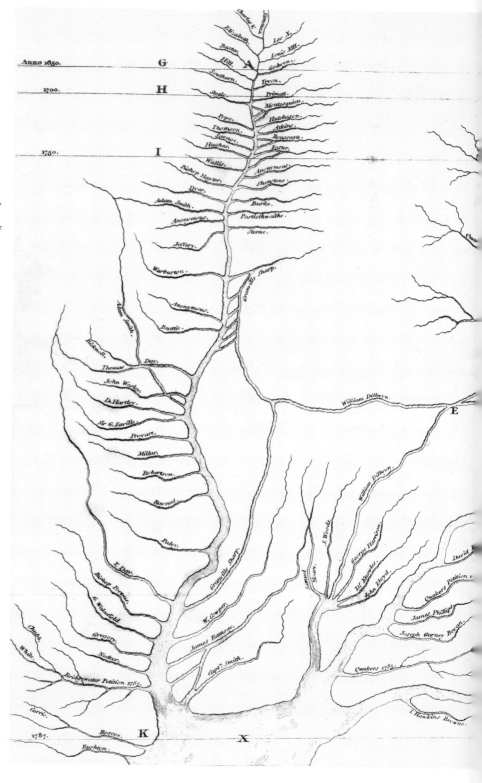

[1.1] Thomas Clarkson del., 'Abolition Map' (copper engraving, 1808). From *The History of the Rise, Progress and Accomplishment of the Abolition of the African Slave-Trade by the British Parliament*

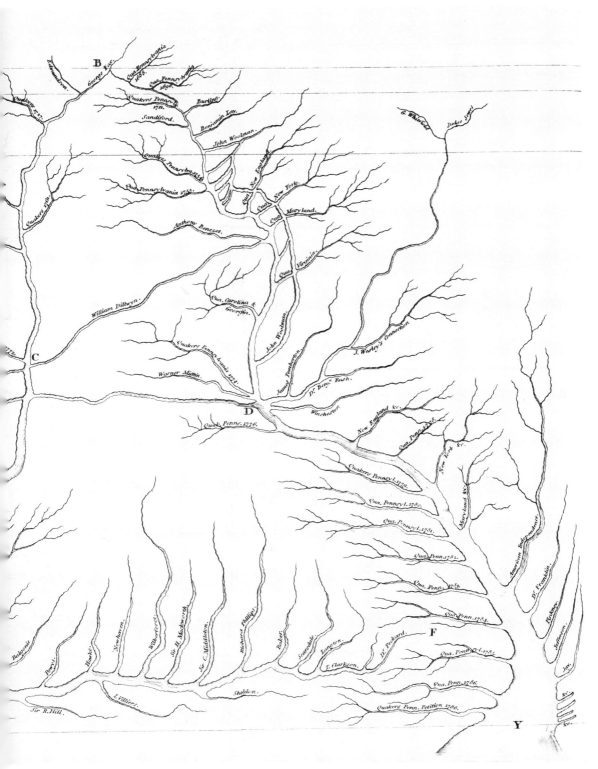

B

george &c.

Edmundson.

Non-Pennsylvania 1688.

Qua. Pennsylvania 1696.

Quakers &c.

Quakers Penns. 1711.

Burling.

Benjamin Lay.

Sandiford.

John Woolman.

G. Whitfield.

Judge Sewel.

Quakers Pennsylvania

Qua. New England.

Qua. New York.

Quakers 1780.

Qua. Pennsylvania 1755.

Qua. Maryland.

Quakers 1780.

Anthony Benezet.

Qua. Virginia.

1775.

William Dillwyn.

Qua. Carolina & Georgia.

John Woolman.

J. Wesley's Connection.

C

Quakers Pennsylvania 1773.

Warner Mifflin.

James Pemberton.

Dr. Benj. Rush.

D

Winchester.

New England &c.

Quak. Penns. 1776.

Qua. Penn. 1778.

New York &c.

Quakers Pennsyl. 1779.

Qua. Pennsyl. 1780.

Maryland &c.

Qua. Pennsyl. 1781.

American Independent.

Qua. Penn. 1782.

Qua. Penn. 1783.

Dr. Franklin.

Qua. Penn. 1784.

Rutoux.

F

Belgonie.

Powis.

Hooks.

Newhaven.

Wilberforce.

Sir H. Mackworth.

Sir C. Middleton.

Richard Phillips.

Bobel.

Scarsdale.

Langton.

Dr. Peckard.

Qua. Penn. & 1785.

Jefferson.

Jay.

&c.

T. Clarkson.

Qua. Penn. 1786.

Sir R. Hill.

L. Villiers.

Sheldon.

Quakers Penn. Petition 1786.

Y

&c.

3

rivers in England and America, and these in turn unite when they flow into the open sea, presumably the sea of emancipation and spiritual renewal. Bickering over the accreditations within the Clarksonian water-canon almost immediately followed.[2]

This map is a good place to start thinking about the central theme of this book, the utterly problematic nature of the visual representation of slavery in Europe and North America. Clarkson's map, like his title page, finds no place for the African or New World slave. Yet as the indefatigable and fearless work-horse of the first phase of British abolition campaigning, and as a pre-eminent anti-slavery propagandist, Thomas Clarkson was in, and felt himself to be in, a unique position to provide an official justification of the movement.[3] His explanation of the design he chose to summarise his version of history is disarmingly simple: 'As the preceding history of the different classes of the forerunners and coadjutors ... may be thought interesting by many, I have endeavoured, by means of the annexed map, so to bring it before the reader, that he may comprehend the whole of it at a single view.' What a vast confidence lies behind the idea that, as far as the collective history of the British slave trade and its abolition is concerned, we may 'comprehend the whole of it at a single view'. Clarkson's disquisition upon his map operates in terms of a stern but optimistic moral didacticism and of a missionary evangelicalism: the map teaches the 'value of religion', that 'the Christian religion is capable of producing the same good fruit in all lands', that 'however small the beginning may appear ... in any good work we undertake we need not be discouraged', 'that no good effort is ever lost'.[4] But when we turn to the map itself it is very hard to see how these pat maxims help with its interpretation. What does the fictional space around the rivers stand for? What do the rivers stand for? If abolition is to be constituted as flowing water, what is the sea into which it flows, and what is the water? Last, but not least, what happened to the slaves?

One way of reading the map is as a colossal genealogy. Much of the first volume of Clarkson's *History* is concerned to provide both a chronological and literary inheritance for abolition. A series of progenitors and patriarchs are laid out. Clarkson trawls through English and French literary and divine writings, claiming Milton and even Pope as abolitionist poets, and erecting an enormous litany of names of those 'involved'. In many ways there is no rhyme or reason to the figures he selects: his attempt to create a self-sufficient cultural history for the cause requires a coherent descriptive model which is capable of overriding the heterogeneity of the names and writings he has furnished. Clarkson's map imposes order on chaos by providing an abolition tree of Jesse. The fruitful loins belong to no single abolitionist but to a mysterious sea, into which, in a strange reversal of the generative metaphor, all the tributaries pour.

Yet while relating to the central image representing biblical genealogy, the map can also be read within the conventions of cartography. As a map of a newly charted land, abolition represents the spiritual colonisation of

England and North America, the Old and the New Worlds. Africa is off the map. The engraving is a wonderful way of escaping from the dilemma of defining 'collective memory' as opposed to 'the actual past'.[5] The only thing that differentiates the graphic representation of one abolitionist's life and work from another is the width and length of the tributary ascribed to him in serpentine lines of black ink. It is a fictional colonisation of the past, a wonderful trick, history combined with geography through a visual sleight of hand. It is a floating metaphor and a dangerous one.

Cartographic theorists increasingly see maps and myths of national power as intertwined. Maps are also read as duplicitous, as inevitably rhetorical, as appropriative fantasies which suspend a multiplicity of meanings which may cancel each other out in terms of the actuality they claim to depict.[6] Clarkson's map, however, goes beyond cartographic debates which turn on the relationship between representation and reality because in terms of its relation to a geographical reality Clarkson's creation is not a map at all, and yet it paradoxically looks very 'real'. This is because the engraving observes the outward forms of a specific late-eighteenth-century and early-nineteenth-century hydrographic style, and is close to many maps which charted the water courses of newly traversed parts of the globe.

Clarkson's water may not, however, be as pure as it looks. Hydrography, no less than any other form of map-making, is not historically or politically innocent. Within the dynamics of empire and exploration water carries a specific political weight. Hydrography was an area of international map publishing intimately reflecting maritime power. Portugal led European hydrography during the period of its maritime ascendancy, to be followed by the Dutch; when Clarkson's map was produced England had gained naval supremacy. The period 1770–1810 had witnessed an explosion of sophisticated and big-selling hydrographic guides: 'Pilots', 'Maritime Atlases' and 'Navigators' flooded out of English presses and were essential to expanding trade and exploration of the Americas, the Caribbean, India, the Pacific Islands and Australia.[7] Atlantic slavery had been only one element in the network of trans-oceanic trade routes established by Britain, with British boats moving out of British ports, across the seas to feel their way up the rivers and tributaries of 'new' worlds. The last three decades of the eighteenth century saw a marked increase in the production of coastal maps, charting recently discovered regions. A British Hydrographic Office was set up in 1795 to centralise and to accelerate the production of coastal charts. Clarkson's map is, on one level, a coastal chart, and as such can be read as a logical extension of the British imperial mission into the area of religious and moral discovery, or rediscovery. In this sense it attempts to recreate the memory of slavery through the new, lean, scientific conventions of late-eighteenth-century hydrography. Each abolitionist is a clean new river with a clear European name.[8]

Clarkson's grand graphic gesture is both a cleaning-up operation and a lie. It might be possible to see in Clarkson's fantastic map an attempt to wipe the national memory clean of the filthy associations with which British maritime expansion had been contaminated by the slave trade. Then conversely it is possible to read in this map the imaginative limitations of British cultural memory. A politico-religious movement as diverse as abolition, which was supposed to find its roots in a selfless philanthropy, can only be historically reconstituted within the conventions of a system for depicting maritime dominance, a graphic system closely related to the slave trade itself. In the end the only thing which seems certain is the difficulty in finding an appropriate way of reading this engraving.

What are we looking at, what can we see?

If this map is not easy to understand then its difficulty is a tiny part of an enormous problem. It may not be possible to find solutions to the questions of how to read, or how to see, visual representations developed out of the Western myths devoted to the memory of slavery. This needs to be emphasised because looking, as opposed to reading, has not, in the context of slavery, been described as an exceptionally problematic activity. Slavery is now a subject generating an enormous number and variety of publications. Books on slavery are profligate in their deployment of imagery. Pictures are used on covers, and frequently inserted in gatherings within the text, subordinate to a written text, colourful, and certainly attractive and entertaining. Rarely, even in serious scholarly studies of the slave trade, abolition, slave narrative or plantation life, does the writer subject quoted imagery (that is to say, reproduced imagery) to the sorts of close reading or technical and theoretical analysis which are applied to quotations from written sources. Maybe this is because there is still an irrational belief that pictures speak for themselves in a way that words do not. There is also the fact that only a tiny proportion of the imagery which was produced to describe slavery might be designated 'high art', and in consequence most of it has fallen beyond the pale for formal art historians, while it has not been taken up by cultural historians or semioticians. In short the imagery of slavery has not been taken as seriously as it should have been.[9]

The material analysed in this book is varied. The criteria for inclusion are, as the title suggests, primarily chronological and geographical, yet the boundaries are also fluid and I have not hesitated to include material from areas outside Britain and North America, or from before 1780 or after 1865, when I felt it was indispensable to developing a specific line of argument. The material discussed ranges from one of the most beautiful and influential academic oil paintings ever made (Turner's *Slavers*, plate 4) to the most ham-fisted and crudely hacked broadside woodcuts (the image of Gordon, 5.39) and takes in early photography (the image of Gordon, 5.36). Criteria of cultural influence, popularity and longevity underlay the choice of materials examined. The images which dominate the discussion – the *Description* of the slave ship *Brookes*, Turner's *Slave Ship*, Biard's *Scene on the African Coast*, the woodcut of the runaway slave carried on slave advertisements and sale notices, the slave in the dirt-eating mask, Gordon's whipped back, Cruikshank's illustrations to *Uncle Tom's Cabin* – have chosen themselves through the ways they have infiltrated the print culture, the popular culture and the intellectual culture of Europe and America during the last two hundred years.

Ignorance is a central theme in this study. The word here carries two primary senses: the familiar one, 'ignorance' as 'a want of knowledge (special or general)' (*OED*, 1A); and 'ignorance' strictly in the sense of what has been deliberately ignored or left unseen. In the latter sense, the act of ignoring conforms to a state of willed blindness: 'to refuse to take notice of … to shut one's eyes to' (*OED*, ignore, 3). Art which describes or responds to trauma and mass murder always embodies paradox. How can aesthetic criteria be applied to describe the torture and mass destruction of our own kind?[10] How is it possible to make something beautiful out of, and to perceive beauty within, something which has contaminated human values to such a degree as to be beyond the assumed idealisations of truth and art, beyond the known facts and beyond the manipulations of rhetoric? The inheritance of slavery, and the memory of the slave trade, cannot be described in the sense of an objective re-creation. The experiences of millions of individuals who were the victims of slavery is not collectable; it is unrecoverable as a set of relics. There can be no archaeology of the memory of slavery that corresponds to an emotional identification with a lost reality. And yet a multitude of images have been made in England and America which purport to describe the history and the experiences of slavery. This book tries to find ways of understanding this material.[11]

The work initially developed out of my increasing sense of the peculiar nature of the English relationship to the slave trade and Atlantic slavery. Slavery has been spectacularly mythologised within English culture, and the production of visual art has been central to the development of a discourse of national aggrandisement. For the British the slave trade, and the 'middle passage' in particular, have a primacy which is unique. From its formal and legal abolition in 1807 the slave trade fairly rapidly developed into a site for national celebration. The perpetration of the trade itself, which had undergone dynamic development for some three centuries until Britain finally dominated it internationally in the period 1730–1800, was overwritten with a triumphalist narrative. The construction of a celebratory historiography focused upon the elite leadership of British abolition was by no means immediate. Indeed the bill passed with very little notice in the press in 1807 and 1808. Abolition remained overshadowed by developments relating to Napoleonic France until 1815. During this period slavery only rarely seized the public imagination; the sudden resurgence of popular abolition activity over the threat of French re-imposition of the slave trade in 1814 provided the most spectacular example.[12] Yet the implementation of an abolition myth was an inexorable cultural process, and by the middle of the 1820s the memory of the slave trade became primarily the memory of its glorious abolition.[13] A similar pattern followed for the abolition of plantation and domestic slavery in the British Caribbean in 1833, North America in 1865 and Brazil in 1888. I have made a deliberate decision not to include a chapter in this book on what David Brion Davis, in a discussion still vital to our understanding of slavery and Western visual culture, has called 'the emancipation moment'.[14] In an important sense the waves of iconography generated in Europe and the Americas by successive emancipation moments do not visually represent slavery or its memory at all. They might more accurately be designated a spasmodic white ejection, a mythic and colouristically inverted analogue to the ink of a squid. The same goes for the visual material devoted to the hagiographic construction of white 'champions' of abolition. Certainly this material must be subjected to a harsh scrutiny, but it must be considered specifically as a white mythology which, to recast the words of Blanchot in the opening epigraph, works hard to deny the possibility of gaining knowledge of the disaster of the Atlantic slave trade.

Our cultures will never know what 'really happened' to the people who endured slavery. We may exhibit and look at artefacts, read lists of cargo, ship tonnages, the entries in punishment books, display caricatures, or paintings or models of slave ships, or the memorabilia of slave torture. There is abolition propaganda focused on anonymous slave sufferers, or on white personalities who spearheaded the abolition movements. There are grand narratives on large academic canvases, and there are heroic sculptures and friezes, almost always built to commemorate the emancipation moment. There are tragic little narratives encased within the texts of runaway slave advertisements. The question remains: are any of these things adequate, or even decent, memory tools? The material in this book is at one level a catalogue of emotional usurpation. The images reproduced mimic the experience of being a slave below deck on the middle passage, on the auction block, in a sugar or cotton field, waiting at table. Yet for each slave the experience was unrepeatable, irreducible and unreproducable: all human suffering exists beyond the vulgarity of the simulacrum. Slavery caused a mass of suffering which the victims might never understand themselves let alone be able to, or wish to, communicate. The attempts of Western painters, sculptors, engravers and lithographers to provide European culture with a record of slave experience is consequently a history fraught with irony, paradox, voyeurism and erasure. The testimony produced by slaves themselves, which is frequently projected through white creative and economic filters, is equally complicated in its relation to whatever we understand as historical truth.

This book tries to find ways of reading images which emerge as ever more contradictory in terms of what they say about white representation of slavery, and what they imply for black and white understanding of this inheritance. There is a vast amount of material to choose from, and this book is not (no single volume could be) an attempt to provide a representative survey of the subject. Instead four areas have been located which have generated particularly contradictory and influential narratives and images. The four sections of the book consequently examine a set of key sites which purport to describe the experience of slavery. These sites are: the middle passage, slave flight/escape, the popular imagery generated by *Uncle Tom's Cabin*, and slave torture/'punishment'. My thematic scheme has excluded some areas of the representation of slavery which relate directly to slave empowerment and resistance, and to European and North American representation of slavery as it was imagined to exist on mainland Africa. These bodies of imagery will require detailed appraisal in the future.

Three excluded areas in particular demand serious study and the first relates to slave rebellion. My discussion of the middle passage does not include analysis of the imagery describing slave insurrections on board ships. A large body of imagery relating to this subject was produced in a variety of publishing forms on both sides of the Atlantic for more than one hundred years. It constitutes a fascinating site for reconfiguring white anxieties relating to the capacities of African slaves to fight for their freedom. This work is also a significant counterpoint to the body of images predicated upon slave passivity and victimhood which this study has foregrounded.

The second significant exclusion is the vast body of imagery which might be described as 'documentary', and which represented day-to-day conditions and life on plantations. This imagery took many forms and much of it is fascinating from the perspective of this book because it lies outside the polemical confines of pro- and anti-slavery debates. Imagery was generated by slave-owners, and by their servants and visitors, and takes the forms of illustrative needlework, patchwork and textile design, casual water-colour sketches and drawings in diaries, or decorative painting on domestic objects and ceramics. Slaves also appear in many forms of engraving in technical manuals relating to agricultural practices, plantation management and the processes of sugar and tobacco refining in particular. Although somewhat better known, there are also the many illustrated travel books, the most beautiful and internationally renowned relating to Brazil, which present slave life through a variety of narrative approaches which are not immediately polemical. All of this imagery is potentially valuable in the work of uncovering the cultural construction of slavery in Europe and the Americas. The last ten years have witnessed a phenomenal increase in books which attempt to describe the minutiae of day-to-day existence on plantations. Slaves, in some plantation contexts, now emerge as groups of people who were capable of sustaining autonomous cultural and artistic activity. Recent accounts suggest ways in which slaves managed, imaginatively, to escape the dehumanising and enclosing surveillance and punishment structures which came to dominate slave systems, and inevitably the visual archive generated by abolition. Non-abolition visual representations of slave culture are consequently emerging as an essential resource in uncovering a record of the probable details of slave life and behaviour.[15] With a few exceptions such material has been purposely omitted from this study for reasons of space, but also because almost all of it stands in an eccentric relation to the criteria which have dictated the inclusion of images in this book. Throughout *Blind Memory* the emphasis has been on images which exerted an immediate, and frequently lasting, cultural impact on Western culture, high and low. In other words I have narrowed the focus to imagery which has, for whatever reason, come to constitute the semiotic core of Western responses to slavery within visual culture, and which has been widely reproduced and culturally reinvented in the eighteenth, nineteenth and twentieth centuries. That this core may expand radically in the near future is an exciting prospect.

The third area that merits detailed examination beyond the covers of this book is the imagery developed around the representation of the African slave trade and the European interaction with this economic phenomenon on the slave coasts of Africa. The European representation of slave forts, in particular, constitutes an extremely varied body of images which certainly demands detailed analysis. The only widely disseminated images relating to the context of African slavery which I discuss in the study are the remarkably popular and internationally marketed engravings made in the early 1790s after George Morland's sentimental oil paintings *The Execrable Human Traffic* and *African Hospitality*. These images highlight the fact that the representations of slaves during the Atlantic crossing were constructed against the background of a series of Western conventions for presenting the African slave trade and the social life of Africans. Recent historiography would indicate that these narrative conventions, whether pro- or anti-slavery, bore little relation to the actualities of either the African slave trade or African social existence.[16] Pro-slavery propagandists presented an internal trade dominated by savageness, heathenism and above all Dahomeyan blood lust and human sacrifice. Abolitionists from the 1780s onwards attempted to construct a counter-mythology prioritising the hospitality and sensibility of Africans in terms which would be reassuring to an educated domestic audience. Morland's work is the *locus classicus* for the latter narrative tendency in the visual arts. Yet despite the initial interest in the cultural constructions of Africans within Africa, this area did not sustain a central relation to the *visual* representation of slavery in England or America until the revival of interest in the 'dark continent' in the context of missionary expansion in the later nineteenth century.[17]

Each of the four sections of *Blind Memory* carries its own introduction and does not require discussion at this point. There are, however, questions which are constantly addressed throughout the book which are as follows. What semiotic codes have been employed in England and America to represent slavery? Why have they been chosen? How has memory been organised visually, and which systemics of visual memory have gained the widest cultural currency? Finally, given what our cultures chose to project and depict, what do we see now?

When trying to work out a method for responding to Holocaust testimonies, Shoshana Felman warns against taking anything for granted or even assuming that we know how to ask the right questions. She talks of living with the effects of the trauma of the Second World War and insists that we must look at 'a history which is essentially *not over*, a history whose repercussions are not simply omnipresent (whether consciously or not) in all our cultural activities, but whose traumatic consequences are still actively *evolving* … in today's political, historical, cultural and artistic scene'.[18] Comparisons between the history of Atlantic slavery and the Nazi Holocaust are precarious and frequently wrong but not always impossible or improper. This book emphasises, in the spirit of Felman's work on the Holocaust, that the historic trauma of transatlantic and plantation slavery must not be encapsulated within a history believed to be stable, digested and understood; this history is also *not over*, and is *evolving*. The hope is that the visual representation of slavery will not continue to be unseen; we must see through the disguises that we impose on our vision. 'Let us wage a war on totality; let us be witnesses to the unpresentable.'[19]

Notes

1 Clarkson must have had the work largely assembled before the final passage of the bill. See David Brion Davis, *The Problem of Slavery in the Age of Revolution 1770–1823* (Ithaca, Cornell University Press, 1975), p. 447.

2 Davis, *Problem of Slavery*, p. 448, fn. 111 alludes to some of the immediate controversies.

3 The best modern summary of the full breadth of Clarkson's obsessive anti-slavery activity, and of the history of his reputation on both sides of the Atlantic, is J. R. Oldfield, *Popular Politics and British Anti-Slavery: The Mobilisation of Public Opinion Against the Slave Trade 1787–1807* (Manchester, Manchester University Press, 1995), pp. 70–91, 160–6.

4 Thomas Clarkson, *The History of the Rise, Progress, and Accomplishment of the Abolition of the African Slave-Trade by the British Parliament*, 2 vols (London, 1808), 1, pp. 262–6.

5 For a contemporary discussion of the limits of this dilemma see Steven Knapp, 'Collective Memory and the Actual Past', *Representations*, 26:1 (1989) 123–47.

6 See J. B. Harley, 'Deconstructing the Map', *Cartographica*, 26:2 (1989) 1–20; 'Responses to J. B. Harley's article, "Deconstructing the Map"', *Cartographica*, 26:3–4 (1989) 89–127; Jeremy Black, *Maps and Politics* (London, Reaktion Books, 1997).

7 See R. V. Tooley, *Maps and Map-Makers* (London, Batsford, 1987), pp. 60–4.

8 See Norman J. W. Thrower, *Maps and Civilisation: Cartography in Culture and Society* (Chicago and London, University of Chicago Press, 1996), pp. 101–10.

9 There are exceptions to this generalisation, the most magisterial being Hugh Honour, *The Image of the Black in Western Art from the American Revolution to World War 1* (Cambridge Mass., Harvard University Press, 1989), 4:1–2. Honour's volumes, as their titles indicate, restrict the material considered almost entirely to Western canons of high art. The most recent short survey of the primary subject areas of the imagery generated in the West by Atlantic slavery is James Smalls, 'Art and Illustration', in Seymour

Drescher and Stanley L. Engerman (eds), *A Historical Guide to World Slavery* (New York, Oxford University Press, 1998), pp. 65–76, which opens with the statement: 'Generally speaking slavery and the slave trade have rarely been the subject for art.' There are some very successful close readings of the encoded ways in which slavery works its way out in the elaborate compositions and narratives of Western academic painting in Albert Boime, *The Art of Exclusion: Representing Blacks in the Nineteenth Century* (London, Thames and Hudson, 1990). His discussion (pp. 28–39) of the relation of Singleton Copley's *Watson and the Shark* to the memory of the middle passage possesses an exemplary delicacy in its approach to the complexities of influence. Jan Nederveen Pieterse, *White on Black: Images of Africa and Blacks in Western Popular Culture* (New Haven, Yale University Press, 1992) provides a useful, although methodologically undefined, survey, which is not frightened to introduce imagery from a variety of contexts not related to high art. Sharon F. Patton, *African-American Art* (Oxford and New York, Oxford University Press, 1998) is a much-needed overview, which for the first time attempts to integrate the statuary, architecture, textiles, musical instruments and paintings produced by slaves in the period 1700–1820 to subsequent art by African-Americans. One effect of this book will be to force reconsideration of how African-American visual art has inflected white American and European visual art. Jean Fagan Yellin, *Women and Sisters* (New Haven, Yale University Press, 1989) reprints an intriguing selection of material relating to the depiction of enslaved women, although the imagery is rarely discussed in any detail. Finally I would single out Henry Louis Gates Jnr., *The Signifying Monkey* (Oxford and New York, Oxford University Press, 1988). The deployment of photographs of the transcultural Esu figure to argue against the European tradition which would read the middle passage as a process of cultural erasure for the slave is deeply responsible.

10 I use aesthetic here in the sense defined by Harold Bloom, *Figures of Capable Imagination* (New York, Seabury Press, 1976), pp. 19–20. In reference to Walter Pater, Bloom states: 'Pater meant us to remember what mostly we have forgotten: that "aesthete" is from the Greek aisthetes "one who perceives" so the aesthetic critic is simply the perceptive critic.'

11 The Jewish Holocaust has generated, and is generating, the most important work to question the possibility of making art about trauma, and to question the possibility of testifying to trauma at all. My thought and methods have been deeply, but frequently indirectly, impressed by the work of among others Primo Levi, Claude Lanzmann, James Young, Shoshana Felman and Kali Tal; points of specific interaction are indicated in the main text.

12 For the complicated popular and elite responses to the passage of the abolition bill in the decade following 1807 see Seymour Drescher, 'Whose Abolition? Popular Pressure and the Ending of the British Slave Trade', *Past and Present*, 142 (1994) 136–66.

13 A thorough historical analysis of this phenomenon is Davis, *Problem of Slavery*, pp. 421–53. For a classic formulation of the triumphalist construction of the heroes of British abolition, see Sir Reginald Coupland, *The British Anti-Slavery Movement* (Oxford, Oxford University Press, 1933).

14 The most trenchant discussion of the conflict between historical process and mythologisation in white constructions of the moment of emancipation is David Brion Davis, *The Emancipation Moment* (Gettysburgh, Gettysburgh College, 1983). Davis is particularly astute in pointing out parallels between British, American and Brazilian rhetoric and iconography celebrating the achievement of slavery abolition. In all cases the Hebraic notion of a climactic moment of jubilee overrides the cautious and drawn-out political manoeuvrings which led up to and beyond the declaration of abolition. See also Boime, *Art of Exclusion*, pp. 153–221.

15 Representative of the remarkable recent work in this field are Larry E. Hudson (ed), *Working Toward Freedom: Slave Society and Domestic Economy in the American South* (New York, University of Rochester Press, 1994); Stephan Palmie (ed), *Slave Cultures*

and the Cultures of Slavery (Knoxville, University of Tennessee Press, 1995); Philip D. Morgan, *Slave Counterpoint: Black Culture in the Eighteenth-Century Chesapeake and Low Country* (Chapel Hill and London, University of North Carolina Press, 1998). Morgan's *Slave Counterpoint* deserves notice for its strategic deployment of a wide variety of visual materials including eighteenth-century plantation maps, representations of slave artefacts and ceramics, narrative embroidery, water-colours and oil paintings of plantations and slave quarters. This body of evidence is not, however, methodologically integrated into the terms of the analysis, and is read as a rhetorically innocent resource which describes social customs and behaviour.

16 The most comprehensive discussion of the growth and operation of the African/Atlantic slave trade is John Thornton, *Africa and Africans in the Making of the Atlantic 1400–1680* (New York and Cambridge, Cambridge University Press, 1998). For the English cultural constructions of Africa across the period of this study see Philip D. Curtin, *The Image of Africa: British Ideas and Action 1780–1850* (Madison, Wisconsin University Press, 1964); Anthony J. Barker, *The African Link: British Attitudes to the Negro in the Era of the African Slave Trade 1550–1807* (London, Frank Cass, 1978), pp. 77–179. For the perception of the African slave coast see Robin Law, *The Slave Coast of West Africa 1550–1750: The Impact of the Atlantic Slave Trade on an African Society* (Oxford, Clarendon Press, 1991).

17 Howard Temperley, *British Anti-Slavery 1833–1870* (London, Longman, 1972), pp. 221–63; Curtin, *Image*, pp. 289–547; Paul E. Lovejoy, *Transformations in Slavery: A History of Slavery in Africa* (Cambridge, Cambridge University Press, 1983); Drescher and Engerman, eds, *A Historical Guide to World Slavery*, pp. 1–5, 32–7, 227–8, 14–15.

18 Shoshana Felman and Dori Laub, *Testimony: Crises of Witnessing in Literature, Psychoanalysis, and History* (New York and London, Routlege, 1992), p. xiv.

19 Jean François Lyotard, *The Post Modern Condition* (Manchester, Manchester University Press, 1984), p. 81.

2 The irrecoverable: representing the 'middle passage'

Death, leave the gates of darkness,
go quickly, to a race chained to despair;
you will not be met with lacerated cheeks
or with lamentation, but in a different way,
with circles beating out dances and with joyful songs
… through the powerful swell of
the deep ocean, let these victims fly
to the special places of pleasure, to their homeland.
There, truly, beside springs and under the lemon groves,
lovers tell each other what terrible things,
being human, they suffered from other humans.

> (Samuel Taylor Coleridge, *Greek Prize Ode on the Slave Trade*
> [author's translation])

Shuttles in the rocking loom of history,
the dark ships move, the dark ships move,
their bright ironical names
like jests of kindness on a murderer's mouth.

> (Robert Hayden, *Middle Passage*)

I was down in the valley of the shadow of the Thames
When I heard the voice of my father, singing
Oh ye wicked men, oh ye wicked men,
Wey you are defend, wey you are defend.
I wanna know about the many, many millions of black people, now,
That went down, down, down, to the bottom of the deep blue sea …

> (Jimmy Lindsay, 'Wey you are defend', *Children of Rastafari*)

The middle passage was initially the primary site for the depiction of the trauma of slavery in terms of the problems it posed for the art and collective consciences of European and American societies. As a theme it occupied a position of unique importance during the first wave of English and French abolition from 1780 to 1807. From the founding of the Society for Effecting the Abolition of the Slave Trade (SEAST) in 1787 to the passage of the bill for abolition of the English slave trade in 1807, the middle passage was a battle ground for pro- and anti-slavery propagandists. Having decided on a strategy of limiting their campaign to slave trade abolition, not general emancipation, abolitionists directed their propaganda drive at proving that the trade was not economic and that the conditions for slaves and the mortality rates for slaves were appalling. Of equal importance was the proof that conditions and mortality rates for British sailors were also bad. The latter argument was intended to disprove the standard pro-slavery position that the slave trade constituted the nursery of British seamanship.[1] While printed texts explored the latter theme in great detail, the plight of the British sailor did not feature in the imagery which the middle passage generated. The most influential pictorial propaganda focused exclusively on the presentation of the slave cargoes, although some early propaganda imagery representing the separation of slave families on the African coast was commissioned by the SEAST in the late 1780s.[2] During the succeeding century the middle passage remained central to representations of slavery by British, French and American abolitionists, and to the representation of slavery in popular visual culture generally.[3]

In asking why these images take the forms they do, the primacy of the written word to early abolition debate needs to be stressed. Abolition writing attempted to evoke the experience of slaves on the middle passage through many methods. The most obvious, the detailing of atrocities from eyewitness accounts, was not always considered adequate even by those who gave the accounts. James Stanfield in his *Observations on a Guinea Voyage*, after giving a series of descriptions which try to explain the sufferings the slaves underwent, states that the task is impossible; experience, as victim or witness, is untranslatable: 'But no pen, no abilities, can give more than a very faint resemblance of the horrid situation. One *real* view – *one* MINUTE, absolutely spent in the slave rooms on the middle passage, would do more for the cause of humanity, than the pen of a *Robertson*, or the whole collective eloquence of the British senate.'[4] Stanfield raises the central question: can horror be described artistically, is there a rhetoric for the description of atrocity beyond that of inventory? William Hazlitt is helpful here: he provided a meditation on the relative operations of Reason and Imagination in the moral sphere, which is centred upon the problem of the imaginative recovery of the experience of the middle passage:

logical truth and practical reason are *disparates*. It is easy to raise an outcry against violent invectives, to talk loud against extravagance and enthusiasm, to pick a quarrel with every thing but the most calm, candid and qualified statement of facts: but there are enormities to which no words can do adequate justice. Are we then, in order to form a complete idea of them, to omit every circumstance of aggravation, or to suppress every feeling of impatience that arises out of details, lest we should be accused of giving way to the influence of prejudice and passion? This would be to falsify the impression altogether, to misconstrue reason and fly in the face of nature. Suppose, for instance, that in the discussion on the Slave-Trade, a description to the life was given of the horrors of the *Middle Passage* (as it was termed), that you saw the manner in which thousands of wretches, year after year, were stowed together in the hold of a slave-ship, without air, without light, without food, without hope, so that what they suffered in reality was brought home to you in imagination, till you felt in sickness of heart as one of them, could it be said that this was a prejudging of the case, that your knowing the extent of the evil disqualified you from pronouncing sentence upon it and that your disgust and abhorrence were the effects of a heated imagination? No. Those evils that inflame the imagination and make the heart sick, ought not to leave the head cool. This is the very test and measure of the degree of the enormity, that it involuntarily staggers and appals the mind. If it were a common iniquity, if it were slight and partial, or necessary, it would not have this effect; but it very properly carries away the feelings, and (if you will) overpowers the judgement, because it is a mass of evil so monstrous and unwarranted as not to be endured, even in thought.[5]

Hazlitt articulates a terrible bind: it is essential that imagination be put to work to create an equivalent of the middle passage, but if the artist succeeds in doing this what would have been created is 'a mass of evil so monstrous and unwarranted as not to be endured, even in thought'. The gap between the historical occurrence and its recovery can only be filled rhetorically with the various compromises which art and language have created. It is the nature of these compromises in visual art which are examined in the following discussion.[6]

This is not a chronological survey of the pictorial representation of the middle passage. The subject is approached via detailed and wide-ranging readings of the two most notorious and influential images generated by the Atlantic slave trade. The discussion consequently falls into two parts. The first considers the engraving *Description of a Slave Ship* (hereafter *Description*); the second considers Turner's beautiful, horrible and difficult oil painting *Slavers Throwing Overboard the Dead and Dying, Typhon Coming On* (hereafter *Slave Ship*). In trying to understand how these works have been read, and why they have become the primary imagistic memorial sites for the West's perpetration of the slave trade, many other prints and paintings are discussed. All this work forces confrontation with methodological and formal questions relating to the depiction of trauma and cultural guilt.

Imaging the unspeakable and speaking the unimaginable: the *Description* of the slave ship *Brookes*

In 1750, as Liverpool moved towards world domination of the Atlantic slave trade, P. P. Burdett drew, and E. Rooker engraved, a view of Thomas Ripley's exquisite little building, the fourth Liverpool Custom House [**2.1**]. On the main steps of this house, up which an elegantly dressed gentleman steps, the city's occasional slave auctions were mainly held.[7] In the bottom left-hand corner of the print two black boys talk and one points either towards the custom house or at a donkey. There is a feeling of relaxed industry about the whole scene, with slavery – its boats, buildings and human merchandise – seemlessly fusing into the life of the city. About 50 yards away two ships, typical of the trading vessels employed in 'the

A View of the Custom House. Taken from Traffords Wyent.

[2.1] P. P. Burdett del., E. Rooker sculpt., *A View of the Custom House* (copper engraving, 1750)

African trade', are docked. England has saved its fastest clipper, the *Cutty Sark*, as a tribute to its East India trade, and it has preserved HMS *Victory* as a tribute to Nelson and the British naval defeat of Napoleonic France. No slave boats were preserved: they were adapted to other trade and sailed on, and when they wore out they were scrapped. Not one plank survives to bear silent testimony to the suffering they contained.

If no slave ship survived to become a site for memory, Liverpool did generate one image in which its slave ships were to be memorialised through the centuries and across continents [**2.2**]. The famous *Description* represented in cross-section, front view and side view, and in a series of overviews of both slave decks, the manner in which slaves could legally be packed onto the Liverpool slaver the *Brookes*.[8] A partial version of the image was first designed in a crude engraving entitled *Plan of an African Ship's Lower Deck with Negroes in the proportion of only One to a Ton* (hereafter *Plan*) produced by the Plymouth Committee of the SEAST in December 1788 and published in January 1789 [**2.3**]. The *Plan* was then taken up by the London Committee of the SEAST and developed into its most widely disseminated form [2.2]. The *Description* was published by James Philips in London in the spring of 1789 and caused an immediate and international sensation.[9] This print was the most famous, widely reproduced and widely adapted image representing slave conditions on the middle passage ever made. It was published simultaneously as a single-sheet copper engraving in an edition of 1,700, and in a run of 7,000 from a wood-engraved impression; both versions were distributed as broadsides.

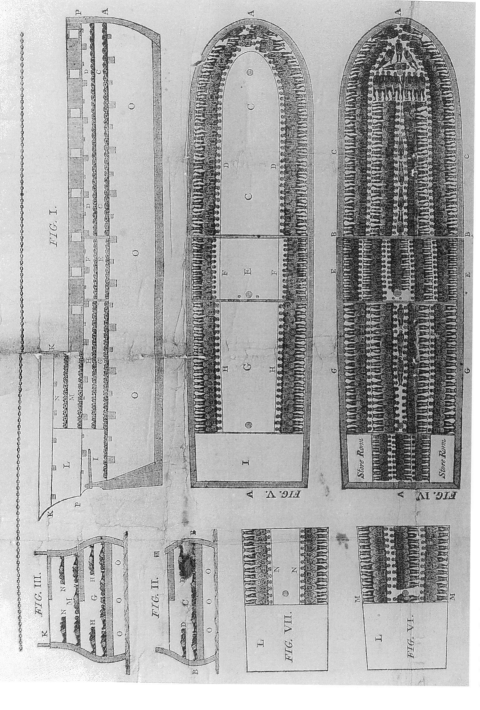

[2.2] Society for the Abolition of the Slave Trade, London Committee, *Description of a Slave Ship* (copper engraving, April 1789)

In the same year that it was published in England a large edition was also
adapted for the French market and distributed in Paris by Thomas
Clarkson, and an American adaptation was mass-marketed in Philadelphia
and led to adaptations in the Northern free states.[10]

The genesis, contemporary reception and subsequent graphic development of the *Description* have not been seen for what they are. This image
supports an abolitionist cultural agenda which dictated that slaves were to
be visualised in a manner which emphasised their total passivity and prioritised their status as helpless victims. The fascination which this print
exerted on its audiences can only be understood if it is considered in terms
of its relation to post-Enlightenment developments in technical drawing, to
established biblical narrative traditions, and finally to aesthetic codes
rooted in Western decorative art. It is a central premise of my argument that
the task of explaining why the middle passage was represented in the way it
was can be related not only to the past but to the present. The discussion
consequently ends by looking at how the *Description* has been deployed in
popular publishing in England and America over the past two centuries.
Twentieth-century adaptations suggest that Western society's memory of
the middle passage may still be dominated by eighteenth-century English
abolitionist models for the memorial reconstruction of the slave trade.

Mechanisms for denial, and for misremembering, still operate within
the European inheritance of the middle passage. An insight of Henry
Louis Gates's is helpful here. Gates sees Western historical perceptions of
the middle passage as an obstacle which prevents an understanding of how
cultural transference from African civilisations to those of New World
slave, and ex-slave, communities may have operated: 'The notion that the
Middle Passage was so traumatic that it functioned to create in the African
a tabula rasa of consciousness is as odd as it is a fiction, a fiction that has
served many economic orders and their attendant ideologies. The full erasure of traces of cultures as splendid, as ancient, and as shared by the slave
traveller as the classic cultures of traditional West Africa, would have been
extraordinarily difficult.'[11] This affirmation raises a lot of questions about
the nature of descriptions of blacks by English abolitionists in the late eighteenth century, and about descriptions of the middle passage in particular.

Pro-slavery fantasy: the middle passage as joy ride

The theory of a '*tabula rasa*' of black culture, the anti-personality which
Gates wonderingly and angrily refers to, was, in its most blatant manifestations, the creation of the propagandists of the pro-slavery lobby in England.

Pro-slavery configurations of the middle passage provided one of the
contexts which dictated the form of the *Description* as a piece of anti-slave
trade propaganda. Leading pro-slavery propagandists, the most persuasive of whom were Robert Norris, Edward Long, Robert Bisset and Bryan
Edwards, produced a body of work which, when it confronted the question of the cultural inheritance of slaves at all, emphasised the corruption,

19

barbarity, childlike simplicity, sexual licentiousness and above all hea-thenism of African peoples. In this they were building upon a body of writing about Africa which had been developed over three hundred years. The middle passage was dealt with primarily as an economic phenom-enon.[12] When discussions moved away from a purely economic analysis an effective way of mispresenting the middle passage was to construct the African slave, and the slave trade, within distorting mythological and artistic conventions. Such disguises could take bizarre forms: a particu-larly powerful example, which combines poetic and graphic forms, occurs in Bryan Edwards's *History Civil and Commercial, of the British Colonies in the West Indies*.[13]

In a lyric preface to his chapter detailing the history and development of the African Atlantic slave trade, Edwards reprints Isaac Teale's poem 'The Sable Venus; an Ode' together with an elaborate illustrative engraving designed by Thomas Stothard [**2.4**].[14] Here, the black slave woman's expe-rience of the middle passage is presented as a version of the Birth of Venus. The rape of slave women is reconstructed in terms of a triumph of the sable

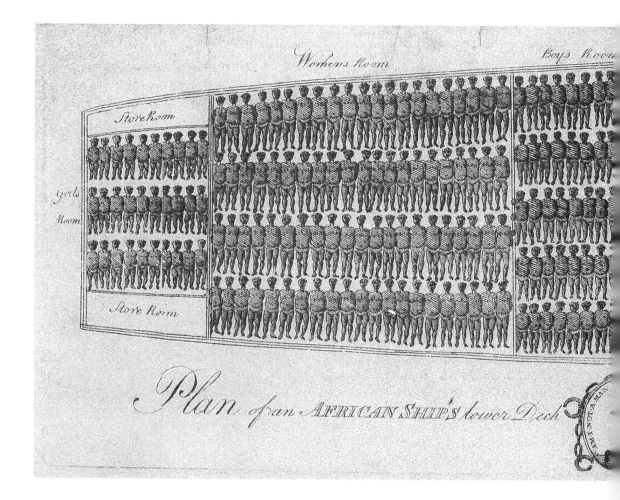

Venus over the slave-owners and traders who are ironically portrayed as her powerless victims. The process begins when Triton, the God of the sea, in order to win Venus 'Assumed the figure of a tar'; the result of their interracial union at sea is a hybrid Cupid.[15] The accompanying plate shows the black Venus as the symbolic representative of all African female slaves. She has a cloud of white cherubs hovering about her and is magically wafted across the Atlantic. The slave ship is transformed into a beautiful scallop shell pulled by frolicking dolphins. This late Baroque extravaganza is, in narrative and descriptive terms, antithetical to the diagrammatic and factual *Description*.[16]

Abolition imagery as African cultural erasure

The development of genuinely popular images attempting to describe the slaves during the middle passage were the achievement not of pro-slavery but of the abolitionists. Yet the images they produced obey a series of

[2.3] Society for the Abolition of the Slave Trade, Plymouth Committee, *Plan of an African Ship's Lower Deck with Negroes in the proportion of only One to a Ton* (copper engraving, January 1789)

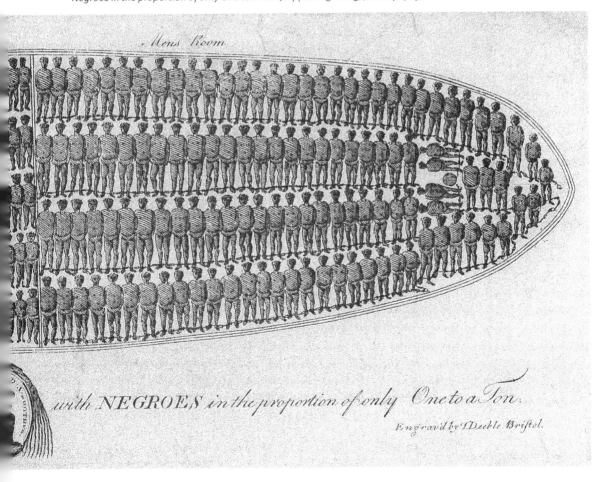

The VOYAGE of the SABLE VENUS, from ANGOLA to the WEST INDIES.

[2.4] Thomas Stothard, 'The Voyage of the Sable Venus, from Angola to the West Indies' (copper engraving, 1793). From Bryan Edwards, *History Civil and Commercial, of the British Colonies in the West Indies*

[2.5] Society for the Abolition of the Slave Trade, London Committee, made by Josiah Wedgwood, abolition seal, 'Am I not a man and a brother?' (cameo in jasper, 1788)

symbolic and narrative codes which deny the slave cultural representation. On 22 May 1787 the London Committee of the SEAST was set up.[17] They rapidly turned their attention to the systematic production of propaganda which drew on every available area of contemporary reprographic technology, and which was particularly inventive in terms of the way it generated visual propaganda. The two central images planned at committee level by the SEAST for mass reproduction and international distribution, the *Description* and the SEAST's official seal, were instantly influential and maintained their centrality in slavery debate in England and America up until the end of the American Civil War. The seal of the SEAST [2.5], with its representation of a kneeling enchained male African beneath the question 'Am I not a man and a brother?', was reproduced as the heading to a great number of anti-slavery publications appearing as stationary, in books, prints, oil paintings, newspaper headings and as a ceramic figurine. In its manifestation as a mass-produced Wedgwood ceramic medallion the image became so generally fashionable in the late 1780s and early 1790s as to be worn as a broach or hairpin by society ladies, and was incorporated into the lids of snuff boxes.[18] What this image shares with abolition propaganda which takes the middle passage as its central focus is a rhetoric which conforms, to a frightening extent, to Gates's description of erasure.

The black as cultural absentee, the black as a blank page for white guilt to inscribe, emerged as a necessary pre-condition for abolitionist polemic against the slave trade.

From the mid-1780s to the early 1790s the symbolic and narrative core of abolition propaganda consisted of descriptions of the middle passage. In pamphlets, books, journals and in the eyewitness accounts submitted during the interminable hearings of the consecutive slave bills in the Commons, a litany of horrors was continually recited, imagined and re-invented.[19] The slave had to be presented in a certain way if his/her cause were to stimulate notions of guilt and culpability on the part of an educated English audience, while at the same time not frightening such an audience off through fear or disgust. Torture and extreme suffering were presented through the personal testimony of predominantly white witnesses. Some of these accounts involved protracted descriptions of the most harrowing violence against women and children. Perhaps equally effective, however, were the approaches which emphasised the dehumanising commodification of the slave though an uncompromising objectivity.[20]

The work of the most rhetorically varied and influential of English abolition poets, William Cowper, bears this out. Cowper's abolition verse presents blacks in ways which essentialise the black's passivity, innocence and docility.[21] An extreme example of the disempowering of the black is in Cowper's bitter, 'Sweet Meat has Sour Sauce: or, the Slave-Trader in the Dumps'. The poem is a monologue spoken by a slave-trader and concludes with a fantasy in which the entire slave cargo is metaphorically transformed into a multitude of dead sprats: 'Twould do your heart good to see 'em below / Lie flat on their backs all the way as we go, / Like sprats on a gridiron, scores in a row'.[22] The slave cargo is to be admired as an exhibition of efficient packaging. And this takes us back to Gates's argument about white myths of the middle passage. Perhaps the most extreme written example of white superscription of the black experience of the middle passage was produced by the ex slave captain and fashionable London divine, John Newton in his *Thoughts Upon the African Slave Trade*. Newton stated that: 'the Slaves lie in two rows, one above the other, on each side of the ship, close to each other, like books upon a shelf. I have known them so close, that the shelf would not, easily, contain one more.'[23] In its emphasis on a library-like order, a display obscene in its seemliness, Newton's metaphor suggests a verbal equivalent of the *Description*.

Real mess and ideal order: the 'right' ways of seeing

The idealising and abstracting tendencies both of Newton's simile and of the *Description* are highlighted if they are set beside the only surviving image made on the spot describing the conditions of slaves in a fully packed slave ship. This is a water-colour made by a young English naval officer, Lieutenant Francis Meynell [**plate 1**]. It obliterates the linear clarity of the *Description* leaving nothing but a horrible mess. The drawing was made in

23

1846, off the coast of West Africa, and depicts the state of slaves on the captured Spanish slaver, the *Albanoz*. The drawing was made thirty-nine years after abolition of the British slave trade and fourteen years after the abolition of slavery in the British sugar colonies. This was a period when national self-doubt and self-loathing over British domination of the slave trade had been effaced and a self-aggrandising mythology reinscribed. The British Navy's African slave patrols were presented as the glorious product of the 1807 abolition bill. The celebration of Britain's disinterested philanthropy allowed for the erection of a pantheon of white abolitionists (Wilberforce, Clarkson, Sharp, Macaulay) and the erasure of national guilt through the active suppression of Spanish, American and Portuguese slave trading. The capture of each foreign slave ship affirmed British enlightenment and disguised the memory of the two hundred years of British domination of the slave trade.[24]

Meynell's drawing has an ungainly power perhaps all the more emphatic in view of the fact that no visual eyewitness account of an English slave cargo has survived from the period before 1807. It is a work which has avoided the vision of the slave deck sanctioned by the Victorian academy. Sir J. Noel Paton's *Capture of a Slave Ship* gives the basic tropes which Meynell evades [**2.6**].[25] White angelic British Tars, bathed in a celestial light, reach down to the slaves who strike classical poses of despair as they wallow mimicking lost souls in the infernal regions. Emotion is at fever pitch and a very British mercy is at hand. The leading rescuer reaches down a bared arm, the finger reaching out like Michelangelo's God creating Adam, but the forearm tattooed with the Crown and anchor.

[**2.6**] Anon., after Sir J. Noel Paton, *Capture of a Slave Ship* (wood-engraving, 1915 based on oil painting, 1867)

CAPTURE OF A SLAVE-SHIP.
(Copied from a picture by Sir J. Noel Paton, by permission of the Glasgow Art Union.)

In Meynell's drawing no white liberating presence is depicted. The slaves have some freedom of movement, in dark corners and crevices, or precariously perched upon rafters and narrow areas of makeshift floor. They appear left to fend for themselves in the misery and the gloom, fitting in around bales of cloth and barrels, their status as cargo self-evident, their powerlessness emphasised by the fact that there is not a chain in sight. More than a maritime prison, with ordered ranks of manacled captives, there is the effect of a shanty town, a haphazard world where depth and colour have been obliterated and where humanity forms part of a seething jumble of goods which will only be sorted, extricated and polished up on arrival. Fatigue, ennui, discomfort and sheer depression are the primary impressions. Not one figure remotely resembles the recumbent lines of the *Brookes*. The marshalled diagrammatics of the *Description* are dispersed, to be replaced with an artistically primitive white representation of suffering chaos. Meynell's image is a private witnessing, the visual equivalent of a diary entry, and it is worth asking whether it possesses an equivalent descriptive power to that of the *Description*. Newton's metaphor and the *Description* both perhaps suggest that it is necessary to go beyond attempts at empathetic emotionalism in order to provide an image which is appropriate to registering the process of the middle passage. The danger of such an unemotional approach is that its extreme reductivism may transform the slaves from people to things.

Myths and origins: the genesis of the Description

To understand how the *Description* was made it is vital to remember that the work represents not an abstract idea but a real boat, the *Brookes*, trading out of Liverpool. This boat was selected by the SEAST Committee in Plymouth as the fitting subject for an illustrated broadside, and then using more detailed facts and measurements, by the London Committee.

The graphic authority of the *Description* results, to a large degree, from the fact that it evolved out of a precise style of naval Architecture. This comes out clearly if the differences between the *Plan* [2.3] produced by the Plymouth Committee in 1788 and the London *Description* [2.2] of 1789 are scrutinised. A detailed comparison provides insights into what qualities gave the final version such appeal to Western audiences over the subsequent two centuries.

The Plymouth *Plan* is simple: it presents a single overview, or plan, of the main slave deck. All except four of the slave bodies are drawn vertically, not packaged efficiently to follow the lines of the ship. The image is also confused in terms of its depiction of the slave bodies by the incorporation of the kneeling slave from the abolition seal who is printed below the image of the ship. This sentimentalised kneeling figure, encircled by a symbolic manacle and cat of nine tails, introduces a set of images which symbolically adulterate the almost abstract depiction of the slave bodies above. In the *Description* the seal and cat have been erased, while the ship itself has now been drawn up according to a precise set of measurements. These measurements are of a completely different nature from the crude rule of thumb proportions upon which the single view of the Plymouth *Plan* was based.

Who actually drew the final version of the *Description* is difficult to establish. The first London Committee minute to refer to the *Description* makes it clear that the responsibility for designing the new version fell to five members: 'Resolved. That is the opinion of this Committee that a description of a Slave Ship with a Plan and Sections be prepared and that the following gentlemen be appointed to execute the same. Mr James Philips, Mr. Harrison, Mr. Woods, Mr. Hoare, Revd. Mr. Clarkson.'[26] Clarkson also, however, goes on to state that 'The committee at Plymouth had been the first to suggest the idea; but that in London had now improved it'.[27] Clarkson then explains that the detailed list of ship measurements, from which the famous London version of the *Description* was drawn up, and which were quoted in the text beneath it, were the work of a professional, one Captain Perry of the Royal Navy. The *Brookes* was chosen because she was at the head of Perry's alphabetical list.[28] When the *Description* came to be developed out of this information it could consequently be drawn using the most advanced techniques of naval architecture. Then, using the equally precise space allocations set out in Dolben's bill for the stowage of slaves, it was possible to work out exactly how many slaves the ship could hold.[29] Where the Plymouth *Plan* gives a single overview of a fictional slave deck of the *Brookes*, the *Description* describes each deck and area of the boat where slaves might be placed. This extraordinary precision is only possible because the design obeys very closely the techniques for depicting a naval vessel set down in late-eighteenth-century naval architecture guides.

The rules of naval architecture were of comparatively recent invention. It was only in 1675 with the publication of Anthony Deane's *Doctrine of Naval Architecture* that a foolproof representational system was developed. This book was groundbreaking and although refined was never really superseded in the eighteenth century.[30] The *Description* obeys the basic conventions, the most radical departure lying in the presentation of two plans, or full views of the decks, from above. The conventional naval plan based on Deane's system would have shown only one half view of the upper deck, and clearly this innovation was made for dramatic impact.[31] Although no single contemporary engraving appears to have incorporated every element of the *Description*, each drawing within it conforms to an already extant architectural model, although the only slave ships which appear to have been drawn in histories of naval architecture are Roman and Venetian slave galleys. The *Description*, in adopting a style of draftmanship used to describe the abstract beauty of ships, relates directly to a discourse of British naval power. Yet in suddenly inundating the clean lines, which describe the ship, with rows of human bodies printed in wedges of black ink, the print simultaneously questions the relation of the

[1] Lieutenant Francis Meynell, *View of the Deck of the Slave Ship Albanoz* (pencil and water-colour on paper, 1846)

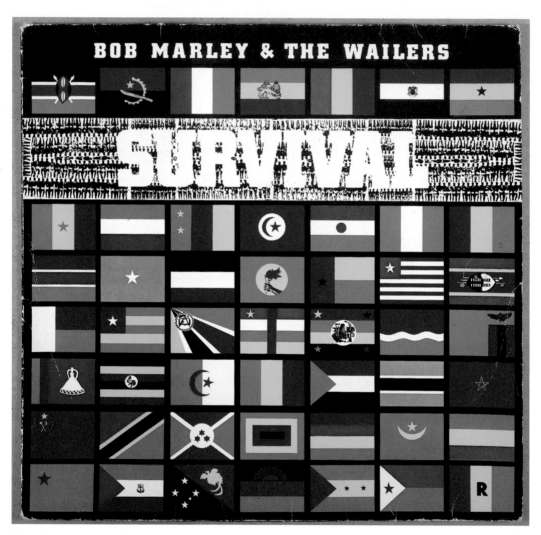

[2] Bob Marley, *Survival* (LP Album cover, photolithograph, 1979)

slave trade to British maritime history. The conjunction of technical engraving with the depiction of a mass of black human flesh is a superb semiotic shock tactic.[32]

The Description *in Paris, and Mirabeau's curious appropriations*

From the moment of its publication the *Description* drew compulsive and highly varied reactions from white European audiences. One French example demonstrates the extent to which fascination went hand in glove with a certain frustration, a frustration at being shown a plan only. In July 1789 William Clarkson travelled to Paris, on behalf of the SEAST, where he remained for a most remarkable year. His *History* gives a detailed account of this period.[33] Clarkson was immediately introduced to leading statesmen and politicians in the circle of the Société des Amis des Noirs. He launched himself into the turbulent political arena of the Revolution and agitated through his contacts in the National Assembly for the immediate abolition of the French slave trade. Clarkson was keen to proselytise the abolition cause and ordered a 'large packet' of propaganda to be sent from England. Besides coloured engravings of slave-related atrocities in Africa, 'it consisted of above a thousand of the plan and section of a slave-ship with an explanation in French'.[34] Many of the leading figures in the Amis des Noirs are quoted as being suddenly shocked into a realisation of the realities of the middle passage as they read the plan naturalistically.[35] The most spectacular response was that of the supreme public orator of the first phase of the French Revolution, Gabriel Honoré de Raqueti Compte de Mirabeau:

> when Mirabeau first saw it [the *Description*], he was so impressed by it, that he ordered a mechanic to make a model of it in wood, at a considerable expense. This model he kept afterwards in his dining room. It was a ship in miniature about a yard long, and little wooden men and women, which were painted black to represent the slaves, were seen stowed in their proper places.[36]

Mirabeau's relationship with English abolition, and with anti-slave trade propaganda, is a fascinating topic in which the *Description* holds centre stage. Mirabeau was a founder member of the Amis des Noirs formed by Brissot in May 1788. Mirabeau was perhaps the most determined and the most courageous member of the Amis des Noirs to attempt to force the National Assembly to confront the problem of the vast French involvement in the slave trade and to force its immediate abolition.[37] By March of 1790 Mirabeau had prepared what was, even by his standards, a mammoth oration upon the slave trade. The speech was to be delivered in a general debate in the National Assembly demanding immediate abolition of the trade. The powerful French planter lobby managed to call off the meeting and demanded a committee review on the question of the admissibility of the slave trade as a subject of open debate.

Mirabeau's speech was consequently never delivered. But the answer as to why he constructed the model mentioned by Clarkson lies within the text of the unperformed speech. Mirabeau was going to demand immediate abolition of the slave trade, and the centrepiece of his rhetoric was to be the presentation before the French National Assembly of his model of the *Brookes*, created from the *Description*. In doing so he was to follow a similar tack to Wilberforce, who had a miniature boat constructed according to the *Description*, with the slave representations from the print pasted flat onto its various decks [**2.7**]. This was passed from hand to hand around the House of Commons during a slave-bill debate but it did not violate the two-dimensional diagrammatic representation of the slaves in the original.[38] Mirabeau's model was much bigger and went further in presenting the slaves in three dimensions. The text of Mirabeau's speech implies that he was suddenly going to reveal his model to the Assembly, much in the manner of a piece of shocking and hitherto undisclosed court evidence. The sight of the ship was then immediately followed up by an extended meditation on its implications:

> Behold the model of a vessel laden with these unfortunate beings, and seek not to turn away your gaze! How they are piled one upon the other! How they are crammed into the between-decks! Unable to stand erect: nay, even seated, their heads are bowed. More than that, they cannot move their members, tightly bound, nor even their bodies; for, partakers of all the wants, of all the miseries of him who shares their irons, each man is attached to another: often to a dying one, often to a dead body! Mark how the vessel when it rolls hurts them, mutilates them, bruises them against each other, tears them with their own chains, and presents thus a thousand tortures in a single picture! They

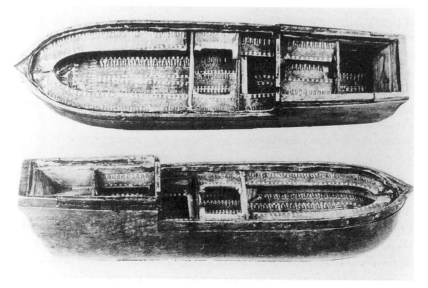

[**2.7**] Anon., model of the slave ship *Brookes* (wood, and pasted copper engraving, 1790)

crouch themselves down, all the space is filled; and the insensate cupidity
which should succour them has not even foreseen that no room for passage
remains, but that it is necessary to tread under foot the bodies of the living victims. Have they at the least a sufficient quantity of wholesome air? Let us cal-
culate it together. A space of a little less than six feet in length, and a little more
than a foot in breadth, is the base of the column of air, the smallest possible,
which has to suffice for the respiration of each one ... The poor wretches! I see
them, I hear them gasping for breath: their parched and protruded tongues
paint their anguish, and cannot further express it! How they hang to, how they
cluster round, the grates! How they endeavour to catch even rays of light, in the
vain hope of cooling themselves thereby, were it only for an instant![39]

Had he ever been able to make this performance Mirabeau would have
achieved a descriptive antithesis to the *Description*. One explanation of
Mirabeau's fusion of psychological realism with the abstract detachment
of the *Description* relates to the mesmeric formal properties of the print.
There is an awful rigour about the design. In purely aesthetic terms the
slaves have no human presence at all; in terms of compositional balance
the white spaces where the slaves are not are as important as the black
spaces of ink which represent their bodies. It is possible that it was precisely this formality, which appears to deny the flesh and blood presence
of the slaves, which led Mirabeau to seek the design's realisation in three
dimensions and then to try to imagine himself as a slave in the hold. In a
sense he was trying to humanise the *Description*, to make it more real, to
give the victims a voice. Again, however, despite the elaborateness with
which Mirabeau articulates his empathy, the slave is culturally void.
Mirabeau's emotions of outrage and pity are a test: he tests his moral and
intellectual capacity for imagining suffering through subjective projection
onto the site of the slave bodies, but the rules for the test are ultimately
laid out by the *Description*. They are rules which allow the black body no
voice which is not the creation of a white observer.[40]

Mirabeau's response is an extreme example of the effect of the
Description as a plan, as an instruction to construct, but I would also argue
that the power of the work grows out of the way it fuses two other elements,
one narrative, the other formal. The *Description* was, as we have seen,
drawn according to the conventions of a relatively new style of naval diagrammatics, but as a boat packed with living things sailing on the ocean for
a set period it is embedded in Christian narrative and myth.

The Description *as parodic ark*

Mirabeau's conversion of the *Description* into a model boat suggests a cor-
relation between the ark and the slave ship. Even in the eighteenth century
the first mythic journey on a boat stowed with all there was of life on this
earth was a familiar plaything. Noah's Ark, the first boat, had been a three-
dimensional children's toy in European households since the late sixteenth
century. Surviving examples from about 1800 have wooden mannequins of

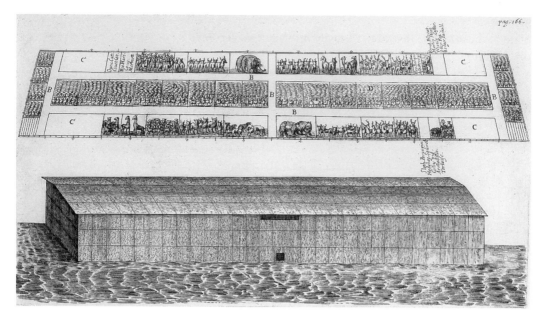

[2.8] Anon., 'Plan of Noah's Ark' (copper engraving, 1668). From John Wilkins, *An essay towards a real character, and a philosophical language*

Noah and his wife naked and painted black. The ark provided not only a mythic base but a narrative and graphic method for the abolitionists.[41]

In the mid-seventeenth century John Wilkins, Bishop of Chester, addressed at length what was, even then, a theological old chestnut: was Noah's Ark big enough to hold all the animals in the world? Wilkins, in developing a naturalistic approach to the description of the ark, adopted the same procedure to prove his case as the abolitionists adopted to give a 'real' account of how many slaves would be put on a slave ship.[42] Wilkins, anticipating the method to be found in Athanasius Kircher's *Arca Noe* of 1675, cites the precise dimensions of the ark as given by Moses in Genesis 6:15; he then provides a table of all the varieties of animal, categorised according to foodstuff, and then an estimate of 'what kind of room may be allotted to the making of sufficient stalls for their reception'.[43] With this information he then produces his diagram [**2.8**], an external view of the entire coffin-like structure and a three-quarter section of the ark, stocked with its living freight, the dimensions and positioning of the different decks indicated by lettering.

There are strong similarities with the *Description*: in both cases the boat designs grow out of a set of printed instructions and a series of measurements; the design constitutes a pictorial realisation of the plan. The delight in providing a diagrammatic explanation of the technical construction of the ark was not limited to the sixteenth century but was carried through and refined in the eighteenth. Indeed increasingly refined versions were being produced right up to the publication of the *Description*. The first edition of the *Encyclopaedia Britannica* in 1773 carried a half-page plate of the ark. The text draws heavily on Wilkins's arguments, and the plate, although more naturalistic than Wilkins's and set in a seascape, appears to have evolved out of Wilkins's basic design.[44]

The publication of the *Encyclopédie*, one of the summarising moments of the Enlightenment in terms of the display of knowledge through text, both in words and images, also took in the plan of the ark. The elaborate plate describing the ark first appeared in the 1777 supplementary volume of plates [**2.9**]. The main design for the ark was directly copied from a French translation of the first edition of the *Encyclopaedia Britannica*.[45] The scenic presentation of the whole boat is accompanied, however, by a series of details giving projected views of sections of the ark. There are cross-sections and three-dimensional spacial projections of the probable layout of individual stalls. The plan was accompanied by precise technical instructions on the construction of the stalls for the animals, right down to how the dung was to be collected and removed.[46] With the *Encyclopédie's* engraving of the ark one arrives at a late-eighteenth-century treatment which in its utilisation of contemporary styles of technical drawing, and its concern with practical detail, parallels the style and thought of the *Description*.

Yet the final power of the *Description* comes not from its similarity to the plans of the ark, but from its essential difference. The slave ship is a precise parody of the ark; to use a term of Jean Baudrillard's it constitutes an 'anti-ark'.[47] The vision of harmony afloat, and of an infinitely extended

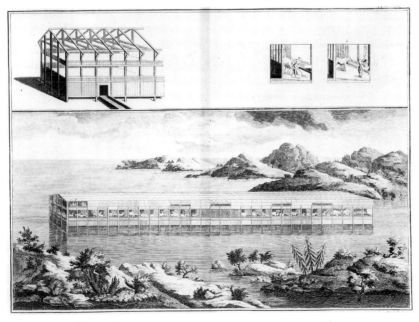

[**2.9**] Anon., 'Arche de Noé' (copper engraving, 1776). From *Supplement À L' Encyclopédie, ou Dictionaire Raisoné des Sciences, des Artes et des Métiers*

familial order with all creation linked two by two, is tortured into a different order. The slave ship as anti-ark embodies a series of balanced antitheses to the ark: greed is substituted for love, exploitation for trust, repetition for variation and sameness for difference. The cargoes of the two boats are perfectly antithetical. The ark emphasised the unique value of each created thing, and each life form aboard is simply unique; the slave ship emphasises the homogeneity of the slave cargo, and each life form aboard is, in its legal status, the same.

The *Description* tells us of a white fascination with its ignorance about a terrible black (and white) experience. For all its familiarity it finally emphasises the indescribable nature of the experience of the middle passage, and that may be what makes it ultimately an appropriate memorial. The *Description* is not a record of black slave experience for such experience is unrecoverable in several ways: firstly in the sense that it could not, decently, be re-invented; secondly in the sense that the experience of each individual on the middle passage was unique and unrepeatable; and finally in the sense that none of us, white or black, should ever consider ourselves to have recovered from this experience. The *Description* is perhaps best understood as a memorial to a disaster, not as a representation of what ever happened. As a memorial it acts as a point of focus for collective historical memory, as a space for meditation, as something clear and clean which paradoxically, as the earlier example of the Meynell drawing insists, has no right to be so.

The Description *as transhistorical hold-all*

The question of how to read the *Description* is further complicated for audiences today because the accreted history of the image which we have inherited is not stable. The *Description* is a protean entity which from the moment of its publication appeared in an enormous number of popular mutations. The mutation continues and the processes of transformation are significant. It is impossible to construct a complete account of the multiple adaptations and reprintings of the original engraving in England, let alone in Europe, and North and South America. Many versions were produced in ephemeral forms such as handbills, broadsides and children's books, and have perished. Some of the most significant surviving translations can be considered as indicators of what, in the course of two hundred years, the *Description* has come to mean.

As we have seen, the image was widely disseminated in France in the year of its first printing. Like the SEAST's seal, it was also printed in North America almost as soon as it came out. As early as May 1789 the magazine the *American Museum* had published a version, which was then readapted from this source almost verbatim by the Pennsylvania Society for the Abolition of the Slave Trade. This enormous Philadelphia edition of 2,500 gave the image currency in North American free states.[48] This version adapted from the primitive English, Plymouth Committee *Plan* went on to serve as the basis for the many adaptations which reappeared in illustrated

pamphlets in North America over the next decade. After this date the
majority of publications which reproduce the slave ship diagram in
America appear to use the version reproduced in Clarkson's *History*.[49]

The American adaptations indicate both the speed with which versions of the *Description* were subsumed into East Coast print culture and
the longevity of the image. It is also striking that the American versions are
remarkably true to their English models. Such adaptive conservatism was
not the case in England where the image underwent a series of bizarre reincarnations, some so extreme that the original content exists on the margins
of legibility. In 1827 the image appeared in *Scenes in Africa for the
Amusement and Instruction of Little Tarry at Home Travellers*. Here the
middle passage was summarised in one succinct paragraph:

> The captain of a slave ship wishes to carry as many as he can at once; the hold
> of his vessel is therefore measured and only sixteen inches each, in width, are
> allowed for the men, and less for the women and children. There they lie, so
> close, that it is impossible to walk among them, without treading upon them.
> They have no more room than a man has in his coffin; you may see by the plan
> of the slave ship how they lie. Numbers die almost every night from such
> close confinement, and the suffocating air it breeds. Nearly half the number
> have died in the passage.[50]

The accompanying engraving [**2.10**], little bigger than a postage stamp,
represents the slave bodies as a series of thin attenuated rectangles with no
human form or feature. In this version the reduction of the human form to
a space allocation is complete. The slaves have literally disappeared as a
human representation to become pure geometrical form.

Throughout the nineteenth and twentieth centuries the image continued to appear in a vast array of published materials relating to the history

[**2.10**] Anon., 'Plan of Slave Ship' (copper engraving, *c*. 1800). From Isaac Taylor, *Scenes in
Africa for the Amusement and Instruction of Little Tarry at Home Travellers*

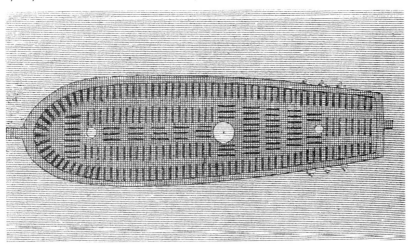

of slavery. It graces a host of abolition publications of the 1850s, including John Cassell's 1852 *Uncle Tom's Cabin Almanack*, which also included a cross-section of an African canoe packed with slaves being transported from the coast to the main slave ship.[51] In terms of naval architecture an extreme adaptation is a plate in Captain G. L. Sulivan's 1875 *Dhow Chasing in Zanzibar Waters* [**2.11**]. The plate shows a cross-section of a dhow captured by a Royal Navy patrol illustrating the mode of smuggling slaves: 'the poor creatures are stowed sometimes in two, sometimes in three tiers on extemporised bamboo decks, not sufficiently distant from each other to allow them to sit upright'. The slaves form an almost completely indecipherable block of ink, a lump of black in the hold.[52]

Over the past three decades the multiple reproduction and adaptation of the *Description* have taken spectacular forms in popular publishing. It has a promiscuous appeal for blacks and whites, for musicians and jewellers, for writers of popular history and elevated literary art. Some of these adaptations attempt to reduce the diagrammatic objectivity of the original, while others exaggerate this quality. Perhaps what they all finally testify to is uncertainty.

A radically reconstructed version of the *Description* formed the central device for Bob Marley's 1979 album *Survival* [**plate 2**]. The central section of the slave ship, reprinted three times and turned into a rectangular strip, dominates the album cover where it stands out in black and white. The word 'SURVIVAL' in white is stencilled over the design obliterating some of the slave bodies in a message of pan-Africanist optimism. The rest of the cover is made of a dancing coloured mosaic of all the flags of the post-imperialist African nations. On the record sleeve the image is printed again, in black and white, over the lyrics. For Marley, or his designer, the image has been rebuilt into a message of hope for contemporary Africa.[53]

The *Description* has been taken up in other politically charged publishing contexts. A recent hard-hitting 'beginners guide' to the history of the Atlantic slave trade, *The Black Holocaust for Beginners*, includes a pen and ink reworking of one of the cross-sections shown in the *Description*, which sits oddly among the otherwise emotionally volatile and realistic imagery [**2.12**]. At the back of the volume there is an advertisement for a miniature cast of the *Description* as a piece of jewellery with cowrie shells attached on springs [**2.13**]. This photograph is accompanied by the advertising copy: 'If you desire a gold, silver or brass pin depicting the Slave ship "Brookes" ... contact *Who Deserves it More Than You?*[54] Here the *Description* has moved into a strange semiotic hinterland where it functions both as a fashion accessory and as a piece of political propaganda.

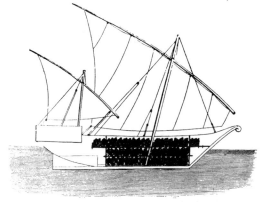

SECTION OF THE DHOW ALLUDED TO AT PAGE 168, SHOWING THE MANNER OF [*Page* 114. STOWING SLAVES ON BOARD.

[**2.11**] Anon., 'Dhow with Slaves' (wood-engraving, 1875). From G. L. Sulivan, *Dhow Chasing in Zanzibar Waters*

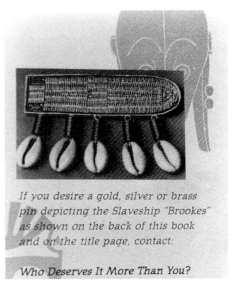

[2.12] Anon., 'African Resistance Continues' (photo lithograph, 1995). From S. E. Anderson, *The Black Holocaust for Beginners*

[2.13] Sista Phyllis M. Bowdwin, 'Who Deserves It More Than You?' (photolithograph, 1995). Advertisement back page, *The Black Holocaust for Beginners*

The *Description* has been deployed in a mass of other publishing contexts. The abstract beauty of the design made it desirable as decorative endpaper for numerous publications on slavery, such as James Pope-Hennessy's 1963 *Sins of the Fathers* or Terence Brady's 1975 *The Fight Against Slavery*, and recently the hardback and paperback editions of Hugh Thomas's *The Slave Trade*.[55] The most elaborate deployments occurred recently when the print was used in a variety of ways inside and outside Barry Unsworth's slave trade blockbuster *Sacred Hunger*, which shared the Booker Prize in 1992. The mass-marketing glut which greeted Unsworth's victory equipped the hardback edition with a dust cover which consisted of three small groups of the slaves from the famous *Description* repeated over and over on a tea-coloured background [**2.14**]. Large blow-ups of this cover in placard form also decorated the display windows of the big booksellers in the weeks following the prize announcement. The endpapers of the book reproduce the design twice in a tasteful combination of greys. Inside the book a section of four manacled slaves has been cut out and used as a little printer's flourish to adorn each chapter title page. Yet the design was not considered appropriate for the merchandising of the paperback edition several months later. This, at least in its English manifestation, carried a garish soft focus pastel portrait of two piratical-looking young black men. One might speculate on the reasons behind the jettisoning of the *Description* at this stage.[56]

This brief excursion into the history of the popular absorption of the *Description* demonstrates the lasting impact of the work but leaves open the

[**2.14**] Anon., dust jacket for Barry Unsworth, *Sacred Hunger* (photolithograph, 1992)

question of how adequate a response to the memory of the slave trade the image finally is. Perhaps all one can say at this stage is that, for better or worse, this image is as close as the abolition movement in Britain got to the creation of a final monument to the middle passage.[57] For Western culture it appears to retain this status, while contemporary late-eighteenth-century high art treatments of the middle passage do not. One reason must be that it was the only eighteenth-century representation of the middle passage that took one not only on board, but inside the hold of, a slave ship. Mainstream abolition imagery on both sides of the Atlantic in the period 1780–1860 was focused primarily on depictions of either embarkation and the separation of slave families on the African coast or the landing of slaves on the Caribbean or American coasts after the voyage.

Capitalising upon the sudden interest in abolition, George Morland produced two oil paintings which described scenes on the African coast, and both pictures were engraved and sold in very large editions, with the active engagement of the SEAST, both in England and after 1794 in France.[58] *African Hospitality* (1791) illustrated a scene from William Collins's poem 'The Slave Trade' in which a shipwrecked white family is hauled to freedom and comforted by an African family. This image of white trauma soothed by African humanity on the beaches of the slave coast existed as a narrative counterbalance to Morland's earlier *Execrable Human Traffic* [**2.15**] of 1788. This painting is a specifically anti-European take on the Atlantic slave trade, which strangely excises Africa from participation. It shows the separation of an African family, the father dragged off under threat of violence while his wife and family look on distracted. The traumatic separation of the Africans is the responsibility of a group of white sailors who appear to be operating as opportunistic kidnappers.

[2.15] John Raphael Smith, *The Slave Trade* (copper engraving, 1789). After George Morland, *The Execrable Human Traffic* (oil on canvas, 1788)

UNITED STATES SLAVE TRADE.
1830.

[2.16] Anon., 'United States Slave Trade 1830' (copper engraving, 1830). From Benjamin Lundy, *Genius of Universal Emancipation*

African participation in the trade, and the organisation of a sophisticated trading network based on slave forts, is absent from the narrative. The scene was accompanied by quotations from Collins framed in a language of heightened emotionalism: 'Lo the poor captive with distraction wild / Views his dear partner torn from his embrace.' Despite its melodramatic base, this work possesses a genuine power in the way it has shifted the narrative of the middle passage from an event which happens on the Atlantic ocean into an event which happens, in ghastly anticipation, within the mind of the victim, on the coast of Africa.

Morland's treatments, based upon anticipation of the voyage, rather than immersion in its horrors, remained a standard element of abolition pictorial rhetoric. Other pictorial accounts of the middle passage came at the event from the other end, concentrating not on embarkation but upon of the slave's arrival and sale. An effective concentration of the primary narrative ingredients in the latter scenario is the widely circulated image 'United States Slave Trade', which was printed as a high-quality single-sheet engraving and as the frontispiece to Benjamin Lundy's *The Genius of Universal Emancipation* [**2.16**].[59] Again the central emphasis is upon family separation. Supercilious planters break up shackled groups of males, females and children, while the slave ship floats offshore, with a ship's boat loaded with slaves rowing to shore. In the background slaves labour on a plantation and are flogged, while the Capitol building can be glimpsed over a hill top, the famous dome flying the star spangled banner. In this work the middle passage has been formally marginalised, one small part of a much larger narrative focusing not upon the horror of the sea trip alone but upon the entire nexus of economic relationships in which the middle passage was embedded. The ship is almost thrust off the edge of the picture to make way for a new abolition agenda rooted in the movement to emancipate slaves in America. Yet significant art had been produced during the first great wave of English anti-slave trade abolition which approached the theme of the middle passage from the slave coasts of the Americas. Both Johan Heinrich Fuseli and William Blake created sophisticated pictorial narratives, which are fairly precisely contemporary with the *Description*, yet which approach the theme of the middle passage in ways which leave the viewer firmly standing on land. Both these works demonstrate that the reduction of the slave ship to a remote presence in the background can be exploited with great power.

In 1796 Blake made an engraving of 'A Negro hung alive by the Ribs to a Gallows' for Captain John Stedman's *Narrative of a Five Years' Expedition Against the Revolted Negroes of Surinam* [**2.17**].[60] This design is an attack on the slave trade which paradoxically makes its point through the visual marginalisation of the slave ship. The design is dominated by the titanic presence of the torture victim. Nothing can hide us from the monumental presence of this man, but the scale of his suspended body is defined in relation both to the objects which surround him on land and to the tiny ship,

Blake Sculp.

A Negro hung alive by the Ribs to a Gallows.

which must soon move off the picture plane to right. A skull on a pole gazes straight out towards the tiny ship in full sail, which sits on a sea of perfectly calm, horizontal, ruled lines. Death stares towards the slave ship; the living, but dying, slave stares out towards the audience, which is left to draw its own conclusions about the relationship between the suffering we witness and the little ship which brought the slave to Surinam. In conjoining the violated body, the death's head and the slave ship, Blake has created his own visual triangular trade.

Fuseli's solution to the presentation of the middle passage is equally confrontational, but also treats the slave ship at a distance. The design was produced both as an oil painting [**plate 3**] and as an engraving. Fuseli was asked to provide engravings for the 1806 edition of Cowper's poems, and the design was intended to accompany one of the popular abolition ballads which Cowper originally composed in the spring of 1788.[61] The poem is the closest Cowper comes to articulating a state of justified anger and vengeful fury in the slave, although he is careful to stop well short of portraying the slave as a full-blooded revolutionary. The widespread belief that the natural cataclysms that struck the land and seas surrounding the slave colonies were a manifestation of divine wrath at the slave trade is taken up by Cowper in a stanza which provides the narrative core for Fuseli's design: 'Hark – He [God] answers. Wild tornadoes / Strewing yonder flood with wrecks, / Wasting Towns, Plantations, Meadows, / Are the voice in which he speaks.'[62] The colossal figure of the black male, wearing a loin cloth, is placed on land in the foreground, accompanied by a lighter-coloured woman. In the painting the female is perhaps white, in the engraving definitely mulatto. The minute upturned hull of the wrecked slave ship floats far below struck by lightning in the midst of the tempest. Fuseli's male slave responds to the disaster with an impassioned victory salute, two clenched fists raised above his head. His companion in a long light gown has one arm curled about his waist while the other is extended in a gesture of warning. The design goes a good deal further in presenting an independent and triumphant image of vengefulness than does Cowper's verse.[63] Fuseli picks up on the fact that Cowper's narrational persona might be male or female by presenting a slave couple, physically relaxed with each other, celebrating the moment of destruction. The middle passage exists as a crime which must be expiated by blood, and there is a millenarian extremity in Fuseli's approach close in spirit to the prophetic pamphlet literature of the 1780s and 1790s which presented London and Liverpool as the doomed Babylon of Revelation because of their relation to the slave trade.[64] While uplifting as an image of black defiance, the painting takes one no nearer to the slave ship and the suffering it contains than does Blake's design. It was to be another thirty-five years before a great Romantic artist provided a treatment of the slave ship, and the suffering it enclosed, while on the Atlantic crossing. When in 1840 Turner created the *Slave Ship* it was in a very different cultural climate from that in which Fuseli and Blake were working.

Monumentalisation, Memorialisation and Slavery:
Turner's *Slavers Throwing Overboard the Dead and Dying, Typhon Coming On*

England's preferred monuments

> The disaster is not sombre, it would liberate us from everything if it could just have a relation with someone; we would know it in the light of language and at the twilight of language with a *gai savoir*. (Maurice Blanchot, *The Writing of the Disaster*)

> The sea. Have you forgotten that pain is a slaughterhouse and the light a whip? I see hollow sun and weary sea, supported on the bleeding of the great and unmysterious Indies. (Edouard Glissant, *The Indies*, XLIX)

J. M. W. Turner's *Slavers Throwing Overboard the Dead and Dying, Typhon Coming On* [plate 4] is the only indisputably great work of Western art ever made to commemorate the Atlantic slave trade, and particularly English monopoly of this trade in the eighteenth century. The painting is inevitably, inexorably, associated with John Ruskin. He owned it for twenty-eight years and devoted one of his most celebrated set pieces to it in the first volume of *Modern Painters*, the book that made his name. But Ruskin wrote about the painting many other times in many other ways. His relationship with the work was deeply tormented, and his torment is educative. Turner's painting and Ruskin's relationship to it are still very misunderstood. Turner has left no substantial record outside this painting of his views on slavery. Ruskin wrote a great deal about slavery and articulated with power a series of attitudes that are now deeply unattractive. His bellicose nationalism, his championing of the British imperial mission, his prominent role in supporting government action over the 1865 Morant Bay rebellion when he took a leading role on the Eyre Defence Committee, his belief that the plight of the British factory labourer was a form of slavery infinitely more regrettable and destructive than that of Africans, all these positions might appear to disqualify him as a critic of the middle passage.[65] The following discussion of the *Slave Ship* argues that it is within the inconsistencies and contradictions of his thought that Ruskin provides a resource for understanding how art can construct slavery.

Leaving Ruskin aside for the moment (in the context of Turner he constitutes a very difficult 'special case'), until very recently the critical history of the *Slave Ship* is an intriguing record of ignorance, misreading and evasion.[66] At its first public viewing at the Royal Academy summer exhibition of 1840, critics in all the big literary journals and major newspapers ridiculed the narrative details which describe the drowning slaves in the foreground. While some lambasted the portrayal of sea and sky as colouristically offensive and technically appallingly sloppy, others, most spectacularly William Makepeace Thackeray, saw in it one of Turner's greatest seascapes and, because of its narrative foreground, one of his

41

greatest follies. The drowning slaves and the glorious sunset were not reconciled.[67]

The painting continued to enjoy mixed fortunes with viewers. On its first public display, in America at the Museum of Fine Arts in Boston in 1875, it again stirred up lively debate over its qualities as art, extracting from Mark Twain the memorable one-liner: 'it reminded him of a tortoise-shell cat having a fit in a platter of tomatoes'.[68] For Twain it was an aesthetic sham, which American art lovers pretended to like because of Ruskin. The blood red sunset is changed into a ludic prop as Twain casts himself as an American bull for whom the painting is a red rag. The objections, put forward with an unmistakably Twainian gusto, are different from those of the early English critics. The slaves do not get a look in. It is not the subject or the narrative that are ridiculous to Twain, but purely the technique, the distance of the painting from nineteenth-century conventions of finish, coloration and verisimilitude: 'floating of iron cable chains and other unfloatable things [the slaves?] … fishes swimming around on top of the mud – I mean water. The most of the painting is a manifest impossibility – that is to say, a lie.' As he toured Europe in the succeeding months, the *Slave Ship* reappears in diary entries that constantly refer to Turner as a force producing nausea and sickness: 'There are pictures here as bad as the *Slave Ship* they give you the belly ache', 'splendid conflagrations of colour have the effect of nauseating the spectator. Turner soon makes one sick at the stomach.'[69] The violence of Twain's dislike, and his sickness in thinking of the painting, constitute a rejection so extreme as to suggest that it had a violent effect on him which had to be submerged. Twain, for whatever reasons, did not want to take the painting on in terms of what it said about the Western inheritance of slavery.

The subsequent absorption of the painting into the Turner canon and its supporting literatures has been less brutally, but more ingeniously, evasive than Twain. The *Slave Ship* has been found a place in the grand works of the Turnerian Romantic project. From the readings of Kenneth Clark onwards, the death of the slaves is seen to constitute one aspect of Turnerian sublimity, his ability to present humanity dwarfed and destroyed by enormous elemental forces. In reading the painting as part of a group of paintings, the uniqueness of its subject is denied. There have also recently been attempts at a narrowly 'political' reading which have set the painting against matter-of-fact imagery depicting industrial developments in Britain or drawn from mid-nineteenth-century anti-slavery propaganda.[70] Yet the painting has refused to be reduced and has recently emerged as a challenge to contemporary audiences, and a trauma point for understanding the relation of race and colour to culture. It has induced a dense and allusive discussion of the relations of its colour symbolism to Herman Melville's, and it has been suggested that the pure white sun of the *Slave Ship* makes whiteness terrifying and destructive, much in the manner of Melville's disquisition on 'The Whiteness of the

Whale' in *Moby Dick*.[71] In a very different and confrontational reading, Paul Gilroy sees the painting as a site which might allow for the dismantling of racially reductive aesthetic agendas. He concludes: 'The picture and its strange history pose a challenge to the black English today. It demands that we strive to integrate the different dimensions of our cultural heritage more effectively.' The painting poses an equally strong challenge to the white English consciousness.

What did mid-Victorian audiences want from a painting of the middle passage? The original public exhibition of the *Slave Ship* is helpful here. In the Royal Academy the *Slave Ship* hung close by the French painter Auguste Biard's *Scene on the African Coast* [**plate 5**] which provided a different and more accessible account of the slave trade. Contemporary reviewers were in no doubt about the merits of the two pictures. Biard's painting received universal applause, and it was bought and presented to Sir Thomas Fowell Buxton.[72] Biard's painting was praised for its clean narrative, its pathos and its cleverness in rendering so many dark complexions. Turner's painting had no such clarity. Several of the reviewers compared the two works.[73] Thackeray's review crystallises those qualities which rendered Biard's work so attractive and Turner's so incomprehensible.[74]

Thackeray's assessment articulates the head-on collision between what Turner was doing with the memory of the slave trade and the official historical memory laid down by Clarkson and Wilberforce's hagiographers and espoused by a rising Victorian imperialist sensibility.[75] Thackeray treated Turner's painting with a mixture of admiration and contempt. While extravagantly praising it on aesthetic grounds for its colouring which is seen as a conflagration ('the most tremendous piece of colour that was ever seen, it sets the corner of the room in which it hangs into a flame'), he described the technique in terms which make it sound like a tubist Auerbach from the early 1960s, ('flakes of white laid down with a trowel; bladders of vermilion madly spurted here and there'). He then followed the fashion in ridiculing it for its presentation of the slaves and the fishes and proves himself the equal of any of the other leading Victorian art critics in terms of his ability to turn a racist pun. The vocabularies of connoisseurship and the slave trade are cleverly but unpleasantly fused: 'horrid spreading polypi; like huge, slimy, poached eggs in which the hapless niggers plunge and disappear. Ye Gods what a "middle-passage."'

Thackeray's review then goes on to make a formal comparison between Turner and Biard. The narrative content of the latter is described with a combination of sentimentalism and rather disgusting relish: 'The scene is laid upon the African coast. King Tom or King Boy has come with troops of slaves down the Quorra, and sits in the midst of his chiefs and mistresses (one a fair creature, not much darker than a copper tea-kettle) bargaining with a French dealer.'[76] The rules for how the slave trade should be presented to a mid-nineteenth-century English audience seem to be as follows. The scene should be exotic and abroad, atrocity should be carried out by

43

foreigners, unchristian Africans should be ridiculed as foolish barbarians whose colour is of its nature risible, and a clear narrative pumped with detail is essential. One detail above all others leads Thackeray into ecstasies:

> Yonder is a poor woman kneeling before a Frenchman; her shoulder is fizzing under the hot iron with which he brands her; she is looking up shuddering, and wild, yet quite mild and patient: it breaks your heart to look at her. I never saw anything so exquisitely pathetic as that face. God bless you Monsieur Biard, for painting it! It stirs the heart more than a hundred thousand tracts, reports or sermons: it must convert every man who has seen it. You British government who have given twenty million to the freeing of this hapless people, give yet a couple of thousand more to the French painter and don't let his work go out of the country, now that it is here. Let it hang alongside the Hogarths in the National Gallery; it is as good as the best of them.[77]

Thackeray's praise names its own price. In this disturbing passage he sets up a peculiar parallelism between this painting and the British Parliament's remuneration of the Caribbean slave-owners upon the passing of the emancipation bill in 1833. Thackeray demands that this image be bought as England's just inheritance in its post-abolition phase; the nation should be rewarded with the purchase of pornography. The extravagant demand is set off by the excitement, the stirring, which he feels in response to the violent abuse of a half-naked black woman. Thackeray reads the image in a way which lays bare his own corrupt narrative expectations. The extraordinary emotional contradiction in the phrase describing her agony – 'shuddering and wild yet quite mild and patient' – embodies Thackeray's voyeuristic duplicity. He wants to see real suffering, but simultaneously he wants his slaves completely passive; there must be no suggestion of rebelliousness even under torture. Where Turner demands the re-examination of English guilt, Thackeray prefers to sit back and enjoy the spectacle of imagined white domination (French not English) and wipe a tear from his eye thanking God for English decency. His call to the nation 'let the friends of the Negro buy this canvas and cause a plate to be taken from it' was rapidly taken up. The picture was purchased for the Abolition Society, and coloured engravings and lithographs circulated internationally for several

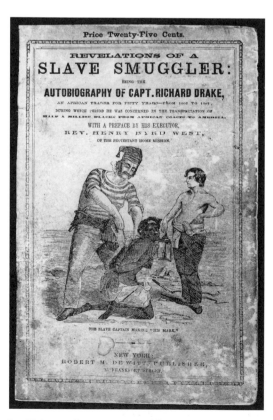

[2.18] Anon., after Auguste Biard (wood-engraving, 1860). Front cover to Richard Drake, *Revelations of a Slave Smuggler*

decades. Thackeray was not alone in singling out the branding of the topless beauty as a point of particular interest. It reappears in woodcut form, cut out from the rest of the picture, in countless variations. The example given here appeared on the front cover of Richard Drake's sensationalising *Revelations of a Slave Smuggler* in America as late as 1860 [**2.18**]. The crude woodcuts published in the popular press and in book form maintained the strange and erotically charged detail of the topless boy, who stands by holding the flame with which the brand was heated. His youth and white nudity appeared to be essential for the sexual frisson which is the central feature of the tableau. The inclusion of an observing infant as an element in the depiction of plantation atrocity became frequent in subsequent French academic painting. Biard's picture is a *locus classicus* embodying the predominant emphases in Victorian imagery describing slavery during the period from 1840 until the outbreak of the American Civil War in 1861 [**2.19**].[78]

Turner's great painting of the slaver was not engraved for the abolition market. Apart from the fact that it was technically untranslatable, it was not engaged with propping up white mythologies which combine sentimentality with eroticism, and overcoat all with a varnish of philanthropic patriotism. The painting is paradoxical, abstract, difficult.[79]

What we remember is defined by what we choose to forget, and how we choose to remember is defined by how we choose to ignore. An elegiac observation by Andre Schwarz-Bart on the impossibility of building monuments to the Holocaust helps in thinking about the sea and sky in Turner's painting: 'So this story will not finish with some tomb to be visited in pious memory. For the smoke that rises from crematoria obeys physical laws like any other: the particles come together and disperse according to the wind, which propels them. The only pilgrimage, dear reader, would be to look sadly at a stormy sky now and then.'[80] The memory of the Holocaust cannot be contained within art or public building. The burning bodies become smoke, the smoke disperses into the air, and this is fact. But this fact is expanded into a notion of mourning which is elemental – the elements in mourning are a memorial beyond human endeavour. Smoke and clouds look similar, and consequently every stormy sky carries within it the association of mass cremation. Beyond this is the reinvention of a great tradition of literary mourning. The storm in Lear, the natural cataclysms following the murders of Julius Caesar and Duncan, the sea dyed red through the blood of one man in the minds of two murderers in Macbeth – Schwarz-Bart claims this inheritance albeit in a modern down-beat language.

Turner's water performs a memorial function similar to Schwarz-Bart's clouds, only his rhetoric is that of a celebratory Romanticism. In concentrating upon the physical processes of drowning and dismemberment, Turner shows that the slaves are to be dissolved in the waters of the ocean, forever inextricably mixed with the element of their destruction. Turner's painting questions the limits of commemorative thought and gesture. Official monuments are built to institutionalise memory, to collectivise

Slave Market Scene on the Kambia River, Coast of Africa.

[2.19] Anon., after Auguste Biard, 'Scene on the African Coast' (wood-engraving, 1860). From Richard Drake, *Revelations of a Slave Smuggler*

suffering and guilt. Monuments to human suffering on a vast scale are diffi-cult affairs. Maya Lin's *Vietnam Veterans Memorial* in Washington – two polished granite walls, inscribed with the birth and death dates of every known combatant in the war – works, for Americans.[81] A list, a pathway, two walls, everyone who died was named and accounted for – it is a ledger of death for the nation, and everyone has a name. But this monument cele-brates absence as much as presence. In one sense the monument only exists in its relation to the other monument that could never be built in this way, because nobody in the Pentagon knew the names. There is a monument yet to be built to every Vietnamese person destroyed by the war. This monu-ment will have to be largely without names. These people existed outside the records of American bureaucracy. England has its own murdered mil-lions to account for in art. The balance sheets in the financial offices of the great maritime slaving ports listed numbers, for insurance purposes, not the names of individual slaves.

Turner's monument to the slave trade is a monument without names, which at least inaugurates the act of mourning. Turner's memorial does not submerge the slaves beneath an unrelenting grandeur but combines the sublime and the ridiculous. He puts the elements in mourning yet his nat-ural world contains many elements, including gaiety and humour. His fore-ground contains a dance of death that is dangerously close to being bathetic.

The fragmentary promises not instability (the opposite of fixity) so much as disarray, confusion. (Maurice Blanchot, *The Writing of the Disaster*)

the leg was to be seen because it was a burning leg. There it is, and it *will* shine through! … the leg that smiles, that winks, is obsequious to you, yet perforce of beauty self-satisfied … is your lord, your slave, alternately and in one. It is a leg of ebb and flow and high-tide ripples. (George Meredith, *The Egoist*)

At the blood-soaked end of mortal avenues an immense treacherous sun laughs derisively. It is humour's sun. (Aimé Césaire, *Poetry and Knowledge*)

The leg in the foreground of Turner's *Slave Ship* [**2.20**] has been more written about than any other aspect of the picture. The critical consensus when the painting first appeared was that the disaster was funny, and a prime site for the exercise of facetious humour. The trigger for this response was invariably the leg. In order to understand one aspect of the painting it is necessary to understand these responses. The foreground is problematic, toying with farce. The first critics were not necessarily wrong to respond to the leg in the way they did. Our problem is that they could not see the relevance of the very absurdity which they detected. The humour is not only a key to the proper interpretation of the leg, but to the tragic dimension of the

[**2.20**] J. M. W. Turner, *Slaver Throwing Overboard the Dead and Dying, Typhon Coming On*, detail (oil on canvas, 1840)

[2.21] Peter Brueghel, *Landscape with Fall of Icarus*, detail (oil on canvas, 1567)

painting as a whole. Turner was not the first or last to see the value of setting death off against slapstick, and shares a vision of tragic amplitude with Brueghel's great depiction of death by water. Brueghel's disaster occurs in a calmer sea, but the leg of his plummeting Icarus is equally ridiculous, and fat [**2.21**]. In both paintings trauma is described as a fall, and both painters choose to isolate that moment at which the body impacts with the water. For contemporary trauma theory this coincidence and this focus on falling have significance. Cathy Caruth sees the figure of the falling body and its relationship to impact to underlie Paul de Man's construction of the relation between traumatic memory, art and critical interpretation. Caruth goes as far as to state that 'the history of philosophy after Newton could be thought of as a series of confrontations with the question of how to talk about falling. And, similarly, the problem of reference, insofar as de Man implicitly associates it, in my interpretation, with this development in the history of philosophy, is: *how to refer to falling*.'[82] One might see in Turner's isolation of a female falling slave, the victim of gravity as well as of the economics of Atlantic slavery, an engagement with the act of falling as it relates to the figuration of traumatic memory. This is not a direction to pursue further here. I want instead to return to the consideration of how falling can comically inflect mortality, and to ask the question: can death involve a comedy beyond 'black' comedy?

One day Ruskin allowed a group of visiting children to look at the *Slave Ship*, and one of them remembered the event:

> Once, when he was showing his 'Turner', The Slave Ship, we asked him cheerfully what all those people were doing in the water. 'Drowning!' he said … But the legs of the slaves were thick, and unlike legs, and so altogether comic, that the more my mother and Mr. Ruskin explained to us that these unfortunates were in mortal anguish and fear of death, the more we giggled. I remember his awe-struck face as he leaned across towards my mother, saying, '*Are* Children Like That?'[83]

What comes out is Ruskin's powerlessness to defend the detail of the leg in the picture, before the tremendous honesty of childish sight and imagination. The leg which the children laugh at is badly drawn, bloated, colossally thick with a tremendous heel, a *lusus naturae* of a leg. But the leg also has a disproportionate narrative power – it overbalances the picture. Contemporary critics could not see beyond the leg, and also responded to it by laughing, although this laughter has a sardonic racial edge: 'Of all the birds in the air and fishes in the sea, what have we in the foreground? It is a black leg thrown overboard, and round it run all the fishes of the sea';[84] 'pomegranate coloured sea, and fish dressed as gay as garden flowers in red and green, with one dusky-brown leg thrown up from this party-coloured chaos, keep the promise of the title';[85] 'the leg of a negro, which is about to afford a nibble to a John Dory, a pair of soles, and a shoal of whitebait';[86] 'The fish claiming their leg-acy is very funny'.[87] If it is funny, why is it funny?

We return to Ruskin's horrified awe as he tries to make children understand what has happened. The children laugh to see such sport. A human being falling, diving, upended, separated momentarily between two elements, and enjoined to them both. The leg like the ship exists between two elements, stitching them together. When this leg is funny it is terribly funny. It is funny because falling in the water at one level must be funny, a cosmic pratfall, a latter-day Icarus amid dancing fish, and because feet, as Georg Baselitz discovered, are funny things if you take them on their own, and legs, as George Meredith proved in *The Egoist*, when isolated for scrutiny, are perhaps even funnier.[88]

Art can isolate legs and feet and do some strange things with them. When Turner painted the *Slave Ship* human fragments were in the ascendant. They had recently assumed an unprecedented potency in European thought, and had become a way of remembering lost greatness. Stone fragments and wrecked sculptures were re-erected in an art of ruins. Shelley's *Ozymandias* opens with the simple declaration: 'I met a traveller from an antique land, / Who said two vast and trunkless legs of stone stand, in the desert.' Fuseli drew a despairing artist gazing disconsolately up at an enormous sculptured foot dwarfing him.[89]

But Turner's leg has no ruined grandeur. It is fleshy and in terms of the legs of Ozymandias very un-grand, yet it lays claim to a different kind of grandeur, and paradoxically makes insignificance significant. The images to which Turner's body parts relate most closely are the two paintings titled *Severed Limbs* which Theodore Gericault made in 1818 [**2.22**]. In Gericault's paintings the body parts are seen in confrontational close-up, discolouring and dominating the whole canvas as they thrust themselves out to the viewer, in dramatic foreshortening and spectacular chiaroscuro, on white sheets. Coldly sweating and sticky with drying blood, these lumps of humanity lie somewhere between the shambles and the operating table. Yet their truncated isolation serves only to amplify their humanity. Dead, discarded, divorced from their human functions, these hands and feet are powerless to prevent the promiscuous continuation of their delicately mortal gestures. The dead meat that was a human body speaks its own sign language; an arm and hand delicately draped around a dead leg cannot help but embrace it.

[2.22] Theodore Gericault, *Severed Limbs* (oil on canvas, 1818)

Although so much further off and bathed in incandescent brine, Turner's leg does share something with Gericault's harsh vision, namely the reduction of the human body to detritus. Where Turner differs from Gericault is in the way he has managed to monumentalise human fragility not by magnifying and isolating the fragment but by pulling away from the overpowering statuesque sensuality of Gericault's macabre still-life, to plunge his leg into a marine theatre of cruelty.[90] While Gericault's work is passionately humourless, the bottom right corner of Turner's painting is a tragi-comic lament on the slave trade which literally foregrounds the reduction of the human form to rubbish, food for fish, but which refuses to leave the fragment isolated in a cold forensic space. This diving leg implores us to try to understand mass murder by picking up the pieces. Turner uses death and dismemberment in ways which would sound again in Carlyle's attempts to recover, or to rediscover, large-scale atrocity during the French Revolution. The isolated human fragment emerges as the transitory, but ironically the most complete, memorial to enormous and anonymous politico/economic processes.[91]

Carlyle's *French Revolution* does not deal intelligently with the slave revolution in San Domingo, yet it does contain varied and uncontrollably daring attempts to communicate atrocity and the mass destruction of human life by other human life. Having approached description of the September Massacres in many rhetorical ways – panoramic, microscopic, confessional – he settles upon a detail which resonates back to Turner's legs and hands raised above the waves:

> Carts go along the streets; full of stript human corpses, thrown pell-mell; limbs sticking up:- seest thou that cold Hand sticking up, through the heaped embrace of brother corpses, in its yellow paleness, in its cold rigour; the palm opened towards Heaven, as if in dumb prayer, in expostulation *de profundis*, Take pity on the Sons of Men! – Mercier saw it, as he walked down 'the Rue Saint-Jaques from Montrouge, on the morrow of the Massacres': but not a Hand; it was a Foot, – which he reckons still more significant, one understands not well why. Or was it as the Foot of one *spurning* Heaven? Rushing, like a wild diver, in disgust and despair, towards the depths of Annihilation? ... 'I saw that Foot,' says Mercier; 'I shall know it again at the Day of Judgement.'[92]

Given his later writings on race and slavery, Carlyle emerges as an ironic figure with which to aesthetically salvage Turner's leg. Yet the applicability of his massive compassion to Turner's treatment of the middle passage indicates the difficulties of coming at the memory of slavery from a narrowly preconceived political or race agenda. It is as if Turner's hands and leg are fused and resurrected here on land, in Carlyle's ambiguous fragment, which is paradoxically both hand and foot. Turner's leg is to be saved from its detractors. It is a lot more important than they could see. Its tenuousness, its fragility and its absurdity are to be admitted in the same spirit of peculiar reverence that Carlyle feels for the foot which transfixed Mercier: its isolated insubstantiality, its severance, its vulnerability, *are* its value.

The near sea: 'fish dressed as gay as garden flowers'

> 'you say he was guiding his boat to the place where the ship went down, which we may surmise to have been a slave ship ... picture the hundreds of his fellow-slaves – or their skeletons – still chained in the wreck, the gay little fish (that you spoke of) flitting through their eye sockets and the hollow cases that had held their hearts. Picture Friday above, staring down upon them, casting buds and petals that float a brief while, then sink to settle among the bones of the dead. (J. M. Coetzee, *Foe*)

> STUDY FOR FISH Coming on at speed, in the Slaver (modern trade?) ...
> (John Ruskin)

If the children laughed only at the leg, the humour of the reviewers was divided between the leg and the fish which feed upon it. The fish take up a good deal more space than all the drowning slaves put together.

Colouristically the fish are the most delicately joyful portion of the canvas yet they constitute one of the most neglected aspects of the painting.

It has been suggested that the poem *Walks in a Forest* by Thomas Gisborne, abolitionist, friend of Cowper, Wilberforce and the leading members of the Clapham sect, might constitute a source for the violent sunset and the beautiful rendering of the fish in the *Slave Ship*. The poem is a good deal more important than this, and provides not only an inventory of the bird and marine life in the picture but an ideological framework which makes sense of Turner's use of this source.[93]

Gisborne's section of the poem entitled 'Summer' opens with a paean to creation as a manifestation of divine love: 'Thy universal love / Pervades Creation; on each living form / Showers down its proper happiness.'[94] This celebration of creation has an unusual gusto for the period and celebrates the processes of mass destruction which permeate the natural world. The passage describing the herring shoals is preceded by an account of the goatsucker who 'its whirring note prolongs, Loud as the sound of busy maiden's wheel: Then with expanded beak, and throat enlarged / Even to its utmost stretch, its customed food / Pursues voracious.'[95] The comparison of the maiden spinning and the bird glutting itself on insects is typical of the strange interchange of human and animal activity in this work. Such odd juxtaposition has relevance for Turner's depiction of the slaves as food for fish. The account of the entire predatory world coming to life to feed on the herring shoals provided Turner with the main elements in his depiction of the devouring of the drowning slaves:

> On warmer climes when herring armies pour
> The living tide of plenty; to the sun
> With gold and green and azure many a league
> When ocean glitters like a field of gems,
> Gay as the bow of heaven, and burns by night
> In every billow with phosphoric fire;
> Their march innumerous foes attend. Behold,
> In light-wing'd squadrons, gulls of every name,
> Screaming discordant, o'er the surface hang,
> And ceaseless stoop for prey … while beneath
> Monsters marine with sanguine inroad gore
> The looser files; and, floating vast, the whale
> Insatiate lops the impenetrable host,
> Unbars his mighty jaws, close-crowded troops
> Ingulfs at once, and clasps the gates of death.[96]

The contemporary editions of this poem, which Turner would have read, carry an extended footnote for the description of the herring armies which is even closer, in some details, to the feeding frenzy in the *Slave Ship*:

> The signs of the arrival of the herrings are flocks of gulls, which catch up the fish while they skim on the surface: and of gannets, which plunge and bring them up from considerable depths. Codfish, haddocks, and dogfish, follow

the herrings in vast multitudes; whales, pollacks and porpoises are added to the number of their foes: these follow in droves; the whales deliberately, opening their vast mouths, taking them in by the hundreds.[97]

Capering and floundering marine life, which engulfs the body in the near sea, is to be seen as re-casting the narrative context of the process of death by drowning. The bodies of the drowned are taken up and transformed into something rich and strange. They become a site not simply for a terrible and ignominious death but for the operations of the life force at work in nature. Yet while Turner maintains every detail of the way the sea creatures devour the herring, he substitutes the bodies of the drowning slaves for the incalculable shoals. One effect of such a transference involves the definition of the absolute equality, or disconcern, with which nature destroys life. If the fish show that in nature death is the necessary exchange for the continuance of the living, does the painting as a whole support the absorption of the pointless death of these human victims as part of an inhuman natural economy?

Another previously unacknowledged source suggests that Turner's fish may operate within a different narrative context, and that they exist as a satirical critique of pro-slavery accounts of middle passage. In such a reading they are a metaphor for the destructive energy of the slave power. Bryan Edwards's *History Civil and Commercial, of the British Colonies in the West Indies*, already mentioned in the context of the *Description*, might also be seen to locate Turner's painting as a passionate satire on pro-slavery fantasies of the Atlantic crossing. Edwards's *History* first came out in 1793 and remained popular in the first half of the nineteenth century. Turner's voracious marine life battening on the body of a drowning woman could be read as a bitter reinvention of Edwards's sable Venus. Isaac Teale's 'Ode to the Sable Venus', which Edwards reprinted and had illustrated, describes the progress of the 'Sable Venus', from Angola across the Atlantic to Jamaica, as an erotic marine idyll. Sea birds, vast fish and dolphins frolic round the black Venus in homage:

> Of iv'ry was the car, inlaid
> With ev'ry shell of lively shade;
>   The throne was burnish'd gold;
> The footstool gay with coral beam'd,
> The wheels with brightest amber gleam'd,
>   And glist'ring round they roll'd.
> […]
> The winged fish, in purple trace
> The chariot drew; with easy grace
>   Their azure rein she guides:
> And now they fly, and how they swim;
> Now o'er the wave they lightly skim,
>   Or dart beneath the tides.

53

[2.23] Anon., 'Deluge' (copper engraving, 1675). From Athanasius Kircher, *Arca Noe*

Each bird that haunts the rock and bay,
Each scaly native of he sea,
   Came crowding o'er the main:
The dolphin shows his thousand dyes,
The grampus his enormous size,
   And gambol in her train.[98]

The dolphin and grampus reappear in Turner's painting, as do the golden sun, and the red of the coral, but transformed into a very different account of the middle passage. It is as if Turner is exacting a furious revenge on the laconic irresponsibility of Edwards's version of the middle passage. The ludicrous panoply of Gods and putti are stripped from Stothard's elaborate illustrational engraving [2.4]. The whale blowing in the far distance and the two frolicking dolphins in the foreground now rush in to engulf the black body in their enormous maws. The body of this sable Venus has travelled in a different sort of chariot from her predecessor and enjoys a very different relationship with a worshipping nature.

   In providing such a violent fate for the black victims Turner is also drawing upon the established conventions for the representation of the deluge, and in a very different manner from the *Description* conducting a dialogue with the story of Noah's Ark. The iconographic tradition within

Western art to which Turner's scene of voracious feeding relates most intimately are the depictions of marine creatures feeding upon the bodies of the drowned during the flood, while Noah's Ark floats on in safety through the storm. For example, the engraving 'Deluge' from Kircher's 1675 *Arca Noe* contains all the basic narrative elements for Turner's painting, including two bent legs from drowned victims which break the surface in Turnerian manner [**2.23**]. These white sinners have drowned because of their wickedness, and are engulfed by whales and dolphins, while Noah within the ark waits in safety. Turner in turning the corpses black, and in having them jettisoned from what should have been the safe haven of the boat, enacts a powerful reversal of the biblical myth. The greed of slavery has turned the interior of the ark from a place of rebirth into a living hell. The sea may be an element of destruction but it is also one of rebirth.[99]

The paradoxical sea in Turner's painting has, however, found one modern intepreter capable of celebrating its combination of beauty and brutality.[100] David Dabydeen's *Turner* was published in 1994 and takes the *Slave Ship* as its central icon and narrative focus. The poem treats Turner's painting with an expansive meditative quality, using it almost as a holy icon, a space for constant re-invention and meditation. He finds a language for the essential energy of Turner's death scene, and for the utter beauty of this violent sea-change:

> but the sea
> Will cleanse it. It has bleached me too of colour,
> Painted me gaudy, dabs of ebony,
> An arabesque of blues and vermilions,
> Sea-squats cling to my body like gorgeous
> Ornaments. I have become the sea's whore
> Yielding[101]

Dabydeen's *Turner* circles around the scene of the drowning, almost as if it is a poetic reincarnation of one of beautifully coloured fish which feed on the slaves, and plays superb games with colour, black and white finally conjoined in the processes of aquatic mutability – sensual, brazen, opulent:

> Jaws that gulped in shoals, demons of the universe
> Now grin like clowns, tiny fish dart
> Between the canyons of their teeth. I should have sunk
> To these depths, where terror is transformed into
> Comedy, where the sea, with an undertaker's
> Touch, soothes and erases pain.[102]

Dabydeen and Turner share with Shakespeare an ability to see beauty in the transformations enacted in death by water. Turner transmogrifies a scene of carnage into a celebration of life, and bathes all in the colours of putrefaction and evisceration. His shamelessly aesthetic response to disaster provided a rich painterly inheritance which has been developed in the context of the Nazi Holocaust by Mordecai Bloom. He has created overtly sensuous depictions of fragmented limbs and gorgeous large-scale aquatic metamorphoses, where bodies transmute into the phosphorescent pigments of marine dissolution.[103]

Yet the fish and the legs are finally only one element in the story Turner tells. The other parts lie in the context which Turner provided for the foreground detail. It is here that we must return to Ruskin, who saw in the fish a darker, erotic and more intimate message than his contemporaries, and who saw in the sea and the sky a terrible and glorious solution to the problem of making art about slavery.

Slavery and property: love and fish – a private narrative and a private betrothal

> How can anyone claim: 'What you by no means know can by no means torment you?' I am not the centre of what I know not, and torment has its own knowledge to cover my ignorance. (Maurice Blanchot, *The Writing of the Disaster*)

The monumental library edition of Ruskin's works first introduces Turner's *Slave Ship* in the form of a narrative of Ruskin's complicated personal relationship with it. This account runs as follows:

> The 'slaver' is also of particular interest in connection with *Modern Painters*. The picture, exhibited in 1840, was enthusiastically described in the first volume; and it shortly afterwards became Ruskin's property, being given to him by his father in gratitude for the success which the book had obtained. 'Its success was assured,' said Ruskin 'by the end of the year [1843], and on January 1st, 1844, my father brought me in the "slaver" for a New Year's gift, – knowing well by this time how to please me'. 'I write,' he notes in his diary (January 1, 1844), 'with the "Slaver" on my bed opposite me – my father brought it in this morning for a New Years present. I feel very grateful. I hope I shall continue so. I certainly shall never want another oil of his. We had a fine washing at it, and got it into beautiful condition, as fresh as can be.' In 1869 Ruskin sold the picture (for £2042, 5s.); the subject – the throwing overboard of the dead and dying, who are seen struggling in the water surrounded by sharks and gulls – had, he used to say, become too painful to live with.[104]

This editor's narrative sets up a series of ways of reading Ruskin's relationship with the painting which combine economic and legal ownership with aesthetics. The painting became Ruskin's aesthetic property as a result of what he did with it in *Modern Painters* I. The description of the *Slave Ship* was the most famous description in the work that made him, as a young man, a critic of international influence, and nationally *the* arbiter of taste and value in landscape art. Once Ruskin had made the painting interpretatively his own, his father then bought the picture for him and provided him with physical ownership.

The *Slave Ship*, placed on his bed, washed, hung in his bedroom and then hung in the hallway, a middle passage between his bedroom and his dining room, became in the end a domestic presence he could not bear to live with, and he sold it. The movement from the most intimate domestic space outwards, firstly into a hallway and then finally to another continent, and another owner, suggests the movements of African bodies, taken from families, bought and sold, transported over and across continents. It might also suggest the domestic movements which map the course of an unhappy marriage.

Ruskin's most uncontrolled and self-revelatory readings of the painting occurred not in the accounts of it in *Modern Painters*, but in the diary entries he wrote immediately around the period of its acquisition. Ruskin's involved relationship with the painting operated at a series of emotional and narrative levels which were activated by contemplation of the mass drowning. During the period when Ruskin's desire for the painting reached a fever pitch, because he was on the verge of possessing it, physically, he was also going through the last stages of an emotional breakdown related to his infatuation with a young woman. He had fallen in love with Adele Domeque, one of the daughters of his father's business partner. During December 1843, when his father was in the process of negotiating with the dealer Griffith to purchase the painting as a New Year gift for his son, Ruskin was still trying to deal with his agony at being rejected by Adele. Ruskin's diary entries over December constantly fluctuate between the two themes: his excitement and pain of anticipation at the idea of owning the painting, and his agony at the loss of Adele, a pain which paralyses him imaginatively and leaves him unable to work.

The tension between the two subjects reaches a climax four days before his father gave him the painting. The remarkable diary entry for 27 December constitutes Ruskin's most intimate, certainly his most self-referential, reading of the *Slave Ship*:

> I have an infernal headache to-night. Did nothing all day; weather close and hot and all wrong. Suspense about Slaver. My heart is all on eyes of *fish* now – it knew something of another kind of eyes once, and of slavery too, in its way. Its slavery now is colder, like being bound to the dead, as in the old Spanish cruelty.[105]

Ruskin articulates a dark fantasy of substitution in which Adele becomes the fish which feed on the slaves, while Ruskin melds himself with the figures of the drowning slaves. The first sentence emerges, in the context of the other diary entries, as a reference to the reappearance of the obsession with Adele. A number of other diary entries in the preceding days refer to terrible headaches brought on by thinking of her, and similarly in the next sentence the inability to work is again a symptom of the obsession. Ruskin's mental state is then related to the weather; here the aberrant weather, hot, calm and tropical, coincides with his emotionally overheated and intellectually becalmed mental state. At this point the second obsessive theme is introduced: 'Suspense about slaver'. The next sentence opens 'My heart is all on eyes of *fish* now'. This bizarre phrase describes the first stage of emotional transference. Adele, who his heart had been 'on', and still was 'on', is replaced by the awful beauty of Turner's painting. But rather than dwell, as he does in *Modern Painters*, on the abstract beauties of the painting, or upon its grand metaphorical design, Ruskin is drawn, for the first time, to isolate the single detail in the painting where the gaze of the viewer meets a returning gaze.[106]

The only eyes in the painting are the eyes of the fish, which are a remarkable, and completely overlooked, aspect of the painting. At least eight of the fish feeding on the drowning bodies stare out, with proportionately enormous eyes, directly at the viewer. The human eyes in this painting are all submerged, out of sight in the sea, in the foreign element that is destroying their owners. The fish, in the enthusiasm of their feeding, heave themselves out of the water as they bite, to stare out, through a foreign element, blindly, hungrily, at the viewer. For Ruskin these eyes have replaced, or have become, the beautiful eyes of Adele Domeque: as he says his heart 'knew something of other eyes [Adele's] once'. With this thought a second level of identification slides in, for the statement 'and of slavery too in its way' places Ruskin within the metaphoric framework as Adele's slave – if her eyes are the fish's eyes, then he is the slave on whom she feeds. This might appear a colossaly self-pitying piece of emotional impropriety, but the thought is embedded in a familiar literary trope. The notion that the lover's heart became enslaved to the beloved, and the conjunction of the literal condition of slavery with the process of being in love, was firmly established by the early seventeenth century. *The Tempest* provides a central early example.[107]

The enslavement of the lover's heart had been explicitly applied to the subject of New World plantation slavery in the eighteenth century. A notorious example is the degenerate poem by James Boswell, *No Abolition of Slavery; or the Universal Empire of Love*, a work which argued, facetiously, that abolition was a non-starter for slavery could never be abolished while his mistress enslaved his heart. The poem concluded: 'The rhapsody must now be ended, / My proposition I've defended, / For slavery must ever be, / While we have mistresses like thee.'[108] While Ruskin's development of the theme in his diary possesses no such whimsical and disgusting satiric control, the final sentence does involve a process of distancing. The heated emotional identification of the initial thought process is rejected for something a deal stranger: 'Its slavery now is colder, like being bound to the dead, as in the old Spanish cruelty.' This is open-ended. Ruskin may mean that 'it' (his heart's slavery) is colder now because he has only his memories of Adele and sense of loss through which to experience his continuing love.

[3] Henri Fuseli, *The Negro's Revenge* (oil on canvas, 1806)

[4] J. M. W. Turner, *Slavers Throwing Overboard the Dead and Dying, Typhon Coming On* (oil on canvas, 1840)

[5] Auguste Biard, *Scene on the African Coast* (oil on canvas, c. 1833)

Yet who or what is the 'dead' to which he is bound: is it the dead love of Adele, his dead love for Adele, his love for Turner's painting, which in comparison to his love for Adele is a dead thing, or is 'it' to be taken as one of the slaves from Turner's painting? Does Ruskin see himself tied to a corpse and his heart to this cold slavery because over the next two decades he was to live with this painting, in all its horror and in all its details, as his closest aesthetic companion?

The last of these suggestions might be placed in the context of the next diary entry, which appears to present the painting as physically usurping the intimate position in Ruskin's life which Adele, ideally, would have filled. Ruskin describes himself as having bedded the painting:

> I write with the Slaver on my bed opposite me. My father brought it in this morning for a New Year's present. I feel very grateful; I hope I shall continue so. I certainly shall never want another oil of his. W. had a fine washing at it and got it into beautiful condition of [*sic*] as-fresh-as-can-be.[109]

It is as if his father has presented him with a wife, or a mistress. His father has procured the painting for him, in order to 'please' him, and the gift also draws an avowal of fidelity. Ruskin declares his intentions in terms of a sort of aesthetic monogamy: 'I certainly shall never want another oil of his [Turner's]'. The scene of intimate transferrals in the diary entry ends with a ritual act of purification: the beloved is bathed, brought into a 'beautiful condition as-fresh-as-can-be', and is now fit for its life of cold slavery with Ruskin. Who is enslaver and who the enslaved is, as Hegel so precisely formulated, sometimes impossible to know.[110]

'Making the green one red': colour symbolism and the aesthetics of violence in Ruskin's reading of the Slave Ship

> I consider myself bound in conscience to bear my testimony at least, and to wash my hands from the guilt which, if persisted in now that things have been so thoroughly investigated and brought to light, will, I think, constitute a national sin of a scarlet and crimson dye. (John Newton)

> Old and young, we dream of graves and monuments … I wonder how mariners feel when the ship is sinking, and they, unknown, undistinguished, are to be buried together in the ocean – that wide and nameless sepulchre? (Nathaniel Hawthorne, 'The Ambitious Guest')

> It is dark disaster which brings the light. (Maurice Blanchot, *The Writing of the Disaster*)

Ruskin provided two extended discussions of the *Slave Ship*. That in *Modern Painters* is familiar, public and was written when Ruskin was young. The second is virtually unknown, and was written when Ruskin was old, yet it provides his personal critique of the aesthetic impulse underlying each of his reactions to the painting.

One of Ruskin's letters provides a history of the development of his thought and imagination.[111] Ruskin provides a technical description of the *Slave Ship* which negates the 'enthusiasm' of the earlier and celebrated description. The argument is complicated:

> there is a certain kind and degree of enthusiasm which alone is cognisant of *all* truth, and which, though it may sometimes mistake its own creations for reality, yet will *miss* no reality, while the unenthusiastic regard actually misses and comes short of, the truth. I am better able to assert this now than formerly, because this enthusiasm is, in me, fast passing away … For instance, there was a time when the sight of a steep hill covered with pines, cutting against blue sky, would have touched me with an emotion inexpressible, which, in the endeavour to communicate in its truth and intensity, I must have sought for all kinds of far-off, wild and dreamy images. Now I can look at such a slope with coolness and observation of *fact* … But it is not all the truth; there is something else to be seen there, which I cannot see but in a certain condition of mind, nor can I make any one else see it, but by putting him into that condition, and my endeavour in the description would be not to detail the facts of the scene, but by any means whatever to put my hearer's mind into that same ferment as my *mind* … One may entangle a description with facts, until you come to pigments and measurements. For instance, in describing 'The Slaver', if I had been writing to an artist in order to have given him a clear conception of the picture I should have said: 'Line of eye two fifths up the canvass; centre of light, a little above it; orange chrome, No. 2 floated in with varnish, pallet-knifed with flake white, glazed afterwards with lake, passing into a purple shadow, scumbled with a dry brush on the left,' etc. Once leave this and treat the picture as a reality and you are obliged to use words implying what is indeed only seen in the imagination, but yet what without doubt the artist intended to be seen; just as he intended you to feel the heaving of the sea, being yet unable to give motion to his colours. And then, the question is, not whether all that you see is indeed there, but whether your imagination has worked as it was intended to do, and whether you have indeed felt as the artist did himself … [112]

This extensive quotation reveals the *Slave Ship* to be at the heart of Ruskin's definition of his visual aesthetics. The argument is similar to that made by Hazlitt when he distinguishes between Reason and the Imagination. Both Hazlitt and Ruskin defend a language of 'enthusiasm' when the subject (in both cases the subject selected is the middle passage) demands it.[113] Ruskin's letter establishes the description of the *Slave Ship* from *Modern Painters* I as the defining example of his enthusiastic mode. Ruskin, then, presents his early description of the *Slave Ship* as a weird, almost mystical, attempt to create through written language what Turner actually felt when he made the picture. It is not an attempt to describe the picture as such, but to recover the thought behind and during its creation. In this sense Ruskin is trying to relive Turner's imaginative response to the middle passage. It is time to see if Ruskin achieved what he claimed to have achieved, or if, as contemporary commentators increasingly claim, he merely celebrated the formal and descriptive qualities of Turner's painting at the expense of its political and historical engagement with slavery.

The assertion that Ruskin relegated the subject of the drowning slaves to a footnote has become commonplace.[114] Some readings have gone further and seen in Ruskin's apparent aestheticising of Turner a sinister precedent for the denial of politics through formal complexity. Turner's painting has consequently been buried in a welter of contemporary facts about slavery. The only way to understand Turner's work is to take it on its own terms. When Benjamin Robert Haydon produced his appallingly wooden mass portrait of *The Anti-Slavery Society Convention, 1840*, he made a work that shares a date with Turner's painting, but absolutely nothing else [**2.24**]. A comparison of the two works makes it thunderously clear that to forget aesthetics when looking at Turner is not to look at him at all.[115] Ruskin reveals Turner to be using colour symbolism, formal organisation of the picture space, and metaphor, to create a meditation on the inheritance of slavery. These formal qualities certainly relate to aesthetics, but Ruskin's explanation of the ways in which they function shows them to be anything but divorced from the subject of the drowning slaves.

[**2.24**] Benjamin Robert Haydon, *The Anti-Slavery Society Convention* (oil on canvas, 1840)

Turner takes up the English slave trade – a history, an economy, a memory, an iniquity – and provides an interpretation of it in pigment on a piece of canvas about 3 feet by 2 feet. Only a fraction of the painting's surface describes anything other than sea and sky, and Ruskin quite sensibly decided that the sea and the sky constitute the core of the picture. Ruskin's interpretation is first and foremost a metaphorical reading. As one might expect from the originator of the concept, it is a triumphant demonstration of the fourth order of the *pathetic fallacy*.[116] The subject, that is, the drowning of the slaves, and the horror of the slave trade, is embodied in a sky made of blood and a sea convulsed with pain. The difficulties in attempting to provide a dignified memorial to mass murder are reflected in the complexities of the seascape, with its contradictory effects of storm and calm, fury and dignity. Ruskin's extended response to the painting, so often referred to, yet never read closely, runs as follows:

> the noblest sea that Turner has ever painted, and, if so, the noblest certainly ever painted by man, is that of the Slave Ship, the chief Academy picture of the Exhibition of 1840. It is a sunset on the Atlantic, after prolonged storm; but the storm is partially lulled, and the torn and streaming rain-clouds are moving in scarlet lines to lose themselves in the hollow of the night. The whole surface of sea included in the picture is divided into two ridges of enormous swell, not high, nor local, but a low broad heaving of the whole ocean, like a lifting of its bosom by deep-drawn breath after the torture of the storm. Between these two ridges the fire of the sunset falls along the trough of the sea, dyeing it with an awful but glorious light, the intense and lurid splendour which burns like gold and bathes like blood. Along this fiery path and valley, the tossing waves by which the swell of the sea is restlessly divided lift themselves in dark indefinite, fantastic forms, each casting a faint and ghastly shadow behind it along the illumined foam. They do not rise everywhere, but three or four together in wild groups, fitfully and furiously, as the under strength of the swell compels or permits them; leaving between them treacherous spaces of level and whirling water, now lighted with green and lamp-like fire, now flashing back the gold of the declining sun, now fearfully dyed from above with the undistinguishable images of the burning clouds, which fall upon them in flakes of crimson and scarlet, and give to the reckless waves the added motion of their own fiery flying. Purple and blue, the lurid shadows of the hollow breakers are cast upon the mist of the night, which gathers cold and low, advancing like the shadow of death upon the guilty* ship as it labours amidst the lightning of the sea, its thin masts written upon the sky in lines of blood, girded with condemnation in that fearful hue which signs the sky with horror, and mixes its flaming flood with the sunlight, and cast far along the desolate heave of the sepulchral waves incarnadines the multitudinous sea.
>
> *She is a slaver, throwing her slaves overboard. The near sea is encumbered with corpses.[117]

Turner's storm is naturalistically described but is also a metaphor for physical torture. To accomplish his reading Ruskin contradicts the painting's title, 'Typhon coming on', and sees the storm as having just passed.[118] He does this because he needs to personify the storm as a torturer. The storm has torn the sky to shreds and broken the back of the sea: Ruskin creates imagery which suggests the effects of a terrible whipping. The sky is the blood on a lacerated back: 'the torn and streaming rain clouds are moving in silent lines'. The sea is described as a torture victim recovering, daring to breathe again, after having the air knocked out of it: 'a low broad heaving of the whole ocean, like a lifting of its bosom by deep drawn breath after the torture of the storm'.

The sea, however, is not only a personification of the tortured slave, but other personifications, simultaneously. The sea has many functions: it is the agent of death, but it suffers with those it makes suffer. The sea in its relation to the dying slaves is witness, executioner, victim and tomb. Ruskin draws out a range of emotion from this seascape appropriate to Turner's ambition.

Ruskin sees a sea that is both grave and agent of mourning for the slaves. The bodies that fight for life in the storm currents mysteriously become the waves themselves, in their eternal battle to rise above the ocean. The following words ostensibly describe the wave motion, but they also re-enact the desperate fight of the manacled groups of drowning slaves in the foreground, as they attempt to rise above the element of their destruction: 'the tossing waves by which the swell of the sea is restlessly divided lift themselves … They do not rise everywhere, but three or four together in wild groups, fitfully and furiously, as the under strength of the swell compels or permits them.' In this disturbing writing there is no division between the agony of the victims and the processes of nature which cause and surround these deaths.

Ruskin explains Turner's overall design. The deaths of the slaves thrown overboard are to be saved from their debased historico-economic context – the painting is an act of artistic salvage. If the squalid story of the slave ship *Zong* was the narrative trigger for the painting then the narrative impulse for the painting is to uncover the evil inherent in a system that could justify mass murder as an insurance loophole.[119] Turner's painting triumphantly redeems these victims from a legal and economic context that is not only wicked but colossally mean. Turner makes these deaths mean something, by bathing them in one of his most terrific seascapes and one of his most sublime sunsets. The gold of the slave trade is shifted into an ironically gorgeous light.

Painting which describes the atrocities committed by humans on humans has to embrace contradiction, and must try to make impossible combinations – pure form with raw emotion, beauty with horror, baseness with ideality, light with dark and black with white. There are different solutions to the painting of mass murder. Picasso's *Guernica* and Goya's *The 3rd of May: Execution of the Insurgents* monumentalise suffering through the grandeur of their scale, the intellectual elegance behind their composition, and the psychological impact of their gestural purity. They also both concentrate on figure painting, and on people's faces. They express the raw terror of their subjects by converting the human physiognomy into a map of suffering. Turner did not paint the human form at all well, and the only face he painted with true insight was his own, in early manhood, once.[120] His solution to the pictorial rendering of mass murder was very different from that of his contemporary, Goya. It lay in providing a seascape which expresses the emotions which man does not, or cannot.

Ruskin's great gift to us is that he was up to the job of explaining the vastly complex messages involved in Turner's narrative use of elemental nature. Above all Ruskin does not let go of the central paradox which animates the work. The sea is a mass grave, a tomb, the waves are dying slaves, the sky is a retributive prophet, but at the same time the sea is only the sea, the sunset is only the sunset, or as Ruskin said elsewhere of Homer's descriptions of the sea, 'Black or clear, monstrous or violet coloured, cold salt water it is always, and nothing but that'.[121] If the sky and the sea are beautifully polluted by the colour of murder, it is the viewer's responsibility to see the mystery of the contradiction and to read myth into it. Ruskin elsewhere observed that one of Turner's chief narrative gifts was the ability to convey the existence of 'an acute sense of the contrast between the careless interests and idle pleasures of daily life and the state of those whose time for labour, or knowledge, or delight is passed for ever'.[122] He develops this *aperçu* on a grand scale in the tension at the heart of his readings of the *Slave Ship*. Which view is right: is the sky just going about its beautiful business, or is it dyed red with rage and guilt? The answer is that the painting holds both these readings and more.

Turner's aesthetic response operates, for Ruskin, at the limits of the pictorial sublime. In Ruskin's narrative the painting describes divine retribution and judgement as they are reflected in the cataclysmic activity of nature. The sky and sea are not just red, they are an eschatological and etiologic expression of the loss, horror, cruelty and mass death of the slave trade. The metaphoric ambition of the writing which attempts to match the painting must be o'er vaulting, and it is no coincidence that it is to Macbeth, and the engulfing fantasy of Macbeth's sanguine hallucinations, that Ruskin turns for the climax of his interpretation: 'that fearful hue which signs the sky with horror … incarnadines the multitudinous sea'.

Ruskin shows what can be done with the transference of metaphor from poetry to painting. He seizes upon the diseased hallucination of Macbeth: blood, symbolic of murder and guilt, saturating and diffusing through the entire ocean. Then, with a vast economy, Ruskin suggests that Turner's analysis of a sordid incident in the history of the British slave trade can most accurately be summed up through a literalisation of the phrase 'the multitudinous seas incarnadine making the green one red'. Ruskin is not, however, merely appropriating one Shakespearean phrase and encrusting it onto his interpretation of the *Slave Ship*. Ruskin's description defines itself in reaction to an associative chain of blood imagery in *Macbeth*. In Shakespeare's examination of the psychology of a mass-murderer and his accomplice, Ruskin finds a set of tools which might be re-used in the attempt to describe Turner's interpretation of a mass murder perpetrated by a nation, and affecting three continents.

The dialogue with *Macbeth* runs deep in the description of the *Slave Ship*. The play, with its extraordinarily rich metaphoric networks for examining the operations of guilt upon the human mind, is an ideal resource. Ruskin transfers the metaphors of universal sanguine contamination, and of an outraged nature in mourning, from Shakespeare to Turner. He also reactivates Lady Macbeth's images of painting with blood in the context of Turner's real activity as a painter.

Ruskin takes up imagery which combines red and gold in the description of murder. This imagery operates through the pun on the word 'guilt' which emerges both as emotion and as the practical product of 'guilding'. When the murder is first planned, Lady Macbeth and Macbeth envisage a literal transfer of guilt from themselves to the two grooms/chamberlains of Duncan. This involves smearing them with Duncan's blood: 'His spungy officers, who shall bear the guilt / Of our great quell … / Will it not be receiv'd, / When we have mark'd with blood those sleepy two / Of his own chamber, and us'd their very daggers, / That they have done it?'.[123] After the murder, when Macbeth is reduced to panic and cannot go through with the plan, the imagery of water, blood and gold begins to develop. Lady Macbeth commands: 'Go get some water, And wash this filthy witness from your hand. / Why did you carry these daggers from the place? / They must lie there. Go carry them and smear the sleepy grooms with blood.'[124]

It is in response to this command that Macbeth refers to the extraordinary power of the sight of blood. It is not the thought of the murder that he cannot bear but the act of *looking* on the blood of the murdered: 'I'll go no more. I am afraid to think what I have done; Look on't again I dare not.'[125] Lady Macbeth's response to this horror of looking involves a move of crucial importance for Ruskin. She converts the scene of the murder into a painting, and the smearing with blood into an act of painting, and in this context introduces the pun on guilding: 'The sleeping and the dead / Are but as pictures; 'tis the eye of childhood / That fears a painted devil. If he do bleed, / I'll guild the faces of the grooms withal, / For it must seem their guilt.'[126]

Guilding, in other words applying gold leaf to a prepared gesso surface, was a technical process in English medieval and Renaissance art. The backgrounds to portrait miniatures, and the representation of heaven as backgrounds in illuminated manuscripts and religious paintings, were commonly made of pure gold, the product of guilding. In Lady Macbeth's pun, the smearing of the blood becomes a gestural act of painting whereby the blood is the gold leaf, and the guilt literally transferred. It is in immediate response to this train of thought and to the sudden knock at the door that Macbeth counters this painterly metaphor of containment – the blood/gold is transferred only to the grooms, and in this way guilt is placed solely on them – with one of infinite expansion. The process of guilding is replaced with that of dyeing, and the potency of the red blood reasserts itself over the gold, to dye the entire sea. When, however, Macbeth pulls himself together and presents his fictive account of the discovery of the murder in order to provide a cover for his immediate murder of the grooms, he returns to Lady Macbeth's pun, this time literalising it by making the blood actually golden: 'Here lay Duncan, / His silver skin lac'd with his golden blood.'[127]

The compounding of blood and gold, through a metaphor of painting, is absorbed into Ruskin's reading of the sky and sea in Turner's *Slave Ship*. The red light is first described in the following words: 'the sunset falls along the trough of the sea, / dyeing it with an awful but glorious light, the intense and lurid splendour which burns like gold, and bathes like blood'. The combination of blood and gold is later extended to incorporate both sky and sea: 'water … now flashing back the gold of the declining sun, now fearfully dyed from above with the indistinguishable images of the burning clouds, which fall upon them in flakes of crimson and scarlet'. The marriage of the elements through ensanguination becomes the climactic focus of Ruskin's response to the painting. The process of 'marking' the grooms with blood is transferred to Turner, who becomes a sort of inverted Lady Macbeth. The painter through his marking of the slave ship in red re-assigns guilt to the slave ship by inscribing it in blood, or in Ruskin's words, 'its [the slaver's] thin masts written upon the sky in lines of blood' while Turner's red paint 'signs the sky with horror'.

The final sentence of Ruskin's description, with its direct Shakespearean allusion, does not only quote but expands the Shakespearean metaphor. Where Macbeth sees the blood he has spilt staining all the oceans of the world ('this my hand / Will rather the multitudinous seas incarnadine / Making the green one red'), Ruskin reads not only the sea but the whole of nature dyed with blood. Turner 'incarnadines' both air and water, through the metaphoric application of sunset: 'that fearful hue which signs the sky with horror, and mixes its flaming flood with the sunlight, and cast far along the desolate heave of the sepulchral waves, incarnadines the multitudinous sea'.

Lady Macbeth uses a metaphor of painting to attempt to create, for Macbeth, a shield from the horror of reality. It is as if Ruskin is violently denying that imaginative option here, developing Lady Macbeth's metaphor of guilding guilt in the context of Turner's description of mass murder. Painting does not make looking less terrible, it does not provide an alternative to reality that hides guilt, but projects British crime on a vast scale. Turner paints guilt in the *Slave Ship*.

Turner's use of red in the *Slave Ship*, worked through by Ruskin as a development of the colour symbolism of *Macbeth*, became a mark to which he returned, almost obsessively, in his subsequent writing. Red hangs over and runs through numerous meditations Ruskin was to produce, as he mulled over and went back to the *Slave Ship*. Ruskin's infatuation with the red-light of Turner's *Slave Ship*, and with the blood and guilt it embodied for him does not exist in an interpretative vacuum but has blood relatives within the literatures which address the inheritance of slavery.[128]

Nature incarnadined, blood diffused in water and in light, resurface as a signification of the guilt, the fury and the enormous sadnesses of slavery, in the context of black writings past and present. Nine years before Turner's painting was exhibited, another Turner, far more intimately connected with the violent extremes to which slavery could drive man, saw nature drenched in blood. Nat Turner, a slave and autodidact preacher, looked for signs from God which would communicate when the time was right for him to lead a slave uprising in Richmond, Virginia. Turner led a group of slaves to massacre several white families. Lingering in prison awaiting execution he provided an account of his motives for a white Lawyer called Gray.[129] In the *Confessions* Turner recounts how he saw the divine signs which vindicated him as an instrument of vengeance and established his prophetic status. These signs would not have been alien to Turner's painterly, or Ruskin's biblical, imagination:

> I discovered drops of blood on the corn as though it were dew from heaven – and I communicated it to many, both white and black in the neighbourhood – and I then found on the leaves in the wood hieroglyphic characters, and numbers, with the forms of men in different attitudes, portrayed in blood and representing the figures I had seen before in the heavens. And now the Holy Ghost had revealed itself to me, and made plain the miracles it had shown me – For as the blood of Christ had been shed on this earth, and had ascended to heaven for the salvation of sinners, and was now returning to earth again in the form of dew – and as the leaves on the trees bore the impression of the figures I had seen in the heavens, it was plain to me that the Saviour was about to lay down the yoke he had borne for the sins of men and the great day of judgement was at hand.[130]

God signs Nature, both in the heavens and on the ground, with hieroglyphics made of blood and water. Christ's suffering and bleeding and the suffering of the slave are united in a symbolic call for retribution. Ruskin sees Turner write the slave ship in lines of blood and sign the sky with horror. But it is not a call to vengeance which Ruskin sees in Turner's *Slave Ship*, rather a lament for the dead and a horror at the guilt of the criminals. In its glorious sorrow the sky in the *Slave Ship* relates

67

not so much to Nat Turner's sky weeping blood as to the pool of light in Toni Morrison's *Beloved*. Sethe, a woman slave who escapes with her children, is detected by slave-catchers. Rather than give herself and her children up and return to slavery, Sethe tries to kill all her children and succeeds in cutting the throat of her baby girl. The memory of this baby, the 'Beloved' of the title, manifests herself as a pool of red light, outside the mother's house, number 124. When an old friend, Paul D, unexpectedly turns up, he sees and experiences the light: 'Paul D tied his shoes together, hung them over his shoulder, and followed her through the door straight into a pool of red and undulating light that locked him where he stood.' The memory of the crime caused by slavery is both horridly frightening and terribly sad:

> 'You got company?' he whispered, frowning.
> 'Off and on,' said Sethe.
> 'Good God.' He backed out the door onto the porch. 'What kind of evil you got in here?'
> 'Its not evil, just sad. Come on. Just step through.'
> …
> Now the iron was back but the face, softened by hair, made him trust her enough to step inside her door smack into a pool of pulsing red light.
> She was right. It was sad. Walking through it, a wave of grief soaked him so thoroughly he wanted to cry. It seemed a long way to the normal light surrounding the table, but he made it – dry-eyed and lucky … Paul D looked at the spot where the grief had soaked him. The red was gone but a kind of weeping clung to the air where it had been.[131]

Morrison shares with J. M. W. Turner the desire to describe murder resulting from slavery and the emotional inheritance it brings. One way she approaches this is through the symbolic use of colour, an all-engulfing redness. Morrison's red is, like Turner's, both light and water, it is both 'pulsating red light' and 'a great wave of grief … that soaked him'. Turner's sky, perpetually frozen on canvas, renders the combination of a pulsating red light in the sunset and within the storm clouds a mist, where one can feel the departing red light and where 'a kind of weeping hung to the air where it had been'. Ruskin saw this, and told us how to see it too.

What must not be forgotten is what a very brave painting the *Slave Ship* is. It was a brave subject to take on board, and to throw overboard in the face of the British artistic establishment. It is still one of the most uplifting solutions to the problem all artists of the disaster must face. In Ziva Amishai-Maisels words, 'How does one combine the artist's pleasure in the act of creation with the horrific subject matter which is the source of the creation? And finally how does one guard against the spectator's being struck primarily by the beauty of the work, lest he/[she] feel that an atrocity can be beautiful?' Yes, how?[132]

Notes

1 The best overview of the propaganda strategies of the initial campaign 1787–96 is Roger Anstey, *The Atlantic Slave Trade and British Abolition 1760–1810* (London, Macmillan, 1975), pp. 256–85. The classic destruction of the 'nursery' argument is contained in *The Substance of the Evidence of Sundry Persons on the Slave Trade Collected in the Course of a Tour Made in the Autumn of the Year 1788* (London, James Phillips, 1789), pp. 60–112. This work was mainly compiled by Thomas Clarkson out of the material gathered in his interviews in slave ports. For a succinct summary of how Clarkson's research, and this publication in particular, buried the nursery argument see James A. Rawley, *The Transatlantic Slave Trade* (New York and London, Norton, 1981), pp. 286–7.

2 For the representation of Africa and the slave trade see pp. 10–11 above, and pp. 36–8, 43–5 below.

3 There are several fine studies which analyse the economics and historiography of the Atlantic slave trade and its position in the abolition debate. For a powerful modern Marxist analysis see Robin Blackburn, *The Overthrow of Colonial Slavery 1776–1848* (London, Verso, 1990), pp. 293–331. The most succinct economic summaries are in Seymour Drescher, *Econocide: British Slavery in the Era of Abolition* (Pittsburgh, University of Pittsburgh Press, 1977), pp. 15–38, 113–25; Philip D. Curtin, *The Atlantic Slave Trade, A Census* (Madison, Wisconsin University Press, 1969), pp. 3–15, 127–205; Rawley, *Transatlantic Slave Trade*, pp. 149–283. The printed propaganda surrounding the slave trade debate in the period 1780–1807 is discussed in Michael Craton, *Sinews of Empire: A Short History of British Slavery* (London, Temple Smith, 1974), pp. 239–85; David Brion Davis, *The Problem of Slavery in the Age of Revolution 1770–1823* (Ithaca, Cornell University Press, 1975), pp. 388–73; Anstey, *Atlantic Slave Trade*, pp. 142–57, 255–86; for abolition poetry see Wylie Sypher, *Guinea's Captive Kings: British Anti-Slavery Literature of the xviii'th Century* (Chapel Hill, University of North Carolina Press, 1942), pp. 156–231. For the production of propaganda on the middle passage by women see Moira Ferguson, *Subject to Others: British Women Writers and Colonial Slavery, 1670–1834* (London, Routledge, 1992), pp. 180, 198, 218, 224, 236, 245. Little serious work has, as yet, been done on the visual propaganda generated by the slave-trade debate. The *Description* is briefly described in James Walvin, *Black Ivory: A History of British Slavery* (London, Harper Collins, 1992), pp. 46–7. The two recent books to include some discussion of the SEAST production of imagery are Hugh Honour, *The Image of the Black in Western Art from the American Revolution to World War 1* (Cambridge Mass., Harvard University Press,1989), 4:1, pp. 62–5; and J. R. Oldfield, *Popular Politics and British Anti-Slavery: The Mobilisation of Public Opinion Against the Slave Trade 1787–1807* (Manchester, Manchester University Press, 1995), pp. 155–85.

4 James Stanfield, *Observations on a Guinea Voyage. In a Series of Letters Addressed to The Rev. Thomas Clarkson* (London, 1788), p. 30.

5 William Hazlitt, *The Complete Works of William Hazlitt in Twenty One Volumes*, ed. P. P. Howe (London, J. M. Dent, 1931), 12, pp. 46–50.

6 For Hazlitt's insights into the dangerously self-serving nature of eighteenth-century empathic 'sensibility', and the relation of this thought to Keats, Godwin and Wordsworth, see Karen Halttunen, 'Humanitarianism and the Pornography of Pain in Anglo-American Culture', *American Historical Review*, 100:2 (1995) 308–9.

7 Gomer Williams, *History of the Liverpool Privateers and Letter of Marque, with an Account of the Liverpool Slave Trade* (London, 1897), p. 474: 'The Custom House, on the east side of the Old Dock, now Canning Place, was built about 1700 … the slave auctions were held on the flight of steps leading to the main entrance.'

8 For an assessment of the manner in which this image has come to dominate the popular, and even many scholarly, conceptions of the middle passage see Rawley, *Transatlantic Slave Trade*, pp. 283–4; Walvin, *Black Ivory*, p. 46; Marcus Wood, 'Imagining the Unspeakable and Speaking the Unimaginable: Visual Interpretation and the Middle Passage', *Lumen*, 16 (1997) 211–45.

69

9 The complicated relationship between the early Plymouth Committee version and that of the London Committee has finally been disentangled by Oldfield, *Popular Politics*, pp. 99, 163–6. The production of the print in London is discussed in *Abolition Committee Minutes*, 3 vols, Add. MSS 21254–56, British Library, London, 2, 24 March – 28 April. For the French and American adaptations see pp. 27–9, 32–6 below.

10 Honour, *Image of the Black*, 4:1, p. 315. For detailed figures on subsequent distribution see Oldfield, *Popular Politics*, pp. 165–6, 181–2.

11 Henry Louis Gates Jnr., *The Signifying Monkey* (Oxford and New York, Oxford University Press, 1988), p. 4.

12 For the pro-slavery construction of Africa and Africans see Robert Norris, *Memoirs of the Reign of Bossa Ahadee, King of Dahomey, An INLAND COUNTRY of GUINEA. To Which are Added the Author's Journey to Abomey, The Capital; and A Short Account of the African Slave Trade* (London, 1789), pp. 10–145; Bryan Edwards, *History Civil and Commercial, of the British Colonies in the West Indies*, 3 vols (London, 1793), 2, pp. 35–100; 3, pp. 303–60; Edward Long, *The History of Jamaica or, General Survey of the Antient and Modern State of that Island*, 3 vols (London, 1774), 2, pp. 338–571. For the middle passage see Norris, *Memoirs*, pp. 150–84; Robert Bisset, *The History of the Negro Slave Trade, in its connection with the commerce and prosperity of the West Indies and the Wealth and Power of the British Empire*, 2 vols (London, 1805), pp. 35–120; Edwards, *History*, 2, pp. 34–59, 112–22; Long, *History*, 1, pp. 499–533. The most comprehensive survey of the construction of Africans in English texts during the period of the slave trade is Philip D. Curtin, *The Image of Africa: British Ideas and Action 1780–1850* (Madison, Wisconsin University Press, 1964). For the influence of Long as racist theorist see Anthony J. Barker, *The African Link: British Attitudes to the Negro in the Era of the African Slave Trade 1550–1807* (London, Frank Cass, 1978), pp. 41–58, 157–71. For the Anglo-French cultural background see Seymour Drescher, 'The Ending of the Slave Trade and the Evolution of European Scientific Racism', in Joseph E. Inikori and Stanley Engerman (eds), *The Atlantic Slave Trade: Effects on Economies, Societies and Peoples in Africa and the Americas* (Durham and London, Duke University Press, 1992), pp. 365–9.

13 For the impact of Bryan Edwards on pro-slavery thought see Davis, *Problem of Slavery*, pp. 185–7.

14 Edwards, *History*, 2, pp. 27–33. The image is discussed Honour, *Image of the Black*, 4:1, pp. 33–4.

15 Edwards, *History*, 2, pp. 31–3.

16 Honour, *Image of the Black*, 4:1, p. 33 states the image is 'after a painting by Stothard'. With the exception of this image, pro-slavery prints focused upon slavery and romantic love do not seem to exist. There is, however, a body of pro-slavery literary satire which develops the trope of love and enslavement, a prime example being James Boswell, *No Abolition of Slavery or the Universal Empire of Love* (London, 1791).

17 The best account of the genesis of the SEAST and its committee structure, and of the centrality of the London Committee to abolition propaganda strategy, is Oldfield, *Popular Politics*, pp. 41–50, 96–113.

18 For a detailed account of the history of abolition propaganda and the various marketing strategies employed see my forthcoming chapter 'The Abolition Blunderbuss', in James Raven, (ed.), *Free Publishing: Contemporary Perspectives* (London, Ashgate, 2001). See also Oldfield, *Popular Politics*, pp. 41–59. The best accounts of the cloudy genesis of the SEAST seal, and its subsequent, though by no means immediate, mass distribution are Honour, *Image of the Black*, 4:1, pp. 62–3; Oldfield, *Popular Politics*, pp. 156–60. There is a fine account of the development and deployment of the women's version of the seal in Jean Fagan Yellin, *Women and Sisters* (New Haven, Yale University Press, 1989), pp. 16–30.

19 Michael Craton, James Walvin and David Wright (eds), *Slavery, Abolition and Emancipation* (London, Longman, 1976), pp. 38–50; *Substance*, pp. 27–117.

20 For extreme examples of the description of atrocity during the middle passage see Thomas Clarkson, *The History of the Rise, Progress, and Accomplishment of the*

Abolition of the African Slave-Trade by the British Parliament, 2 vols (London, 1808), 2, p. 269. Anstey, *Atlantic Slave Trade*, pp. 27–33.

21 For an exception to this generalisation see my discussion of *The Negro's Complaint* p. 272 below.

22 William Cowper, *The Poems of William Cowper*, ed. John Baird and Charles Ryskamp, 3 vols (Oxford, Clarendon Press, 1980–95), 3, pp. 16 and 286 n., which states 'Cowper's description is accurate; see plan with elevations of the slave ship *Brookes*'.

23 John Newton, *Thoughts Upon the African Slave Trade* (London, 1788), p. 19. For a recent historical account which equates Newton's metaphor with the *Description* see Rawley, *Transatlantic Slave Trade*, p. 283.

24 British valorisation of the slave patrols after 1807 has not been adequately examined but is mentioned in Curtin, *Atlantic Slave Trade*, pp. 231 49; Blackburn, *Overthrow*, pp. 313–16, 409–10, 475–6, 545–7; Rawley, *Transatlantic Atlantic Slavery*, pp. 419–22; Hugh Thomas, *The Slave Trade: The History of the Atlantic Slave Trade 1440–1870* (London, Picador, 1998), pp. 570–89. For a Victorian account see Charles D. Michael, *The Slave and his Champions* (London, S. W. Partridge, 1915), pp. 115–59.

25 A wood-engraving based on the painting is reproduced Michael, *The Slave*, p. 49.

26 *Abolition Committee Minutes*, 2, 17 March.

27 Clarkson, *History*, 2, p.111, and for a further account 2, pp. 28–9.

28 Clarkson, *History*, 2, pp. 112–13.

29 Williams, *Liverpool Privateers*, pp. 585–6. Peter Fryer, *Staying Power: The History of Black People in Britain* (London, Pluto Press, 1984), pp. 480–3.

30 Richard A. Mansir, *A Modeler's Guide to Naval Architecture* (New York, Moonraker, 1983), pp. 6–8. Deane's system was brought to perfection by Frederik Henrik af Chapman, *Architechtura Navalis Mercatoria* (Stockholm, 1768).

31 Patrick Miller, *The Elevation, Section, Plan and Views, of a Triple Vessel, and of Wheels with Explanations of the Figures in the Engraving* (Edinburgh, 1787), pp. 1–10, and plate.

32 For the type of vessels used in the trade see M. K. Stammers, 'Guineamen: Some Technical Aspects of Slave Ships', in Anthony Tibbles (ed.), *Transatlantic Slavery Against Human Dignity* (London, HMSO, 1994), pp. 35–42; for the minimal alterations to the boat required to take a slave cargo see John Newton, *The Journal of a Slave Trader*, ed. Bernard Martin and Mark Spurrell (London, Epworth Press, 1962), pp. 10–12; for the depiction of slave galleys in naval architecture at the time of the plan see John Charnock, *An History of Marine Architecture … from the Earliest Period to the Present*, 3 vols (London, 1800), 1, p. 114; 2, p. 220.

33 Clarkson, *History*, 2, pp. 118–66.

34 Clarkson, *History*, 2, p. 151.

35 Clarkson, *History*, 2, p. 153.

36 Clarkson, *History*, 2, p. 153.

37 The most convenient English overview of Mirabeau's involvement in abolition is Barbara Luttrell, *Mirabeau* (Hemel Hempstead, Harvester Wheatsheaf, 1990), pp. 199–201. For a more extended but inaccurate account see John Stores Smith, *Mirabeau: A Life History*, 2 vols (London, 1848), 2, pp. 138–57. The majority of the text of Mirabeau's planned speech on abolition of the slave trade is printed in *Mémoires Biographiques, Littéraires et politiques de Mirabeau Écrits par Lui-Même, Par son Père, son oncle et son fils adoptif*, 8 vols (Paris, 1834), 7, pp. 103–208.

38 Wilberforce's model of the *Brookes* is discussed in *Slavery Living History Fact Pack*, ed. Elizabeth Frostick (Hull, Wilberforce House, Hull City Museums and Art Galleries, 1989), item G 19/9. The model is on permanent public display in Wilberforce House.

39 Smith, *Mirabeau*, pp. 150–2.

40 For Wilberforce's similar attempt to animate the plan through fantasy see Honour, *Image of the Black*, 4:1, pp. 65–6.

41 For ark as toy see Antonia Fraser, *A History of Toys* (London, Weidenfield and Nicolson, 1966), pp. 90, 97, and for black Noah plate 109.

42 For Kircher and the developments of realistic depictions of the ark, see Norman Cohn, *Noah's Flood: The Genesis Story in Western Thought* (New Haven and London, Yale University Press, 1996), pp. 38–46.

43 John Wilkins, *An essay towards a real character, and a philosophical language* (London, 1688), p. 164.

44 *Encyclopaedia Britannica*, 3 vols (London, 1773), article 'Arc' and plate opposite 1, p. 425.

45 *Supplement À L'Encyclopédie, ou Dictionaire Raisoné des Sciences, des Artes et des Métiers*, 3 vols (Amsterdam, 1776), 1, p. 534. This states 'ARCHE DE NOÉ, On trouvera dans *les Planches d'antiquités Sacrées de ce Supplément, Pl. I.* un plan de *l'arche*, qui nous paroit representer le mieux cet ancien batiment. Nous l'avons tiré de la grande *Histoire Universelle, traduite de l'anglois, tom. I.*' For the image 'Antiques Judaiques', Suppl. vol. 'Planches' (Paris, 1777), plate 7.

46 The plate describing the ark is reprinted and discussed in detail in D. Kocks, 'L'esthétique des planches de l'*Encyclopédie*', in Peter-Eckhard Knabe and Edgar Mass (eds), *L'Encyclopédie et Diderot* (Verlag Koln, DME, coll. 'Kolner Schriften zur Romanischen Kultur 2/Textes et Documents', 1985), p. 131. I am most grateful to Benoît Melançon of the University of Montreal for bringing to my notice the treatment of the ark in the *Encyclopédie*.

47 Jean Baudrillard, *America*, trans. Chris Turner (London, Verso, 1987), pp. 18–19. Baudrillard suggests that Noah's Ark is a metaphor which, in its balance and optimism, demands a nemesis. Baudrillard finds that nemesis in contemporary Manhattan. 'This is the anti-Ark. In the first Ark, animals came in two by two to save the species from the great flood. Here in this fabulous Ark, each one comes in alone – it's up to him or her each evening to find the last survivors for the last party.'

48 I am grateful to Philip Lapsansky of the Library Company of Philadelphia for my knowledge of the history of the adaptation of this image in the United States. The early examples of the reproduction of the Plymouth Committee's version of the seast's original are outlined in Phillip Lapsansky, 'Graphic Discord: Abolitionist and Anti-abolitionist Images', in Jean Fagin Yellin and John C. Van Horne (eds), *The Abolitionist Sisterhood: Women's Political Culture in Ante-bellum America* (Ithaca, Cornell University Press, in collaboration with the Library Company of Philadelphia, 1994), p. 204.

49 For the pamphlet adaptations of the *Description* see Lapsansky, 'Graphic Discord', p. 204. See also Thomas Branagan, *The Penitential Tyrant* (Philadelphia, 1807) and Samuel Wood, *Tyranny Exposed* (New York, 1807). Also Clarkson, *History*, 2, p. 112. For later adaptation see Richard Drake, *Revelations of a Slave Smuggler: Being the Autobiography of Captain Richard Drake, An African Trader* (New York, 1860), p. 69.

50 Isaac Taylor, *Scenes in Africa for the Amusement and Instruction of Little Tarry at Home Travellers By the Reverend Isaac Taylor* (New York, 1827), p. 63.

51 *The Uncle Tom's Cabin Almanack or Abolitionist Memento* (London, 1853), pp. 50–1. For later reproductions of the plan see Dicky Sam (pseud.), *Liverpool and Slavery* (Liverpool, 1884), p. 31.

52 The dhow appears as a full-page plate. G. L. Sulivan, *Dhow Chasing in Zanzibar Waters and on the Eastern Coast of Africa: Narrative of five years experiences in the suppression of the slave trade* (London, 1875), plate opposite p. 114.

53 Bob Marley, *Survival* LP Album cover and record sleeve (Island Records, 1979).

54 S. E. Anderson, *The Black Holocaust for Beginners* (New York, Writers and Readers Publishing, 1995), p. 167.

55 James Pope-Hennessy, *Sins of the Fathers: A Study of the Atlantic Slave Traders 1441–1807* (London, Weidenfield and Nicolson, 1967), front and back endpapers. Hugh Thomas, *The Slave Trade* (London, Picador, 1997), hardback dust cover, and

endpapers; *The Slave Trade* (London, Picador, 1998), paperback front cover, and end-papers. Although the *Description* is lavishly deployed in the book's packaging, it is not included in the illustrations within the text.

56 Barry Unsworth, *Sacred Hunger* (London, Hamish Hamilton, 1992), dust cover and endpapers. Barry Unsworth, *Sacred Hunger* (London, Penguin, 1992), paper cover. This edition still includes the vignette of the three slaves as a repeated chapter heading device; there is no other use of the *Description*.

57 The *Description* has been taken up in several recent museum and art gallery installations. The image appears as a wall panel before the viewer enters a three-dimensional mock-up of the slave deck of the *Brookes* in the 'Transatlantic Slavery Gallery' in the Maritime Museum in Merseyside, Liverpool. It also features in video displays within the gallery. One of the most formally extreme re-deployments of the *Description* in a fine art context was the collage and assemblage work *Passage* made by David Boxer, and exhibited at the University of the West Indies, Mona, Jamaica, in 1998. This consisted of a cabinet, with shelves, the shelves were covered with glasses, and some of the glasses contained live fish. The bottom shelf contained a cow skeleton painted white. The walls and curved interior surfaces of the cabinet carried a collage composed of torn-up photocopies of the *Description*, and pieces of sheet music. I am grateful to Mark Stein, of the University of Frankfurt, for photographic documentation of this event. For the slave ship image in contemporary black American performance and video, see Timothy Murray, *Drama Trauma: Spectres of Race and Sexuality in Performance, Video and Art* (London and New York, Routledge, 1997), pp. 159, 180.

58 For the engraving of the images see Oldfield, *Popular Politics*, pp. 168–71.

59 *The Genius of Universal Emancipation*, 4:1 (1830) 1. This reproduces the frontispiece opposite p. 1, while the text contains a detailed account of the various forms in which the image was disseminated.

60 Blake would probably have based the design to some degree on a preparatory drawing by Stedman himself. None of Stedman's drawings for Blake's designs survives. See Boime, *Art of Exclusion*, p. 341.

61 For publishing history and the popular tune to accompany the poem see Cowper, *Poems*, 3, p. 13 and commentary.

62 Cowper, *Poems*, 3, p. 14.

63 Albert Boime, *Art in an Age of Revolution* (Chicago and London, University of Chicago Press, 1987), pp. 305–6 argues that the 'superhuman' scale of these figures indicates that Fuseli was presenting them according to the conventions normally applied to his mythical heroes. For Fuseli's engraved version in Cowper see Gert Schiff (ed.), *Johann Heinrich Füssli 1741–1825 Text und Oeuvrekatalog*, 2 vols (München, Verlag Berichthaus, Zürich, 1973), 1, pp. 567, 579; 2, pp. 389, 421.

64 For the treatment of the destructive tempest in popular abolition verse, and for Fuseli's possible use of Thomas Day's *The Dying Negro*, see Honour, *Image of the Black*, 4:1, pp. 93–4. For popular millenialism and slavery see J. F. C. Harrison, *The Second Coming: Popular Millenarianism 1780–1850* (London, Routledge and Keegan Paul, 1979), pp. 65, 68, 84.

65 For Ruskin on slavery as '*a natural and eternal inheritance* of a large portion of the human race' see *The Library Edition of the Works of John Ruskin*, ed. E. T. Cook and A. Wedderburn, 39 vols (London, George Allen, 1903–12), 17, pp. 247–61. For a comparison between sailors on a man of war and middle passage see *Works*, 28, p. 585. For relations between domestic service and slavery see *Works*, 19, pp. 520–4. For Eyre and the Jamaica insurrection see *Works*, 18, pp. 550–4. The classic formulation of artistic slavery as an ultimate evil is the opening of the chapter 'The Nature of the Gothic' from *Stones of Venice*, in *Works*, 10, pp. 189–200. Another version appears in *The Cestus of Aglaia*, in *Works*, 19, pp. 104–6. The most unrelenting recent assault on Ruskin's imperialist theory is in Edward Said, *Culture and Imperialism* (London, Vintage, 1994), pp. 94–5, 123–6.

66 The best summary of this critical history is in *The Paintings of J. M. W. Turner*, ed. Martin Butlin and Evelyn Joll, 2 vols (New Haven and London, Yale University Press, 1984), 2, pp. 236–7.

67 For detailed discussion of the contemporary reviews see pp. 43–4, 49 below.

68 Quoted in Jerrold Ziff, 'Turner's "Slave Ship": "What a red rag is to a bull"', *Turner Studies*, 3:4 (1984) 28. Although Twain ironically attributes the comment to an anonymous journalist he first formulated it in a notebook entry in 1878, 'Slave Ship – Cat having a fit in a platter of tomatoes', quoted Ziff, 'Turner's "Slave Ship"', p. 28. The best account of the debate in American journals is Albert Boime, 'Turner's *Slave Ship*: The Victims of Empire', *Turner Studies* 10:1 (1990) 42. Critical exchanges are documented, p. 43, fn. 48. For American reviews of the 1850s and for Herman Melville's relationship with the painting see Robert K. Wallace, *Melville and Turner: Spheres of Love and Fright* (Athens and London: University of Georgia Press, 1992), pp. 447, 449.

69 Both quoted in Ziff, 'Turner's "Slave Ship"', p. 28.

70 Kenneth Clark, *The Romantic Rebellion* (London, John Murray, 1973), pp. 223–63. For the *Slave Ship* as 'ironic deluge painting' see Andrew Wilton, *The Life and Works of J.M.W Turner* (London, Academy Editions, 1979), p. 218. Jack Lindsay, *J. M. W. Turner, his Life and Work: A Critical Biography* (London, Long Adams and Mackay, 1966), pp. 189–90 provides the most detailed analysis of the literary context for the painting and states 'Turner is recognising that the guilt of the slave trade was something too vast to be wiped out by any belated act of parliament' (p. 250). His analysis also, however, places the picture as one small part of an overall critique of capitalism. This aspect of Lindsay's argument anticipates the cultural history readings of Albert Boime, 'Turner's *Slave Ship*', p. 42 where Turner's masterpiece is described as a 'hell and brimstone sermon, subsuming human suffering to the taste for high tragedy'.

71 See Wallace, *Melville and Turner*, pp. 396–400, 520–5.

72 For Buxton see Boime, *Art of Exclusion*, p. 68.

73 See *Blackwoods Magazine* (Sept. 1840) 380, 384.

74 Thackeray's review first appeared in *Fraser's Magazine* (June 1840) 731–2. For a fine analysis of the painting as an inventory of abolition stereotypes see Boime, *Art of Exclusion*, pp. 83–4.

75 Turner's painting came out almost contemporaneously with the publication of the two textual bulwarks of abolition mythology, the *Life of Wilberforce* by his sons and Clarkson's *History of the Abolition of the Slave Trade*, originally published in 1808 and republished 1840 in single volume form.

76 *Fraser's Magazine* (June 1840) 731.

77 *Fraser's Magazine* (June 1840) 731.

78 For Biard's caricatured presentation of blacks see Boime, *Art of Exclusion*, pp. 64–5. For pornographic French flagellatory abolition academy painting see the discussion of Marcel Verdier pp. 000–00 below. For Biard in American adaptation, *Revelations of a Slave Smuggler* (New York, Robert De Witt, 1860) front cover and plates opposite pp. 60, 74.

79 Art historians insist on a connection between Turner's choice of subject and a hunt for royal patronage. Butlin and Joll, *Turner*, 2, p. 237, Boime, *Art of Exclusion*, p. 42. If he were on such a hunt he went about it strangely: in recalling the *Zong* he chose a subject which must have been positively malodorous to the British establishment and painted it in a style considered incomprehensible.

80 Schwarz–Bart is quoted in James E. Young, *The Texture of Memory: Holocaust Memorials and Meaning* (New Haven and London, Yale University Press, 1993), p. 1.

81 For a sensitive discussion of the work conducted in relation to the monuments surrounding it see author Charles L. Griswold, 'The Vietnam Veterans Memorial and the Washington Mall: Philosophical Thoughts on Political Iconography', in Harriet F. Seine and Sally Webster (eds), *Critical Issues in Public Art: Content, Context, and*

Controversy (New York, Harper Collins, 1992), pp. 70–100. See also Marita Sturken, 'The Wall, the Screen, and the Image: The Vietnam Veteran's Memorial', *Representations*, 35:3 (1991) 118–42.

82 Cathy Caruth, *Unclaimed Experience: Trauma, Narrative and History* (Baltimore and London, Johns Hopkins University Press, 1996), p. 76.

83 Ruskin, *Works*, 23, p. xxv.

84 *Blackwood's Magazine* (Sept. 1840) 380.

85 *The Athenaeum* (16 May, 1840) 400.

86 *The Times* (6 May, 1840).

87 *Blackwood's Magazine* (Sept. 1840) 380.

88 George Meredith, *The Egoist* (London, Constable, 1897), pp. 11–13. Meredith's ultimate arbiter of taste within fashionable circles, Mrs Mountstuart Jenkinson, a lady 'certain to say the remembered if not the right thing', has her powers challenged in the second chapter of *The Egoist*. She is required to form an epithet to encapsulate the qualities of the 'young Sir Willoughby', who is too perfect for words: 'And, says Mrs. Mountstuart, while grand phrases were mouthing round about him: "*You see he has a leg*"'. For Georg Baselitz's foot paintings see *Georg Baselitz* (Hamburg, Benedikt Taschen, 1990), pp. 67–9.

89 For the literary background to the fragment in Romantic literature see Annie Janowitz, *England's Ruins: Poetic Purpose and the National Landscape* (Oxford, Basil Blackwell, 1990), pp. 10–15, 48–70, 127–9. For the Fuseli image see Schiff (ed.), *Füssli*, 1, p. 579; 2, p. 421.

90 For a sensitive reading of Gericault's aesthetic humanisation of the fragment in these works see Richard Leppert, *Art and the Committed Eye: The Cultural Functions of Imagery* (Oxford and Boulder, Westview Press, 1996), pp. 149–52.

91 For a detailed socio-political reading of Gericault's severed limb paintings in the context of the aesthetic debates of post-revolutionary France see Nina Athanassoglou-Kallmyer, 'Gericault's Severed Heads and Limbs: The Politics and Aesthetics of the Scaffold', *Art Bulletin* 74:4 (1992) 599–618.

92 Thomas Carlyle, *Centenary Edition of the Works of Thomas Carlyle in Thirty Volumes* (London, Chapman and Hall, 1896), 4, p. 42.

93 John Gage, *Turner 1775–1851* (London, Tate Gallery, 1974), p. 188. For Turner's possible literary sources for the *Slave Ship* see Jack Lindsay, *The Sunset Ship: The Poems of J. M. W. Turner* (London, Scorpion Press, 1966), pp. 50–2.

94 Thomas Gisborne, *Walks in a Forest* (London, 1794), p. 54.

95 Gisborne, *Walks*, p. 56.

96 Gisborne, *Walks*, pp. 56–8.

97 Pennant, *British Zoology*, quoted in Gisborne, *Walks*, p. 57.

98 Isaac Teale, 'The Sable Venus', in Edwards, *History*, 2, pp. 29–30.

99 Honour, *Image of the Black*, 4:1, pp. 32–3 responds to Stothard's image of the Sable Venus with admirably frank outrage. For a reading of Teale's poem in relation to contemporary gender and hybridity debates see Robert J. C. Young, *Colonial Desire: Hybridity in Theory, Culture and Race* (London, Routledge, 1995), pp. 152–8.

100 For representations of the deluge see Cohn, *Noah's Flood*, pp. 1, 37, 40, 44–6, 105, 107.

101 David Dabydeen, *Turner and Other Poems* (London, Cape Poetry, 1994), p. 14.

102 Dabydeen, *Turner*, p. 21.

103 For Bloom see Ziva Amishai-Maisels, *Depiction and Interpretation: The Influence of the Holocaust on the Visual Arts* (Oxford, Pergamon, 1993), pp. 80–3.

104 Ruskin, *Works*, 3, p. lv.

105 John Ruskin, *The Diaries of John Ruskin*, ed. Joan Evans and John Howard Whitehouse, 3 vols (Oxford, Clarendon Press, 1956–59), 1, p. 255. Paul Gilroy, *Small Acts* (London, Serpent's Tail Press, 1993), p. 82 meditates the relevance of the *Slave Ship* to contemporary debates on race and racial consciousness, black and white.

106 Ruskin returned to the fish in the Catalogue of the Ruskin Collection, under the entries for 'His Drawings by Turner'. Two fish studies are interpreted allegorically, perhaps

satirically: *Works*, 13, p. 469: '108. STUDY FOR FISH Coming on at speed, in the Slaver (modern trade?) 109. STUDY FOR THE SLAVER Looking up to the sky, in the Slaver (modern philosophy?).'

107 *The Tempest*, III, i, 59–66.

108 Boswell, *No Abolition of Slavery*, p. 24.

109 Ruskin, *Diaries*, 1, p. 257.

110 G. W. F. Hegel, *The Phenomenology of Spirit*, trans. A. V. Miller (Oxford, Clarendon Press, 1977), pp. 111–17.

111 Parts of this letter were reprinted in Harold Bloom, *The Ringers in the Tower: Studies in Romantic Tradition* (Chicago and London, University of Chicago Press, 1971), pp. 176–7. Bloom argues that the first part of this letter is a Ruskinian weak re-reading of Wordsworth's *Ode: Intimations of Immortality*. Bloom does not refer to the second half of the letter in which Ruskin expands his argument in the context of an art/life antithesis which is focused on the *Slave Ship*.

112 Ruskin, *Works*, 36, pp. 80–1.

113 For Hazlitt's distinction in the context of the middle passage see pp. 15–16 above. In the nineteenth century 'enthusiasm' still carried the meanings 'Possession by a god, supernatural inspiration, prophetic or poetic frenzy' (*OED*, 1). Its relation to literary Romanticism and popular millennialism have been written about at length. See, for example, Jon Mee's discussion of Blake and enthusiasm in *Dangerous Enthusiasm* (Oxford, Oxford University Press, 1993).

114 Dabydeen, *Turner*, p. ix: 'Ruskin … wrote a detailed account of the composition of the painting … the subject, the shackling and drowning of Africans, was relegated to a brief footnote in Ruskin's essay. The footnote reads like an afterthought, something tossed overboard.' Paul Gilroy, *The Black Atlantic: Modernity and Double Consciousness* (London, Verso, 1993), p. 14: 'It is important, though, to draw attention to Ruskin's inability to discuss the picture except in terms of what it revealed about the aesthetics of painting water. He relegated the information that the vessel was a slave ship to a footnote in the first volume of *Modern Painters*.' Tim Hilton, *Ruskin: The Early Years* (New Haven and London, Yale University Press, 1985), p. 77 talks of Ruskin 'relegating the ostensible subject of the picture to a footnote'. For a more sympathetic reading see Wilton, *Life and Works*, p. 218.

115 Albert Boime, 'Turner's *Slave Ship*', pp. 36–41 constitutes the most narrowly political reading of the *Slave Ship*, which is set against a backdrop of contemporary imagery relating to the slave trade and factory labour. Boime considers Hayden's hopelessly wooden mass portrait of the world anti-slavery convention of 1840 as politically superior to Turner, claiming 'As a statement on slavery, it [Haydon's *The Anti-Slavery Society Convention, 1840*] has a more practical and more concrete political message than the Turner'.

116 In his definition of the operation of the 'pathetic fallacy' Ruskin, *Works*, 5, p. 209, describes the fourth order of creative mind as that which encounters a subject so terrible that it enters the mode of prophecy (enthusiasm), where the adoption of metaphoric personification is no longer an indication of creative inferiority: 'And thus in full there are four classes: the men who feel nothing, and therefore see truly; the men who feel strongly, think weakly and see untruly (second order poets); the men who feel strongly, think strongly and see truly (first order of poets); and the men who, strong as human creatures can be, are yet submitted to influences stronger than they and see in a sort untruly because what they see is inconceivably above them. This last is the usual condition of prophetic inspiration.'

117 Ruskin, *Works*, 3, pp. 571–3.

118 Ruskin, *Works*, 3, p. 42, sets up a series of tables providing estimates of the time of day and weather conditions in each of Turner's important paintings. For the slaver the verdict is 'Evening … Ten minutes before sunset. Tumultuous spray of illumined rain cloud.'

119 For the relation of the history of the *Zong* to the *Slave Ship* see Butlin and Joll, *Turner*, 2, p. 237, and Boime, 'Turner's *Slave Ship*', p. 36.

120 Reproduced, Butlin and Joll, *Turner*, 1, plate 19, discussed 2, p. 22.

121 Ruskin, *Works*, 5, p. 222.

122 Ruskin, *Works*, 6, p. 381.

123 *Macbeth*, I, vii, 71–6.

124 *Macbeth*, II, ii, 43–7.

125 *Macbeth*, II, ii, 47–9.

126 *Macbeth*, II, ii, 50–3.

127 *Macbeth*, II, iii, 112–13.

128 For obsessive reworkings of the sanguinary imagery of the *Slave Ship* see Ruskin, *Works*, 18, p. 24; 34, p. 45; 6, p. 381.

129 Henry Irving Tragle, *The Southampton Slave Revolt of 1831: A Compilation of Source Material* (Amherst, University of Massachusetts Press, 1971), pp. 300–1.

130 Tragle, *Southampton Slave Revolt*, p. 309.

131 Toni Morrison, *Beloved* (London, Picador, 1987), pp. 8–10.

132 Amishai-Maisels, *Depiction and Interpretation*, p. xxxi.

3

Rhetoric and the runaway: the iconography of slave escape in England and America

I will never run from another thing on this earth. I took one journey and I paid for the ticket. (Sethe in Toni Morrison, *Beloved*)

There's no problem in life so big that you can't run away from it. (Dillwyn Smith, in assessing when he considered one of his paintings finished)

Running away, in Western culture, is a pejorative concept customarily associated with desertion, cowardice, retreat and failure. The slave 'runaway' is disadvantaged through the associations of his/her titular epithet before the first step towards escape has been taken. Yet slave escape is deeply embedded within the historiography and imagery created by Western culture to remember slavery, and its representation is a bundle of contradictions.

The narrative combinations of escape, flight, recapture, punishment, renewed escape, and life after escape, provide basic structures for the art and literature of anti- and pro-slavery propaganda. This inheritance is ultimately the historic achievement of slave revolutionaries. Without 'runaways' there would have been no Maroons and no Maroon wars in Jamaica, no Zumbi, no Palmares and no Quilombos in Brazil, no Dred Scott decision and no fugitive slave law in North America. The literature and art generated by slavery would not exist without 'runaways'. Aphra Behn could not have written *Oroonoko*, John Stedman would never have gone to fight 'the Revolted Negroes of Surinam', and his sensational travelogues, novellas and the dramas based on this experience would not have thrilled London at the turn of the eighteenth century. Richard Hildreth could not have written *Archie More or The White Slave*, Harriet Beecher Stowe could not have written *Uncle Tom's Cabin* (a novel in which every major slave character runs away or thinks about why, or why not to, run away) or *Dred, A Tale of the Dismal Swamp*, Dred himself being a strangely mythologised and sanitised version of the insurrectionary and finally fugitive Nat Turner. The slave narratives, in which the act of escape is pivotal, would have had no authors, and William Still no materials to compile his magisterial *The Underground Railroad*. If Margaret Garner had not escaped and killed her three-year-old child to avoid recapture, Toni Morrison would consequently not have built *Beloved* the way she did. Without runaways there would also have been no runaway advertisements.

For the slave-owner the presentation of the runaway through advertisement was outwardly straightforward, and constituted the announcement, within the terms of an established legal code, of an act of theft, albeit a paradoxical self-theft. For the abolitionist, whether black or white, ex-slave or born-free, the runaway had to be created against the rhetorical backdrop of a legal history, and in terms of the law's most obvious popular rhetorical manifestation, runaway advertising. The clashing semiotic practices which the runaway generated are the subject of the following work. The texts and imagery of runaway advertising emerge as endemic in the ways they inflect, to a greater or lesser extent, all visual representations of the slave fugitive.

When abolition was established in the late eighteenth century as a concerted movement in England and North America the slave advertisement emerged as a primary target for the abolitionists. The processes through which abolitionists converted the imagery and texts of slave advertising into anti-slavery propaganda became increasingly sophisticated. The following analysis consequently begins by providing a contextualising survey of the literary satire which attacked slave advertising in England and America from the late eighteenth to the mid-nineteenth century. This discussion also requires articulation of why the runaway slave advertisement, in its combination of text and image, was so effective in its nullification of the figure of the fugitive slave. Illustrated slave advertisement effectively presented the runaway as disempowered, and abolitionists consequently developed methods for subverting the power of this form, many of the most effective examples working through imagery.

It is further argued that a survey of the strategies of English and American anti-slavery propaganda reveals the most radical and semiotically revolutionary recasting of the iconography of slave escape to have been generated within the major slave narratives. Many of these employed imagery in very different ways from other mainstream abolition texts created solely by whites. The imagery in slave narratives is shown to reformulate, and frequently to ironise, a series of general interpretative and methodological issues relating to the presentation of the runaway. This discussion consequently concludes with detailed readings of the interactive roles of text and imagery in rendering the 'runaway' in the narratives of Frederick Douglass, Henry Bibb and Henry 'Box' Brown. The *Narrative of Frederick Douglass* is used to set up the discussion in terms of its rhetorical ironising of both Southern and Northern constructions of the fugitive. Yet the radical redefinition of the act of running away in this text is shown to be finally powerless to resist absorption into the iconographic reductions of the popular print market. The *Narrative of H. B. Brown*, and the various popular texts it generated, show how a personalised iconography could be developed in prints, children's books, almanacs, newspapers and even the public stage, to develop a mythology of escape as resurrection.

Brown's representation within the iconography of the English and American popular press emerges as fraught with narrative and symbolic paradoxes which ultimately hinge on Brown's strategies for maintaining his own black cultural hegemony. Finally The *Narrative of Henry Bibb* is seen to present something quite different – an assault, through ironic quotation, on the conventionality of the Northern repertoire of imagery relating to the runaway.

Re-marking the market: white abolitionist uses of the texts of slave advertisements from Coleridge to Dickens and Stowe

> What a History! Horses and Negroes! Negroes and Horses! It makes me tremble at my own Nature! (Samuel Taylor Coleridge)

As soon as black chattel slavery was established, slaves escaped, and advertisements publicising their descriptions were produced. The scale of the advertising reflected the scale of the phenomenon. From the earliest days of colonial labour in the Americas, runaways, white and black, had posed a problem big enough to influence the form of the slave codes. Winthrop Jordan summarises: 'The codes devoted much attention to the most persistent and potentially dangerous problem of slave control – running away. Probably more time, money, and energy was expended on this problem by white slave owners, legislators, constables, jailers, and newspaper printers than on any other aspect of administering the slave system.'[1] The print cultures of eighteenth- and nineteenth-century Brazil, the Caribbean and the Southern United States teemed with notices for runaway slaves.[2] They were also current in the late-eighteenth-century English newspapers published in slave ports, most significantly Liverpool.[3] The advertisements embodied the hard-nosed business approach of owners to the loss of valuable property. Slave advertisements were composed of a descriptive text, or an image and a text. The images, type-cast or wood-engraved, remained largely standardised over two continents and two centuries. A male was represented by a running clothed figure, carrying a bundle of goods on a stick and passing a tree [**3.1**]. A female was represented, most commonly, by a seated clothed figure, resting, and holding a bundle [**3.2**]. The images were also sometimes used as eye-catching devices for notices for slave auctions, or as advertisements for slave purchase. These two images enjoyed a remarkable longevity and an intercontinental and transcultural currency.

Representations of the fugitive slave, and the formulae for prose descriptions of escapees, had been developed out of the conventions of advertisements for runaway white indentured servants advertised commonly in colonial papers from the mid-eighteenth century.[4] Advertisement sections frequently provided a concrete expression of the precise legal equation between slaves and other forms of livestock. As Coleridge's

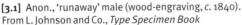

[3.1] Anon., 'runaway' male (wood-engraving, *c.* 1840). From L. Johnson and Co., *Type Specimen Book*

[3.2] Anon., 'runaway' female (wood-engraving, *c.* 1840). From L. Johnson and Co., *Type Specimen Book*

prefatory quotation to this chapter emphasises, newspapers and broadsides advertised lost horses, and other livestock, alongside escaped slaves in the same columns. In order to facilitate identification, the majority of advertisements also tended to emphasise physical peculiarities. Distinguishing marks resulted from disease, accident, or from branding and physical punishment, whether deliberate torture or casual brutality. The scars and deformities listed recreated the slave's body as a living and moving text. The advertisements constituted a perpetual catalogue of the abuse of the slave body and as such had the potential to be subverted by anti-slavery authors.

The visual propaganda focused on runaway slave advertising in the mid-nineteenth century developed out of a long-standing and sophisticated tradition of textual engagement with the form of the advertisements. The satiric potential of slave advertisements was explored as early as 1795 by the English radical polemicist William Cobbett in the pamphlet *A Bone to Gnaw for the Democrats*.[5]

The first interest in the use of runaway advertisements as a source for abolition propaganda occurred in the context of English abolition in the early nineteenth century. In 1808 Samuel Taylor Coleridge produced the satire 'Hint for a New Species of History' in which he provided contributions to a projected volume 'A History of the Morals and (as connected therewith) of the Manners of the English Nation from the Conquest to

81

the Present'.[6] The book was also intended to chart the moral degeneracy of the age and as a key example Coleridge quoted a section of the *Kingston Mercantile Advertiser*. Three advertisements for slaves headed 'RAN AWAY' and 'STRAYED' are interspersed with an advertisement for 'a small bay HORSE' and 'a bright dun He-MULE'. Coleridge responded:

> What a History! Horses and Negroes! Negroes and Horses! It makes me tremble at my own Nature! – Surely, every religious and conscientious Briton is equally a debtor in gratitude to Thomas Clarkson, and his fellow labourers, with every African: for on the soul of every individual among us did a portion of guilt rest, as long as the slave trade remained legal.[7]

Coleridge punches home the outrageous fusion of man and animal in the blunt rhetoric of his inversion 'Horses and Negroes! Negroes and Horses', for the horses come first. In the prefatory comments to this article Coleridge goes further and creates an ironic frame which allows the discussion to edge into satire. He states that 'the moral being has sometimes crawled, sometimes strolled, sometimes walked, sometimes run; but it has at all times been moving onward. If in any one point it has gone backward, it has only been to leap forward in some other.' But human progress does not move so easily when set next to slavery.

The progress of the 'moral being' is enacted through a series of verbs of motion, from the infantile 'crawled' through the casual 'strolled' and pedestrian 'walked' to 'run'. The metaphor of the virile figure of moral progress running and leaping carries a burden of irony, and its optimism is cut down by the introduction of a new and very different form of running. The slaves in the advertisements are not running forward with progress, but away from the 'progressive' civilisation which enslaved them. The three advertisements headed 'RAN AWAY' which immediately follow on from Coleridge's definition of 'human progress' describe not only the flight of the slaves, but the flight of white society from progress. The runaway emerges as a metaphor for white moral failure. Coleridge turns this power back upon slave societies and slave government through satire. In doing so he opened up the way for a satire growing out of the mediation of slave advertising.

Nearly two decades after Coleridge's satire, Thomas Clarkson published his 1824 pamphlet *Negro Slavery*.[8] He attacked plantation slavery through the minute analysis of the advertisements in a single issue of the *Royal Gazette of Jamaica* for June 1823. His main focus was the standard pro-slavery argument comparing the condition of British labourers unfavourably with that of West Indian slaves.

Clarkson settles on the repeated statement that slaves have 'run away' and overhauls it. With a grim humour that mounts to an almost Cobbettian reiterative ferocity he converts the term 'run away' into the centrepiece for this stage of his argument:

> I find in this Gazette, that *more than one hundred slaves are advertised as
> having run away from their masters,* and as then detained in the gaols or
> workhouses of the different parishes where they were taken up!!! What a fact
> is this!!! *More than a hundred runaways appear in one Gazette to have been
> taken up and committed to gaol!!!*
>
> But I may ask, runaways *from what?* Why, according to the accounts of
> our opponents they must have been *runaways from happiness – runaways
> from comfort* ... [9]

This is hard-hitting moral satire. Clarkson begins with the un-ironic application of the term 'runaway', as it is used by the masters, as it appears in the
press, but rapidly moves on to incorporate the phrase in his own sarcastic
verbal compounds: 'runaways from happiness', 'runaways from comfort'.

At this point Clarkson switches to a systematic analysis of the content
of the advertisements, isolating the elements of degradation and brutality
which they disclose. Four categories are established which consist of
'branding', 'description of apparatus', 'whipping scars' and 'burning
scars'. Each category is introduced with the increasingly ironic phrase 'We
are struck ...'. It is, of course, the slaves who are struck first, then the traces
of their suffering in their turn 'strike' the reader of the advertisements.
Clarkson forcefully redefines activities which are assumed to be unproblematic by re-interpreting them with an innocent eye:

> we are struck, on examining the advertisements in this Gazette, with the
> descriptions given of many of these runaway slaves. Numbers of them appear
> to have been branded with the initials of their owner's names, and other
> marks, *on the naked flesh,* with a *heated iron,* in the same manner as young
> horses or cattle are branded when they are turned into our forests. The oper-
> ation, however, is probably much less painful when performed upon a brute,
> than when performed on *one of the human species.* Some of these brand-
> marks upon these slaves, consisting, as they often do, *of several letters,* must
> have tortured no inconsiderable portion of the flesh ... Tom, again a Nago
> (African), is said to be 5 feet 2 inches high, and marked apparently RG on the
> shoulders, and PYBD on the right, and apparently LB on the left breast.
> Thus we see in this last instance *one individual branded with no less than ten
> capital letters.* [10]

Clarkson establishes branding as a key element within the descriptive
apparatus of the runaway advertisement. In doing so he isolates a site of
violence which was to remain central to abolitionist polemic. [11]

Clarkson's pamphlet provided a basic method for subsequent abolition propaganda in Europe, America and Brazil. The advertisements for
runaways were a perpetual manifestation of the cold economic assumptions
and unacknowledged cruelties underlying slave systems, and a great part of
their appeal related to the fact that they were produced by the slave-owners
themselves. They were increasingly recognised by abolitionists as providing an ever-rolling, self-generating flood of evidence which damned the
slave-owners out of their own mouths. The consistencies in the repetition of

evidence testified to the equality, in ignominiousness, of all systems of black plantation slavery from the sixteenth to the nineteenth century.

Abolitionists developed increasingly sophisticated ways of reconstituting runaway advertisements in various types of publication. The *New York Anti-Slavery Almanac* used slave advertisements in a series of articles.[12] The *Boston Anti-Slavery Almanac* for 1837 carried a series of runaway advertisements accompanied by cuts of a runaway slave with a stick. This is headed with one of the earliest examples of a parodic runaway advertisement:

$ 100,000 REWARD,

Will be paid to any one who will prove to an impartial jury that the system of slavery, of which the following advertisements exhibit a specimen, is any less wicked, less cruel, or any less worthy of unqualified abhorrence, than the foreign slave trade, which the Congress calls Piracy.[13]

The culmination of the use of the slave advertisements in American abolition publications was *American Slavery As It Is, Testimony of a Thousand Witnesses*, published in New York in 1839 by the American Anti-Slavery Society. The brainchild of Theodore Dwight Weld and Angelina and Sarah Grimke, it was a daring book which shattered the unspoken proprieties which had previously governed the approach of American abolitionists to slavery propaganda.[14] Moral suasion, emphasising the spiritual and practical benefits which would ensue from abolition, was replaced by the citation of acts of cruelty by slave-owners. This pamphlet had a vast influence in terms of the way it legitimated the graphic representation of violence against slaves in subsequent abolition publication. It sold more than one hundred thousand copies in America, came out in many English editions, was announced by Garrison as the most significant of abolition publications, and Harriet Beecher Stowe purportedly kept it under her pillow while writing *Uncle Tom's Cabin*.[15]

The majority of material in *American Slavery* was extracted from Southern newspapers in the form of advertisements and articles. The volume was consequently an organised literary collage, a catalogue of arbitrary suffering on an enormous scale which was presented in a number of different styles ranging from confessional narrative by ex-southerners to the blunt inventories of provincial newspaper advertising. The commentary combines nineteenth-century legal language and evidential procedure with the rhetorical conventions of Protestant martyrology.[16]

Weld's attempts to claim legal status for the evidence he provides is a well-documented aspect of *American Slavery*. What has not been considered is the extent to which the book looks to another tradition of witnessing. The book attempts to ennoble the casual violence inflicted on slaves with the status of martyrological suffering – in some ways it succeeds in doing this. The great tradition of Protestant martyrology, enshrined in the thought, literature and rhetoric of England and North America by

Foxe's *Actes and Monuments*, and by its innumerable popular manifestations in the reduced and accessible versions of the *Book of Martyrs*, lies behind the inventory of violence and suffering constructed by Weld.[17]

American Slavery can be read as a latter-day *Actes and Monuments* for the slave constructed out of the testimony of slave advertisements. The section entitled 'General Testimony to the Cruelties inflicted Upon Slaves' is an organisational *tour de force*. Every category detailing the records of violence on the bodies of slaves is set out as a double column under the titles 'witnesses', 'testimonies'. The former consists of the name of the slaveholder and details of the paper in which the advertisement appeared. The latter consists of a quotation from the advertisement under the relevant heading of 'flogging', 'mutilation of teeth', 'Tortures, By Iron Collars, Chains, Fetters, Handcuffs, &c.'.[18]

The slave advertisement is thus absorbed into a set of linguistic and institutional conventions which transform it. The rhetoric of the Church and of the Law suddenly ennoble what was before the transient language of journal advertising. The very bureaucratic processes which the state enforces for the recapture of slaves are appropriated by the abolitionists, and redefined. The slave-owners are anthologised as the authors of a comprehensive martyrology of the sufferings of their victims. It is a martyrology for the new print age, the age of advertising. Unlike Foxe's great agglomeration, and unlike the slave narratives which proliferated in the 1850s and 1860s, there is no rhetorical structure of celebration, no individual apotheosis, and the slave/martyr never testifies for himself. There is simply the unending process of fact piled on fact. Martyrdom is built into the Western Christian consciousness – it is the original Christian gesture, grand, personal, an act of the triumphant will. The monumentalisation of suffering is encoded in the very title of Foxe's *Actes and Monuments*: the act is to be martyred and the act, if carried through properly, makes the monument. *American Slavery* created an alternative way of memorialising mass secular black martyrdom. As with the records that remain of the victims of the Nazi Holocaust, this monument is culled from the arbitrary bureaucratic fall-out created by the system which created the victims. Weld realised that within the ephemeral columns of advertisements the raw materials for a horrifying monument to the individual suffering of the slaves lay entombed.[19]

The influence of *American Slavery* ran deep, but imitators missed the crucial point – that the power of the publication came out of the way it allowed its sources to speak for themselves. When, in 1842, Dickens wrote the chapter of *American Notes* entitled 'Slavery', he drew directly on the catalogue method of Weld's pamphlet.[20] Yet he prefaced his list of advertisements with an assault on 'Public Opinion' which in its self-involved hysteria leaves little room for the slave:

Public opinion! Why, public opinion in the slave States *is* slavery, is it not?
Public opinion, in the slave States, has delivered the slaves over to the gentle

mercies of their masters. Public opinion has made the laws, and denied the slaves legislative protection. Public opinion has knotted the lash, heated the branding-iron, loaded the rifle, and shielded the murderer. Public opinion threatens the abolitionist with death, if he venture to the South; and drags him with a rope around his middle in broad unblushing noon, through the first city in the East. Public opinion has, within a few years, burned a slave alive at a slow fire in St. Louis; and public opinion has to this day maintained upon the bench that estimable Judge who charged the Jury, impanelled there to try his murderers, that their most horrid deed was an act of public opinion, and being so, must not be punished by the laws the public sentiment had made. Public opinion hailed this doctrine with a howl of wild applause …[21]

Quite rapidly 'Public Opinion', so traduced, so generalised, so dragged out of context, and through event, ceases to mean anything at all. Dickens's attempts to whip himself into an escalating expression of outraged, and outrageous, irony are a distraction. Abolition had to wait for the publication of *Uncle Tom's Cabin* in 1852 for a text which gave expression and form to a pure, and economically expressed, contempt for the slave advertisement and all it enshrined. Stowe, as so often in *Uncle Tom's Cabin*, used her fictional framework to break the mould of abolition propaganda. Here, rather than condemn the form of the slave advertisement through foaming fulmination, she calculatedly spits on it:[22]

> 'Ran away from the subscriber, my mulatto boy George. Said George six feet in height, a very light mulatto, brown curly hair; is very intelligent, speaks handsomely, can read and write; will probably try to pass for a white man; is deeply scarred on his back and shoulders; has been branded in his right hand with the letter H.
>
> 'I will give four hundred dollars for him alive, and the same sum for satisfactory proof that he has been killed.'
>
> …The long-legged veteran … took down his cumbrous length, and rearing aloft his tall form, walked up to the advertisement, and very deliberately spit a full discharge of tobacco juice on it.
>
> 'There's my mind upon that!'

[3.3] Hamatt Billings, 'Spitting on a runaway advertisement' (wood-engraving, 1853). From *Uncle Tom's Cabin* (Sampson Low)

Some editions carried graphic representations of the incident [**3.3**].[23] The coarseness of the insult has a self-sufficient finality which cannot be bettered. Yet the form of the slave advertisement could not always be so easily inverted because it frequently did not function through a printed text alone, but through the combination of text and image. It is the problematic nature of this combination which needs to be uncovered.

The battle for the runaway: white abolition assaults on the semiotics of illustrated slave advertisement

Slave power semiotics: going nowhere in a hurry

The slave power's construction of the runaway is encapsulated in one pair of images [3.1 and 3.2]. The slave advertisement is based upon a paradox. To recognise an escaped slave and prove her/his identity she/he must be described as an individual. The most obvious way to particularise a slave so that they can be recognised by a stranger is to describe distinguishing marks. But, as the adjective suggests, such marks distinguish the slave as an abused individual, at the same time that they point her or him out to the potential slave-catcher. The texts of slave advertisements consequently elaborate the unique human status of, and the particular signs of suffering on, the body described. Even descriptions of slave dress, or the clothing taken on departure, could become a celebration of the slave's individuality.[24]

Slavery, as a legal and economic phenomenon, was premised upon the denial of personality, and of a personal history, to the slave. The texts of the runaway advertisements challenged the abstraction of slave into property because they foregrounded the personal peculiarities of slaves. Consequently the legal and economic anonymity of the slave needed to be reasserted. The icon of the runaway provided the solution. This advertising logo is an image of appalling force, a statement that in the eyes of the law, and the eyes of the slave power, one runaway is the same as every runaway, while the act of running away always takes the same literal form. The image is part of a commercial nexus in which the North was as deeply implicated as the South.

Until abolition was well established this image signified the runaway, and beyond this it signified the advertisement of a reward for the apprehension of a runaway. It was standardised to the extent that it was quite simply a typographic character. The printer's stock books which came out in the big Northern cities, from the 1830s right up until the eve of abolition, carried this image at a variety of prices in a variety of sizes. The small versions appeared top left of the text in newspaper advertisements [**3.4**]. The larger versions in woodcut form were used on handbill and broadside runaway announcements [**3.5**]. Northern printing firms sent their specimen books down South and printed up orders for the Southern market.

The image had a European origin. In England advertisements for 'runaway' or 'strayed and missing' persons were so familiar that by the early nineteenth century the form could be used as the basis for anti-state political satire.[25] During the early decades of colonial expansion on the East Coast of America a high proportion of the white servants who were shipped over from Europe arrived under indenture contracts which made them not that much better off than slaves.[26] Not surprisingly runaways were common and the forms of advertisement rapidly became standardised. By the middle of the eighteenth century advertisers, mainly under the influence of the advertising methods of the entrepreneurial Benjamin Franklin, began to

$100,000 REWARD,

Will be paid to any one who will prove to an impartial jury that the system of slavery, of which the following advertisements exhibit a specimen, is any less wicked, less cruel, or less worthy of unqualified abhorrence, than the foreign slave trade which Congress calls PIRACY.

RUNAWAY SLAVE IN JAIL. Was arrested and committed to the parish jail of Ascension, ... Thomas Mills, about 25 yrs old, &c. States he is FREE, and he was left off the Paul Jones on her way up. The *owner* is requested to comply with the LAW and take him away. *Ascension, Oct. 22, 1835.*   J. L. Comstock, Jailer.

NOTICE.

WAS committed to the Jail of Wilkinson co. on Wednesday, Jan. 27, 1836, a negro man named NED, about 24 years of age, ... *very much marked with the* WHIP *on his thighs and buttocks.* The owner, &c.   WM. T. LEWIS, Sh'ff.
Woodville, Mississippi, Jan 30, 1836.

FIFTY DOLLARS REWARD. Runaway from the subscriber his Negro Man Pauladore, commonly called PAUL. ... I understand Gen. R. Y. HAYNE has PURCHASED his WIFE & CHILDREN from H. L. PINCKNEY, Esq. and has them now on his plantation at Goose creek, where, no doubt, the Fellow is frequently lurking. The above reward will be paid, on his being lodged in the work house of Charleston, or gaol at Georgetown. All persons are cautioned against harboring him under penalty of the law.   T. DAVIS.

TWENTY-FIVE DOLLARS REWARD. Ranaway from the Subscriber, a Negro woman, named Matilda. It is thought she may be somewhere up James River, or lurking above the Basin, as she was CLAIMED AS A WIFE by some boatman in Goochland.   J. ALVIS.

STOP THE RUNAWAY!!!—$25 REWARD.—Ranaway from the Eagle Tavern a negro fellow named NAT. He is a carpenter by trade, ... and has an intelligent countenance. He is a shrewd, sensible negro, and is no doubt attempting to follow his WIFE, who was lately SOLD TO A SPECULATOR, named "Redmond." The above reward will be paid by Mrs. LUCY M. DOWNMAN, of Sussex co. Va.

[3.4] Anon., 'runaway' advertisement (type metal cut, 1842). From the *Anti-Slavery Almanac*

introduce small woodcuts to attract the readers' attention.[27]

The runaway male was presented dressed up in a frock coat and three-cornered hat, carrying a bundle on a stick and walking along in a pastoral landscape with a small stunted tree to his bottom right. Distinguishing features and relevant details of biography were given, as in the slave advertisements, and white runaways are often described as wearing iron collars. Examples in mid-eighteenth-century journals indicate how precisely the runaway slave advertisements develop out of the white runaway servant notices. The advertisement illustrated here is for an indentured male Irish runaway [3.6]. Similarly formulaic advertisements existed for women [3.7].[28] As with the conventions of the slave advertisements, the

$150 REWARD

RANAWAY from the subscriber, on the night of the 2d instant, a negro man, who calls himself *Henry May*, about 22 years old, 5 feet 6 or 8 inches high, ordinary color, rather chunky built, bushy head, and has it divided mostly on one side, and keeps it very nicely combed; has been raised in the house, and is a first rate dining-room servant, and was in a tavern in Louisville for 18 months. I expect he is now in Louisville trying to make his escape to a free state, (in all probability to Cincinnati, Ohio.) Perhaps he may try to get employment on a steamboat. He is a good cook, and is handy in any capacity as a house servant. Had on when he left, a dark cassinett coatee, and dark striped cassinett pantaloons, new---he had other clothing. I will give $50 reward if taken in Louisvill; 100 dollars if taken one hundred miles from Louisville in this State, and 150 dollars if taken out of this State, and delivered to me, or secured in any jail so that I can get him again.   WILLIAM BURKE.
Bardstown, Ky., September 3d, 1838.

[3.5] Anon., 'runaway' advertisement (woodcut, broadside, 1838)

woman is shown full face and stationary. As the century progressed and the number of white indentured servants declined, they were replaced by a flood of advertising for black slave runaways. The development of a mass advertising industry in America during the first half of the nineteenth century saw the iconic absorption of the slave, who constituted a tiny particle in a semiotic sea which increasingly flowed over the expanding new republic.

The seamless integration of the slave into the day-to-day economic transactions of North and South is represented with a terrible graphic finality in the sheets of trade icons which concluded Northern printer's stock books. These books provided the basic visual vocabulary for trade and product advertisements in mid-nineteenth-century America. The significance of advertising for the print culture of America in the first half of the nineteenth century is difficult to overestimate. The American print industry was very different from that of Europe, for its basis was not recreational or literary, but utilitarian. Its methods were brash and crude and intensely visual. The book trade was not, in terms of technology or distribution, well developed, while the centrality of advertising and the

[3.6] Anon., advertisement for male runaway servant (wood-engraving, January 1818). From the *New York Gazette*

[3.7] Anon., advertisement for female runaway servant (wood-engraving, January 1818). From the *New York Gazette*

necessity of disseminating information over vast spaces meant that broadsides, pamphlets, chapbooks and newspapers had an importance in facilitating communication very different from the role of such 'ephemeral' publishing forms in Europe. The first three decades of the nineteenth century have been described, in terms of printing history, as the '"Classified Ad Period"'.[29] Looking at American newspapers and broadsides, the visual elements of display are striking. It is significant that the first known American printers' specimen book, published by Binny & Ronaldson in 1809, is wholly composed of cast type ornaments, most of them trade icons for press and broadside advertisements.[30] The message is plain to see: pictures come first, the words can be fitted in afterwards. American type specimen books continued to devote a large portion of their pages to the display of icons which would immediately locate an advertisement for the reader. Given the prevalence of runaway slave advertisements, the trade cuts of slaves, in all shapes and sizes, became a standard element of print culture [**3.8** and **3.9**].

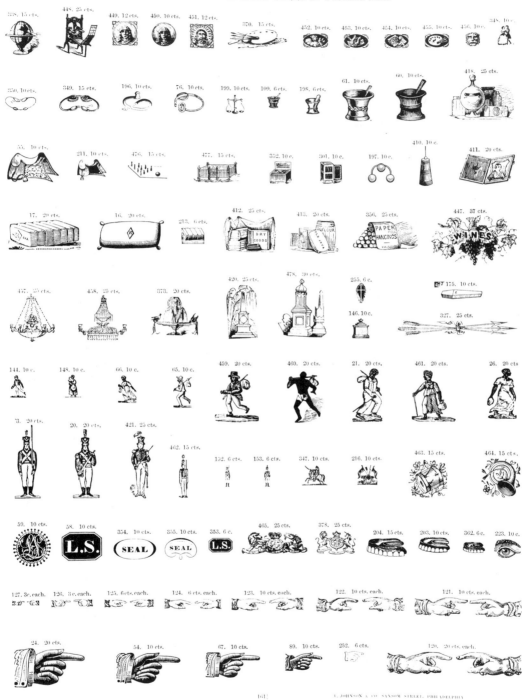

[3.8] Anon., specimen page (cast, type metal ornaments, 1840). From L. Johnson, *Specimens of Printing Types*

[6] Thomas Moran, *The Slave Hunt* (oil on canvas, 1862)

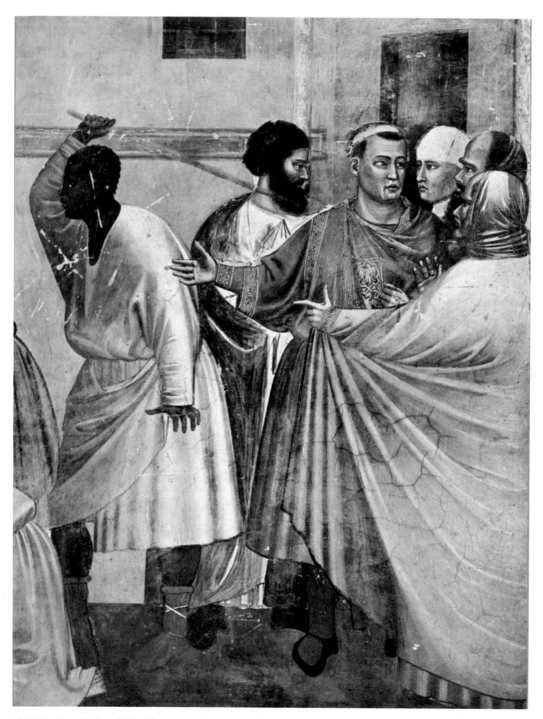

[7] Giotto, *Flagellation of Christ* (fresco on plaster, 1303–6)

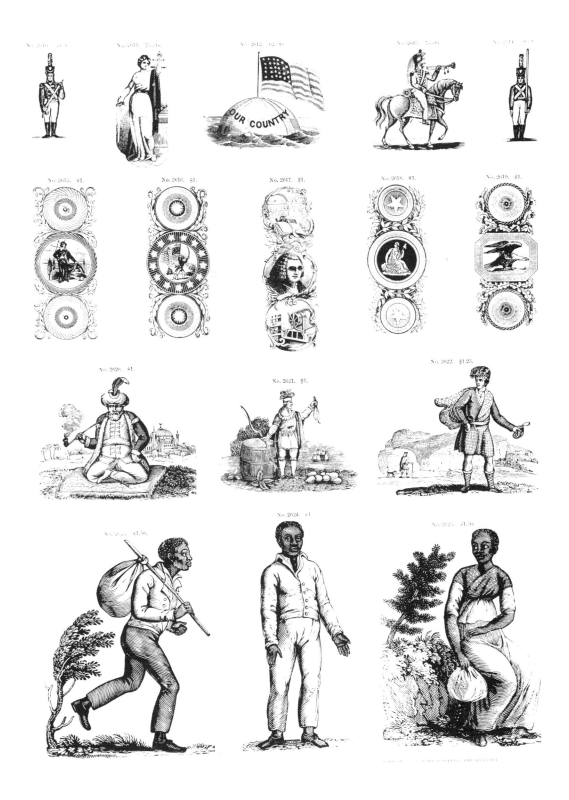

[3.9] Anon., specimen page (cast, type metal ornaments, 1840). From L. Johnson, *Specimens of Printing Types*

A little man or woman, clothing in outline, head and hands a solid black space of ink, runs, sometimes to left and sometimes to right. Above them and below them, in perfect parallels, run lines of other images representing the activity and myriad commercial interests of the industrially expanding North. The consumer jamboree that was, and is, American society is there in its certain, clean-cut, indomitable, expansive nineteenth-century essence. Household items float in space: sofas, desks, tables, chests, bags, keys, mortars and pestles, bottles, chairs, combs, gloves, cutlery, guns and slaves. Some things make sense: watches next to coffins, glasses next to bottles, anvils next to horses, Chinamen next to tea caddies, chains next to slaves.

The consistency with which these images were transcribed from decade to decade, and from country to country, is a testament to their practical efficacy. The familiarity and ready availability of the woodcut of the woman runaway comes out powerfully in the way it was used as a basis for political print satire. An 1836 mock election ticket printed in Ohio for the presidential campaign, and attacking Richard M. Johnson, focused on his mulatto wife Julia Chin [**3.10**]. Beneath the heading 'Carrying the War into Africa' the stock cut of the runaway woman slave resting is reproduced [3.2]. A speech bubble written in travesty of black dialect announces 'let ebery good dimicrat vote for my husband, and den he shall hab his sher ub de surplum rebenu wat is in my bag'. The suggestion that Johnson has creamed off funds illegally for himself is made through reference to the runaway's bag of belongings, the implication being that Johnson has stolen from the people just as the slave has stolen her master's property in order to make good her escape.

The simple reproduction of the runaway image as a portrait of Julia Chin is the whole extent of the satire. The equation underlying this gesture is that any person with a degree of black blood may be represented by the anonymous woodcut of the runaway slave, and that this symbol is synonymous with stupidity, dishonesty and public betrayal. Because she has black blood Julia Chin does not, as with white male politicians, merit the honour of personal caricature but is presented as a race stereotype. This print underlines the difficulty abolitionists faced in attempting either to appropriate or to overturn the semiotic inheritance of the slave advertisement. The images of the runaway were so familiar that they possessed a terrible semiotic inertia, the reassuring familiarity of a currency worn smooth with handling.[31]

The image of the male runaway was more frequently employed than that of the female. Its fame has provided it with a symbolic fluidity similar to that of the famous *Description* of the slave ship *Brookes*. Like the *Description*, it has been incorporated into the covers and advertising materials used in promoting a variety of nineteenth- and twentieth-century publications. The sources of its fascination run deep beneath Western narrative and symbolic structures.[32]

"Carrying the *War* into Africa."

Let every good dimicrat vote for my husband, and den he shall hab his sheet ub de surphim rethenu wat is in my bag.

She plucks Dick—and Dick plucks you—and Van plucks Dick.

Jinnoorine

JOHNSON TICKET.

This picture of a poor fugitive is from one of the stereotype cuts manufactured in this city for the southern market, and used on handbills offering rewards for runaway slaves.

THE RUNAWAY.

To escape from a powerful enemy, often requires as much courage and generalship as to conquer. One of the most celebrated military exploits on record, is the *retreat* of the ten thousand Greeks under

[3.10] Anon., 'Carrying the War into Africa' (wood-engraving, *c.* 1850)

[3.11] Anon., 'The Fugitive Slave' (wood-engraving and letterpress, July 1837). From *The Anti-Slavery Record*

The image has a power that stretches beyond the proclamation of legal ownership and relates to the strange effects latent in the depiction of frozen motion. The ecstatic hopelessness of the motionless lover who Keats apostrophises in the *Ode on a Grecian Urn* finds a most sinister reincarnation in the runaway. He will be perpetually running, until he is re-instated in his legal position as a slave. This is the *locus classicus* for the slave-holder's view of the runaway. In its literalisation of the concept of 'run-away' it is a negation of the slave's most radical anti-slavery gesture. The slave does not guilefully depart under shade of night, but stands out bold and stupid on the bleak white background of the printed page. He does not steam on a boat, like Ellen and William Craft, or travel, like Henry 'Box' Brown, by train, or ride, like David Barrett, on a horse. Comic, trivial, pathetic, and always the same, with his bundle of goods and one foot eternally raised, he proclaims his inadequacy for the task he has set himself. The very engraved lines which make up the slave are running round in circles, running everywhere and nowhere. One arm and the legs form triangles

93

thrusting forward; the stick, bundle and other arm form another set of triangles hanging back. The net result is that the head – poised, straining,
perfectly still – is itself a motionless O.

Abolition counter-rhetoric

One of the remarkable achievements of abolition propagandists, in both
North America and Brazil, was that they did, to a degree, accomplish the
reactivation of the runaway icon within the context of anti-slavery rhetoric.
The front-page illustration for the July 1837 issue of the *Anti-Slavery
Record*, edited by Elizur Wright and published in New York, carried a
woodcut of a runaway slave [**3.11**]. The print is taken from a stock cut,
identical in every detail with contemporary cuts appearing in type specimen books in Cincinnati, New York, Boston and Philadelphia [3.1].
Wright attempts the semantic reconstitution of the image in the context of
the battle for abolition. The twelve pages of text which follow the quotation of this notorious badge of bondage rethink it. Wright makes a striking
and extended comparison between the act of running away and the tactical
retreat of the Greek military commander Xenephon:

> To escape from a powerful enemy, often requires as much courage and gener-
> alship as to conquer. One of the most celebrated military exploits on record is
> the *retreat* of the ten thousand Greeks under Xenephon, for a great distance
> though an enemy's country. The sympathy of the reader is wonderfully
> drawn out for these disappointed Greeks, returning chop-fallen and woefully
> beset from their unsuccessful attempt to put one Asiatic despot on the throne
> of another. But the retreat of the ten thousand native Americans now living in
> Upper Canada, escaping from worse than Asiatic tyranny, and having to pass
> hungry, and hunted, through the wide domains of false freedom, is far more
> worthy of being placed upon record. We trust, too, that in a land of Christians
> these peaceful fugitives will not receive less sympathy than those murderous
> old Greeks, in their brazen helmets and bull-hide shields …[33]

For Wright this is bad history, and a history of the bad. Wright's attack
gains satiric force from the very prominence of the model he debunks. The
flight of the ten thousand was a standard site for the literary rendition of
classical heroism, imported from England to New England. Its availability
and status are underlined by its foregrounding in Emerson's 'Essay on
History'. Wright's use of this episode to launch a forthright criticism of the
barbarity of Classical Greece in the context of North American chattel
slavery creates a dialogue with Emerson's celebrated discussion. For
Emerson Xenophon's men are exemplary, they are a typological prolepsis
for the American frontiersman and an ultimate example of white self-suffi-
ciency at its most unassailable:

> What is the foundation of that interest all men feel in Greek history? … The
> manners of that period are plain and fierce. The reverence exhibited is for
> personal qualities, courage, address, self-command, justice, strength, swift-
> ness, a loud voice, a broad chest … A sparse population and want make every

man his own valet, cook, butcher, and soldier, and the habit of supplying his own needs activates the body to wonderful performances. Such are the Agamemnon and Diomid of Homer, and not far different is the picture Xenophon gives of himself and his compatriots in the Retreat of the Ten Thousand: 'After the army had crossed the Teleboas in Armenia, there fell much snow, and the troops lay miserably on the ground, covered with it. But Xenophon arose naked, and taking an axe, began to split wood; whereupon others rose and did the like.' Throughout his army seemed to be of a boundless liberty of speech … Who does not see that this is a gang of great boys, with such a code of discipline and such lax discipline as great boys have.[34]

Emerson's Xenophon celebrates independence, strength, courage and simple moral rectitude which are mirrored in the American myths of the pioneer as king of the wild frontier. This universal great-boy represents a simplicity of existence not dependent upon service of any sort. Domestic service is singled out by Emerson as unknown to the warrior Greek who is 'his own valet, cook, butcher'. These are Greeks without slaves. Wright cuts at the heart of this fiction through bold re-appropriation and provides a bitter answer to Emerson's opening rhetorical gambit, 'What is the foundation of that interest all men feel in Greek history?' Those very qualities of initiative and self-dependence which Emerson claims jointly for Greek hero and American frontiersman are, for Wright, to be relocated and reacquired for the runaway slave. This appropriation is seething with irony: the tradition of Spartan heroism is denied white America, because the very virtues of independence celebrated by Emerson are contradicted by the corrupt dependants of the slave system. The literary notion of the American frontiersman, Fenimore Cooper's great clean white boys, fit to associate with noble savages, but not with slaves, must now battle it out with fugitive blacks, in the literary and political imagination of the free states.[35]

Wright overturns the extant association of the image used in slave advertisements in a forthright manner. Yet his approach is not typical of abolition attempts to highlight the plight of fugitive slaves through the use of imagery. From the 1830s until the 1860s there was a consistent abolitionist attempt to create an alternative image bank for the presentation of the runaway. Yet, with the exception of the use of imagery in slave narratives, and Eastman Johnson's magnificent but anomalous *Ride of Liberty*, it is noticeable that these images frequently disempower the black subject.[36] A favourite area for the construction of visual counter-narratives was the representation of the failed escape attempt as heroic, an approach which, although ultimately analogous to Wright's, consisted of the application of the conventions of European academy painting to the subject of the fugitive.

The second half of the nineteenth century saw a series of academic oil renditions of the slave hunt which use the conventions of academic history painting to create the slave, run to ground, furiously defending his life and family. A powerful and influential rendition of this theme was Richard

[3.12] Richard Ansdell, *Hunted Slaves* (oil on canvas, 1861)

Ansdell's 1861 *Hunted Slaves* [**3.12**]. Much of the power of this design comes from the explicit absence of the slave power in any form except the dogs. In this elemental scene, a magnificently muscled black man, standing in swampland, battles ferocious nature in order to protect his woman. The savage bloodhounds are not merely hounds of hell reared on the plantation, but are the metaphorical embodiment of the absent owners, who are, presumably, about to burst into the picture plane in order to prevent their property, both dogs and slaves, from destroying each other.[37] This design certainly liberates the runaway from his imprisonment within the advertisement woodcut – he stands and fights. Yet it is possible to read a troubling ambiguity in the way the picture celebrates the black man as violent and powerful. The absence of white people from the picture makes it possible to read the design within the tradition of paintings which present the black as an exotic and ferocious natural phenomenon fighting with savage beasts. In such a reading the cornered black desperately battling dogs relates to the Western academic tradition of the hunt, as typified in Landseer's *The Stag at Bay*. Ansdell's picture does not present the confrontation of suffering humanity with ferocious nature but the battle of ferocious beasts. The purest example of the insertion of the black body into this type of painting is George Dawe's *A Negro Overpowering a Buffalo, a Fact which Occurred in America in 1809*, showing a naked black man triumphantly wrestling a buffalo to the ground with his bare hands.[38]

Other narrative conventions of academic painting were applied to the runaway theme in ways which are not straightforwardly positive. Sublime landscape painting could be employed as a metaphor for the overwhelming odds and terrifying plight of the fugitive. The most beautifully painted example is Thomas Moran's 1862 *The Slave Hunt* [**plate 6**], where the gloomy giganticism of natural forms dwarf human endeavour.[39] In creating this conception of a trapped family forging on in the full knowledge of their failure, Moran has recreated the runaway family as a sort of latter-day adaptation of John Martin's *Sadak in Search of the Waters of Oblivion*. Yet again it is difficult to know the extent to which this image finally supports the slave subject. Here the slave is presented surrounded by a nature which is hostile and destructive, and which seems allied to, even to aid, the slave power.

Such high-art renditions of the captured fugitive are not typical of visual representation of the failed slave escape in the abolition press. It is also significant that they occurred late in the day, on the eve of, or most frequently after the achievement of, abolition. In this sense they are historically conditioned – the aggrandisement of the slave, and of the slave's quest for liberty, is now incorporated into the mythology of the victorious North. They are a *postfacto* justification of Union policy and history. The black is absorbed into the general mythological aftermath of war and the sub-text to these academy paintings seems to be that, despite appearances, these black people really had been worth fighting for.[40]

In the popular market the woodcuts and lithographs which proliferated in the anti-slavery almanacs, children's books and print satires, particularly in the wake of the 1850 fugitive slave act, almost universally present disempowered images of the slave. The emphasis is upon suffering and failure: the slave is an innocent victim who might have been saved had he or she reached the North but who is now a prime site for sentimental lamentation as a victim of Southern savagery. These prints give a new twist to the verbal compound 'run-away' which is by no means straightforward in terms of the image of the slave it projects. This can be quickly illustrated in the following two examples from the New York Anti-Slavery Society's compendium, *The Legion of Liberty*, the illustrated juvenile periodical *The Slave's Friend* and the mock abolition children's book *The Gospel of Slavery* [**3.13**, **3.14** and **3.15**]. In all these images, and they are representative of literally thousands of other cuts and prints brought out in Boston and New York in the 1850s, the slave is shown running away from pursuers, brought down from behind by dogs, or shot in the back. Pathetic and brutal it certainly is, but in narrative terms one is invited only to feel aggression towards the aggressor and sorrow for the suffering. The black slave is a figure to be protected and not admired, a victim who chooses to run away; even when there is no more practical point in running, he/she runs rather than stand and fight. Some images emphasise black confusion and powerlessness in a particularly bleak manner. One harrowing little cut in the *American Anti-Slavery Almanac* shows a black male hanging from a tree wearing an enormous slave collar carrying bells [**3.16**].[41] He is suspended in a clearing in a vast pine forest and a flock of carrion birds fly about his body pecking at

[3.13] Anon.,
'F is for Fugitives'(wood-engraving,
1864). From Iron Gray, *The Gospel of
Slavery*

[3.14] Anon.,
'Letting the Oppressed Go Free' (wood-
engraving, April 1857). From *The Legion
of Liberty*

[3.15] Anon.,
'The Fugitive Slave' (wood-engraving,
April 1833). From *The Slave's Friend*

[3.16] Anon.,
'The Slave Paul' (wood-engraving, April
1838). From *The American Anti-Slavery
Almanac*

F Stands for *Fugitives* hasting from wrath,
And furies are hot on their dangerous path.

THE
SLAVE'S FRIEND.

VOL. III. No. IX.   WHOLE No. 33.

Letting the oppressed go free.

THE FUGITIVE SLAVE.

The slave Paul had suffered so much in slavery, that he chose to encounter the hardships and perils of a runaway. He exposed himself, in gloomy forests, to cold and starvation, and finally hung himself, that he might not again fall into the hands of his tormentor. [See Ball's Narrative, 2d Edit. p. 325.]

it. The overpowering gloom of the American wilderness drives the slave to despair and suicide: 'The slave Paul had suffered so much in slavery, that he chose to encounter the hard-ships of a runaway. He exposed himself in gloomy forests, to cold and starvation, and finally hung himself, that he might not again fall into the hands of his tormentor.' The story held out is that if you suffer horribly in slavery, you may suffer even more badly as a runaway in the wilderness. The sub-text is that the slave needs the help of a free North to succeed.

There are rare exceptions to this popular iconography of passivity and dependency. Yet the overall patterns of the presentation of the fugitive as passive victim in the white abolition press hold true. More involved and challenging re-examinations of the graphic representation of the theme of 'running away' occurred not within the problematics of patronisation which underlie the propaganda, produced by whites, for whites, but in the black slave narratives which employed illustration.

Is there a true story to tell? Black developments of the imagery of the runaway in the context of the white market-place: Frederick Douglass, Henry Bibb and Henry 'Box' Brown

Slave narratives are notoriously difficult to locate in terms of form, and in terms of the 'truth' of their content. They are also difficult to classify when examined in the contexts of genres to which they relate closely, such as confessional and spiritual autobiography, travel literature, the novel of adventure and novelistic romance. What is their relation to memory and to literary form – do they recover the events which they describe, or do they merely rehearse a body of knowledge within rhetorical parameters with which a white readership was already familiar after decades of European and American abolition publicity?[42] A growing body of scholarship, with William Andrews's *To Tell a Free Story* at its centre, has begun the process of uncovering the linguistic denials and erasures, and the performative paradoxes, within slave narrative. Work on slavery and African-American memory has become increasingly sophisticated.[43] Insight into the difficulties of remembering and representing trauma within the context of slavery has been facilitated by the growing willingness of some intellectuals to consider parallels between slavery and the Holocaust. Considering the inheritance of slavery, Paul Gilroy suggests that the work of Primo Levi 'might be used in a preliminary way to locate the parameters of a new approach to the history of those modern terrors that exhaust the capacity of language'.[44]

One of Levi's crucial points is that the forms of mnemonic distortion of victim and victimiser are very different: 'The memory of a trauma suffered or inflicted is itself traumatic because recalling it is painful or at least disturbing: a person who was wounded tends to block out the memory so as not to renew the pain; the person who has inflicted the wound pushes the memory deep down, to be rid of it, to alleviate the feeling of guilt.'[45] The experience of the

Holocaust is something that has required the survivors and the families of the victims to assume a peculiar cultural status. To use Levi's term, 'the memory of the offence' has required extraordinary approaches to language and to history. Recent black artists and intellectuals, while not denying the unique status of the Holocaust, have argued that the accreted history of slavery has performed a no less intense transformation on the thought and art of American and European blacks. Gilroy goes so far as to say that this history has 'marked them [ex slave populations] out as the first truly modern people'.[46] For Toni Morrison, talking of the approaches to the memorial reconstruction of slavery which operated in her novel *Beloved,* the experience of slavery forced the slave to think and act in what we would now term a set of postmodern behavioural and intellectual codes: 'black women had to deal with post-modern problems in the nineteenth century and earlier. These things had to be addressed by black people a long time ago: certain kinds of dissolution, the loss of and the need to reconstruct certain kinds of stability ... These strategies for survival made the truly modern person. They're a response to predatory western phenomena.'[47] But it is worth asking to what extent these qualities of dissolution and instability are registered within the slave narratives themselves. Morrison's and Gilroy's claims can be tested against the work produced by escaped slaves for what were predominantly white Northern audiences in the mid-nineteenth century. The following analysis focuses on an area that has, so far, been largely omitted from these memory/slavery debates: the question of the pictorial representations of slave experience within slave narrative. Looking at the manner in which printed imagery has been deployed to describe escape in three slave narratives, it is argued that Morrison's claim that slave experience was proleptically 'postmodern' are powerfully born out.[48]

Frederick Douglass, the secret sharer

> I have frequently been asked how I felt when I found myself in a free State. I have never been able to answer the question. (*Narrative of the Life of Frederick Douglass*)

The pictures in slave narratives written by blacks often resist, or recast, established illustrational and graphic codes for the depiction of slave escape. In order to provide a context for a discussion of this process, the rhetoric of Frederick Douglass is a necessary starting point. The *Narrative of the Life of Frederick Douglass* highlights, through an astounding deployment of white rhetorical strategies, the big difficulties which face an ex-slave who tackles the theme of running away and who consequently attempts to describe escape, or punishment upon being captured, or the achievement of freedom.[49]

In many ways Douglass's *Narrative* gave models of how *not* to give the white Northern abolitionist readers what they wanted or expected. Douglass challenged the frameworks of the nineteenth-century slave narrative, and ironised the descriptive and linguistic codes invented to describe the act of escape. Douglass comes at these conventions from a number of directions, and in earlier parts of his narrative provides several set pieces which are so perfect in the way they enact the established patterns for describing slave escape that they are parodic.

The slave hunt provides one example. The incidents of melodrama, excitement, savagery and horror central to the Romanticised depiction of the slave hunt are frequently rehearsed in the abolition literature of the runaway. This is true both of slave narratives themselves (*Narrative of the Life and Adventures of Henry Bibb* is a good example) and in the abolition novel from Hildreth's *White Slave* to Stowe's *Uncle Tom's Cabin* and *Dred*. In Douglass's narrative, this troping of the act of running away in the form of a grand hunt scene is not presented in terms of Douglass's own experience. Instead he provides a breakdown of the narrative ingredients of the slave hunt in the form of the communal fantasy which is acted out by himself and a group of fellow slaves planning an escape. It is as if they are as much victims of the white rhetoric surrounding slave escape, as of slavery itself. The rehearsal of potential dangers takes the form of a litany of the stock elements of fugitive slave narrative:

> The case sometimes stood thus: At every gate through which we were to pass we saw a watchman – at every ferry a guard – on every bridge a sentinel – and in every wood a patrol. We were hemmed in on every side. Here were the difficulties, real or imaginary – the good to be sought and the evil to be shunned. On the one hand, there stood slavery, a stern reality glaring frightfully upon us, – its robes already crimsoned with the blood of millions, and even now feasting itself greedily upon our own flesh. On the other hand way back in the dim distance, under the flickering light of the north star, behind some craggy hill or snow covered mountain, stood a doubtful freedom – half frozen – beckoning us to come and share its hospitality. This in itself was sometimes enough to stagger us; but when we permitted ourselves to survey the road, we were frequently appalled. Upon either side we saw grim death, assuming the most horrid shapes. Now it was starvation causing us to eat our own flesh; – now we were contending with the waves and were drowned; – now we were overtaken and torn to pieces by the fangs of the horrible blood hound. We were stung by scorpions, chased by wild beasts, bitten by snakes, and finally, after having nearly reached the destined spot, – after swimming rivers, encountering wild beasts, sleeping in the woods, suffering hunger and nakedness, – we were overtaken by our pursuers, and, in our resistance, we were shot dead upon the spot! I say, this picture sometimes appalled us and made us
> 'rather bear those ills we had
> Than fly to others that we knew not of.'[50]

In this peculiar passage the slaves' contemplation of escape raises a series of imagined, almost obsessively personified horrors in which fact and fiction are elided. Slavery as a cannibalistic metaphor implicates both slaves and enslavers. Slavery, personified in ensanguined robes devouring its own kind, like some latter-day Saturn, merges into the slaves, who as starving fugitives are forced to literalise the cannibalistic excesses metaphorically applied to the slave power, and to eat each other. Escape becomes a subject too terrible to think about, a confrontation with horrors which are so over-powering that the process of thinking about them is enough to legitimate the present state of slavery as a preferable option. Hamlet's neurotic meditation on the possibility of an after-life is not quoted ironically here but as a precise account. Slavery is at least life in a known form; flight and escape are to a large extent meaningless, because they cannot be imagined, any more than Hamlet can imagine life after death. It is not slavery which emerges as an equivalent for death, but, in Douglass's terrific Shakespearean quotation, escape and the achievement of freedom.

This passage hints at the motives behind Douglass's elaborate refusals, within the text of the *Narrative*, to describe the details of his escape. To sub-stitute an account of the 'real' experience of escape would be to deny, to dis-lodge, the fictions of escape with which the narrative is replete. It would move outside the rhetorical formulae which his audience expected and which Douglass himself manipulated so darkly, to describe the indescrib-able. When Douglass does explicitly raise the question of how to describe the feeling of freedom, he does so only to deny that it can be answered: 'I have frequently been asked how I felt when I found myself in a free State. I have never been able to answer the question.' Another silence, another gap, opens up.[51]

The final irony is that the free North did everything it could to fill, indeed to obliterate in clamour, the silences which Douglass created around his escape, and his response to his escape. If he could not or would not tell, then Jesse Hutchinson Jnr. certainly would. Douglass's lecturing and his *Narrative* brought celebrity. In the same year that it was published he was already a big enough name to merit the production of popular sheet music in his honour. Hutchinson's elaborate *The Fugitive's Song* purports to tell us, in four pages of ecstatic verse, exactly what Douglass's senti-ments were on reaching the North. This projected monologue invents the runaway, or more precisely purports to have Douglass reinvent himself, as the grateful product of New England abolition. Douglass's escape is care-fully controlled by the clichés of abolition rhetoric:

> New England! New England! thrice blessed and free,
> The poor hunted slave finds a shelter in thee,
> Where no blood thirsty hounds ever dare on his track;
> At thy stern voice, New England! the monsters fall back!
> In the Land of New England I'm free from your wrath,
> And the sons of the Pilgrims my deep scars shall see,
> Till they cry with one voice 'Let the Bondsmen go free?'[52]

Slavery is represented by 'bloodthirsty hounds' and 'monsters', while Northern abolitionists are 'Sons of the Pilgrims' and Douglass himself is 'the poor hunted slave'. The final act of disempowerment exacted on Douglass lies in the image on the cover. Frederick Douglass's *Narrative* was unillustrated with the exception of a frontispiece, a poor-quality engraved portrait of Douglass.[53] The only popular image to represent his escape is consequently the lithograph designed to sell *The Fugitive's Song* [**3.17**]. Douglass, no matter what the real facts of his escape might have been, is still entrapped within the iconography of the runaway slave advertisement. Dressed in trousers and striped shirt but carrying the stick and bundle of the classic woodcut figure, and with the inevitable bush at bottom left, he runs up a river bank, while a hunting party complete with dogs and horses is stranded on the far river bank. There could be no clearer testimony to the weight with which the traditional image of the runaway sat on the collective memory of the North.

'All right': the battle of the box in the Narrative of Henry Box Brown

> I heard a man say 'let us rap upon the box and see if he is alive;' and immediately a rap ensued and a voice said, tremblingly, 'Is all right within?' to which I replied 'All right'. (Henry 'Box' Brown,
> *Narrative of Henry Box Brown*)

The climax of the *Narrative of Henry Box Brown* provided an image which became one of the most widely disseminated pictures in the abolition publications of the 1850s, on both sides of the Atlantic. The image of Brown, emerging from the packing case in which he was incarcerated for the duration of his trip, from slavery in Richmond, Virginia, to Philadelphia and freedom, was reproduced in print satires, children's books, abolition almanacs, newspapers, and as the climactic image for the enormous panorama of oil paintings with which Brown toured the towns of the Free North of America, and later Europe [**3.18**]. Why was the imagery describing the celebratory conclusion to Brown's escape open to such a variety of interpretations in such very different media?

Brown, in his own inimitable way, gave abolition perhaps the most potent single metaphor it possessed for the displacement of the traditional image of the 'runaway' slave in the popular imagination. Brown, emerging like a hybrid Lazarus/jack-in-the-box from a freight case, stood in opposition to the

[**3.17**] Anon., *The Fugitive's Song* (song sheet cover, stone lithograph, 1845)

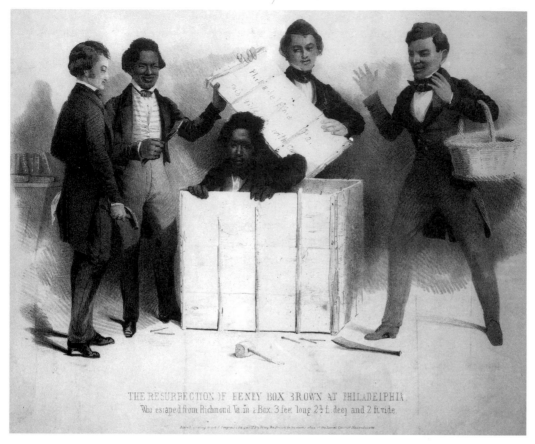

[3.18] Anon., *The Resurrection of Henry Box Brown at Philadelphia* (stone lithograph, 1850)

woodcut carried on runaway slave advertisements [3.1]. The semiotic associations of the stock runaway image were, as we have seen, difficult for the abolitionists to overturn and the image of Brown's resurrection provided one way of doing this. Yet the textual constructions of his escape are not straightforward; the ways in which his experience was interpreted, both by Brown himself and by the abolition and popular press, can be used to uncover tensions between free-white and black-ex-fugitive approaches to the experience of bondage. There were fundamental differences between the ways in which Brown saw and wished to tell his story and the ways in which white abolition desired to design the product. Some of these tensions emerge if the first American edition of the *Narrative* is set against the first English edition. Brown's story appeared as a book in Boston in 1849, under the heavy authorial influence of Charles Stearns, and was titled the *Narrative of Henry Box Brown, Who Escaped from Slavery Enclosed in a Box 3 Feet Long and 2 Feet Wide.* The first English edition appeared in 1851 in Manchester as the *Narrative of the Life of Henry Box Brown, Written by Himself.*[54]

The two editions provide an opportunity to consider which linguistic and narrative elements Brown felt impelled to redevelop or introduce once he was composing his story away from the persuasive advisory presence of Stearns. Brown presents an intriguing case in terms of how his narrative is to be constructed as testimony, as literature or as historical truth. The rightfully influential categorisations which Robert Burns Stepto has established for the comparative analysis of these qualities within slave narrative can be usefully applied to the two editions. Brown may be seen fighting his way out of Stepto's 'first phase basic narrative' or 'eclectic narrative', where an apparatus of authenticating documentation is simply appended to the tale, and where the prescriptive editorial controls subjugate the slave voice, and into his 'second phase basic narrative' or 'integrated narrative', where these materials are integrated into the main text. Yet Brown's story is much bigger than any single text which represents it.[55]

Conventional narrative categorisation does not really provide a way of accommodating the proliferation of textual forms in which Brown's story emerged. Brown's rewriting of his narrative, and his multiple reconstructions of it, not simply as a book, but on stage as a panorama, a ballad, or literally as performance when he emerged from his packing case to lecture, are all in their different ways 'true' stories. Once Brown's story spirals into the world of transatlantic popular print culture, let alone that performative area which straddles the art gallery, the theatre and the lecture hall, it becomes a phenomenon in which the whole is greater than its parts. It may be missing the point to look for the authenticated truth in such a collection of texts – it is the process of mythic generation itself which constitutes their final, and dangerously relative, truth. What concerns me here is the distance between what the English and American abolitionists wanted to take from Brown, and conversely what Brown wanted to make of himself.

In 1848 Brown was working as a slave in a tobacco factory in Richmond, Virginia, when he was suddenly informed that his master had sold his wife and three children to a Methodist minister. This was too much for him and Brown determined on flight. His method was both novel and sensational. He was mailed north to Philadelphia and freedom in a packing case, by Adams Express, with the help of a white shopkeeper, Samuel Smith, who was later imprisoned for his part in the escape. Brown's journey took twenty-seven hours, during which time he was several times turned up the wrong way and nearly suffocated. He was eventually received and liberated in Philadelphia by James McKim and the black abolitionist William Still.[56]

Brown immediately became an abolition fixture, touring the East Coast as a lecturer and performer. He arrived on the scene at a point when black ex-slaves had only recently become accepted in influential numbers and positions within the North American abolition movement. The popular climate had also changed, and white audiences across the North developed a thirst for a wide range of writings and performances from ex-slaves, although there were tensions over the level of narrative independence to be allowed ex-slave orators.[57] Brown clearly possessed entrepreneurial flair and flung himself into the task of advertising his legend as widely as possible. Not content with publishing his narrative and with lecturing, he also organised the production of a colossal travelling panorama, *The Mirror of Slavery*. Produced in collaboration with the painter Josiah Walcott, the panorama reputedly covered more than 50,000 square feet of canvas. It consisted of a series of descriptions of the atrocities of the slave system and culminated in an account of his journey to freedom.[58] Brown and the abolitionists immediately saw the publicity potential of this eccentric mode of escape. Brown kept the famous box and toured the abolition lecture circuit with it. On occasions he would begin a lecture by leaping out of it. By January 1850 he had become a star-turn and entertained the Anti-Slavery Mass Convention of the Abolitionists of New York with an oration and a performance of the popular ballad he had composed about his escape. He performed in company with a free black, J. C. A. Smith, who had helped 'pack' Brown originally and who had then proceeded north, having been cleared of his part in the affair by a court in Virginia.

Brown's story developed an even more sensational twist when, in the autumn of 1850, as a direct result of the passage of the new Fugitive Slave Law, an attempt was made by slave-catchers to kidnap him. Brown almost immediately left for England. He toured the British Isles for four years, lecturing, singing and showing the panorama. Brown's performances in England and his refusal to succumb to the established norms for black ex-slave performers on the abolition lecture circuit uncover a great deal about the expectations of his audience and the creative impulses behind Brown's radical refusal to meet those expectations.[59]

The British Anti-Slavery Society had narrow ideas about how it expected black ex-slave lecturers to behave and publicise their experiences. Black abolitionists had to arrive with letters of introduction from white Northern abolitionists and were expected to present themselves as sober Christians intent on bettering themselves in white society. They were even encouraged to move on to work as missionaries in Africa, and several American ex-slaves took this option.[60] Henry Box Brown appears, however, to have kicked against the pricks and to have been very much his own man. He delighted in showmanship, and in the performance of his escape. He had, after all, endured the agony of seeing his family sold South, and considered himself, after his traumatic journey in the box, to have triumphed over an experience which very nearly destroyed him, and to have achieved a second birth.[61] His abilities at self-promotion were phenomenal. While in England he went so far as to re-enact his escape during a lecture tour of the North. He travelled from Bradford to Leeds, crated up in his box, to emerge triumphantly, like a jack-in-the-box, an embodiment of surprise and the unconfinable.[62]

Brown's flamboyant style, showy dressing, and propensity to interlard his lectures with anti-slavery songs and spirituals, brought him into conflict with the more 'respectable' element of his English audiences. He shattered the ceremonial and rhetorical proprieties of the formal lecture hall. He introduced the elements of his own art and folk culture and fused them with the visual conventions of the circus, beast show and pictorial panorama. Brown challenged the accepted framework for the presentation of the ordeal of the runaway.[63] He went beyond the formal pale in the relation of his experiences and consequently forsook the suspension of racist animosity enjoyed by the majority of ex-slave lecturers on the abolition circuit.

The articles about Brown in the *Wolverhampton and Staffordshire Gazette* described his panorama as a 'gross and palpable exaggeration ... a jumbled mass of contradictions and absurdities, assertions without proof, geography without boundary and horrors without parallel', while the South appeared as 'a series of inquisitorial chambers of horrors – a sort of Blue Beard, or a giant despair den, for the destruction, burning, branding, lacerations, starving and working of Negroes' and those who held slaves were depicted as 'demi-fiends, made of double distilled brimstone'.[64] *The Herald* went further to attack Brown as a '"bejewelled darky" whose portly figure and overdressed appearance bespeak the gullibility of our most credulous age and country'. It later described him as a 'bejewelled and oily negro, whose obese and comfortable figure and easy nonchalance, reminds one of various good things and sumptuous living', and moved on to even more bare-faced racism in describing Brown's 'nocturnal antics' performed with 'ludicrous and semi-baboonish agility' to delight the 'juvenile ragamuffins' who constitute his audience.[65]

Brown's spectacular performances may have been out of kilter with British notions of what should constitute the behaviour of a black ex-slave on a lecture platform, but Brown's approach brings out the extent to which he was in tune with the spirit of the time. He drew on commercial and creative resources which white abolitionists shied away from. When a reviewer opines against the fact that Brown's audience included 'juvenile ragamuffins' there is an assumption that abolition is territory in need of strict control, that if black ex-slaves generate an appeal beyond the respectable and educated white abolition societies, the appeal is of its essence debased and worthless. Without guidance and surveillance the black will lose his precarious grip on respectability and fall into the chaotic and degenerate world of popular entertainment. This world had, after all, ordained certain roles for blacks in London: if they were lucky, servants, pugilists, nigger minstrels; if not, crossing sweepers, beggars and the other avenues for survival open to the destitute.[66]

Yet Brown fought attempts to close down the languages and images in which he decided to narrate his experiences at both a textual and a performative level. Brown had spirit, in the true gospel sense, and his religious interpretation of his escape was reverent and awe-filled, but also full of joy and even a certain element of low comedy. Brown's gifts as a self-dramatist, and his ability to draw on linguistic and artistic resources unique to North American slave culture, come out clearly if the account of the moment of his liberation in the 1851 text of the *Narrative* (which it would appear he wrote entirely himself) is set against that which he co-wrote two years earlier with Charles Stearns. In the 1851 text the first words he spoke on his release registered his physical well-being: 'A voice said "Is all right within?" to which I replied "all right".' Revealingly these first words are given as 'All right sir' by one of the witnesses in the introduction, and by William Still.[67] Brown then immediately fainted and on recovering consciousness his first extended response was to break into his own gospel rendition of the fortieth psalm.[68] Brown's ecstatic arrangement of scripture is quoted in full in his own version of the *Narrative*. The compulsive reiteration reinvents the psalm as a hymn of heart-breaking innocence singing praise at the coming of a personal Jubilee:

> I waited patiently, I waited patiently for the Lord, for the Lord;
> And he inclined unto me, and heard my calling:
> I waited patiently, I waited patiently, for the Lord;
> And he inclined unto me, and heard my calling:
> And he put a new song in my mouth,
> Even a thanksgiving, even a thanksgiving, even a thanksgiving unto our God.
> Blessed, Blessed, Blessed, Blessed is the man, Blessed is the man,
> Blessed is the man that has set his hope, his hope in the Lord;
> Oh Lord my God, Great, Great, Great, Great, …
> … Let all those that seek thee be joyful and glad,
> Let all those that seek thee be joyful and glad, be joyful
>   and glad, be joyful and glad, be joyful, be joyful, be joyful, be joyful, be
> joyful and glad
> – be glad in thee …[69]

Brown had chosen this text because in its original version the theme of resurrection from the pit had a precise relevance: 'I waited patiently for the Lord; and he inclined unto me and heard my cry. He brought me up as of an horrible pit, out of the miry clay, and set my feet upon a rock and established my goings. And he hath put a new song in my mouth even praise unto our God.'[70] But Brown takes a creative approach to his source, seizing on key phrases and extemporising. They were, however, not words which easily fell on the ears of the East Coast gentry halfway through the nineteenth century. In the 1849 edition the hymn was not included in the main text of the narrative at all, but hidden in the introductory apparatus of prefaces, dedicatory letters and testimonials. Even within the stylistically less fastidious parameters of the American ballad market, Brown's performance of scripture was not allowed free reign. Beneath the caption 'Engraving of the Box in which Henry Box Brown escaped from slavery in Richmond, Va. Song, *Sung by Mr. Brown on being removed from the box*', a Boston street ballad gave a formal translation of verses one, four, five, eleven and sixteen of the fortieth psalm, and completely avoided Brown's ecstatic repetitions. The ballad was headed with a simple engraving of the box, inscribed 'Philadelphia Pa. Right side up with care'. The box itself is shown emphatically sealed with five heavy black bands, and Brown presumably is to be imagined still safely inside it[**3.19**].[71]

There are several other examples of Brown's determination to re-invent his experience using vernacular forms and language which his white editors had denied the first edition of his *Narrative*. The main text of Brown's 1851 *Narrative* concludes with the retelling of his escape in the form of a popular ballad which he has composed himself, and apparently sang when at public meetings. Sung to the tune of the popular air 'Uncle Ned', and carrying a comic chorus, the ballad concluded:

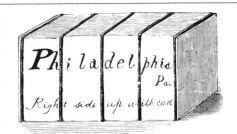

Engraving of the Box in which **HENRY BOX BROWN** escaped from slavery in Richmond, Va.

S O N G,

Sung by Mr. Brown on being removed from the box

I waited patiently for the Lord ;—
And he, in kindness to me, heard my calling—
And he hath put a new song into my mouth—
Even thanksgiving—even thanksgiving—
    Unto our God !

Blessed—blessed is the man
That has set his hope, his hope in the Lord !
O Lord ! my God ! great, great is the wondrous work
    Which thou hast done !

If I should declare them—and speak of them—
They would be more than I am able to express.
I have not kept back thy love, and kindness, and truth,
    From the great congregation !

Withdraw not thou thy mercies from me,
Let thy love, and kindness, and thy truth, alway preserve me—
Let all those that seek thee be joyful and glad !
    Be joyful and glad !

And let such as love thy salvation—
Say always—say always—
The Lord be praised !
    The Lord be praised !

Laing's Steam Press, 1 1-2 Water Street, Boston.

[**3.19**] Anon., 'Song sung by Mr. Brown on being removed from box' (illustrated long ballad, wood-engraving and letterpress, 1849)

> The friends gathered round and asked if all was right,
> As down on the box they did rap,
> Brown answered them, saying, 'yes all is right!'
> He was then set free from his pain.
> *Chorus* – Brown laid down the shovel and the hoe,
>   Down in the box he did go;
>   No more Slave work for Henry Box Brown,
>   In the box *by Express* he did go.[72]

Again this ballad was not considered appropriate for printing in the 1849 American edition, although it was printed as an illustrated broadside. Brown's narrative initiated the multiple retellings and simplifications of his story which rapidly spread in the English and American press, primarily in visual forms. In the very process of retelling his story he provided it with the comic and folkloric elements which were to typify its popular assimilation. Above all Brown had the confidence to embrace the bathetic elements of the tale. A man shipped in a box, turned on his head, tumbling out ruefully having tricked the entire force of the slaveholding south, is, at one level, the stuff of slapstick. But it is the potent slapstick of the triumphant underdog: Brown is a kind of Brer Rabbit figure, with his nose in exuberant performance and his tale in African and African-American folklore. He is a cunning as well as heroic ex-slave. He didn't have to run away, but used the most advanced high-tech machinery and travelled, as his delighted italics announce, '*express*'. Now there will be no more 'Slave work' – he will work for himself.

If some members of contemporary audiences were suspicious of Brown in the flesh, the narrative of his escape was full-bloodedly embraced in the abolition and popular press. It is within the imagery of these popular adaptations that the power of Brown and his mythic box emerge with the most vitality. Brown's narrative had a ready-made metaphorical dimension lacking from other slave narratives. The process of his escape was a paradoxical embodiment both of the experience of bondage and of the experience of freedom. His imprisonment in the box was not simply an ingenious method of escape, it was a symbolic entombment – Brown in the box was Brown's soul, and the soul of every slave, in a state of bondage. Brown coming out of the box was not simply the emergence of one spirited fugitive but the spiritual and physical liberation of every escaped slave, and by implication of the American spirit emerging from the moral entombment of slavery. Brown's escape was propagandistically reconstituted as an enormous mythological embodiment of national liberation, a national moral apotheosis. It was the emancipation declaration in microcosm and proleptically performed. Hence its appeal to free white audiences on both sides of the Atlantic was fundamentally rooted in a language of Christological resurrection and apotheosis. Brown is both miraculous escape artist and divinely ordained for liberation from the living death of slavery, metaphorically sacred and profane, fact and myth, Houdini and Lazarus.[73]

In the avalanche of visual representations of Brown's escape which appeared in American and English publications, the key moment of the emergence from the box inevitably holds centre stage.[74] The largest and most polished of the single-sheet print representations of the scene is a lithograph which shows clearly in its title how Brown, in the popular imagination, already enjoyed symbolic status as one returned from the dead. *The Resurrection of Henry Box Brown at Philadelphia. Who escaped from Richmond Va. in a Box 3 ft. long, 2½ ft deep and 2½ ft wide* neatly combines the facts with the nascent myth. Brown emerges looking shaken but very serious and stares straight at the audience. The iconographic inheritance within religious painting to which this scene relates most closely are the representations of the emergence of Noah from the ark [**3.20**]. Noah in biblical typology prefigures the Resurrection of Christ, and consequently Brown's association with this part of the narrative of the flood is most appropriate. Yet having said this, the print and broadside representations of Brown's emergence duplicate early Christian paintings of Noah's emergence from a small box-like ark with an almost uncanny precision.[75]

Despite this elevated ancestry, the tone of *The Resurrection of Henry Box Brown*, as with so many of the popular prints of the subject, is hard to pin down. Brown is impeccably dressed and a little dishevelled pushing out of the crate to the general delight of a no less fashionably attired audience of four. The audience are presented as amused – their expressions exist somewhere between smirking incredulity and laughter. It is difficult to determine if the print contains a satiric edge. What is certain is that like the introductory letters it is fixated with the precise physical details of Brown's packaging and un-packaging. One spectator holds a claw hammer, Frederick Douglass, who has been opportunistically introduced to the scene, a crow bar, and another spectator carries a wicker basket for the tools. A discarded mallet and several long nails litter the foreground.

[3.20] Anon., *Noah in the Ark* (egg tempera on quick lime, *c.* 200)

Part of the print's fascination lies in the way it provides a total contrast to the customary iconography of the runaway as manifested in the single-sheet political print, and indeed in print culture generally. The passage of the Fugitive Slave Act by Congress in September 1850, which put new obligations on the population of the free North to return fugitive slaves, elicited a mass of propaganda in the North, including political prints. Slaves are invariably shown being harried, pursued, shot down or chased by dogs. A print such as *Effects of the Fugitive-Slave-Law* [3.21] is a typical example.[76] Skilfully drawn, and using the potential of stone lithography to pick up the subtle shading of chalk and crayon drawing, this print

[3.21] Anon., *Effects of the Fugitive-Slave-Law* (stone lithograph, 1850)

nevertheless presents blacks as victims. They are presented as butchered martyrs, sacrificed on the altar of freedom. The crucial point is that *Effects* is a print semiotically still confined within the dialectic of the runaway advertisement – the slaves still run on foot, and their act of flight is still futile – and in this sense it returns to its iconic ancestry, the famous woodcut generated in the slave states to describe lost property [3.1]. The depiction of Brown's escape substitutes stasis for flight, jubilation for agony, and technology for shanks's pony. Brown may have suffered but he let white technology do the work of moving for him. He has broken out of the metaphoric space of the runaway, and arrives in that of the industrialised North.

Cheap woodcut versions soon followed. The same cut was used several times in the *Liberty Almanac* with different texts. The volume for 1851 carried a woodcut showing Brown surrounded by four white men [**3.22**].[77] Douglass has disappeared from this cut, Brown is reduced to shirt sleeves,

[**3.22**] Anon., 'On Receiving the Box' (wood-engraving, 1851). From *The Liberty Almanac*

HENRY BOX BROWN.

The following remarkable incident exhibits the cruelty of the slave system, while it shows the ingenuity and desperate determination of its victims to escape from it :—

A few months ago, a slave in a Southern city managed to open a correspondence with a gentleman in a Northern city, with a view to effect his escape from bondage. Having arranged the preliminaries, he paid somebody $40 to box him up, and mark him, "This side up, with care," and take him to the Express office, consigned to his friend at the North. On the passage, being on board of a steamboat, he was accidentally turned head downward, and almost died with the rush of blood to the head. At the next change of transportation, however, he was turned right side up again ; and after twenty-six hours' confinement arrived safely at his destination. On receiving the box, the gentleman had doubts whether he should find a corpse or a living man. He tapped lightly on the box, with the question, "All right?" and was delighted to hear the response, "All right, sir." The poor fellow was immediately liberated from his place of burial.*

and heaves himself out of the box holding on to the arm of one of the spectators. A short paragraph below gives the outline of the escape, ending with the words:

> On receiving the box the gentleman had doubts whether he should find a corpse or a living man. He tapped lightly on the box with the question 'All right?' and was delighted to hear the response 'All right sir.' The poor fellow was immediately liberated from his place of burial.*
> *His name has received an addition since this occurrence, and he is now known as Henry *Box* Brown.[78]

This may seem innocent enough, but Brown's account has undergone some sinister modifications. The account of M. McRoy from the testimonial letters has been substituted for Brown's, and his first words are given as 'All right sir' rather than Brown's unsubservient 'All right'. Brown's confident and assertive phrase has been transposed to 'the [white] gentleman' who released him, a detail not to be found in any of the original editions of Brown's narrative. In fact a subtle switch of viewpoint has been made for the narration of the climactic liberation. The whole thing is seen, not from Brown's viewpoint, but from that of his liberators. Firstly we are given an insight into the suspense and fear of the liberator ('he had doubts whether he should find a corpse or a living man'), then we are given his sensitively proposed question as he 'lightly tapped' the box and said 'All right', then an account of his 'delighted' response to hearing Brown's respectful 'All right sir'. Brown's exodus is not a personal triumph; it is not presented actively at all. Brown is simply a 'poor fellow' who is 'liberated'. Brown's resurrection is thus seen from the viewpoint of the white abolitionists – he does not resurrect himself, but is 'liberated from his place of burial' by them. This process of appropriation is very thorough. Even Brown's renaming in the context of his escape is presented, not as something he generated, or as an act over which he has any control, but as the imposition of white society, an imposition relegated to the position of a final footnote. Again the passive form dominates – Brown has not taken a new name, but 'his name has received an addition'. His name, the name slavery had bestowed on him, has now been updated by a white Northern society, which through the remodification of his nomenclature claims him for its own. The internecine processes of white appropriation and redefinition seep into Brown's story as it seeps into the popular market. In this context Brown's publication of his own version of his story two years after that officially sanctioned by a white writer, and his decision to open his tale to the narrative operations of performance and popular self-advertisement, might be seen as both politically responsible and pragmatic.

The same woodcut of Brown's escape was repeated at the bottom of a stirring article in the 1852 edition of *The Liberty Almanac*.[79] This piece entitled 'Emancipation' gives a roll-call of the most celebrated escaped slaves, and celebrates the 'self-emancipation' of 'Pennington, Douglass,

Bibb, Brown, and the Crafts'. Brown is given pride of place as the article concludes:

> The escape of Henry *Box* Brown, who was boxed up and forwarded by express to a free State, is well known. Who, on reading such interesting facts, will not exclaim, as Brown did to the kind inquirer to whom the box was consigned, 'All, right, sir.' Here is Brown, leaping from his emancipation-box.[80]

Although it doesn't bear out what we see in the illustration, this last sentence does at least restore Brown as the active and celebratory focus of his own narrative. Even here, however, Brown is still given the strangely formal if not subservient form 'All right, sir'.

The image of Brown's escape had the semiotic fluidity of true popularity. Perhaps the final proof of the extent to which Brown's narrative was transferred into the currencies of popular culture lay in the rapidity with which he was absorbed into the children's book market. Little wood-engravings showing Brown bounding out of the box featured in a variety of children's anti-slavery literature. The absorption of his narrative into *Cousin Ann's Stories for Children* was particularly ingenious, because of the way the plates marry it to a well-established didactic abolition trope.

Cousin Ann's Stories, published in Philadelphia in 1849, was a moralistic children's book preaching temperance and anti-slavery. Slavery is first introduced through an analogy with the capture of animals. This parallelism between slavery and the caging of wild animals was used extensively by the British abolitionists.[81] It also relates to the English satiric tradition, originating in the eighteenth century, where prints, most famously Hogarth's *Four Stages of Cruelty*, made direct comparisons between cruelty to animals and moral depravity and criminality in human society. Abolitionists had taken up the theme in a variety of contexts, and American abolition publications actually reproduced cheap woodcut versions of the Hogarth designs [**3.23**].[82] In *Cousin Ann's Stories* the 'voluntary' self-caging of Henry Box Brown, as a means of final liberation, is cleverly set against the story of Howard and his pet [**3.24**]. The account of Howard is given in verse:

PROGRESS OF CRUELTY.

THE FIRST STAGE OF CRUELTY.

What various scenes of cruel sport
The infant race employ,
What future baseness, must import
The tyrant in the boy.

Behold a youth of gentler look,
To save the creature's pain,
'Oh take!' he cries, 'here take my book,'
But tears and book are vain.

Learn from this fair example, you
Whom savage sports delight,
How cruelty disgusts the view,
While pity charms the sight.

[**3.23**] After William Hogarth, *The Four Stages of Cruelty* (1751), plate 1, 'The First Stage of Cruelty' (wood-engraving, 1843). From *The Legion of Liberty*

Our Howard had a little squirrel,
Its tale was long and grey,
He put it in a wiry cage,
And there it had to stay.

Its hickory nuts and corn it ate
From out its little paw,
And such a funny active thing,
I think I never saw.

But Howard thought he should not like
A little slave to be;
And God had made the nimble squirrel,
To run and climb the tree.

[…]

A bird or squirrel in a cage
It makes me sad to see;
It seems so cruel to confine
The creatures made so free.[83]

A few pages later there follows a greatly con-
densed version of Brown's narrative [**3.25**].
The majority of the tale is in the form of an
adventure story detailing his physical hardships in the box. The, by now de rigeur, litany
of the precise dimensions of the box is recited
and the details of Brown's hardships in transit
are provided with an intense eye for detail:
'While on the river boat the box is put on its
head, it was placed so that Henry's head and
back were down … He lay in this way, while the
boat went twenty miles and it nearly killed him,
he said the veins in his head were great ridges
that felt nearly as big as his finger.'[84] The text
accompanying the woodcut illustration and
giving an account of his liberation is as follows:

After he had bathed himself and ate breakfast,
he sang a hymn of praise, which he had kept in
his mind to sing if he should ever get to a land of
freedom and safety. The first lines were,
    I waited patiently for the Lord
    And he inclined and heard me
Henry was a strong fine looking man. He was
named Henry Box Brown because he came
nearly three hundred miles in a Box. We call
people heroes who do something brave and
great, and Henry is a hero. Every body but the

HOWARD AND HIS SQUIRREL.

Our Howard had a little squirrel,
    Its tail was long and grey,
He put it in a wiry cage,
    And there it had to stay.

Its hickory nuts and corn it ate
    From out its little paw,
And such a funny, active thing,
    I think, I never saw.

But Howard thought he should not like
    A little slave to be;
                1D

[**3.24**] Anon., 'Howard and His Squirrel' (wood-engraving,
1849). From *Cousin Ann's Stories for Children*

HENRY BOX BROWN.

I will tell you the story of Henry Box
Brown. It is a strange tale, and it is all true.
Henry was a slave in Richmond, Virginia, and
then his name was Henry Brown. He had a
wife and four little children whom he loved
very much.

[**3.25**] Anon., 'Henry Box Brown' (wood-engraving, 1849).
From *Cousin Ann's Stories for Children*

slaveholders seems glad of his escape from slavery. Henry will be well off in the free states but his heart will always ache when he thinks of his wife and dear children. No one in Carolina is allowed to teach a child to read or write; so he will never get a letter from any of his family, and it is not likely they will hear from him, or ever know that he is free.[85]

This rearrangement of the narrative firmly replaces Brown centre stage, and in its quotation of the opening of his hymn appears to be based directly on a reading of the first English edition. However, the detail of the bathing and eating of breakfast is entirely innovative. Perhaps the most intriguing addition lies in the way the narrative returns to the theme of Brown's separation from his wife and children in a way in which Brown's own account adamantly refuses to do. The reintroduction of the theme operates powerfully on the woodcut images of Howard and Henry. Howard, the free white child, claps as he watches his little squirrel run up the tree. Brown emerges from his box to greet two white men, not his own family; for Brown's wife and children there is no representation and no liberty.

Brown was proud of what he had done, he was famous for what he had done, and in a very real sense he *was* what he had done. When looking him up in the *British Library Catalogue of Printed Books* he is given under the heading 'Brown, Henry Box'. The box, and all it stood for, is part of his name. He had brought about the conditions for this renaming, but had not so named himself – the delighted and genuinely popular audiences of England and America had applied the sobriquet. Brown had overturned, through a single imaginative act, the sober anonymity of the image of the runaway and replaced it with something replete with both mythic grandeur and low comedy. Contemporary abolitionists were not slow to make comparisons with classical figures, and English children's versions of Brown's narrative make multiple comparisons between Brown's capacities for endurance and those of the ancient Spartans.[86]

If the wider interpretative response to Brown's self-publicity which this piece advocates is adopted then it is possible to argue that Brown is, artistically, the most forward-looking of all abolitionist propagandists. He had two big experiences, the loss of his family and his subsequent escape from slavery. In marketing this material in the context of abolition he used the full range of media available to him at the time: the panorama (and Brown's was one of the biggest), the lecture, the poetry and music of the plantations, nineteenth-century sentimental verse, prayer, hymns, stage performance, slave narrative, graphic satire, children's books, broadsides, woodcuts and lithographs, and the latest technology related to travel. His escape constituted an immediate metaphor that combined spiritual autobiography, resurrection narrative, travel narrative and farce.

We live in a period where the contemporary visual arts have increasingly explored the didactic potential of installation and performance art. The recent incorporation of a modern replica of Brown's 'box' as an installation within the Whitney Museum's New York exhibition, 'Black Male:

representations of masculinity in contemporary American Art', indicates the manner in which Brown appeals to post-Duchampian installation art in the West.[87] Yet it is in the area of performance that the most useful parallels might be drawn. The great German post-war artist Joseph Beuys dominated European performance art in its most overtly political manifestations from the mid-1960s until his death in 1988.[88] Beuys's life and work provides a new perspective from which to consider and understand a little more about the extent of Brown's achievement. When Brown had himself crated up and sent from Bradford to Leeds, re-enacting his original escape, he was very close to the methods and thought of Beuys.

One way to read Brown's narrative is as providing a metaphor of hope and healing for nineteenth-century America in much the same way that the work of Beuys provided metaphors of healing for the German people, and more widely the European and American people, in the 1960s and 1970s as their cultures struggled with the inheritance of the Second World War. Beuys claimed to have located the trauma point of North America in the figure of the coyote, a deity to the Native American tribes, vermin to the white man. Picked up from the airport in an ambulance, delivered into a cage at a New York gallery, he lived for several days in this cage with a wild coyote. He repeated the performance in Glasgow, where he also collaborated around this performance with Jimmy Boyle, Scotland's most wanted man.[89] Brown's body as he travelled North might be seen as an embodiment of the trauma of slavery, his resurrection to offer a symbol of healing and hope to a society which would have to come to terms with the inheritance of slavery and Civil War. The criticisms of crassness and showmanship levelled against Beuys, by the American and European establishment, were not dissimilar from those aimed at Brown. Both men introduced elements of performance and showmanship to their storytelling, and with both men their motives are finally obscure and not innocent of commercial elements. Brown was at one level a public entertainer who made money from his shows. He was also, however, a gifted public educator who offered audiences, on both sides of the Atlantic, exposure to his uniquely varied and inventive slave testimony.

'You've seen one you've seen them all': picturing truth in the Narrative of the Life and Adventures of Henry Bibb

> Reader, believe me when I say that no tongue, nor pen, ever has or can express the horrors of American Slavery. Consequently I despair in finding language to express adequately the deep feeling of my soul, as I contemplate the past history of my life. (*Narrative of the Life and Adventures of Henry Bibb*)

> What is Truth? Said jesting Pilate; and would not stay for an answer. Certainly there be that delight in giddiness, and count it a bondage to fix a belief; affecting free will in thinking, as well as in acting. (Francis Bacon, *Of Truth*)

The *Narrative of the Life and Adventures of Henry Bibb, An American Slave, Written by Himself* can be used as a test case to reveal how the deployment of pictures in slave narrative can resist, or recast, the established illustrational and graphic codes which permeate white abolition publication.[90] A bizarre relationship between words and images emerges. The semiotic challenge of the images in Bibb's *Narrative* grows out of the fact that with the exception of the portrait on the title page, few and maybe none of the engravings originally depicted Bibb or any of the characters in his work. The woodblocks used had already appeared in a variety of other publications, or had been adapted from earlier woodcuts and etchings in abolition literature. It is my contention that the peculiar status of the images used in Bibb's narrative violently challenges the audience, but that this challenge was not taken up by contemporary readers. It would appear that there is a double standard operating, that the requirements of truth within the printed text, and the requirements of truth within narrative woodcut and copper plate engraved 'illustration', operate in different ways.

Bibb's *Narrative* gives multiple accounts of escape, recapture and punishment. The iconographic operations of these images throw into sharp focus the problematic nature of the overriding authorial 'truth' which all slave narratives claim, and which their white readerships, within the prefatory apparatus of testimonial letters and reviews, claimed for them. This discussion of the subversion of the rhetoric of the runaway in slave narrative concludes with a set of images which approach the theme of slave flight in very different ways. These images demonstrate the profoundly destabilising operations of the printed imagery in this text, but it is important to preface the analysis of the plates with a consideration of the gap between how contemporary audiences read Bibb's narrative, and how he invited it to be read.

The book was read as an unproblematic account of Bibb's life.[91] For Garrison's *Liberator*, the book was 'we doubt not … in every essential particular true'. Elizur Wright's *Chronotype* similarly states: 'We believe this to be an unvarnished tale, giving a true picture of slavery … the book is written in perfect artlessness.'[92] The reviews express an unruffled faith in the idea that Bibb gives a complete description of the experience of being a slave. Bibb's text enables the reader to relive the experience of slavery, yet, with the exception of a single mention of 'sundry pictorial illustrations' in the *Liberator*, the illustrations were completely bypassed and did not register as part of this record. Two features of Bibb's narrative might be isolated in this context. Firstly it contains passages, of which my prefatory quotation is typical, which constantly reiterate the impossibility of setting into words, or language of any sort, the experiences which it describes. In this sense the text constantly denies its own truth.[93] Secondly, despite the fact that Bibb's book carries more images than any other slave narrative produced in North America, and as far as I know in

Engraved by P.H. Reason

Henry Bibb

Stop the runaway 'where is he' &c. &c. Reward for him

Daniel Lane after Henry Bibb in Louisville Kentucky June 1838
The object was to sell Bibb in the slave market but Bibb turned
the corner too quick for him to be evened

[3.26] Anon., double portrait of Henry Bibb (copper engraving, with stipple, and wood-engraving, 1849). From *Narrative of the Life and Adventures of Henry Bibb,* frontispiece

the history of eighteenth- and nineteenth-century slave narrative, all the wood-engravings appear to have been grafted into the book from other sources at points of more or less thematic relevance.[94] These images did not grow out of any direct illustrational engagement with Bibb's life yet are placed in direct relation to his written version of that life. What then do they mean and how should they be read?

Bibb's text contains twenty-one pictures consisting of twenty wood-engravings and a frontispiece. This frontispiece contains a large and technically fine metal-engraved portrait of Bibb, and directly below this a postage-sized woodcut of a runaway pursued at night down an alley [**3.26**]. With the exception of this frontispiece, the images have been drawn from a popular reservoir of wood-engraved blocks employed by the white abolitionist press. The majority of them relate to the theme of running away and subsequent recapture and punishment. Bibb achieves perhaps the most complicated subversion of the image of the runaway in any slave narrative.

Nearly all the wood-engravings have personal histories which stretch out backwards and forwards, through anti-slavery almanacs, through mainstream abolition periodicals and through sensational anecdotal accounts of plantation atrocity. What needs to be addressed is their iconic and narrative status once they have been brought together in Bibb's autobiography. The initial reasons for adopting the blocks containing these images were probably economic: they were already available and make the book look interesting and dramatic. But these images raise a lot of narrational conundrums and can also be read as a pictorial confirmation of Bibb's constant restatement that beyond the external circumstances describing the event, nothing can be told. The multiple application of these woodcuts is a testament to the impersonality of the facts of slave life. These facts are repeated in ever varied words in the body of slave narratives but are outside the experience of the audience. It is as if the formulaic wood-engravings are saying every whipping is like every other whipping, every failed escape the same, and every fugitive in court is repeating the same futile confrontation with the law. While Bibb's text stresses that there is not a spoken or written language which can describe slave experience, these images set down a parallel disavowal. They testify that there is no pictorial language to do justice to the horror of slave life, only a series of well-circulated, well-digested stereotypes. Beyond this, however, is the disturbing truth that the re-duplication of the blocks suggests that there is a currency in language and in imagery for the description of pain which is accepted and familiar to the Northern abolitionist readership. There is a mythology of slave experience which for the Northern American and English reviewers constituted an unproblematic realism.

Bibb's eighth chapter concludes with a vignette of a slave running away from three men in tail coats and top hats [**3.27**]. A blank placard floats incongruously above the fugitive's head. This plate, as far as it represents

them away with me.

[3.27] Anon., (wood-engraving, 1849). From *Narrative of the Life and Adventures of Henry Bibb*

anything in the accompanying writing, appears to relate to Bibb's statement that he could have escaped had he wanted to: 'while they were shifting me from one boat to another my hands were some time loosed, until they got us all on board – and I know that I should have broke away had it not been for the sake of my wife and child who was with me'.[95] In fact he didn't break away, because his wife, Malinda, and his child, were about to be sold with him, and he wanted to stay with them as long as possible. But the engraving does not represent a fantasy of Bibb as runaway. In its initial incarnation it did not describe Bibb and his family, but was a piece of anti-colonisation

[3.28] Anon., 'For Liberia' (wood-engraving, 1839). From the *Boston Anti-Slavery Almanac*

propaganda for 1839 concerning the enforced emigration of liberated slaves to Liberia. The original woodblock carried the headline 'FOR LIBERIA' within the placard, and the sub-title read '"NUISANCES" GOING AS "MISSIONARIES," "WITH THEIR OWN CONSENT"' [**3.28**].[96] The narrative clarity is compromised not only by the failure of image and language to relate to each other, but by the physical deterioration of the block.

The runaway is approached from a very different direction in another set of images. The most extreme and humorous reapplication of an old plate occurs in the context of Bibb's description of his recapture and appearance in a local court in Cincinnati. Having again run, and then been retaken by slave-catchers, Bibb is taken to the local justice to be identified:

> These ruffians dragged me though the streets of Cincinnati, to what was called a justice office. But it was more like an office of injustice.
>
> When I entered the room I was introduced to three slaveholders, one of whom was a son of Wm. Gatewood, who claimed me as his property. They pretended to be very glad to see me.
>
> They asked me if I did not want to see my wife and child; but I made no reply to any thing that was said until I was delivered up as a slave. After they were asked a few questions by the court, the old pro-slavery squire very gravely pronounced me to be the property of Mr. Gatewood.
>
> The office being crowded with spectators, many of whom were colored persons, Mr. G. was afraid to keep me in Cincinnati, two or three hours even until a steamboat got ready to leave for the South.[97]

This account is provided with a full-page wood-engraving [**3.29**]. It carries the caption 'Squire's Office'. Bibb is held by one of the slave-catchers, while a man, presumably Gatewood, moves across to Bibb to claim him as property. A fat and impassive squire appears to be seated in a grand seat of justice, while several white officials, not mentioned by Bibb in his writing, and carrying long staffs, gaze at the scene. There seem to be no black people in the court. An even more puzzling question relates to Gatewood's costume: why is he dressed in an eighteenth-century peruke, a fashion accessory nearly a century out of date? The reason is ludicrously plain – this illustration, again printed from a block on the verge of breaking up, doesn't depict Bibb or the scene in Squire's office. It is a wood-engraved interpretation loosely based on an oil painting of some renown depicting one of the most famous episodes of English abolition. J. Hayllar's painting of Granville Sharp rescuing the slave Jonathan Strong was a classic abolition image, describing an event which occurred in 1765. It showed the moment when Kerr, the planter, was attempting to lay hold of Strong to take him back to Jamaica as a slave. Granville Sharp in turn laid his hand on Kerr's shoulder and accused him of assault on a free man. Wood-engraved versions of the painting occurred in British abolition literature throughout the nineteenth and until well into the twentieth century.[98] The woodblock used in Bibb's narrative had appeared in America in the 1843 edition of the abolition anthology *The Legion of Liberty* [**3.30**] and carried the following caption:

Squire's office.

THE FIRST SCENE IN BRITISH EMANCIPATION.

Granville Sharpe rescuing a young African, claimed as a slave, from his tyrant, in presence of the Mayor of London.

[3.29] Anon., 'Squire's Office' (wood-engraving, 1843). From *Narrative of the Life and Adventures of Henry Bibb*

[3.30] Anon., 'The First Scene of British Emancipation' (wood-engraving, 1843). From *The Legion of Liberty*

THE FIRST SCENE OF BRITISH EMANCIPATION

Granville Sharp rescuing a young African, claimed as a slave, from his tyrant, in presence of the Mayor of London. Sharp pursued his humane course and his elaborate researches produced the work entitled, 'The injustice and dangerous tendency of tolerating slavery,' and procured the grand and glorious decision from the British courts of justice published in 1769, in the face of Europe and the world, 'That every slave was free as soon as he set foot on British ground.'[99]

This remarkably over-simplified account of the Mansfield decision concerning the status of colonial slaves on British soil was printed as the first half of a narrative diptych. The second part printed on the next page reproduced a popular print of the 'emancipation moment' in the British Caribbean under the title 'THE LAST SCENE OF BRITISH EMANCIPATION'.

The interpretative gulf between the original setting and the use of the print in Bibb's book is bewildering. Granville Sharp has gone through a protean, and rather disturbing, transformation – he has moved from hero of abolition in an English court, to representative of the slave power in Cincinnati. This can be constructed as a triumph for the semiotic flexibility of the nineteenth-century American publishing environment, but then again might simply constitute an example of visual insensitivity verging on insensibility. It is difficult to know what this image means in the context of Bibb's narrative. The print can be seen to enact a glorious fusion of Jonathan Strong in England in 1765 and Henry Bibb in Cincinnati in the 1830s. In such a reading the pictorial conflation forms a narrative bridge which tells us that the plight of the recaptured fugitive in a white court is always essentially the same.

One of the crucial narrative realignments which occurs in Bibb's text, and which gives it a claim to uniqueness if it is set against other male slave narratives, is the way in which it describes the traumatic effects of Bibb's marriage and subsequent fatherhood while still a slave. Bibb's horror at falling in love with a slave woman, and having a child by her, because of the way these actions compromise beyond recall his personal quest for liberty, dominate the narrative.[100] The depictions of Bibb's attempts to escape with his family are consequently of particular force. As a slave and as the father of a slave, Bibb's quest for freedom is always psychologically and morally compromised. His slave marriage and parenthood are set out in the majority of the narrative as having excluded him from the possibility of the achievement of an unproblematic liberation from slavery. Even when free himself he will always be responsible for the continuing endurance of his family within slavery. For William Andrews it is the ways in which Bibb's narrative approaches this bind that give it a tragic amplitude lacking in other male slave narratives. Frederick Douglass's narrative, for example, is typical in constituting an unproblematically heroic tale of initiative and self-liberation. As Andrews points out, Bibb can only finally gain a sense of completeness and satisfaction in his freedom when his wife Malinda gives up waiting for him to liberate her and enters an adulterous relationship with a new owner. At this point Bibb declares her 'theoretically and practically dead to me as a wife'.[101] From then on Bibb presents himself as psychologically liberated from this relationship, and free to take a new wife in the free North. He marries an abolition activist and gains the kind of complete break with his enslaved past which typifies the majority of male slave narratives. Both his wife Malinda and his daughter Mary Frances cease to register in the final pages of the narrative – they are sealed within that part of the text which precedes Bibb's revelation of Malinda's 'adultery'.

Malinda as a narrative presence is deployed with great strategic power to bring out the compromised nature of Bibb's existence once he has committed himself to loving her. Bibb lays bare the way in which slavery has enmeshed him in a web of emotional interdependencies which render the act of running away deeply problematic. The cost of unsuccessful escape and the slave's disempowerment once recaptured is described though his inability to protect Malinda. In one section Bibb, having successfully escaped to the North, returns to attempt to take his wife and child out of slavery, but is recaptured and sold to the slave-trader Madison Garrison, who then takes the entire family down south to sell in the slave market of New Orleans. Bibb is kept in the slave prison at Louisville for several months while

See p. 27.

A punishment, practised in the United States, for the crime
of loving liberty.

[3.31] Anon., (wood-engravings, 1843). From *Narrative of the Life and Adventures of Henry Bibb*

[3.32] Anon., 'The Flogging of Females' (wood-engraving, 1835). From *The Anti-Slavery Record*

[3.33] Anon., 'Scenes in the City Prison of New York. Stephen Downing' (wood-engraving, 1835). From *The Anti-Slavery Record*

[See page 63.]

SCENES IN THE CITY PRISON OF NEW YORK

Garrison attempts to sell either Bibb or his whole family, but Bibb's reputation as a runaway has made him unsaleable.[102] Garrison's exasperation leads him to victimise Malinda and Bibb gives a detailed account of her abuse. Two images originally deployed in the *Anti-Slavery Record* are placed on a single page opposite the description of Malinda's torture; they bear no captions [**3.31**]. The upper image, showing a male slave suspended from a tree and beaten with the paddle, originally appeared in the March 1835 issue under the title 'A punishment practised in the United States, for the crime of loving liberty' [**3.32**]. The lower image shows a black man and woman striking submissive poses before a figure in a top hat carrying a staff. It originally illustrated the tale of the loyal wife of the slave Peter Martin imploring bail for her runaway husband while he languished in prison and it appeared on the front cover of the May 1835 issue [**3.33**].[103] In the *Narrative* the images are to be read together in the context of a single paragraph:

One day while I was in this prison, Garrison got mad with my wife, and took her off in one of the rooms, with his paddle in hand, swearing that he would paddle her; and I could afford her no protection at all, while the strong arm of the law, public opinion and custom, were all against me. I have often heard Garrison say, that he had rather paddle a female, than eat when he was hungry – that it was music for him to hear them scream, and to see their blood run.[104]

Presumably the lower image is to be taken emblematically as a representation of Bibb and Malinda hypothetically and unsuccessfully imploring 'the strong arm of the law, public opinion and custom', all represented in the figure of the official with staff and hat. The top illustration relates to Malinda's paddling, although the text backs off from giving a an account of this, and once Malinda disappears into one of the rooms neither Bibb nor his audience is allowed to follow. The man shown being paddled suspended from a tree is, in pictorial terms, almost as tangential an approach to the scene. Yet both image and text are preceded by a perfectly factual account of the operation of paddling, the relevance of which only becomes apparent retrospectively:

> The paddle is made of a piece of hickory timber, about one inch thick, three inches in width, and about eighteen inches in length. The part which is applied to the flesh is bored full of quarter inch auger holes, and every time this is applied to the flesh of the victim, the blood gushes through the holes of the paddle, or a blister makes its appearance. The persons who are flogged, are always stripped naked, and their hands tied together ... the paddle is applied to those parts of the body which would not be so likely to be seen by those who wanted to buy slaves.[105]

While Bibb does not describe the flesh and blood torturing of his wife, this precise and studiously objective treatment of the process she was forced to endure suddenly springs back into the mind of the reader to animate the frozen figures of the woodcut. The cost of running away on those left behind has never, perhaps, been more forcefully narrated. The narrative relations between text and image contain terrible gaps. Bibb could not see what went on behind the closed doors of that room but has witnessed the process on other bodies and he wants his audience to perform some form of imaginative equivalent to the horror which he had to recreate for himself. The book provides a description, an image and an event, and leaves the reader, in the position of witness, to put the three together.

This is very sophisticated narrative, yet one cannot help asking where it leaves Malinda, whose torture is described in such a way that she appears paradoxically to be denied any relation or reaction to her own suffering. In this context it is worth asking the extent to which Malinda is ever allowed to function as a psychological reality at any point in the narrative. When Malinda is introduced it is in terms of the formulae of the romantic novella. Bibb's first mention of her is as a traditional temptress. His idealism in wanting to escape is 'turned aside by the fascinating charms of a female'.

She is a 'highly interesting girl', a 'dear girl' with a 'gentle smile upon her lovely cheek'. The following sentence could have been lifted out of any number of romantic novellas and dropped into Bibb's narrative by a helpful ghost writer: 'I could read it [her love] in the language of her bright and sparkling eye, pencilled by the unchangeable finger of nature, that spake but could not lie.'[106] If Bibb is talking about experiences too painful to remember then perhaps it is appropriate that he presents them in terms of a formulaic language developed to pretend to describe romantic love while describing nothing but its own generality. It is in this context that the images used to describe Malinda are relevant. As the text does not really describe Malinda at all, but presents her through an overused linguistic currency that might apply to any woman at any time, so the plates that 'describe' Malinda and Bibb describe merely an anonymous pair of runaways, frozen in woodblock, perpetually reproducible for a Northern audience in any runaway narrative.

There are two full-page illustrations which purport to give descriptions of Bibb and Malinda attempting flight. Again, neither of these blocks in their original manifestations described Bibb and his wife at all. The source plates appear, confusingly, in a volume entitled *The Suppressed Book About Slavery* which was finally published in 1857, although it is claimed in the preface that it was completed and ready for press many years earlier. Several of the Bibb plates rework areas of the detailed, highly finished and formally elaborate etchings, which illustrated this volume.[107]

The first plate showing Bibb attempting escape with his wife is supposed to represent Bibb fighting off a pack of wolves while his wife and daughter cower in the background [**3.34**]. In the printed text this passage is one of the most potent exempla by which Bibb is convinced of the existence of a divine providence which watches over the slave in the wilderness.[108] But the woodcut cannot easily be seen to provide an imagistic parallel for this inspirational episode. The plate is a crude adaptation of one part of an etching which described a slave family apprehended by slave-catchers [**3.35**]. The woman in the background is shown cowering, whereas Malinda is described holding a club in Bibb's narrative. The wolves were originally a slave-catcher's hounds, and the family surrounded by armed mounted and unmounted whites. The plate in the *Narrative* is very difficult to read since the wolves/dogs have virtually disintegrated into the fractured mesh of the block. The plate has been placed vertically on a single page, although it was obviously made to be displayed and viewed in landscape format in another publication. The quality of the printing is appalling, and the plate does not show Bibb and Malinda at all but some generic approximation of a scene of runaway apprehension.

When Bibb does describe the capture of himself and his family by the slave-catchers sent out by Deacon, the prose is accompanied by another

[3.34] Anon., 'Bibb and Malinda Escaping' (wood-engraving, 1843). From *Narrative of the Life and Adventures of Henry Bibb*

cut adapted from *The Suppressed Book About Slavery* [**3.36** and **3.37**]. Bibb and his family are reduced to anonymous representatives of slave flight and capture. Any group of mother, father and child, caught by any group of slave-catchers, could be represented by this design. The juxtaposition of the impersonal and crude woodcut, showing just another slave family pursued and captured, could be seen as a method for stressing the psychological realism and autobiographical particularity of Bibb's account of his concern for his family. There is also the sense that the right-hand side of this plate, showing two little figures hopelessly running, inevitably to be caught, is still trapped within the semiotics of the runaway slave advertise-

[3.35] Anon., 'The Bloodhound Business' (etching, designed *c.* 1840, published 1857). From *The Suppressed Book About Slavery*

[3.36] Anon., 'Bibb and Malinda Captured' (wood-engraving, 1843). From *Narrative of the
Life and Adventures of Henry Bibb*

ment.[109] While Bibb's narrative indefatigably fleshes out and humanises
his repeated attempts at escape, while he tries to give each attempt to break
out of slavery a detailed particularity, the existence of these plates under-
cuts the effect. If these plates relate powerfully to the slave power's construction of the runaway then it is must be asked what Bibb would have
meant to his free Northern readers. Would he always be just another fugitive involved in the inevitable processes of flight and recapture? The plates
lower a terrible kind of certainty over Bibb's writing. In their repetitive
quotation they offer reassurance to a white audience, they imply that the
experiences of slavery are always essentially the same and are emotionally

[3.37] Anon., 'Running Away' (etching, designed *c.* 1840, published 1857). From *The
Suppressed Book About Slavery*

recoverable for a white Northern reader. Yet such reassurance is bought at a terrible cost in terms of the way Bibb's experience is imprisoned within a set of descriptive pre-conditions. On at least one occasion, however, Bibb's book manages to triumph over the descriptive limitations which its peculiar mode of illustration imposes. The frontispiece quotes, and simultaneously destroys, the ability of the image of the runaway slave to depersonalise its subject.

The contrast between individuality and sameness in the representation of the black fugitive, which, I have argued, in so many ways activates the relation between text and imagery in Bibb's book, is precisely defined in the frontispiece [3.26]. Opposite the title page is a highly accomplished engraved portrait of Bibb as a free man. The portrait was executed by the black abolitionist and engraver Patrick H. Reason, who produced a mass of engraved work for American abolition societies.[110] Printed on separate paper, tipped in, and framed in octagonal format, the print celebrates Bibb as an individual. Bibb is shown dressed soberly yet expensively, with a knife-edge shirt collar and starched shirt-front printed in gleaming unadulterated white, a loose cravat and brocade waistcoat. A strong and beautifully manicured hand rests on the top of a volume, his own *Narrative*, which is held vertically. Bibb stands with his body in three-quarter profile, but his head is turned to look at the reader full face. His hair, apparently straightened, is elegantly parted and frames a strikingly delicate face, with beautiful lips, a strong jaw, and sad eyes which nevertheless look out with determination and assurance. The contours of the face and the skin tone are described with great delicacy.

The print has the clarity and precision, especially in its rendering of tonal range, of a photograph. This results from the technique used to render the face. That this is a high-quality engraving in the style of the most exclusive European print houses is borne out by the technical means used to represent the face. While the rest of the print is line engraved with the burin, the standard procedure for portrait engraving, the face was engraved solely by the use of stipple. This form of intaglio print-making involved using a hammer, or specially modified arched burin, with a tiny needle sharp point. Minute pricks were then incised in the surface of the copper. The force with which the stipple tool was applied defined the depth and circumference of the hole made and consequently the relative size and darkness of each printed dot. The technique was extremely labour-intensive and required great skill; until the development of photography it provided the most delicate means of rendering half tones in printing, and in this context it was even more refined than mezzotint. The method was used for the delineation of faces in the most expensive and acclaimed engraved portraiture.

It was a technique perfected by Bartolozzi in eighteenth-century England in the context of his superb full-scale reproductions of Holbein's portrait drawings of Henry VIII's court, and had been used to depict the engraved faces of every important European since the 1780s.[111] The English engraver David Edwin brought the technique of stipple engraving to the United States at the turn of the eighteenth century, producing technically exquisite engraved portraits after paintings by Gilbert Stuart.[112] During the first two decades of the nineteenth century the technique was brought to a high technical standard in the larger East Coast cities, and was used for portraits of distinguished individuals, as well as for the portraits in expensive historical and biographical publications such as Delaplaine's *Repository of the Lives and Portraits of Distinguished American Characters.*[113] Yet Reason may well have learned the technique in Europe, for he was sponsored by the New York Anti-Slavery Society to study engraving techniques in England.[114] Reason's application of stipple to depict the skin tones and facial characteristics of an escaped slave is intensely moving, and rather important in terms of how the print functions. Bibb, once anonymous property, is proclaimed as a unique personality. This image in its technical quality and descriptive subtlety proclaims that Bibb has established himself in white society. He has got somewhere and he is someone. Below the portrait is the engraved inscription of the artist's name, and directly below this an engraved facsimile of Bibb's signature. Proclaiming that he can write, the signature announces his textual individuality as his portrait testifies to his physical individuality. In its grandeur and psychological clarity the image stands in direct descent from the frontispiece to the first great slave narrative to be written in the West. Olaudah Equiano's *Interesting Narrative* carried a portrait of a fashionably attired and confident Equiano, seated before an open book, in this case the Bible [**3.38**]. As with Bibb the face is described in stipple, and the image is a proclamation that the author has arrived, as a personality, in English culture. The engraving was, in fact, worked up from a very fine miniature oil portrait.[115]

[**3.38**] Anon., portrait of Olaudah Equiano (copper engraving with stipple, 1/89). From *The Interesting Narrative of Olaudah Equiano*

Bibb's image relates to a wider context: the portraits of distinguished blacks which originated in England in the late eighteenth century, with oil paintings of, among others, Equiano and Ignatius Sancho, and which continued in the context of the abolition lecture circuit in England and America in the mid-nineteenth century. Yet Bibb takes the empowerment which this portrait tradition represents a stage further by providing it with a powerfully ironic context. Bibb's triumphant profession of freedom is set off against the defining codes of the runaway slave advertisement. The bottom of the page resurrects this imagery in explicit terms in order that Bibb's destruction of its force in the example of his life and writings may be more fully celebrated [**3.39**]. The final trailing flourish which underlines Bibb's signature plunges vertically into the top of the highest gable of a row of houses. These houses form the background to a little narrative vignette describing the scene of Bibb in flight from Daniel Lane. The image is flanked either side with the exclamations 'Stop the runaway! Where is he!' and '$50 Reward for him'. The tiny crude engraving shows a night scene with two figures running round a corner; one, running in a pool of light, is a completely black figure of a slave less than a centimetre high, carrying a bundle on a stick. In this portrait Bibb is the little black anonymous figure of the runaway, reduplicated countless times in runaway slave advertisements, forever frozen, forever pursued, forever property. The double portrait which this frontispiece embodies carries an emphatic message. The power of the runaway slave advertisement is finally overturned. The individual whose monumental presence stares out in the top two-thirds of the design is, yet paradoxically is not, the same man as the little hunted refugee at the page bottom.

Despite the triumphant frontispiece, the relation between printed word and image in Bibb's book as a whole is deeply troubling and finally perhaps unresolvable. It could be argued that I have given too much

[**3.39**] Anon., double portrait of Henry Bibb (copper engraving, with stipple, and wood-engraving, 1849). From *Narrative of the Life and Adventures of Henry Bibb*, frontispiece, detail

significance to the multiple deployment of these images. Common sense dictates that once the source has been located the status of the image is irrevocably altered, the 'illustration' is false, its reality lies outside, in a different and earlier text and context. The images in Bibb's *Narrative* are therefore reduced, their significance general and decorative. The re-deployment of blocks can be explained through the economics of publishing. It was important for Bibb and his abolitionist supporters to get the story of his life out as quickly as possible. Wood-engravings under commission were expensive, while abolitionists possessed a reservoir of blocks describing the most common abuses of slave life. The same cuts appear reprinted again and again in illustrated anthologies, periodicals, children's books and magazines. The easiest way to produce a heavily illustrated and cheap edition of Bibb's narrative rapidly was to use these blocks, whenever they seemed appropriate, according to the rationale that they may not have represented Bibb's individual experiences, but they give the general idea. Yet this sensible explanation of how the images got into the narrative does not provide any way of reading them, either in relation to Bibb's words or in the context of the history of their having been misread.

Given their multiple narrative status it is finally very difficult to know how to read any of the woodcuts. The extended interpretations above read them in parallel with Bibb's words, but the images may represent something more obscure, more uncertain. They may be a testament to the dismaying truth that the atrocity suffered by slaves can only be recounted according to a set of technical and imaginative lowest common denominators. These images reduce slave experience to a set of repeated scenes; they constitute an essentialist base for the depiction of slave life within abolition semiotics. Experience becomes translated into webs of engraved lines which can be set into any text considered to be thematically relevant.

One way of approaching the meaning of these recirculated images is to see in them a realisation of one of the processes of erasure and facelessness through repetition which Derrida works with in 'White Mythology'.[116] As with the words that Derrida explores, these images had a precise value within a currency, they are still passed around from hand to hand as part of that currency, but have been worn smooth, characterless, through handling and re-handling. Derrida poses the question: 'In effect, there is no access to the usure of a linguistic phenomenon without giving it some figurative representation. What could be the *properly named usure* of a word, a statement, a meaning, a text?'[117] Are Bibb's pictures an answer to this question, are they the 'figurative representation' of the erasure of language (both as image and as written word) through use, which Derrida asks for? Taken as such the pictures are a commentary upon, perhaps even a solution to, Bibb's repeated statements of the impossibility of describing the experiences of slavery, statements which are, as I argued earlier, insistently reiterated within the narrative to a point where they go beyond a merely popular rhetoric of disavowal. The images in Bibb's book have an iconic currency but are valueless, faceless; they are quite specifically not what they are; they are typical to the point of meaninglessness; they form a visual redefinition of the very processes of incommunicability which his text continually articulates and simultaneously denies. They hold no message, or two messages at once, one of which denies the existence of the other. In this sense perhaps the pictures, because they hold in each case an absent second meaning, are a physical embodiment of white mythology itself, as defined by Derrida: 'White mythology – metaphysics has erased within itself the fabulous scene that has produced it, the scene that nevertheless remains active and stirring, inscribed in white ink, an invisible design covered over in the palimpsest.'[118]

These images communicate the terrible certainty that in one way there is nothing that can be said and thought which will describe what Henry Bibb had to live through. What he produced was part self-justification, part contribution to a political movement, part confessional narrative; it was not and never can be the 'truth' which his first reviewers claim. The fact that these illustrations are what they are, in other words that they are quite precisely not what they claim to be – an account of Bibb's experience – leaves all readers of the narrative in a difficult position. The silent illustrations seen, but not read, by generations of readers, must be seen for what they are if we are to understand what Bibb and his publishers ended up telling us.

Notes

1 Winthrop D. Jordan, *White Over Black: American Attitudes Toward the Negro, 1550–1812* (Harmondsworth, Penguin, 1968), p. 107. For a detailed account of runaway slave legislation see A. Higginbottom Jnr., *In the Matter of Colour: Race and the American Legal Process in the Colonial Period* (New York, Oxford University Press, 1980), pp. 12–13, 27–8, 33–5, 176–9, 198–9, 236–40, 254–5. For an overview of North–South legal relationships over fugitives see Paul Finkelman, *An Imperfect Union: Slavery, Federation and Comity* (Chapel Hill, University of North Carolina Press, 1981) and *Slavery in the Courtroom* (Washington, Library of Congress, 1985). For runaways in the Chesapeake area see Philip D. Morgan, *Slave Counterpoint: Black Culture in the Eighteenth-Century Chesapeake and Low Country* (Chapel Hill and London, University of North Carolina Press, 1998), pp. 75–8, 446–51, 464–8, 480–4, 541–9.

2 Several collections of slave advertisements have now been published. For eighteenth-century American slave advertisements see Lathan A. Windley (comp. and ed.), *Runaway Slave Advertisements: A Documentary History from the 1730s until 1790*, 4 vols (London, Greenwood Press, 1983). See also Billy G. Smith and Richard Wojtowicz, *Blacks who Stole Themselves: Advertisements for Runaways in the Pennsylvania Gazette, 1728–90* (Philadelphia, University of Pennsylvania Press, 1989) and Philip D. Morgan, 'Colonial South Carolina Runaways: Their Significance for Slave Culture', *Slavery and Abolition*, 6:3 (1985) 57–79. For Brazilian runaway advertising see Gilberto Freyre, *Os Escravo nos Anúncios de Jornais Brasileiros do Século XIX*, 2nd edn (São Paulo, Companhia Editoria Nacional, 1979). For Jamaican slave advertisements see Orlando Patterson, *Slavery and Social Death: A Comparative Study* (Cambridge Mass. and London, Harvard University Press, 1982), pp. 59, 94, 270, 432, 447; Michael Craton, *Searching for the Invisible Man: Slaves and Plantation Life in Jamaica* (Cambridge Mass., Harvard University Press, 1978), pp. 245–54.

3 See Gomer Williams, *History of the Liverpool Privateers and Letter of Marque, with an Account of the Liverpool Slave Trade* (London, 1887), pp. 475–6. Peter Fryer, *Staying Power: the History of Black People in Britain* (London, Pluto Press, 1984), pp. 60–4.

4 For the development of woodcuts in early American runaway advertising see Clarence P. Hornung and Fridolf Johnson, *220 Years of American Graphic Art* (New York, George Brazillier, 1976), pp. 16–17.

5 See Leonora Nattrass, *William Cobbett: The Politics of Style* (Cambridge, Cambridge University Press, 1992), p. 52.

6 Samuel Taylor Coleridge, *The Table Talk and Omniana of Samuel Taylor Coleridge* (Oxford, Oxford University Press, 1917), pp. 353–4.

7 Coleridge, *Omniana*, p. 356.

8 Thomas Clarkson, *Negro Slavery. Argument, That the Colonial Slaves are better off than the British Peasantry* (London, 1824).

9 Clarkson, *Negro Slavery*, p.1.

10 Clarkson, *Negro Slavery*, p. 2.

11 For the semiotics of branding within abolition visual culture see pp. 246–50 below.

12 *New York Anti-Slavery Almanac* (New York, 1839) 31–2.

13 *Boston Anti-Slavery Almanac* (Boston, 1837) 16.

14 [Theodore Dwight Weld], *American Slavery As It Is* (New York, American Anti-Slavery Society, 1839). For the background to *American Slavery As It Is* see Robert Abzug, *Passionate Liberator: Theodore Dwight Weld and the Dilemma of Reform* (New York, Oxford University Press, 1980), pp. 210–18. Also Dwight Lowell Dumond, *Anti-Slavery: The Crusade for Freedom in America* (Ann Arbour, University of Michigan Press, 1961), pp. 241–56. For a detailed account of the martyrological inheritance of abolition see pp. 241–71 below.

15 For Stowe's use of *American Slavery* as the source for her presentations of slave torture see Bruce E. Kirkham, *The Building of Uncle Tom's Cabin* (Knoxville, University of Tennessee Press, 1977), pp. 101–3. For the relation of slave advertisement to slave narrative, in the context of *American Slavery*, see William L. Andrews, *To Tell a Free Story: The First Century of Afro-American Autobiography, 1760–1865* (Chicago, University of Illinois Press, 1988), p. 62. For publishing figures see Dumond, *Anti-slavery*, pp. 249–50.

16 Weld and the Grimkes went through more than 20,000 issues of Southern papers in six months. See Abzug, *Passionate Liberator*, pp. 210–18.

17 For political aspects of martyrology in *Actes and Monuments* see Frances A. Yates, 'Foxe as Propagandist', *Encounter*, 27:4 (1966) 78–86; also William Haller, 'John Foxe and the Puritan Revolution', in Richard F. Jones (ed.), *The Seventeenth Century: Studies in the History of English Thought and Literature from Bacon to Pope* (Stanford, Stanford University Press 1965), pp. 209–24; Warren W. Wooden, *John Foxe* (Boston, Twayne, 1983), pp. 41–76; D. M. Loades, *John Foxe and the English Reformation* (London, Scolar, 1997).

18 Weld, *American Slavery*, p. 72.

19 For a discussion of the memorialisation of the Holocaust in terms which raise precisely these problems see James E. Young, *The Texture of Memory: Holocaust Memorials and Meaning* (New Haven and London, Yale University Press, 1993), pp. 132–5.

20 Charles Dickens, *American Notes* (Oxford, Oxford University Press, 1987), p. 230.

21 Dickens, *American Notes*, p. 230.

22 Stowe's effective satiric use of slave advertisement here contrasts sharply with her cumbrous treatment in her *Key to Uncle Tom's Cabin* (London, 1853), pp. 239–57 where the protracted assault on 'Public Opinion' carries Dickensian traces.

23 See *Uncle Tom's Cabin. or, Life Among the Lowly by H.B.S. Illustrated Edition Complete in one Volume Designs by Billings* (London, 1853) p. 142.

24 See Shane White and Graham White, 'Slave Clothing and African American Culture', *Past and Present*, 148 (1995) 155–61. Note in particular the extraordinary advertisement for Lucy, p. 156.

25 See Marcus Wood, *Radical Satire and Print Culture 1790–1822* (Oxford, Clarendon Press, 1994), pp. 202 3.

26 Morgan, *Slave Counterpoint*, pp. 8–9, 303–6, 400–1, 261, 263, 271.

27 For Franklin's centrality in introducing woodcuts to press advertising see Hornung and Johnson, *American Graphic Satire*, p. 25; George Henry Preble, *Our Flag: The Origin and Progress of the Flag of the United States* (New York, 1872), pp. 214–15.

28 These advertisements are reproduced in Hornung and Johnson, *American Graphic Satire*, p. 24. The best account of white runaway advertisements in the context of black slave runaways is in Abbot Emerson Smith, *Colonists in Bondage: White Servitude and Convict Labour in America 1607–1776* (Chapel Hill, University of North Carolina Press, 1947), pp. 265–70.

29 Hornung and Johnson, *American Graphic Satire*, p. 36. They also state 'a single issue of the *New York Gazette* for 1 Jan. 1818 contained 538 ads, occupying 25 out of 28 columns'.

30 See Hornung and Johnson, *American Graphic Satire*, p. 37.

31 For the promiscuous deployment of the runaway in nineteenth-century Brazilian print culture see Boris Kossoy and Maria Luiza Tucci Carneiro, *O Olhar Europeu O Negro na Iconographia Brasileira do Século XIX* (São Paulo, Universidade de São Paulo, 1994), plates 17, 18.

32 Some relevant examples are: Osvaldo Orico, *O Tigre da Abolição* (Rio de Janeiro, Grafica Olimpica, 1953), front cover and title page; Freyre, *Os Escravos*, dust jacket; Finkelman, *Imperfect Union*, front cover.

33 *Anti-Slavery Record*, 3:7 (July 1837) 1–2.

34 Ralph Waldo Emerson, *The Collected Works of Ralph Waldo Emerson, Volume II, Essays, First Series*, ed. Alfred R. Fergusson and Jean Fergusson (Cambridge Mass., Belknap Press, 1979), pp. 14–15.

35 For a discussion of the extent to which Frederick Douglass engages with and reinvents Emersonian hero narrative see Henri Louis Gates Jnr., 'Binary Oppositions in Chapter One of *Narrative of the Life of Frederick Douglass an American Slave Written by Himself*', in Dexter Fisher and Robert B. Stepto (eds), *African American Literature* (New York, Modern Language Association of America, 1979), p. 238. Gates's emphasis on the centrality of military exploits to the genre of white European autobiography, and of the relation of slave narrative to this theme, is also important here.

36 For Johnson and Civil War imagery attempting to valorise slave escape see Albert Boime, *The Art of Exclusion: Representing Blacks in the Nineteenth Century* (London, Thames and Hudson, 1990), pp. 115–17; Hugh Honour, *The Image of the Black in Western Art from the American Rev olution to World War I* (Cambridge Mass., Harvard University Press, 1989), 4:2, pp. 222–4.

37 For a reading of the painting as an unproblematic assimilation of narrative conventions of Western academic history painting, see Honour, *Image of the Black*, 4:1, pp. 211–12.

38 See Honour, *Image of the Black*, 4:2, pp. 25–7. For other examples 4:1, pp. 89–91. For the social and narrative conventions of ritual hunting pictures see Richard Leppert, *Art and the Committed Eye: The Cultural Functions of Imagery* (Oxford and Boulder, Westview Press, 1996), pp. 74–83.

39 Honour, *Image of the Black*, 4:1, pp. 208–9. For Moran's Turnerian influences see Honour, *Image of the Black*, 4:1, p. 212.

40 The only example in oils from the 1850s is John Adam Horton, *The Fugitive Slave*. See Honour, *Image of the Black*, 4:1, p. 210.

41 *American Anti-Slavery Almanac for* 1838, Boston, page for April.

42 The two central studies to raise these questions in the context of Afro-American and Anglo-African slave narratives are Charles T. Davis and Henry Louis Gates, Jnr. (eds), *The Slave's Narrative* (Oxford and New York, Oxford University Press, 1985) and Andrews, *Free Story*. For authenticity in slave narrative see 'Narration, Authentication, and Authorial Control in Frederick Douglass' *Narrative* of 1845', in Fisher and Stepto (eds), *African American Literature*, pp. 178–211; Gates, 'Binary Oppositions', pp. 212–32, sets the slave narrative against the developing forms of nineteenth-century

popular fiction. For white cultural and literary paradigms for the construction of black-ness see George M. Fredrickson, *The Black Image in the White Mind* (New York, Harper and Row, 1971) and Toni Morrison, *Playing in the Dark* (London, Picador, 1993). For the reception of Afro-American slave narratives by white British audiences see R. J. M. Blackett, *Building an Anti-Slavery Wall: Black Americans in the Atlantic Abolitionist Movement, 1830–1860* (Ithaca and London, Cornell University Press, 1983).

43 Toni Morrison's construction of the term 'rememory' focuses debate on this issue. There have been many attempts to unpack this concept, the most valuable of which are Mae G. Henderson, 'Toni Morrison's *Beloved*: Re-Membering the Body as Historical Text', in Hortense J. Spillers (ed.), *Comparative American Identities: Race, Sex and Nationality in the Modern Text* (London, Routledge, 1991), pp. 62–86, and Asnaf Rushdy, '"Rememory": Primal Scenes and Constructions in Toni Morrison's Novels', *Contemporary Literature*, 31 (1990) 300 23. For the problematising of the memory of trauma see Primo Levi, *The Drowned and the Saved*, trans. Raymond Rosenthal (London, Abacus, 1988), pp. 11–12.

44 Paul Gilroy, *The Black Atlantic: Modernity and Double Consciousness* (London, Verso, 1993), pp. 205–23 considers the appropriateness of Jewish/Black historical paral-lelism. For the first detailed, and highly controversial, treatment of this theme see Stanley Elkins, *Slavery: A Problem in American Institutional and Intellectual Life* (New York, Grosset and Dunlap, 1963), pp. 98–130.

45 Levi, *The Drowned*, p. 12.

46 Gilroy, *Black Atlantic*, p. 216.

47 Paul Gilroy, *Small Acts* (London, Serpent's Tail, 1993), p. 178.

48 Of the major academic studies of the slave narratives, Andrews, *Free Story*, is the only relatively heavily illustrated volume, but the images reproduced are not considered to be an integral part of the 'text' of the narratives in which they are included. A large number of slave narratives carried separately engraved whole sheet plates which illustrated key events, for example Solomon Northrup, *Twelve Years a Slave, Narrative of Solomon Northrup, A Citizen of New York, Kidnapped in Washington City and 1841, and Rescued in 1853* (Auburn, 1853) and Frederick Douglass, *My Bondage My Freedom* (Auburn and New York, Miller Orton and Mullington, 1855). Many others, the first being *A Narrative of the Adventures and Escape of Moses Roper*, carried wood-engravings set into the text. The most spectacularly illustrated volume by an African-American in the nineteenth century to accumulate imagery around slave escape was William Still, *The Underground Railroad: A Record of Facts, Authentic Narratives, Letters, Narrating the Hardships Hair-Breadth Escapes and Death Struggles of the slaves in their efforts for Freedom, as related by themselves and others, or witnessed by the author* (Philadelphia, Porter and Coates, 1872).

49 This discussion is inflected by the arguments of Henry Louis Gates's 'Binary Oppositions'. Rather, however, than stress binary opposition as a central linguistic device for the examination of the slave's relation to a readership, I focus upon parody. In doing so I shift the emphasis to parts of Douglass's narrative where stylistic mimesis, in the form of rhetorical appropriations and reversals of white discourse, replaces opposition as the primary linguistic impulse. For Douglass and Hegelian parody see Leonard Cassuto, *The Inhuman Race: The Racial Grotesque in American Literature and Culture* (New York, Columbia University Press, 1997), pp. 87–95.

50 Frederick Douglass, *Narrative of the Life of Frederick Douglass* (London, Penguin, 1986), pp. 123–4.

51 Douglass, *Narrative*, p. 143.

52 Jesse Hutchinson Jnr., *The Fugitive's Song* (Boston, 1845), p. 5.

53 The engraved portrait to the first edition of *My Bondage My Freedom* is in contrast a high-quality engraving, the face executed in stipple.

54 See James Olney '"I was born". Slave Narratives, their Status as Autobiography and as Literature', in Gates and Davis (eds), *The Slave Narrative*, p. 173, fn. 12. The two ver-sions of the narrative within the main text are referred to as 1849 and 1851.

55 See Robert B. Stepto, *From Behind the Veil: A Study of Afro-American Narrative*, 2nd edn (Urbana, Chicago and London, University of Illinois Press, 1979), pp. 3–31.

56 The first eyewitness account of Brown's release, apart from his own, is that recounted by Still, *Underground Railroad*, p. 84. Standard accounts of the career of H. B. Brown are in Blackett, *Anti-Slavery Wall*, pp. 158–9, 169–70; Andrews, *Free Story*, pp. 99–100; C. Peter Ripley (ed.), *The Black Abolitionist Papers*, 5 vols (Chapel Hill and London, University of North Carolina Press, 1985–92), 1, pp. 174–5 n.

57 For white control of black lecturing see Ripley, *Black Abolitionist Papers*, 3, pp. 26–30.

58 For a discussion of the adaptation of Brown's narrative by American abolitionists see Cynthia Griffin Wolff, 'Passing Beyond the Middle Passage: Henry "Box" Brown's Translations of Slavery', *Massachusetts Review*, 37:1 (1996) 23–43. For the shifting impact of blacks in the American abolition movement see Philip S. Foner, *History of Black Americans from the Emergence of the Cotton Kingdom to the Eve of the Compromise of 1850*, 3 vols (Westport and London, Greenwood, 1983), 2, pp. 479–535. For a good contextualising analysis of the effect of Weld's *American Slavery As It Is* see Foner, *History*, 2, pp. 411–14. For an overview of the shift in the role of black abolitionists 1830–50 see Ripley, *Black Abolitionist Papers*, 3, pp. 27–57. For Brown's panorama and the Walcott collaboration see Nancy Osgood, 'Josiah Walcott, Artist and Associationist', *Old Time New England*, 76:264 (1998) 15–20.

59 A full list of all black abolitionists in the British Isles 1830–65 is given in Ripley, *Black Abolitionist Papers*, 1, pp. 571–3, for a detailed account of the experiences of ex-slave lecturers in England pp. 5–35. For the role of J. C. A. Smith, and his quarrel with Brown in England, see Ripley, *Black Abolitionist Papers*, 1, pp. 293–7, 298 n. Brown's panorama is also discussed at some length in this correspondence. The catalogue to Brown's panorama has not survived, but that of William Wells Brown, first printed in London, and titled *A Description of William Wells Brown's Original Panoramic Views of the Scenes in the Life of An American Slave*, has survived. This was on a similar scale to, and contemporaneous with, 'Box' Brown's, and is reproduced in Ripley, *Black Abolitionist Papers*, 1, pp. 190–224. For the commodification of black ex-slaves within abolition publicity structures see Wolff, 'Passing Beyond the Middle Passage', pp. 23–4, and Michael Newberry, 'Eaten Alive: Slavery and Celebrity in Antebellum America', *English Literary History*, 61:1 (1994) 159–87.

60 The best discussion of the relation of black abolitionists in England and America to missionary and emigrationist policy is Blackett, *Anti-Slavery Wall*, pp. 162–94. For a brief consideration of Brown and the interrelations between public performance and slave narrative in the context of Garrisonian evangelical abolition see Andrews, *Free Story*, pp. 99–100. For the rise of black ex-fugitives on the professional lecture circuit in America, and the behavioural and linguistic codes surrounding them, see Benjamin Quarles, *Black Abolitionists* (New York: Oxford University Press, 1969) and Larry Gara, 'The Professional Fugitive in the Abolition Movement', *Wisconsin Magazine of History* 48:2 (1965) 196–204. The introduction to Ripley, *Black Abolitionist Papers*, 1, pp. 3–36 provides a solid historical and social analysis of the role and activities of black American abolitionists in Britain. For the cultural associations of the jack-in-the-box see Philip Thompson and Peter Davenport (eds), *The Dictionary of Visual Language* (London, Bergstrom and Boyle, 1980), p. 134.

61 For the extent to which blacks could still, at this late date, market themselves as exotic and strange exhibits within the London show world, see Richard D. Altick, *The Shows of London* (Cambridge Mass., Harvard University Press, 1978), pp. 268–87.

62 See Blackett, *Anti-Slavery Wall*, p. 15 and n. 22.

63 See Blackett, *Anti-Slavery Wall*, pp. 159–60. Blackett sees it as significant that none of the other black ex-slaves in Britain at the time came to Brown's defence.

64 All these press quotations are from Blackett, *Anti-Slavery Wall*, pp. 159–60. Against construction of the panorama as absurd melodrama one might set the reaction of Justin Spaulding: 'the real *life-like* scenes presented in this PANORAMA, are

admirably calculated to make an unfading impression upon the heart and memory, such as no lectures, books, or colloquial correspondence can produce', in Brown, *Narrative* (1851), p. 4.

65 This material was brought to light in Blackett, *Anti-Slavery Wall*, p. 159, from which I quote. Blackett does not consider the implications of Brown's performative approach to abolition publicity in the context of the formulae laid down in England for the public appearance of ex-slaves.

66 See, James Walvin (ed.), *Black and White: The Negro and English Society, 1555–1945* (London, Penguin, 1973).

67 See M. McRoy's account in Brown, *Narrative* (1851), p. iii; also Still, *Underground Railroad*, p. 83: 'The proceedings commenced. Mr. McKim rapped quietly on the lid of the box and called out "All right!" Instantly came the answer from within. "All right, sir!"'.

68 Still, *Underground Railroad*, p. 84 gives a different account from Brown's, stating that he had planned this performance long before: 'Very soon he remarked that, before leaving Richmond he had selected for his arrival hymn (if he lived) the Psalm beginning with these words: "*I waited patiently for the Lord, and He heard my prayer.*" And most touchingly did he sing the psalm, much to his own relief, as well as to the delight of his small audience.'

69 Brown, *Narrative* (1851), pp. 57–8.

70 Psalm 40, 1–3.

71 American Antiquarian Society, Holdings: BDSDS (1849), 'Song sung by Mr. Brown on being removed from box.' I am grateful to Georgia B. Barnhill of the American Antiquarian Society for bringing this ballad to my notice.

72 Brown, *Narrative* (1851), p. 61.

73 For a detailed account of these textual reinventions see Marcus Wood, '"All Right!": The Narrative of Henry "Box" Brown as a test case for the racial prescription of rhetoric and semiotics', *Proceedings of the American Antiquarian Society*, 107:1 (1997) 65–104. Wolff, 'Passing Beyond the Middle Passage', p. 28 argues that Brown's embowment can be read as a metaphor for the middle passage; curiously no contemporary accounts I have seen make this connection. Cassuto, *Inhuman Race*, p. 105 provides and ironic reading of Brown's embowment, pointing out that he has literally to turn himself into an object in order to make himself a person.

74 *The Resurrection of Henry Box Brown at Philadelphia. Who escaped from Richmond Va. in a Box 3 ft. long, 2½ ft deep and 2½ ft wide* (Boston, 1849), stone lithograph, in Bernard F. Reilly (ed.), *American Political Prints 1766–1876: A Catalog of the Collections in the Library of Congress* (Boston, G. K. Hall, 1991), 1850–54.

75 See Norman Cohn, *Noah's Flood: The Genesis Story in Western Thought* (New Haven and London, Yale University Press, 1996), pp. 22–7, and plates.

76 *Effects of the Fugitive-Slave-Law* 1850, stone lithograph, LC 1850–55, in Reilly (ed.), *American Political Prints*.

77 *The Liberty Almanac for* 1851 (New York, American Anti-Slavery Society, 1851) 15.

78 *Liberty Almanac* (1851) 15.

79 *The Liberty Almanac for* 1852 (New York, American Anti-Slavery Society, 1852) 25.

80 *Liberty Almanac* (1852) 25.

81 The linking of cruelty to animals with cruelty to slaves in anti-slave trade publicity goes back to the seventeenth century. Thomas Clarkson drew attention to a central example: 'Dr. Primatt in his "Dissertation on the Duty of Mercy, and on the Sin of Cruelty to Brute-animals," … takes occasion to advert to the subject of the African Slave-trade.' *The History of the Rise, Progress, and Accomplishment of the Abolition of the African Slave-Trade by the British Parliament*, 2 vols (London, 1808), 1, p. 48. For a detailed discussion of the slave/child/animal conflation in abolition children's literature see pp. 271–6 below.

82 The first and third plates of Hogarth's series were reproduced in crude wood-engraved form in *The Legion of Liberty* (New York, New York Anti-Slavery Society,

1843) unpaginated. For a particularly forceful articulation of the English obsession with the connection between the suffering of slaves and of animals see the fiery pamphlet by the radical and abolitionist Elizabeth Heyrick, *Cursory Remarks on the Evil Tendency of Unrestrained Cruelty Particularly on that Practiced in Smithfield Market* (London, Darton and Harvey, 1823). See also James Turner, *Reckoning with the Beast: Animals, Pain and Humanity in the Victorian Mind* (Baltimore and London, Johns Hopkins University Press, 1980), pp. 1–39.

83 *Cousin Ann's Stories for Children* (Philadelphia, 1849), pp. 12–14.

84 *Cousin Ann's Stories*, p. 24.

85 *Cousin Ann's Stories*, p. 24

86 John Rylands, 'Raymond English Anti-Slavery Collection', Box 7, item 3, no. 9. consists of no. 8 of the 'Juvenile Anti Slavery Series'. This is a retelling for children of the history of Henry Box Brown. This carries a crude wood-engraved frontispiece illustration based on the American lithograph and showing Henry Box Brown emerging from his crate. The narrative gives the essential facts but constantly seeks to stress Brown's heroism through comparisons with the Spartan and Roman codes of endurance, and stoicism. For the comparison of the runaway with Xenophon's retreat of the 10,000 see the *Anti-Slavery Record*, 3:7 (1837) 1–2.

87 See Thelma Golden (ed.), *Black Male: Representations of Masculinity in Contemporary American Art* (New York, Whitney Museum of Art, 1994).

88 For an overview of Beuys's aesthetic theory and performances see Caroline Tisdall, *Joseph Beuys* (London, Thames and Hudson, 1979); David Thistlewood, *Joseph Beuys: Diverging Critiques* (Liverpool, Liverpool University Press and Tate Gallery Liverpool, 1995); Alain Borer, *The Essential Joseph Beuys* (London, Thames and Hudson, 1996).

89 The beautiful photographs documenting the first performance are published in Caroline Tisdall, *Joseph Beuys Coyote* (Munich, Schirmer Mosel, 1976). For Boyle's account of the performance see Jimmy Boyle, *A Sense of Freedom* (London, Pan Books, 1977), p. 258.

90 The first edition of Bibb's narrative is used: *Narrative of the Life and Adventures of Henry Bibb, An American Slave, Written by Himself with an Introduction by Lucius C. Matlack* (New York, 1849).

91 The standard study of Bibb's *Narrative* as 'truth' by a modern scholar is Robert Burns Stepto, 'I Rose and Found My Voice: Narration, Authentication, and Authorial Control in Four Slave Narratives', in Davis and Gates (eds), *The Slave's Narrative*, pp. 225–31. Bibb's narrative is taken as the central illustrative text for Stepto's first and most unproblematic phase in the narrative morphology of slave autobiography. Bibb's work is representative of 'Basic Narrative (a) "Eclectic Narrative" – authenticating documents and strategies (sometimes including one by the author of the tale) are *appended* to the tale' (p. 227). Stepto's analysis of Bibb consists of a paraphrase of the statements of authorial intention in the preface to the *Narrative*, and of authorial achievement as expressed in the press reviews. These statements of what Bibb says he is going to do, and what the reviewers say Bibb has done, are taken as representing what in fact conditions the narrative operations of Bibb's work. The shortcoming of this approach is that it takes highly accented critical accounts of the text for the text itself. The rhetorical shifts within the main body of Bibb's narrative, which ironise the introductory apparatus, are consequently overlooked, as are the images.

92 These reviews were included in the unpaginated review section appended to the end of the third edition of the *Narrative of Henry Bibb* (New York, 1850).

93 For Bibb's rhetoric of denial in the printed text see Marcus Wood, 'Seeing is Believing or Finding "Truth" in Slave Narrative: The Narrative of Henry Bibb as Perfect Misrepresentation', *Slavery and Abolition*, 18:3 (1997) 174–211.

94 I append below a table of the plates from Bibb's narrative, with the sources so far detected.

Narrative of Henry Bibb	Source
plate p. 19	*American Anti-Slavery Almanack* (Boston, Isaac Knapp, 1838), page for August.
plate p. 22	Source undetected.
plate p. 45, upper	*The Anti-Slavery Record* (New York, Anti-Slavery Society, 1835), 1:5, p. 5, 'Cruelties of Slavery'.
plate p. 45, lower	*The Anti-Slavery Record* (New York, Anti-Slavery Society, 1835), 1:10, p. 109. 'The Flogging of Females'.
plate p. 53	Source undetected.
plate p. 63	*The Legion of Liberty* (New York, Anti-Slavery Society, 1843), 'The First Scene of British Emancipation'.
plate p. 71	*American Anti-Slavery Almanac* (Boston, Isaac Knapp, 1839), page for September.
plate p. 81	Source undetected (this block was embossed in gold on the front cover, red morocco, of the Library Company of Philadelphia's first edition. This block may well have been made for the edition and gives a rough likeness of Bibb).
plate p. 100	*Anti-Slavery Almanac* (New York, Anti-Slavery Society, 1839), p. 29, 'Nuisances Going as Missionaries of Their Own Account'.
plate p. 104, upper	*The Anti-Slavery Record* (New York, Anti-Slavery Society, 1835), 1:3, p. 3, 'A Punishment Practised in the United States for the Crime of Loving Liberty'.
plate p. 104, lower	*The Anti-Slavery Record* (New York, Anti-Slavery Society, 1835), 1:7, p. 73, 'Scenes in the City Prison of New York. Stephen Downing'.
plate p. 111	*The Slave's Friend* (New York, Anti-Slavery Society, n.d. *c.* 1830), 1:2.
plate p. 113	*Anti-Slavery Almanac* (New York, Anti-Slavery Society, 1840), p. 7.
plate p. 115	*Anti-Slavery Almanac* (New York, Anti-Slavery Society, 1840), p. 17.
plate p. 124	*The Suppressed Book About Slavery* (New York, 1857), 'Bloodhound Business', opposite p. 289.
plate p. 129	*Suppressed Book*, 'Running Away', opposite p. 345 centre.
plate p. 133	*Suppressed Book*, 'Flogging the Negro', opposite p. 240.
plate p. 140	*American Anti-Slavery Almanack* (Boston, Isaac Knapp, 1838), page for October.
plate p. 148	Source undetected.
plate p. 201	Source undetected.

95 Bibb, *Narrative*, p. 100.
96 *New York Anti-Slavery Almanac* (New York, 1839) 29.
97 Bibb, *Narrative*, pp. 64–5.
98 See Charles D. Michael, *The Slave and his Champions* (London, S. W. Partridge, 1915), embossed front cover and frontispiece.
99 *Legion of Liberty*, unpaginated.
100 This aspect of the book is convincingly analysed in Andrews, *Free Story*, pp. 150–60.
101 Bibb, *Narrative*, p. 189.
102 Bibb, *Narrative*, p. 105.
103 *Anti-Slavery Record*, 1:3 (1835) 3; 1:7 (1835) 73.
104 Bibb, *Narrative*, p. 105.
105 Bibb, *Narrative*, p. 103.
106 For an interpretation of the influence of the nineteenth-century novel of sentiment on Bibb's narrative, including the citation of this passage, see Olney, 'I was born',

pp. 163–5. For Olney the combination of the style of the novel of sentiment with 'a realistic presentation of the facts of slavery … produces something that is neither fish nor fowl' (p. 164).

107 *The Suppressed Book About Slavery* (New York, 1857) contains a series of plates which provide the sources for illustrations in the *Narrative of Henry Bibb*. See relevant items in footnote 6.

108 For Bibb's use of prayer and biblical typology in relation to other slave narratives see Melvin Dixon's 'Singing Swords: The Literary Legacy of Slavery', in Davis and Gates (eds), *The Slave's Narrative,* pp. 298–317. For the citation of this passage see pp. 311–12.

109 For a detailed analysis of the development and cultural influence of this image see pp. 87–94 above.

110 For the attribution see Sharon F. Patton, *African American Art* (Oxford and New York, Oxford University Press, 1998), pp. 77–8.

111 For the history of stipple see Campbell Dodgson, *Prints in the Dotted Manner* (London, British Museum, 1937); Jean Adhemar, *Graphic Art of the Eighteenth Century* (London, Thames and Hudson, 1964).

112 See William Dunlap, *History of the Rise and Progress of the Arts of Design in the United States,* 3 vols (New York, 1834, reprinted Dover, 1969), 2, pp. 66–70.

113 For an account of the role of stipple in nineteenth-century American print culture see Frank Weitenkampf, *American Graphic Art* (New York, Macmillan, 1970), pp. 61–9.

114 Patton, *African American Art*, p. 77.

115 The extent to which the portrait actually reinvents Bibb as white is hard to determine. Certainly Bibb's proximity to a conventional notion of European whiteness in this image was a big point in his favour for some contemporary reviewers. The anonymous reviewer of the *Anti-Slavery Bugle* commented: 'Henry Bibb is a bright, mild looking gentlemanly sort of man, about 34 years of age, not more African than European in his lineage, and in fact, doubtless having some of the finest Kentucky blood in his veins.' Quoted in Gates and Davis (eds), *The Slave's Narrative*, p. 29. When looking at the use of stipple in Bibb's portrait it is significant that the portrait in the first edition of the *Narrative of Frederick Douglass* is executed entirely in line engraving while the face in the far more elaborate portrait to the first edition of *My Bondage My Freedom* is very finely done in stipple. For both the painting and engraving of Equiano see Honour, *Image*, 4:1, pp. 30, 387 n. 5.

116 Jacques Derrida, *Margins of Philosophy*, trans. Alan Bass (Brighton, Harvester Wheatsheaf, 1982), pp. 207–19.

117 Derrida, *Margins*, p. 209.

118 Derrida, *Margins*, p. 213.

Beyond the cover: *Uncle Tom's Cabin* and slavery as global entertainment

4

not so much a book as a state of vision (Henry James)

Slavery in the market-place: *Uncle Tom* and the leisure industries

The analysis of visual responses to Atlantic slavery must engage with the resources and limits of cultural representation. Abolition thought was constantly absorbed into nineteenth-century English and American culture, frequently in ways which now appear visually bizarre, ethically inconsistent and morally disastrous. Strange conflations resulted when the newly expanding Victorian leisure and entertainment industries engulfed abolition texts. By the middle of the nineteenth century the mass publishing industry had the power to absorb anything and to reinvent it on its own, or its audience's, terms.

Harriet Beecher Stowe's *Uncle Tom's Cabin* is the key site for the examination of what popular audiences in the mid-nineteenth century wanted to see as, and what publishers wanted to impose upon, the representation of blacks within slave systems. During the 1850s abolitionist rhetoric in England, presenting American slaves, crystallised around *Uncle Tom's Cabin*. The power and technical intricacy of the original novel was, to a remarkable degree, drowned in a visual rhetoric of colossal vulgarity, which encrusted itself onto the ineradicable structures which white supremacy and philanthropy had established for the presentation of the black. When *Uncle Tom's Cabin* appeared in 1852, the treatment of Africans and African-Americans within Western cultural forms had significantly shifted over the preceding twenty years. Scientific racism had substantially developed and had infiltrated art and literature on both sides of the Atlantic. For the first time the basic precepts of a general theory of black inferiority were being absorbed into popular culture at many levels.[1] The following discussion explores how, and why, Stowe's book was so strangely transformed within visual representation. The visual legacy of *Uncle Tom's Cabin* and its adaptations provide a cultural index of how England and America desired to remember slavery and black people, and of how the languages of racism had altered in the period 1830–50.[2]

The absorption of *Uncle Tom's Cabin* into the exploding print environment of Victorian England is a complicated affair. It is probably impossible to clarify what the appeal of the novel was to different levels of society and what the interfaces were between different levels of reaction. England already had well-established traditions for representing blacks. Seventeenth- and eighteenth-century representational codes fed into abolition propaganda, which in its turn became increasingly conflated with propaganda concerning the operations of the missions amongst blacks in both the Caribbean and in Africa. Abolition itself had, since the 1780s, frequently taken an ambivalent position in terms of its utilisation of the languages and theory of scientific racism. The huge success of Stowe's novel within the British Isles can partly be explained by looking at the ways it contributed to, and interacted with, these traditions. When considering the cultural absorption of *Uncle Tom's Cabin* it must be remembered that the period 1780–1865 witnessed not only the occurrence of European and American abolition but the development of, and by the 1860s mass belief in, scientific racism.[3] It should also not be forgotten that England had very constrained and prescriptive notions of what was and what was not appropriate black behaviour, and Stowe's novel, particularly in its consistent emphasis on the policing role of Christianity, enforced these.[4]

Outside the 'educated' responses to blacks evolved by abolitionists and missionary philanthropists, there was a range of popular responses which involved the stereotyping of black sexuality, morality, history and character traits. The various simplified and bowdlerised treatments of Stowe's novel and its characters often disappeared into these sinister simplifications.[5] The novel would have been known to large parts of the population in the form of a play, or an illustrated song sheet, popular ballad or even a ceramic statuette. Yet while Uncle Tom appeared in several guises in the popular entertainment market, it is difficult to say whether Tom infiltrated the public sphere or whether it irresistibly consumed him. When *Uncle Tom's Cabin* was absorbed into popular ballads the novel moved in a print environment which had already appropriated blacks, a white version of black dialect, and black history, in a variety of ways which work bafflingly against each other. One of the indications of the genuinely popular interest in the abolitionist cause lies in the survival of illustrated ballads, printed in the cheapest possible manner, which concerned the miseries and evils of slavery. For a music hall audience in the mid-nineteenth century blackness was almost inevitably associated with slavery, and the imaging of black people was involved in a cultural backlash against previous decades of abolition propaganda.[6] Yet such popular ballads coexisted alongside ballads very much in the 'jump Jim Crow' tradition. Here blacks, familiar as street entertainers since the late eighteenth century, and then re-invented by white actors in black-face in the mid-nineteenth century, are depicted as unfeeling, comic, high-energy buffoons talking a pidgin' dialect of its essence hilarious, especially when applied to the expression of the 'finer emotions'.[7]

Uncle Tom's Cabin was first published in weekly serial form in *The National Era* from June 1851 to April 1852. Harriet Beecher Stowe made up, as she went along, a story which she and the editor had originally envisaged as running for fourteen weekly instalments. Within nine months of its publication in single volume form the book was so successful, on both sides of the Atlantic, that Charles Briggs wrote an article for *Putnam's Monthly* in January 1853 devoted to explaining a new phenomenon. Briggs saw immediately that *Uncle Tom's Cabin* was not just a successful book.[8]

Briggs's critique is far-reaching in terms of the way it grasps the economic and political impact of *Uncle Tom's Cabin* in England and America. Briggs stated that the book's success not only reflected, but was made possible by, advances in printing technology and reading markets which were, quite simply, unprecedented. He considered the book not as a single text but analysed the entire 'Tomist' phenomenon. 'Uncle Tomitudes', the myriad popular inventions developed out of the book, are put forward as an uncontrollable colonising force.[9] But for Briggs, *Uncle Tom's Cabin* does not autonomously generate its success; rather it is an indicator of developments in printing, advertising, communications technology and the expectations of reading publics. He raises the notion of instantaneous world domination by a single text, with technology, in the form of the telegraph, enabling a kind of textual imperialism. Success is measured in terms of bulk: 'The publishers have kept four steam presses running night and day, Sundays only excepted, and at double the ordinary speed ... they keep two hundred hands constantly employed in binding Uncle Tom, and he has consumed five thousand reams of white paper, weighing seventy-five tons.'[10] The prose possesses a strange racially charged tension. Despite the efforts of two hundred pairs of hands to bind him, Uncle Tom, the furiously hungry black personification, eats 'reams of white paper'. Elsewhere Briggs goes further with metaphors of destructive voraciousness, metamorphosing Uncle Tom into a disease, racing indiscriminately through the world's population:

> One of our newspaper critics compares the Uncle Tomific, which the reading world is now suffering from, to the yellow fever, which does not strike us as a very apt comparison, because the yellow fever is confined wholly to tropical climes, while Uncle Tom, like the cholera, knows no distinction of climate or race. He is bound to go; and future generations of the Terra-del-Fuegans and Esquimaux will be making Christmas presents at this season of the year, of *Uncle Tom's Cabin* in holiday bindings.[11]

Uncle Tom bursts out of the containing geographically determined pathology of tropical disease metaphor – the yellow fever is a disease of slave societies in Africa, South America and the Caribbean. Uncle Tom is more sinister and invades the domestic geography of Western urban centres in the form of a cholera epidemic. Briggs's concern with the book not simply as printed text, but as a catalyst for technology, focuses attention on a difficult question. Because of the scale and rapidity of the book's success, and the variety of forms and materials in which it was produced, it is very hard to define where the text of *Uncle Tom's Cabin* begins and ends.

Uncle Tom's Cabin is a title which covers all the different printed forms and merchandising spin-offs which mushroomed around it. It was such 'translations' which were responsible for the dissemination and mythologisation of key scenes and characters to a mass audience, firstly in the States, then in England, and by 1853 all over Europe.[12] The Tomist phenomenon is a central archive for late Victorian popular fantasies of slave culture, and as such one of the central depositories of the West's blind memory.

During the second half of the nineteenth century the text had proliferated throughout Europe and the Americas in printed forms which included serials, illustrated editions and children's books. In Brazil, at the height of the final drive for abolition in São Paulo in the late 1880s, the peculiar abolitionist guerrilla leader Antonio Bento still considered *Uncle Tom's Cabin* so central an abolitionist didactic text that he serialised it on the front page of *A Redemção*, the broadsheet which was the organ of his mystical abolitionist sect the Caiphases.[13] At the same period in Europe and America Stowe's book had become so well assimilated into the mainstream of sentimental children's fiction that editions of Anna Sewell's *Black Beauty*, sponsored by the humane societies, bore the title *Black Beauty: His Grooms and Companions; the 'Uncle Tom's Cabin' of the Horse*.[14] Such a comparison of cruelty to animals and cruelty to slaves revived a standard association to be found in English abolitionist children's texts of the late eighteenth and early nineteenth centuries, and would not necessarily have carried the same tastelessness that it now does.[15] The fragmentations and adaptations of the text in England were even more diverse than in the States. There was abolition stationery with envelopes featuring illustrative cycles composed of all the most popular scenes; there were *Uncle Tom's Cabin* jigsaw puzzles and even board and card games in which players represented characters from the novel and had to decide how to act at key moments in the plot. In one of these games, *Justice*, the characters have been reduced to five 'players' bearing the titles 'Tom', 'Little Eva', 'Legree', 'Massa George' and 'Topsy' [**4.1**]. It is significant that there are no mature white or black women who survive from Stowe's original into the final cast list. We are left with three melodramatic white roles (two aristocratic whites, one a child, one an adolescent, and a mature white male villain innocent of irony) and two black stereotypes, Tom and Topsy, both of whom receive their moral validation through their projected and abject devotion to Little Eva. The 'winner' of the game was inevitably the player holding Eva, Tom and Justice. By 1853 the marketing of Tom had run out of control. There was Uncle Tom wall paper, repeating the most notorious scenes in an endless decorative cycle. A London store sold 'Uncle Tom's pure unadulterated coffee', another 'Uncle Tom's

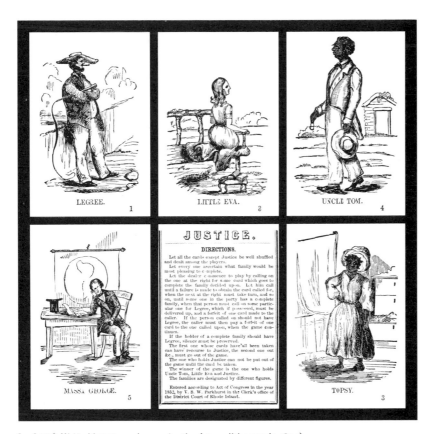

[4.1] V. S. W. Parkhurst, card game *Justice* (stone lithograph, 1852)

Shrinkable Woollen Stockings'. Tom's appeal was not restricted to new items – there was even a clothes shop advertising 'Uncle Tom's New and Second Hand Clothing'.[16]

From 1852 until the present day *Uncle Tom's Cabin* has remained a children's classic, adapting to changing racial and moral emphases and to different styles of illustration. The book led to sermons, liturgical arrangements in church services, endless poetic developments of the novel, which habitually reunited Tom and Eva in Heaven. There was an equally large variety of parlour songs which similarly concentrated on Eva's relationship with Tom. In the late nineteenth century Tom plays were a national institution in the States and the standard stage adaptations of Aiken and Lemon were still commonly performed in England.[17]

Uncle Tom's Cabin had very rapidly become international property to an extent which takes it beyond conventional notions of authorship and form. Henry James, musing upon the compulsive effects which *Uncle Tom's Cabin* exerted upon him as a child (he was nine when it first appeared), emphasises the suspended status of the work. He cast around for the right terms in which to encompass it. In its dramatic manifestations it was 'a fish, a wonderful leaping fish' that 'had simply flown through the air'. But James finally presents *Uncle Tom's Cabin* as outside any single metaphor, almost as a cultural hallucination: 'There was for that triumphant work no classified condition'; it 'had above all the extraordinary fortune of finding itself, for an immense number of people, much less a book than a state of vision'.[18] The phrasing 'less a book than a state of vision' is precise and important. This notion of a popular visionary quality superseding or engulfing the text, constantly reinventing it, is central to its cultural adoption. But the vision is a dangerous one.

Rossetti's Tom-foolery

The visual representation of slavery can take many forms beyond the canvas or the page. Dante Gabriel Rossetti's relationship with *Uncle Tom's Cabin* generated a number of visions, each of which sucks Stowe's text into a pathological parodic environment. Take, for example, the following account of Rossetti at a boxing match in London in the 1860s:

> we took our places among a lot of sporting 'bungs', *en evidence* of about as low an audience as could be found even in London. Rossetti reclined on his chair and hummed to himself in his usual absent manner as he looked at the roughs around him ... Presently there stepped forward a negro. After his round he sat in his corner and was attended to by his friends, who fanned and otherwise refreshed him. While he was being fanned the 'nigger' assumed a seraphic expression which was most comic. 'Look,' cried Rossetti in a loud voice, 'Uncle Tom aspiring to heaven, by Jove!' The whole house 'rose' with delight. One of the 'patrons' seated by us wanted to stand us a pint apiece.[19]

This is 'catch 22' racism. The qualities which white society legitimates for blacks within the context of pugilism – physical prowess, suffering and heroism – are instantaneously subsumed into white neurotic laughter via the catalyst of a reference to a farcical Tomist stereotype. Rossetti's opportunistic joke pulls the rug out from under everybody's feet. The enabling mechanism lies within the fictive martyrdom of Uncle Tom at the conclusion of Stowe's novel, and the travestying of that martyrdom in the stage versions of the novel. Tom, singing and smiling, rising to Eva's arms, is a disempowering fantasy, the preposterous sentimentality of which has become, as Rossetti cynically realised, the stuff of pantomime. The final scene of Aiken's stage version of *Uncle Tom's Cabin*, one of the most popular of the English stage adaptations, consisted of no dialogue but simply a visual tableau: 'Gorgeous clouds, tinted with sunlight. Eva robed in white is discovered on the back of a milk white dove, with expanded wings, as if just soaring upward. Her hands are extended in benediction over St. Clare and Uncle Tom who are kneeling and gazing up to her. *Expressive Music. Slow Curtain.* THE END.'[20] For Rossetti this travesty was not the end but the beginning.

Tom, utterly passive, on his knees, gazing Eva-wards, exists in strange relation to a powerful black athlete, demonstrating strength, skill and aggression on terms of complete equality, if not superiority, to whites, in London's underworld. The instantaneous applause for Rossetti's joke by an assembled crowd, emphasised as consisting of the lowest whites around, suggests that by 1857 Uncle Tom had, as a folkloric presence, been subsumed into a general currency of racist humour which is cut adrift from Stowe's novel. Or is it?

Rossetti's intensely visual relationship with *Uncle Tom's Cabin* exhibited an almost obsessive desire to reinvent it as a series of grotesque fantasies. He produced a snide attack on the book in the form of a parody of a popular black-face minstrel song:

> Dere was an old nigger, and him name was Uncle Tom,
> And him tale was rather slow;
> Me try to read the whole but me only read some,
> Because me found it no go.
> Den hang up de auther Mrs Stowe,
> And kick de volume wid your toe –
> And dere's no more public for poor Uncle Tom,
> He am gone where de trunk lining go.
>
> Him tale dribbles on and on widout a break,
> Til you hab no eyes for to see;
> When I reached Chapter 4 I had got a headache,
> So I had to let chapter 4 be.
> Den Hang up, etc.
>
> De demand one fine morning for Uncle Tom died,
> De tears down Mrs. Stowe's face ran like rain;
> For she knew berry well, now dey'd laid him on de shelf,
> Dat she'd neber get a publisher again.
> Den hang up, etc.[21]

Stowe's book is travestied on the grounds that it is boring, badly told and written for profit. The basis of the joke is that Rossetti poses as a black man trying to read a book written about a black man. Stowe's version of black American dialect is superscribed by Rossetti's version, and Rossetti's version is encrusted onto Uncle Tom from the music hall. The popular black-face ballad 'Old Ned', which begins, 'Dere was an old nigger, and him name was Uncle Ned / And him died long long ago …', provides the linguistic model, not Stowe's writing.[22] Perhaps the most sinister aspect of Rossetti's squib lies in the way he presents a parody of a black man, parodying Rossetti's own experience of reading the novel and finding it worthless. The crazy cynicism of such a position is magnified when one remembers that Rossetti probably never read the book at all.[23] The final irony is that this simply doesn't matter, for Rossetti, as for an enormous public market, *Uncle Tom's Cabin* is not a book, but a convenient iconic storehouse.

The basis of Rossctti's racism is a feigned carelessness about colour. His brother describes his views on blacks as founded in a terrible flippancy: 'My brother had no very settled ideas about negroes, their rights and wrongs: he knew, and was much tickled by, Carlyle's "Occasional Discourse on the Nigger Question".'[24] Of course this tells us that Rossetti did indeed have very precise ideas about black people, their rights and wrongs. Educated society in mid-nineteenth-century Britain and the Northern States of America was outraged and disgusted by Carlyle's scandalous assault on the effects of black emancipation in the English sugar colonies. The Southern states were delighted by a text which seemed to legitimate the continuation of slavery as a necessary and benevolent patriarchy.[25] Rossetti doesn't much care either way – he is 'tickled' – because black people are visible only when they are funny or aesthetically useful. Rossetti did, for example, paint a sensitive portrait of an androgenous black child in his 1866 oil *The Bride*. Yet the decision to include the black related purely to issues of colouristic balance. The child was designed to set off the pure whiteness of Rossetti's sensual female models. Rossetti explained his decision with the exclamation: 'I mean the colour of my picture to be like jewels and the *jet* would be invaluable'.[26] A hint into the flesh and blood callousness of Rossetti's approach emerges in his brother's account of the fortuitous effects of misery on the black child model: 'whilst sitting the tears would run down his cheeks: the skin as if it absorbed them as blotting paper, would look darker'. If the '*jet* is invaluable' what value have the tears that polish it?[27]

Rossetti's blindness to his own colour blindness took some strange turns. For Rossetti the characters from *Uncle Tom's Cabin* which were absorbed into theatrical low comedy could be readapted within the context of his own clowning and buffoonery with his young Pre-Raphaelite disciples. Rossetti envisioned the notoriously tousled William Morris as Topsy, a sobriquet which once invented was rapidly adopted as a group nickname when the second generation of Pre-Raphaelites, under Rossetti's leadership, painted the roof of the Oxford University Student's Union.[28] Morris's pursuit of Jane Lipscombe, later to be Janey Morris, was ridiculed in doggerel which equates Morris's visual clumsiness with Topsy's illiteracy: 'Poor Topsy has gone / To make a sketch of Miss Lipscombe, / But he can't draw the head / And don't know where the hips come.'[29] All good fun no doubt, but the substitutions involved are not harmless – Morris, real, rich, white, free, amorous and male, becomes Topsy, fictional, destitute, black, enslaved, unsexual and female. *Uncle Tom's Cabin* was indeed a state of vision for Rossetti, but a diseased one, and the disease was endemic.

The pictorial interpretation of *Uncle Tom's Cabin* in book form provides a further context in which to confront the ways in which difficult aspects of Stowe's book were subsumed into extant visual paradigms for the perception of blacks in America and England. To move beyond the covers of the printed book, and into that area of general adaptation which fascinated Henry James, is to approach a mysterious point at which entire cultures obliterated Stowe's work through the sheer force of collective fantasy.

Graphic conditioning: George Cruikshank, *Uncle Tom's Cabin* and the limits of racism

When Stowe's novel caused a sensation in England in 1852 George Cruikshank was the most famous graphic artist in the Western world. The publishing entrepreneur John Cassell secured Cruikshank as the artist who would spearhead the publicity campaign surrounding his pirated editions of the book. Cassell's choice of artist, and the work which resulted, can be used to uncover a good deal about why and how the book was acquired by the popular English imagination.[30]

Uncle Tom's Cabin appeared at a defining moment in the expansion of European visual culture. The period 1830–60 saw the mass development of cheap illustrated journalism.[31] The various forms of pictorial illustration, from cheapest wood-engraving to the most elaborate colour printing, grew emphatically. The visual semiotics of the press rapidly developed. In certain areas people began to read through pictures, and to expect pictures to tell them how to read.[32] *Uncle Tom's Cabin* provides a central illustration of the remarkable variety of forms in which text could be produced as pictures in England by the middle of the nineteenth century.[33]

Cassell is a good place to start when considering the English marketing of *Uncle Tom's Cabin*. He was notably inventive and fed Stowe's work into the most fashionable illustrated book markets. His employment of Cruikshank as an illustrator highlights problematic areas within the English assimilation of the book. A limited number of scenes from the novel were singled out for mass exploitation in ways that had consistent tendencies. Cruikshank's illustrated edition was one of the most popular and long-lived. His twenty-seven whole-page designs, reproduced as wood-engravings, concentrated upon the scenes which were to provide the basic matrix for the majority of subsequent illustrated editions: Little Harry doing comic impressions before Mr Shelby and the slave-trader Haley; Eliza's escape with her child; George's sister, topless, whipped for refusing her master's advances; a slave mother leaping to her death with her child in her arms over the side of a paddle steamer; Eva converting the little black Topsy while her father and aunt watch through a window; Topsy capering in a turban before Miss Ophelia's mirror; the death of Eva; the hunting down of Scipio with slave dogs; Uncle Tom decorated by Eva with a wreath of flowers; Tom sweating over his Bible; the shooting and subsequent fall down a precipice of Tom Loker; the auction of Tom and Emmeline; Tom's flogging, vision of Christ, and death by torture; and finally George Shelby liberating his slaves.

These scenes determine a set of visual priorities for the book that define its popular essence, and which are founded in sentimental humour, violence and sex. They substantiate its orthodoxies at the expense of its more revolutionary and indigestible elements. The characters are reduced to racial types and the action to a set of tableaux. The characters in the book who actively seek their freedom are an octoroon male, George, who is so white he has to blacken his skin at one point to pass for a Spaniard, and a quadroon woman, Eliza, who is also, for the purposes of illustration, chalk white. Mid-nineteenth-century commercial wood-engraving leaves little room for subtle distinctions in the representation of degrees of skin tone, and George, Eliza and Harry consequently appeared in illustrated editions, prints and ceramics as an ideal white family.

Cassell reprinted *Uncle Tom's Cabin* repeatedly over forty years, while several other editions copied and lifted Cruikshank's designs. Yet in terms of his ideological sympathies, and his graphic abilities to draw blacks, Cruikshank was a significant choice of artist. While his name guaranteed book sales, his graphic pedigree now appears ambiguous in terms of the way it qualified him as illustrator for the foremost abolitionist text of the nineteenth century. Cruikshank's graphic representations of blacks in *Uncle Tom's Cabin*, and their appeal for an English Victorian readership, are only partially understood outside the context of Cruikshank's overall career. He drew black people for over sixty years, and his first depictions grew out of the graphic environment and traditions of English Regency satire, in which he matured.[34] His illustrations for Stowe's novel when viewed as the logical culmination of this experience emerge as problematic. It is argued here that Cruikshank's appeal to a popular market as an interpreter of Stowe's black characters largely resulted from his skill in importing long-established graphic formulae into the conventions of sentimental fiction. The hybrid resulting from Cruikshank's fusion of these traditions was irresistible to English and American audiences, but the appeal was not innocent. In the following discussion Cruikshank is used as the central focus for an analysis of the shifting semiotics of black representation within the graphic print market during the most dynamic period of English debates over slavery.

Blacks in post-Hogarthian English print satire: Cruikshank's apprenticeship

The prints which Cruikshank made before 1830, connected with slavery and depicting blacks, relate to a series of contexts for the European representation of race and slavery which emerged during the second half of the eighteenth century and which both diversified and intensified during the Revolutionary period. The years 1780–1832 saw not only the rise and fall of British print satire, but coincided with the birth and subsequent development of the mass movements for abolition of the slave trade and subsequently abolition of slavery within the British Caribbean colonies. The prints dealing with blacks during this period could draw on the inheritance of pro- and anti-slavery propaganda. The work was also inflected heavily by political developments, primarily in France, but also in French San Domingo, from 1792 until black independence was finally achieved. The energy and variety with which blacks are represented in social and political prints during this period also reflect the considerable black populations in London, Liverpool and Bristol. For the first time English graphic artists were looking at and drawing blacks as social familiars.[35]

It can consequently be argued that the work of Cruikshank, James Gillray, Thomas Rowlandson and Richard Newton, who constitute the most powerful of the print satirists working from 1790 to 1815, is iconographically, stylistically and aesthetically uniquely rich in its portrayal of blacks and slavery. Looking at the work of these artists, Regency print satire might be seen to stand apart from Hogarthian and Victorian graphic treatments of blacks in its anxiety, energy and complexity. This is not to deny that the majority of Regency prints are deeply troubling to a late-twentieth-century Western audience in their parading of racial and sexual codifications which denigrate blacks. Yet these prints do operate in a social culture and a print culture which are profoundly engaged with representational codes surrounding blacks and slavery in ways which previous and succeeding print cultures do not seem to have been.

Blacks were certainly present in print satire during the Hogarthian period, but as the work of David Dabydeen and Hugh Honour reveals, blacks emerge as fairly rigidly codified in the high and low art of the first half of the eighteenth century. In popular prints they occupy the positions of servants, or exist within the murky areas of London lowlife, cropping up as itinerant labourers, whether street vendors, crossing sweepers, prostitutes, or within popular entertainment, most commonly as singers, dancers and boxers. The late eighteenth century did see certain exceptional black figures become the subject of formal academic portraiture by leading artists. The black man of letters and artistic socialite Ignatius Sancho was painted by Sir Joshua Reynolds, and Olaudah Equiano also had his portrait painted in an exquisite miniature oil, which then formed the basis for the multiple engraved portraits in the different editions of his *Interesting Narrative*. Yet such dignified and empowering images of black men are exceptional when viewed within the overall perspective of eighteenth-century portraiture. In society portraits by the most fashionable artists from the 1670s to the 1780s, from Lely through Hogarth to Reynolds, blacks were commonly included not as the central character, but as an exotic element, frequently in parallel with fine bred domestic animals. Blacks constituted a status symbol, a pet for the glamorous and youthful aristocrat at the picture's centre, and there was keen competition to gain the blackest black, in order to set off the whiteness of the aristocratic complexion. Like domestic pets, black children's primary attractions were seen to lie in their beauty, their biddableness and their entertainment potential. In fact so commonplace was the eighteenth-century iconography presenting blacks as toys that it served as the basis for abolitionist visual satire on both sides of the Atlantic until well into the nineteenth century. The print *Little Scipio: a favourite plaything in the family of Égalité, Duke of Orleans*, attacking the decadent aristocratic treatment of a black child 'favourite', was reproduced in a variety of English and American publications [4.2]. For the English this image had the added bonus of an anti-Gallic frisson, its sexual undercurrent justified by its geographical setting. As the eighteenth century progressed black iconography became increasingly sexualised, and blacks were introduced both in high and low art to signify overt and frequently socially compromised sexual unions.[36]

George Cruikshank consequently entered a graphic world well used to presenting blacks. He was born in 1792, the year racial tensions finally exploded into mass violence in San Domingo, and throughout his career he produced prints upholding European stereotypes concerning the physical and intellectual make-up of blacks. But his work produced up until the mid-nineteenth century encapsulates not so much conscious hypocrisy, as the confusion, and paradoxically the subsequent creative richness, of English visual responses to slavery. Cruikshank worked in his father Isaac's print workshop and was producing signed work for him by the age of seven. Isaac was an accomplished print satirist working in London at the time when Thomas Rowlandson and James Gillray dominated the field. Given the topicality of slavery during the great slave-trade abolition debates of the 1780s and 1790s, and the large black populations in major English ports, particularly London, it is not surprising to see virtually every significant print satirist taking up the abolition debate and representing blacks in a number of other contexts in social and political satires. This work provides many insights into the extent to which the representation of the black body had become a site of cultural contestation.

[4.2] Anon., 'Little Scipio: a favourite plaything' (wood-engraving, 1834). From *The Oasis*

Little Scipio: a favorite plaything in the family of Egalite, Duke of Orleans.   Page 139.

James Gillray's approach to the depiction of blacks anticipates the complexity of Cruikshank, in that while he does repeat many stereotypes his prints can be paradoxical and anarchic. In *Anti-sacharites or John Bull and his brother leaving off the Use of Sugar*, he ridiculed the royal family for their adoption of a no sugar stance during the period when the abolitionists recommended total abstention from slave produce.[37] The theme is used to satirise the notorious meanness of the King, suggesting that his motives for avoiding sugar might have more to do

[4.3] James Gillray, *Barbarities in the West Indies* (hand-coloured etching, 1791)

with domestic economy than abolition. The engagement with abolition ideology, let alone the suffering of black slaves on the plantations, appears ephemeral.

Yet Gillray did produce atrocity prints attacking slavery. The 1791 *Barbarities in the West Indies* appears, on the face of it, to be an assault on the West Indian plantocracy [4.3].[38] Gillray performs a fantasy of dismemberment upon the slave – fragments of black bodies are pinned to the back wall, while the overseer boils over with vindictive fury which he expresses not only in his outrageous actions but in a depraved monologue which is not to be found in the parliamentary evidence reporting the case: 'B—t your black Eyes! what you can't work because you're not well? – but I'll give you a warm bath to cure your Ague, & a Curry-combing afterwards to put spunk into you.' The nailed up body parts in the top right-hand corner are hyperbolic, and, it has been argued by Ronald Paulson, may parody abolitionist claims.[39] A more sinister reading would go further and see Gillray, through an apparent abolition sympathy, enacting a fantasy of execution and dismemberment upon an anonymous set of black bodies, a fantasy in which the viewer is invited to participate. Racial ambiguities saturate other Gillray prints. The 1796 *Philanthropic Consolations on the Loss of the Slave Bill* is an attack on William Wilberforce in the wake of yet another recent defeat of the bill for the abolition of the slave trade [4.4].[40] Gillray here turned upon the

155

[4.4] James Gillray, *Philanthropic Consolations on the Loss of the Slave Bill* (hand-coloured etching, 1796)

perceived leader of English abolition, attacking Wilberforce both as an abolitionist and as a supporter of Pitt's repressive administration. Gillray's lack of
sympathy for Wilberforce was mirrored in the attitudes of most radicals who
were convinced that Wilberforce's close friend, the Prime Minister Pitt the
Younger, was using abolition as a smoke-screen to direct attention away from
the miseries of the white labouring classes in England.[41] But contemporary
politics aside, the humour of this print is more primitive and attempts to
exploit British horror at, and consequent comic dismissal of, miscegenation.
Wilberforce and the Bishop of Westminster frolic with two black women.
They are flanked by the signs of sexual decadence: on the left a black page
boy, on the right a volume of pornography *Rochester's Jests*, alluding to the
sexual escapades of the notorious restoration rake and erotic poet John
Wilmot, Earl of Rochester. The bathetic elements underlying Gillray's fascination with interracial sexuality are stripped down to their lowest common
denominators in *Cymon and Iphigenia*, this time focusing on a relationship
between a black woman and a lower class white man [**4.5**]. This basic scenario, an imbecilic white man confronted by an engulfing black female sexual
presence, is repeated in many contemporary prints including work by
Rowlandson and Richard Newton. In *A Nice Bit* Newton took the scene
inside the bedroom but the crude humour repeats Gillray's model, and

prints which rely on exactly the same formula pepper Rowlandson's social satires.[42]

While Rowlandson never developed an intellectual engagement with black subject matter, many of Newton's prints reveal his approach to blacks and abolition to have been no less complicated than Gillray's. Newton, who died when only twenty-one and who had made significant print satires before he was ten, produced his first print on slavery in 1788, when he was eleven. *The Slave Trade* was an opportunistic attack on the sudden vogue for abolition, and the print suggests that the mass support for slave trade abolition was a political manoeuvre on the part of Pitt and Dundas to gain the approval

[4.5] James Gillray, *Cymon and Iphigenia* (hand-coloured etching, 1796)

of King George III [4.6]. The King is encircled by sycophantic politicians: the most excessive obsequiousness comes from Pitt, who prostrates himself and kisses George's foot, and Dundas in the foreground, dressed in a kilt, who kisses the King's arse. The only figure with a white face is George, while every politician has his face shaded. What this shading signifies is difficult to work out. Obviously it indicates the politician's supposed sympathy for the African slaves, but within the semantics of the political print blackness also carries association of corruption and

[4.6] Richard Newton, *The Slave Trade* (etching, 1788)

[4.7] Richard Newton, *A Real San Culotte* (hand-coloured etching, 1792)

[4.8] Richard Newton, *The Full Moon in Eclipse* (hand-coloured etching, 1797)

even, as we shall see, has a diabolic dimension. To blacken the face of one's enemy is also a graphic device of great primitive power, suggesting the erasure of the features, the graphic destruction of personality. It is significant that the shading is not uniform: Dundas has been darkened far more intensely than the other politicians, suggesting greater corruption and hypocrisy. While the shading is open in terms of its precise race significations, there can be no doubt that in Newton's world to be black is to carry a series of negative cultural associations.

Blackness itself is not straightforward in its application to the human body, which is to say that not all the black bodies are in fact African. A bank of imagery dating back to the twelfth century, that is before there had been significant European contact with African peoples, linked blackness with the devil. This basic colour symbolism is very much alive in eighteenth-century satire.[43] Newton's devils appear inevitably blackened up, and are in fact painted with an identical deep bluish grey to that used for several African and Caribbean blacks.[44] The fluid symbolic status of black as it hovers between devil and African is at the heart of *A Real San Culotte*, which uses the old graphic device of splitting a figure down the middle to reveal true identity [4.7]. Here the jolly-looking revolutionary is revealed as a black devil, with its hoof planted in post-revolutionary America. The print was made at the end of 1792 when British anxiety over reports of the slave massacres of whites in San Domingo were at their height. The devil as black barbarian and cannibal who shades into the European white is a highly charged conjunction which equates French Jacobin and San Domingan slave revolutionaries. Similar rhetorical conflations are commonplace in Burke's foaming 'Letter to a Noble Lord' and 'Letters on a Regicide Peace', and saturate the pro-slavery propaganda of the 1790s.[45]

Newton's prints which do show African bodies inevitably carry sexual meaning. The exhibition of the black female body, unclothed, as essentially comic, but ultimately threatening, is taken furthest in *The Full Moon in Eclipse* [**4.8**]. Newton's print is a development of a long-standing literary tradition relating to the construction of the black woman as a force and form capable of negating the conventional attributes of female beauty, and of putting out the sun and moon. The conceit is succinctly articulated as early as 1508 in William Dunbar's poem 'Ane Blake Moir', a stanza of which runs: 'Quhen schou is claid in reche apparrall / Schou blinkis als brycht as ane tar barrell; / Quhen schou was born the son tholit clippis, / The nycht be fain faucht in hir querrell.' This seems to be the only one of Newton's outrageously bawdy prints to retain popular circulation in the more bluntly racist print environment of Victorian Britain, where it was reproduced in an even more crudely drawn form, as a description of the steatopygous buttocks of the Hottentot Venus.[46]

Black male sexuality is not as central to Newton's prints, although it does infiltrate *The First Interview* of 1797 in a particularly horrific manner [**4.9**]. Newton's print infers sodomy between black and white males – here shockingly white royalty is abusing a black child. Prince Frederick Charles approaches the Princess Charlotte with legs spread wide and his huge belly stuck out. Bent beneath the belly and with his buttocks tightly pressed against the royal groin, the black page boy screams out, 'O lord, O lord, my neck will break, I cannot carry it any farther'. The inference that it is not

[**4.9**] Richard Newton, *The First Interview* (hand-coloured etching, 1797)

merely the Prince's belly that the boy is being forced to carry is strengthened by the bawdy monologue of the carpenter in the background who speculates 'How he will reach her God only knows, I suppose he has some German method' – the German method is clearly being demonstrated before our eyes. It is difficult to finalise Newton's race agenda here: is the black to be pitied, does he represent racially disadvantaged and abused childish innocence, the powerless fall-out from the slave trade, or is it just all good fun, and as a black is he ridiculous anyway? It is only possible to speculate on the extent to which Newton is aware of what he has done.[47]

Newton's central contribution to the abolition debate is no easier to decode in racial terms. *A Forcible Appeal for the Abolition of the Slave Trade*, of April 1792 [5.31], is perhaps the most difficult of his works to read in terms of the way it combines interracial sexuality, pornography and the rhetoric of abolition. The print purports to expose the inhuman punishment of slaves in the West India plantations in order to argue for the cessation of the slave trade, but the treatment of flagellation is erotically charged.[48] A similar ambivalence exists at the heart of the extraordinary 1792 *The Abolition of the Slave Trade* [**4.10**]. Made by Cruikshank's father, Isaac, the print carried the alternative title *The inhumanity of Dealers in Human flesh exemplified in*

[**4.10**] Isaac Cruikshank, *The Abolition of the Slave Trade* (hand-coloured etching, 1792)

The ABOLITION of the SLAVE TRADE.
Or the Inhumanity of Dealers in human flesh exemplified in Cap.t Kimbers treatment of a Young Negro Girl of 15 for her Virj. Modesty

Captain Kimber's treatment of a Young Negro Girl of 15 for her Virgin modesty, and concerns a notorious case brought before the House of Commons. In parliament Wilberforce accused Kimber of murdering a teenage slave-girl. She had refused to 'dance' on the deck of his slave ship, the common form of exercising slaves, and as a result it was claimed he flogged her to death. In the subsequent case, very inefficiently handled by the abolitionists, Kimber was in fact cleared, but the caricaturists took up and travestied the story. Isaac Cruikshank introduces sexual elements: the girl is strung upside down virtually naked before the leering captain and apparently punished for refusing Kimber's advances, an element which did not appear in any official evidence. Her agony and degradation are the stimulus merely for bawdy innuendo on the part of her torturers, one of whom, while gazing between her legs, makes an allusion to the availability of white women in the London docks: 'Jack our girlies at Wapping are never flogged for protecting their modesty.' / 'By God that's too bad if he had taken her to bed with him it would have been well enough.'[49] While the young black woman hangs mute and inverted she is flanked by grinning, fully clothed, white males. The title *Abolition of the Slave Trade* bears an ironic relationship to what is shown in the print. The viewer's sympathies are invited to be with the white men; the black girl, whose breasts and buttocks are fully exposed, is not permitted to show her face.

As material for the graphic satirist blacks are a strange combination of the familiar and unfamiliar. Part of the semiotic inheritance has represented them as alien beings, mysterious objects, of their essence funny, but the site for terrible anxieties and repressions involving white sexual confusion and guilt about the slave trade. But as well as being represented within this confused iconographic inheritance, blacks were also very much a social reality. Blacks were part of urban society; in London and the big slave ports they were visible in a variety of social contexts, still to some extent fashionable as servants, and a striking part of the London underworld of the Regency.[50] Blacks occasionally surface in social satire as empowered and subversive forces, a challenging presence within urban communities, a radical reminder of the cultural transplantation of the slave trade. For example, the anonymous *The Rabbits* published by Sayer in 1792 has a text which is charged with subversive sexual innuendo [**4.11**]. A fashionably attired busty white woman lifts a dead rabbit with spread legs to her nose and announces to the kneeling black salesman 'O la, how it smells – sure it's not fresh', to which the black responds 'Be Gar miss, dat no fair, – If Black Man take you by Leg so – you smell too'. This is bold stuff: the white woman is confronted with her own animality; the black man turns the world, or at least his interrogator, upside down, and his suggested examination implies intimacy. The print shatters the taboo on the discussion of black male / white female sexuality.

It is within the context of the labouring poor, and of the urban underworld, that black characters most commonly feature in Cruikshank's early

[4.11] Anon., *The Rabbits* (copper engraving, 1792)

[4.12] George Cruikshank, *I was barn in St. Kitts* (etching, *c.* 1805)

work. His first surviving representation of a black is the handbill *I was barn in St. Kitts* [**4.12**], showing the black giant Sam Springer carrying an advertisement for himself and accompanied by a punning verse which ironically suggests that black freedom in London boiled down to passing oneself off as a freak:

> I was barn in St. Kits an' fram slabery ran
> To Engellan, where I was free,
> Ware dey shows me about, a 'black giant' for fun:
> Now I get's my board as you see.[51]

Cruikshank, during the early part of his career, was an inveterate haunter of gin palaces, brothels, prize-fights and the various attractions of the London underworld.[52] Other etchings of his, most notably the renowned illustrations for Pierce Egan's accounts of the capers of the two Regency bucks Tom and Jerry, feature black boxers and entertainers. Cruikshank drew on direct observations to make these prints, and Sam Springer indicates how early his interest in depicting blacks had been kindled. But his habits of drawing increasingly became conditioned by generalised formulae for the description of blacks which relate to the emergence of scientific racism. Cruikshank's blacks exhibit rolling eyes, shining teeth, grimacing thick lips, protruding jaws and low foreheads. They are shown dancing, gesticulating or involved in various forms of buffoonery of the Jim Crow variety.[53]

During the second decade of the nineteenth century, when Cruikshank had taken over from Gillray, who went insane in 1811, as the foremost print satirist in London, he produced several prints which address interracial sexuality. Many are along the lines of Gillray's *Cymon and Iphigenia*, and based on the premise that the matching of black females and white European males was of its essence hilarious. In 1818 he created *Puzzled Which to Choose!! or the King of Timbuctoo Offering one of his Daughters* [**4.13**], where the blacks are provided with all the accoutrements of nineteenth-century assumptions about black phrenology and anatomy: enormous backsides and lips, low foreheads and so on.[54] The print was an early product of Cruikshank's brief collaboration with Frederick Marryat, and enjoyed a long-lasting and international success.[55] This coarse line of miscegenetic humour was central to Cruikshank's comic exploitation of popular racist attitudes. The joke is repeated a quarter of a century later in 1844 in *Probable Effects of Over Female Emigration or importing the fair sex from the Savage Islands in*

[**4.13**] George Cruikshank, *Puzzled Which to Choose!! or the King of Timbuctoo Offering one of his Daughters* (etching, 1818)

[4.14] George Cruikshank, *Probable Effects of Over Female Emigration* (etching, 1844)

Consequence of Exporting all our own to Australia [**4.14**]. Again the white male, modest and perplexed, is threatened by rapacious black women. In this print, however, Cruikshank had developed an interest in depicting various types of African headgear and facial adornment, including lip discs and nose rings.[56]

One of Cruikshank's most bizarre prints concerning black female sexuality appeared in 1819: *The Court at Brighton á la Chinese!!* [**4.15**], an elaborate development of Gillray's *The Reception of the Diplomatique and his Sweet at the Court of Pekin*.[57] In 1816 George, Prince Regent, had increasingly retreated to his private fantasy world within the Brighton Pavilion. George's oriental obsessions allow Cruikshank to convert him into a Chinese potentate, who dominates the print, yet there is a second portrait of George in the background which draws him into contemporary racist discourse. George faces away from a black woman who is a caricature of Saatje, the Hottentot Venus, whose steatopygous figure caused a sensation a decade earlier when she was paraded around London and Paris. She rapidly became a standard symbol within comparative anatomy, a branch of scientific racism which ascribed

[**4.15**] George Cruikshank, *The Court at Brighton* (etching, 1819)

over-developed and primitive sexual organs to the black woman. In this print she is shown in profile balanced against a figure of George who has similarly accentuated buttocks.[58] The joke had been exhaustively developed in 1810 when the widely predicted parliamentary coalition which was to be led by Lord Grenville had been dubbed 'The Broad Bottoms'. This had in turn caused a number of caricaturists to use Saatje as the basis for a racist visual pun. Charles Williams and William Heath produced several prints on the theme and one of them, *A Pair of Broad Bottoms* [**4.16**], provided Cruikshank with the compositional basis for his comparison in *The Court at Brighton*.[59]

The chaos of Cruikshank's response to black-white relations is most fully expressed in the furious events of *The New Union Club* of 1819 [**4.17**].[60] The print again grew out of Cruikshank's collaboration with Marryat, and took as its direct inspiration a recent anti-abolition pamphlet by the young naval captain's

[**4.16**] William Heath, *A Pair of Broad Bottoms* (etching, 1810)

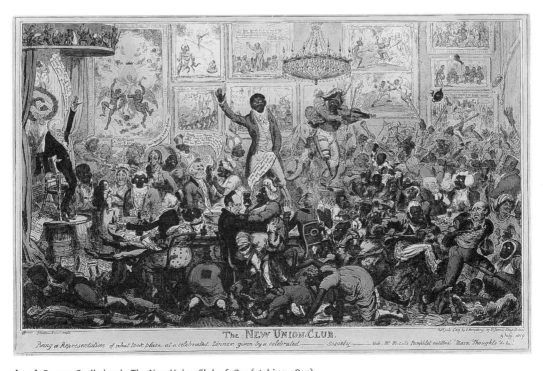

[**4.17**] George Cruikshank, *The New Union Club of 1819* (etching, 1819)

father Joseph Marryat.[61] The print supposedly caricatures a genuine incident, a meeting of the philanthropic African Institution, which was supposed to have got out of hand. This specific stimulus is drowned, however, in the intensity of Cruikshank's anti-black fantasies.[62] The white abolitionists are, with only a few exceptions (the most notable being the figure of Wilberforce, standing at the table's head and raising a glass), largely presented as victims of unbridled black hedonism. They look on bemused at the outrageous antics of the blacks. The white as victim of black violence, libidinousness and drunken sexuality is not restricted by class. Cruikshank's warning of the effects of black freedom extend to the assault of the poor mutilated sailor, kicked out of the picture bottom right, by a fit and well-dressed old black sailor. The implied argument here is one of the most familiarly repeated in anti-abolition polemic. Wilberforce and the Saints, while concentrating on the miseries of the black slave, forget the suffering of honest white English labourers.

The print illustrates virtually every stock negative assumption about the nature of blacks and the potential ills not only of miscegenation but of black and white fraternisation. Blacks are sensual, drunken, violent and vindictive. Beyond this they are obsessed with the destructive pursuit of everything that is white: white ceremonies, white sexual partners, white

[4.18] William Hogarth, *Election Entertainment* (copper engraving, 1755)

dress codes, white employment – in the end the print is a gibbering assault on the very concept of whiteness itself.

Formally the print draws on many traditions of religious painting. It constitutes both an apotheosis of black chaos and a vision of a hell for white people; it is a last judgement for abolition. The print is further complicated by the way it is embedded in a tradition of satiric prints depicting political meetings which have degenerated into orgies. The sources for Cruikshank's print underline how complicated and interracial the basic vocabularies of graphic racism can be. The tradition began with Hogarth's *Election Entertainment* of 1755 [**4.18**]. This general attack upon the corruption of English election festivities held to bribe the voters included a detail which anticipated many of the central tropes which Cruikshank was to develop. The tip of the banner, middle left, bearing the slogan 'Liberty and Loyalty', points at the head of a leering black man. With his left hand he caresses the head of a hideous gap-toothed prostitute, while she is making up to a dissolute but despondent aristocrat. With his right hand the black cunningly empties the contents of his pipe into the aristocrat's wig. Lecherous, wily, destructive and above all chasing white female flesh, he is the germ which grew into Cruikshank's print, yet not before Gillray had provided a racial bridge in the form of his *Union Club* of 1801 [**4.19**]. This print shows a drunken debauch attended

[**4.19**] James Gillray, *Union Club* (hand-coloured etching, 1801)

by Irishmen and leading supporters for the Act of Union. Gillray's assault on Irish political aspiration is highly significant as a source, and Cruikshank had complicated motives for choosing this print as the basis for his assault on black freedom. Gillray's print indicates that the graphic vocabularies of racist denigration which had been evolved around the Irish could effectively be transferred to blacks. In Cruikshank's print the traditional butt of English racism, the Irish, are substituted by blacks, blacks occupying the very bottom of an appalling semiotics of prejudice.[63] By the time Cruikshank produced the *New Union Club* it was also the case that the figure of the French Jacobin, given the history of the preceding thirty years, had superseded even the Irishman as a figure of depraved and violent low life, possessed of a physiognomy combining all the ingredients of anti-black caricature. From Gillray's incandescently violent series of etchings, *Promis'd Horrors of a French Invasion*, to Johan Zoffany's 'Invasion of the Cellars of the Louvre, 10 August 1792', engraved in mezzotint by Earlom, there was a sophisticated tradition of prints showing scenes of mass carnage engendered by intoxicated ultra-revolutionary Frenchmen. Yet Cruikshank is doing a lot more than merely turning his Jacobins black.[64]

In terms of its formal organisation the print moves quite literally from a parodic heaven, a black heaven, to an unironic black hell. At the top left of the design, just to the right of Wilberforce's raised glass [**4.20**], Cruikshank

[**4.20**] George Cruikshank, *The New Union Club of 1819*, detail (etching, 1819)

[**4.21**] James Gillray, *The Apotheosis of Hoche* (hand-coloured etching, 1798)

has created a parody of Gillray's brilliant attack on the excesses of
Revolutionary France *The Apotheosis of Hoche*. Gillray's original showed
the eponymous French general rising heavenwards, carrying a guillotine in
place of a harp, a hangman's noose replaces the aureole above his head, and
he is surrounded by a myriad of decapitated heads, with wings, the Terror
having generated thousands of parodic cerubini [**4.21**]. Cruikshank entitled his parody of the print *Apotheosis of W. W.* and replaced Hoche with the
naked figure of Wilberforce, who sits perched astride the strong arms of two
enormous grinning black and winged angels. His genitals touch the naked
black flesh – it is as if he has engendered the blacks, while they appear, quite
literally, to have caught him by the balls. As opposed to the noble feathered
wings of his angelic porters, Wilberforce is given puny insect wings. Above
and below him severed grinning black heads with thick white lips hover on
wings – the black Jacobins of the San Domingo revolution have replaced the
white Jacobin victims of the Parisian Terror.

The middle ground of *The New Union Club* [4.17] throbs with the
products of miscegenation and with abused white bodies. Just to the right
of Wilberforce's knee a black and white couple sit, holding a confused and
disconcerted looking infant who is divided vertically into a black and white
half. Behind them a Quaker and a Negress in madras turban have produced a spotted baby; the Quaker raises his hand and proclaims, 'hail
piebald pledge of love'.[65] Just to their right a Negress, portrayed in hideous
simian distortion, besmirches the face of a stern and affronted James
Stephen with black cork, and announces '*Really now Massa Teven you
right say be sham'd you own colour! You no know how amsum you bis look
black now!!*' Slipping across the print diagonally from top left to bottom
right the black assault on white becomes more extreme and literal.

In the brawl at middle right two blacks battle it out using half-caste
children as clubs. The foreground of the print shows the descent into a hell
of intoxication and bestialism. As the action becomes more gross, and the
caricature more extreme, so the graphic technique gets coarser, the callig-
raphy wilder and the lines more fiercely bitten. The critique of black personality extends to, indeed increasingly focuses upon, black women and
children. This aspect of the print separates Cruikshank's anti-black satire
from the anti-Gallic satire of Gillray's *Union Club*. While Gillray's print is
an adults-only and all-male affair, Cruikshank shows black children below
the disabled white sailor's legs battling it out for a bone with a dog. The
most charged assault on received notions of black gender roles lies in the
presentation of the two battling black women in the central foreground
[**4.22**]. Drawn and then bitten in great thick black lines, which enclose
their subjects like prison bars, two ferocious black females grapple with
the fixed and pointless intensity of Goya's 'Duel with cudgels' from the
Quinta del Sordo. Their hinged, piranha-like jaws are set open revealing
rows of sharp teeth. The prone female attempts to gauge out the eyes of her
enemy, who sits astride her raising what looks like an enormous saveloy,

[4.22] George Cruikshank, *The New Union Club of 1819*, detail (etching, 1819)

[4.23] George Cruikshank, *The New Union Club of 1819*, detail (etching, 1819)

club-like, in their right hand. The upper woman's naked breasts swing with erected nipples, and a voracious naked black infant lies flat, its thick lips fastened onto the left breast. This bizarre scene neurotically foregrounds white male anxiety concerning the physical strength and mythic mammary abundance of the black woman. Anxiety over black male domination of the white male collapses to a comparable nadir in the bottom left foreground [4.23]. An insensible Quaker lies flat out on the floor, his face drawn out into a frozen open-mouthed expression, perhaps a scream, perhaps a yawn. Above him, leaning forward, right arm extended as if in a gesture of explanation, an elaborately dressed black footman, with narrowed eyes, vomits into the white's open mouth.

What comes across most strongly is the caricaturist's profound fear of black rebellion – the shadow of San Domingo is still heavily cast. Indeed the bottom print hanging on the right side of the wall is entitled 'The King of Hayti and his Black-guards', making the association explicit. The print is, however, at an opposite extreme from the illustrations to *Uncle Tom's Cabin*, and stands outside the representational platitudes for the depiction of blacks which were increasingly to emerge in the 1830s. For all the bestiality, the blacks in *The New Union Club* are strangely empowered – it may be a diabolic empowerment, but they are to be taken very seriously. The characters Cruikshank drew thirty years later to illustrate Stowe's novel are altogether more passive, ludicrous and respectable – they have been effectively Victorianised.

To a large extent the iconographic paradigms for the passive depiction of black slaves which lie behind Cruikshank's illustrations for *Uncle Tom's Cabin* had been put in place by the abolitionists in the late eighteenth century. Perhaps the central icon was the seal of the Society for the Abolition of the Slave Trade [2.5].[66] Cruikshank used the image as the basis for a savage anti-state satire in the wake of the Peterloo massacre, the 'Peterloo Medal' [4.24].[67] Cruikshank took up the celebrated Waterloo campaign medal, the first medal distributed to all troops, and based his satiric design for a Peterloo Medal on the composition and inscription of the famous seal of the Society for the Abolition of the Slave Trade.

A soldier, with face blackened and caricatured black features, raises a dripping axe above a kneeling figure in rags. The victim asks, in the words of the slave, 'Am I not a man and a brother?', to which the black soldier replies, 'No you are a poor weaver'. While the satire might be read as an ironic commentary on the status of black slave and white industrial labourer, its racial message was more probably aggressively anti-black. It was a commonplace of radical rhetoric to attack Wilberforce and the Abolition Committee's efforts on behalf of the slave as a deliberate distraction which allowed the plight of the labouring poor in England during the crisis years after Waterloo to be ignored. Cruikshank's woodcut might be seen to conform to this argument, ironically taking up the slogan of the oppressed black and reapplying it to the poor white, while equating state

[4.24] George Cruikshank and William Hone,
Peterloo Medal (wood-engraving, 1819)

[4.25] George Cruikshank, *Plantation Scene* (wood-engraving, 1829)

military aggression with pro-black sentiment. How it was read would finally have depended upon the political sympathies of the viewer.

'Puzzled which one to choose': Cruikshank's blacks, 1830–1850

In the two decades leading up to Cruikshank's employment on *Uncle Tom's Cabin*, the graphic environment in London changed radically. The single-sheet etching died out, and graphic artists had to rely on the demand for illustrated periodicals and newspapers. Sexual and satiric codes changed as well and the extremity of Regency satire gave way to the benignity and cod moralism of Victorian periodicals. The abolition movement turned its energies outward and attempted a global assault on slavery in India, Ceylon, China and the Americas. The popular representation of blacks became increasingly prescribed within the emergent codes of popular scientific racism.[68] Cruikshank's depiction of blacks was inflected by contemporary developments. The final passage of the emancipation act in 1833 was preceded by a resurgence of popular graphic propaganda and Cruikshank contributed several lacklustre images to the campaign [**4.25**].[69] The violence and weirdness of *The New Union Club* was not repeated, but gave way to a whimsical and lazy approach to the depiction of blacks. The application of facial and gestural stereotypes takes on a pronounced generality. The following three examples from *Cruikshank's Comic Almanack* brought out from 1844 to 1853 suggest Cruikshank's slackness in depicting blacks by this stage.

The eccentric advertising campaigns of the notorious 'Black Doll' rag and bone shop inspired Cruikshank's *De Black Dollibus* of 1847 [**4.26**].[70]

This is a world turned upside down, where a white nurse tends a black rag doll, where the cooks of England worship before the idol of a black doll, and where black dolls in frilled bonnets mimic a black-face minstrel group. The text, parodying the Black Doll advertisements, makes the identification between the dolls and black Londoners explicit. Opposite this article is a full-page spread, *The Banquet of the Black Dolls* [**4.27**], in which Cruikshank's reductivist approach to the delineation of black physiognomy reaches its apogee, and closely anticipates the manner in which he was to draw Topsy.[71]

Blacks form a basic comic ingredient in *Cruikshank's Comic Almanack* and relate to the generalised racial stereotyping in mid-Victorian graphic art. The conventions for these stereotypes came out of physiognomical and phrenological representation. As we have seen, there also existed a repertoire of tricks for the depiction of the Irish as a form of low life related to apes, a tradition to which Cruikshank enthusiastically contributed.[72] Yet within such a graphic systematics Cruikshank does seem to have developed a particular style for the presentation of the American plantation slave. A plate such as the 1846 *The Country Here is Swarmin' with the Most Alarmin' Kind o Varmin* [**4.28**] shows Cruikshank, six years before working on Stowe's novel, to have a graphic repertoire for the display of the plantation 'darkey' for a mass English audience.[73] This print is accompanied by a text which opens 'It was too late. Their fearful enemy, that scourge so dreaded by the negro race of the Southern States, the terrible Land-Crab, was upon them.' Eyes are white and bulge, faces are spherical and noseless, obesity is general. At least a quarter of the plates for *Uncle Tom's Cabin* are no more than variations on this print.

Cruikshank on the 'Uncle Tom' band wagon

Cassell's employment of Cruikshank as an illustrator for his major edition of *Uncle Tom's Cabin* highlights the tensions and

[**4.26**] George Cruikshank, 'De Black Dollibus' (etching, 1847). From *The Comic Almanack*

[**4.27**] George Cruikshank, 'The Banquet of the Black Dolls' (etching, 1847). From *The Comic Almanack*

THE BANQUET OF THE BLACK DOLLS

The country here is swarmin' with the most alarmin' kind o' varmin.

[4.28] George Cruikshank, 'The Country Here is Swarmin' with the Most Alarmin' Kind o Varmin' (1846). From *The Comic Almanack*

collusions between anti-slavery sentiment and the rapidly evolving forms of Victorian racism which inflect much of the English assimilation of the book.[74] Cassell wanted a big name illustrator and in landing Cruikshank he had captured the biggest. The title page of Cassell's first edition of 1852 gives as much space to the information relating to the plates as it does to the author and title, while Cruikshank's name is blazoned in type double the size of that provided for Stowe.

Cassell used *Uncle Tom's Cabin* as a platform for a variety of publications which capitalised on the revived interest in abolition generated by the novel in order to harp upon the triumphs of British abolition, and to introduce a roll-call of the heroes of the new generation of American activists.[75] Cruikshank was put to work on a variety of projects apart from the illustrations to the main edition. He produced a large and beautifully drawn etching, presumably an advertising broadside for Cassell's edition of *Uncle Tom's Cabin* [**4.29**]. The design is formally disciplined: divided into two strict geometrical sections, a lower rectangle surmounted by a triangle, or pyramid. The pyramid is capped by the figure of Eva bearing a laurel wreath, with which she is about to crown Stowe, whose ringleted bust, enclosed in an oval frame or shield, dominates the design and stares the viewer squarely in the face. Along the diagonal to Eva's right, in supplication, stands Miss Ophelia, while beneath her is Tom, hands clasped, and below him the kneeling Chloe accompanied by a black infant. On the balancing diagonal to Eva's left is a grimacing Topsy, followed by a very white George, Eliza and Harry Harris. Again the woman and child kneel. The support for this pyramid consists of a rectangle depicting a female with a lamp, presumably representing reason, but reason in the guise of Eva. She illuminates, and dispels, typical scenes of plantation horror,

Mrs HARRIET BEECHER STOWE,
THE AUTHOR OF
"UNCLE TOM'S CABIN".

Who, by this work of fiction, founded on facts, has shown, to the world, clearly, for the

first time, & in it's true light, the hideous character of
SLAVERY.!

Designed by George Cruikshank.
Engraved by John Thompson.

Published by John Cassell
Ld Belle Sauvage Yard London

first proof George Cruikshank

[4.29] George Cruikshank, advertising broadside for Cassell's edition of *Uncle Tom's Cabin* (etching, 1852)

[**4.30**] George Cruikshank, 'Mose and Pete foil Shelby' (wood-engraving, 1852). From *Uncle Tom's Cabin* (Cassell)

inevitably featuring the flagellation of a topless female. Cruikshank was also commissioned to produce the illustrations for the remarkable *Uncle Tom's Cabin Almanac*, a spectacular hodgepodge of abolition horror stories past and present with contemporary woodcuts. Yet the centrepiece of Cruikshank's work for Cassell was the illustrations to the most expensive of his editions of *Uncle Tom's Cabin*. These consisted of twenty-seven full-page wood-engravings which Cruikshank thought about deeply and prepared meticulously. The preparatory sketches and proof states show Cruikshank working through different conceptions for the character of Eva, and trying out a number of scenes and compositions which were finally rejected. The sketches also show Cruikshank struggling with the depiction of black faces in the treatment of Tom and Topsy. His inability to decide whether Tom was to be drawn with the traditional features of an Anglo-Saxon hero or as a grinning Blackface, there being no stylistic middle ground, was never resolved.[76]

Overall the plates are a testimony to Cruikshank's inability to move beyond the narrow conventions he had lately adopted for the description of blacks. The excessive formularisation and comic basis of Cruikshank's black portraiture is amply expressed in the plate describing Mose and Pete's successful attempts to prevent the slave-catcher Haley from pursuing Eliza and her child [**4.30**]. The full-face portraits consist of a series of concentric circles. The heads are spherical, the eyes white circles with the black circles of pupils standing out within them, the mouths white rings. When drawing profiles of blacks, Cruikshank repeatedly recurred to the conventions of scientific racism and the facial angle popularised by Petrus Camper. This angle was constituted by drawing a horizontal line

through the orifice of the ear and the lower part of the nose. The angle
formed between the intersection of this and the line of facial profile, i.e.
the line cutting the mean of forehead, nose and lips, indicated intelli-
gence. Introduced in the context of purely aesthetic speculation by Petrus
Camper as a measurement for facial beauty, the theory was subsumed
into racist discourse as the standard method for measuring relative intelli-
gence in the races. The closer the angle approached to the horizontal the
more degenerate the subject.[77] Cruikshank was well acquainted with the
technical operations of this theory, and his use of extreme facial angles in
his drawings of blacks was not theoretically casual. Thirty years before
working on *Uncle Tom's Cabin*, he deployed the theory as the basis for a
satire directed against the State in William Hone's parodic newspaper *A
Slap at Slop*. The text opens: 'FEROCITY EXEMPLIFIED, by COM-
PARATIVE ANATOMY; or, an Illustration of the facial line in Man and
the Brute, showing the natural gradation from the ferocious to the human
being, with the domestic habits of the Savage' [**4.31**].[78]

Cruikshank's solutions to the problems posed for him by black portraiture took a number of directions. Firstly there was the option for several of the most important characters of transforming them
unproblematically to whites. George, Eliza, their little boy Harry, Cassy
and Emmeline, all characters described in the text as of differing shades
of lightness, are drawn throughout the illustrations as white people.
Secondly there was the option of drawing all minor black characters in
terms of comic stereotypes. Hence the majority of illustrations featuring
several black Africans show them behaving *en masse* according to behavioural types. They are most commonly either dancing, laughing,
shouting or singing in groups. Of the eleven plates which focus primarily

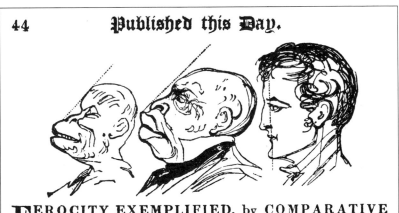

**FEROCITY EXEMPLIFIED, by COMPARATIVE
ANATOMY; or, an Illustration of the FACIAL LINE in Man
and the Brute, showing the natural gradation from the ferocious to the
human being, with the domestic habits of the Savage.**

[**4.31**] George Cruikshank, mock advertisement for *A Slap at Slop* (wood-engraving, 1821)

At midnight Tom waked with a sudden start. Something black passed quickly by him to the side of the boat, and he heard a splash in the water.

[4.32] George Cruikshank, 'Lucy's Suicide' (wood-engraving, 1852). From *Uncle Tom's Cabin* (Cassell)

on apparently full-blooded black African-Americans, five show blacks in low comic 'Jim Crow' guises.

The failure of the illustrations to *Uncle Tom's Cabin* shows Cruikshank to be strangely insensitive to Stowe's book. Cruikshank habitually possessed a protean ability to submerge himself in the essential character of a novel. The great differences in the technical approach to the illustrations to *Oliver Twist*, the first English edition of *Grimm's Fairy Tales*, and Ainsworth's *Jack Shepherd*, to take but a tiny sample, show his imaginative versatility and a capacity to move beyond melodrama and whimsy. It is, then, worth thinking in more depth about exactly how and why Cruikshank's visual interpretations of Stowe's novel fail so completely.

A test case: Lucy versus the drunkard's daughter

Given the tragic dimensions of black slave experience in Stowe's narrative, the plates in which Cruikshank was forced to go outside his caricatural experience of black representation must carry a special weight. An extended analysis of the plate showing the death of Lucy uncovers many of the shortcomings of Cruikshank's representation of slave suffering.

One of the most disturbing accounts of a personal disaster growing out of slavery in *Uncle Tom's Cabin* is the story of the slave Lucy's suicide by drowning, when she cannot bear living after the sale of her child [**4.32**]. Cruikshank chooses to show Lucy at the point when she leaps off the boat into thin air. The choice of incident relates to the great success of a print Cruikshank had made four years before. The design for Lucy's suicide is a weak reworking of the wonderful lithograph showing the end of the drunkard's daughter from Cruikshank's temperance work *The Drunkard's Children* [**4.33**].

Everything in this image works. The vertical fall of the girl is exaggerated by being set off against the parabolas of the bridge arch behind her, which sweep from top left to bottom right. The massive and calm geometry of the bridge frames a perfect quarter circle in the bottom left, and within this framed space floats the pure white circle of a full moon, across which two thin sharp clouds drift, an image of violent severance which anticipates the opening of Dali and Buñuel's *Un Chien Andalou*. The corners of this print are used magnificently. In the top right two figures strain into the composition helpless to assist, with a tiny patch of grey sky squeezed in above them. In the bottom left the glimpse of the final mast top in a row of tall ships suggests the enormous scale of the girl's drop. Her terror is expressed in the pathetic gesture of covering her eyes with a handkerchief so that she won't see the approaching impact, or the distance she must fall. The style used to describe the girl is in sharp contrast to the hard geometrical outlines of the stone bridge behind. Soft fabrics, flowing hair and ribbons, stream out; the back edge of the dress is like some fantastic sea shell, the front edge held hard by the pressure of the wind against the soft outline of her thigh and knee. Cruikshank's eye for pathetic detail was never sharper than in his rendering of the little boot on the outstretched leg, the bonnet, placed centrally, flying upwards amid more ribbons, and the pinpoint of white skin poking through the threadbare elbow of the black jacket.[79]

In the Lucy plate for *Uncle Tom's Cabin* everything has gone wrong. There is no imaginative empathy with the subject. There is far too much going on, and it is all going on at the same clumsy graphic pitch. The geometric purity of the earlier print has been replaced with narrative clutter, the superstructure of the highly unconvincing boat blocks out too much sky, and there is no sense of depth – it is impossible to tell where the water ends and the sky begins. Tom's posture and expression are ridiculous and siphon attention from the central figure; the woman's gesture of clasped

THE DRUNKARD'S CHILDREN.

[4.33] George Cruikshank, 'The poor girl, homeless, friendless, deserted and gin-mad' (stone lithograph, 1848). From *The Drunkard's Children*

hands is melodramatic. Lucy's arms, shoulders and breasts form a perfect diamond but this framing device serves only to call attention to the caricatural extremity, the travestying, of the facial expression.

Cruikshank's woodenness emerges if the print is set against the way Stowe's text moves in and out of rhetorical positions. She opens with a plain factual rendering of the disappearance of the child, and Haley's brutally frank explanation to the mother. Stowe sets an emphatic narrational account of the woman's shock on being told her child has gone against Haley's obscene practicality in attempting to find language which will calm her. The monumental inadequacy of Haley's language, Lucy's ghastly politeness in requesting she be *allowed* to grieve in peace without the grotesque emotional pollution of Haley's banalities, and Haley's final retreat into the non-communication of internal monologue have great power:

> But the woman did not scream. The shot had passed too straight and direct through the heart, for cry or tear.
>
> Dizzily she sat down. Her slack hands fell lifeless by her side. Her eyes looked straight forward, but she saw nothing. All the noise and hum of the boat, the groaning of the machinery, mingled dreamily to her bewildered ear, and the poor, dumb stricken heart had neither cry nor tear to show for its utter misery. She was quite calm ...
>
> ... 'I know this yer comes kinder hard, at first, Lucy,' said he; 'but such a smart, sensible gal as you are, won't give way to it. You see, it's *necessary*, and can't be helped!'
>
> 'O! don't, Mas'r don't!' said the woman, with a voice like one that is smothering.
>
> 'You're a smart wench, Lucy,' he persisted; 'I mean to do well by ye and get ye a smart place down river; and you'll soon get another husband, – such a likely girl as you –'
>
> 'O! Mas'r if you only won't talk to me now,' said the woman in a voice of such quick and living anguish that the trader felt that there was something at present beyond his style of operation. He gave up, and the woman turned away and buried her head in her cloak.
>
> The trader walked up and down a little while and occasionally stopped and looked at her.
>
> 'Takes it hard, rather' he soliloquised 'but quiet tho'; let her sweat a while; she'll come right, by and by!'[80]

Stowe has succeeded in describing an anguish beyond words, with words. The pain of an ultimate abuse must be endured in a state of powerlessness. Lucy cannot escape her uncomprehending torturer, she cannot express anger, all she can do is plead with him for silence in order that mourning for her loss may, at some level, begin to occur. It is the lack of privacy, even at the moment of despair, which defines the limits of property ownership within the slavery relation. Stowe is to be credited with opening up unhealed emotional wounds, inflicted by slavery, which English and American culture have only now begun the work of searching.

It is not that Cruikshank could not find images and techniques to describe the fear and trembling of the individual facing absolute misery or the fear of death. His depiction of Fagin in the condemned cell for *Oliver Twist* is an enduring testament to his ability to conjure up absolute horror. Why he failed with Lucy is finally, surely, a question of race, nationality and gender. Where Cruikshank could accomplish the task of depicting the solipsistic despair of a young white female alcoholic, unable to endure the misery of her own life, he was incapable of empathy with the despair of a black slave mother unable to endure an enforced and final separation from her child.

The gulf between an appropriate graphic response to slave mother suicide and Cruikshank's plate can be brought out by looking at an early-nineteenth-century abolition text which had provided a powerful prototype. The illustration in Jessey Torrey's 1817 *A Portraiture of Domestic Slavery in the United States* gives a stark rendition of the suicidal leap of a slave mother unable to endure separation from her children [**4.34**]. This print has great force, perhaps growing out of the way the woman's almost relaxed position, sitting suspended in space, almost uncannily anticipates the photographs of actual suicide leaps now in police files, images which Andy Warhol drew on for a number of his screen prints.[81] The figure in Sharpe's engraving is uncontaminated by extraneous elements. The clear geometry, the crude clarity of engraving style, the utter absence of any other human presence, the crispness of the single light source, somehow capturing the desolate quality of moonlight, all these elements combine to conjure up the simple desperation of the act. These qualities complement the uncluttered narrative text, where Torrey gives the woman's final words, her own testimony to trauma: 'I inquired of her, whether she was asleep, when she sprang from the window. She replied, *"No, no more than I am now."* Asking her what was the cause of her doing such a frantic act as that, she replied, *"They brought me away with two of my children, and wouldn't let me see my husband – they didn't sell my husband, and I didn't want to go; – I was so confuse and 'istracted, that I did'nt know hardly what I was about – but*

[4.34] Anon., 'Slave mother suicide' (copper engraving, 1817). From Jessey Torrey, *A Portraiture of Domestic Slavery in the United States*

I didn't want to go and I jumped out of the window; – but I am sorry now that I did it; they have carried my children off with'em to Carolina.[82] Maybe by the mid-nineteenth century neither English nor American popular journalism and graphic art could endure such hard-hitting purity. The padding and obfuscations of Victorian stylistic giganticism protected audiences from the horror of slavery.

The genealogies of Tom: degenerative transmissions in England and America

Semantic chaos in the sexual translations of 'old Prue'

Cruikshank was one of many sucked in by the vision of Uncle Tom, and the money to be made in rendering that vision. Surveying the mass of editions of *Uncle Tom's Cabin* which came out in the first eighteen months of its appearance, two things stand out: firstly their formal variety and secondly the domination of illustrated editions. The majority of big English publishers got in on the *Uncle Tom's Cabin* act while the book was cut up among the whales and minnows of professional book illustration. While the prestige plates, and particularly the title pages, often went to a big name such as Cruikshank, John Leech and Hablot K. Brown, the rest of the plates were doled out to lesser talents.

The edition of Adam and Charles Black is typical of the marketing strategies. This company commissioned Phiz to produce an ornamental and allegorical title page, while leaving the main body of illustrations in the text to the lesser known Sears. By 1853 the marketing fever led publishers to smother their covers and endpapers with Tomist advertisements. 'Clarke and Beeton's popular 1 s. Edition' demonstrates the extent to which the text was being carved up into a variety of heavily illustrated forms:

> *7s. 6d. The illustrated edn. by Mrs Harriet Beecher Stowe. with forty magnificent engravings.*
>
> *4s. Cloth Extra. 'The People's Illustrated Edition'. By Mrs. HARRIET BEECHER STOWE. Embellished with Fifty Full Page Engravings.* [and continued on the back cover] *The Cheapest Book Ever Published. In one handsomely bound 8 vo. volume containing fifty illustrations. This edition may be had in Penny Numbers. Each number contains two splendid page engravings and sixteen pages of letter press, printed in large Type. The whole may also be had complete in Twenty-five Numbers; or in six parts at sixpence each.*
>
> *1s. Ornamental Boards. UNCLE TOM'S CABIN by Mrs. HARRIET BEECHER STOWE. New Edition with twenty Characteristic Engravings.*
>
> *6d. Sewed. UNCLE TOM'S CABIN by Mrs. HARRIET BEECHER STOWE. Pocket Edn.*[83]

Clarke followed Cassell's lead in using editions of the book as a central focus for a general Tomistic merchandising campaign. Clarke offered a whole series of associated publications including a portrait of Mrs Stowe by Lynch at 5s, proofs a hefty 8s and 6d, the *Key to Uncle Tom's Cabin*, and the Reverend W. Goodall's 'Companion to the Key to *Uncle Tom's Cabin*'. Stowe's book also galvanised the market-place in terms of a revival of interest in earlier plantation novels. Richard Hildreth's remarkable 1837 plantation blockbuster and novel of adventure, *The White Slave*, underwent a renaissance.[84]

Throughout the latter half of the nineteenth and into the twentieth century the first sets of illustrations continued to be compiled and rearranged, with a peculiar tenacity. An examination of all English editions from 1852 to 1910 puts Henry Anelay, George Cruikshank, George Thomas and the American illustrator and abolitionist Hammatt Billings as firm favourites. Billings illustrated the original American edition of *Uncle Tom's Cabin* which came out in July 1852 and then a more elaborately illustrated edition which the authorised publishers brought out for the Christmas market in December 1852. It was this edition, full of small wood-engraved vignettes set into the text, which became the mainstay of popular editions in Britain, throughout the 1860s, 1870s and 1880s. Billings was first adapted in a fairly lavish edition by Sampson Low.[85]

The final testament to Billings's English success resides in the phenomenal plagiarism of his work. Billings's refusal to incorporate caricature into his depiction of blacks contrasted starkly with Cruikshank's work. The popularity of Billings's images on both sides of the Atlantic over a period of several decades indicates that audiences were open to an imagery which did not involve the illustrative reductions of Cruikshank and his imitators. Shilling editions of *Uncle Tom's Cabin* by Simpkin and Marshall produced in the mid to late 1850s carry woodcut adaptations of the Billings plates set in ovals and roundels within the text [**4.35**]. The Simpkin and Marshall editions were then in their turn plagiarised in the editions brought out by Ward Locke and Co. in the 1860s and 1870s. These retained the majority of the Billings designs. Ward Locke's editions are at the end of the adaptive food chain, and represent the most over-developed form of life, in terms of the novel's transmission into cheap illustrated book form. As such they are a very informative document in terms of what they tell us about the essence of the book's popular appeal as it was progressively passed down through the transformative processes of popular illustration. Billings's designs are now printed in crudely cut form two to a block, on single sheets, and not incorporated into the text. His comparatively documentary approach to the depiction of slave life was also powerless to protect itself against new tendencies in the publishing market. Billings's designs were frequently incorporated as one element within an illustrative jamboree which drew on racist and pornographic tendencies in contemporary illustration. The Ward Locke edition also introduces new illustrational material which relates both to the tendency of adaptations of the novel increasingly to idealise the Harris family as white and to dwell pruriently on the sexual exploitation of black slave women. Full-page colour lithographic plates featuring Eliza, George

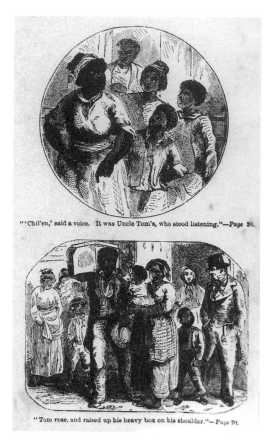

"'Chil'en,' said a voice. It was Uncle Tom's, who stood listening."—*Page* 38.

"Tom rose, and raised up his heavy box on his shoulder."—*Page* 70.

"'What now! Why those folks have whipped Prue to death.'"—*Page* 157.

[4.35] Hamatt Billings, plagiarisms, 'What's this Dinah?' and 'I had to put it away in a kind of garret, and it cried itself to death' (wood-engravings, 1867). From *Uncle Tom's Cabin* (Ward Locke and Co.)

[4.36] Anon., 'What now! Why these folks have whipped Prue to death' (wood-engraving, 1867). From *Uncle Tom's Cabin* (Ward Locke and Co.)

and Harry as an idealised Victorian white middle-class family are introduced and there is also a new whole-page wood-engraving **[4.36]**. This shows 'old Prue' being whipped to death. The cut is a powerful example of the processes of illustrational slippage by which the book could pander to the expectations of plantation pornography.

In the novel the death of Prue is one of the most disgusting and terrifying episodes. Prue is a minor character glimpsed only once in the direct action. She is a tall, bony, scarred and ancient black slave. She has suffered through watching slavery take away and destroy her children: 'in Kentuck. A man kept me to breed chil'en for market, and sold 'em as fast as they got big enough'. She had to listen to the sound of her final infant crying itself to death while she was powerless to help it. After this she became an alcoholic. As a result of her alcoholism she is whipped nearly to death then left in a cellar to be consumed alive by flies. Stowe introduces this ghastly end incidentally in the form of a short aside from the woman who has taken Prue's place delivering rusks: 'Well you mustn't tell nobody. Prue, she got drunk agin – and they had her down cellar – and tha they left her all day; and I hearn 'em saying that the *flies had got to her* – and *she's dead!*[86] The powers of the market-place have operated a remarkable transformation on this scene when it comes to be illustrated. Prue is now a very shapely, young and top-less woman whipped by a white gentleman in elegant clothing. In the fore-ground another man gazes on, clutching a pair of scissors in his right hand, with which he has just sliced off Prue's clothing; the remainder of her dress appears about to slide off her hips. A grinning crowd enjoys the spectacle, and there is the appalling inference that we are meant to join them.

Altogether this edition is a pretty dense illustrational hybrid with something for every taste, and not much fastidiousness about how closely the pictures it carries relate to the letter of Stowe's text. The book has become an illustrational playground in which the responsible and unmelo-dramatic style of Billings is melded with new, slick and sexually equivocal subject matter. Yet the development of sexual fantasy around whipping is not trivial and relates to the book's increasing absorption into European psychopathology. The extent to which the scenes in *Uncle Tom's Cabin* describing the flagellation of women and children had, by the late nine-teenth century, worked their way into the sexual fantasies of Europeans is under-researched. It is relevant, however, that the originator of the terms 'sadism' and 'masochism', Richard von Krafft-Ebbing, described how one patient attributed his first sexual arousal as a pubescent to encountering *Uncle Tom's Cabin*. Freud also revealed that several of his patients shared the common fantasy that 'a child is being beaten' and that Stowe's novel was the point of origin for this. The extent to which the text or the images were responsible for these fantasies has never been analysed.[87]

These illustrated editions tell us that the book operated on a basic level of entertainment, that its plot was gutted for the elements with the biggest emotional kick. They reveal Stowe to have constructed a book which contained all the ingredients of a Victorian best-seller: a hero and heroine who both die tragically and as good Christians, and villains of the darkest die, all of whom come to no good, or if they do survive, then, like Tom-Loker, they are converted. The book incorporated two sub-plots involving intrepid escapes and much disguise, and a lot of low comedy and buffoonery, as well as sentimental humour and outraged satire. Yet as a piece of slavery propaganda Stowe's novel appeared in a society which had been periodically saturated with different types of abolition propaganda since the first great drive to abolish the British slave trade in the 1780s. *Uncle Tom's Cabin* had the uncanny ability to tap into a whole variety of genres dealing with blacks and slavery.

The culpability of Stowe's book in the processes of its own popular transformations is an issue here. James Baldwin's furious assault on Stowe's book in terms of its encoding of a series of deeply damaging racist assump-tions has never been refuted. Baldwin emphasises the book's superstitious approach to religious fanaticism and its insistence on a conventional

Christianity as an overriding mechanism of control for the presentation of blacks. In doing so, even with the tenaciousness of despair, he foregrounds an aspect of the book to which contemporary criticism appears increasingly blind. His arguments may be framed in a confrontational rhetoric but their essence holds together.[88] Stowe's book, in its cultural and structural bones, within its very creative genes, contains assumptions about race endemic in Massachusetts in the early 1850s. *Uncle Tom's Cabin* is best approached as a cultural sample, as a culture in which the bacteria of nineteenth-century racism flourished. There will never be a clear-cut answer to the question of the extent to which Stowe's book enabled the degenerative racist common-places which infested its adapted visual forms. What is undeniable is that these forms exist, and a lot can be learned by tracing their generations. The representation of reading provides an educational site.

'Oh Uncle Tom, what funny things you are making there': imaging Tom's lessons with George and Eva

The presentation of the slave's relation to language in Stowe's book is by no means innocent. Tom's first appearance in the novel finds him at school in his own eponymous cabin, taught by a white boy:

> He was very busily intent at this moment on a slate lying before him, on which he was carefully and slowly endeavouring to accomplish a copy of some let-ters, in which operation he was overlooked by young Mas'r George, a smart bright boy of thirteen, who appeared fully to realise the dignity of his position as instructor.
>
> 'Not that way, Uncle Tom – not that way,' said he, briskly, as Uncle Tom laboriously brought up the tail of this g the wrong side out; 'that makes a a q you see.'
>
> 'La, sakes, now, does it' said Uncle Tom, looking with a respectful admiring air, as his young teacher flourishingly scrawled *q*'s and *g*'s innumer-able for his edification; and then, taking the pencil in his big, heavy fingers, he patiently recommenced.
>
> 'How easy white folks al'us does things!' said Aunt Chloe, pausing while she was greasing a griddle … [89]

The written word, which comes so easily to white people, will always be a difficult and deformed thing in Tom's ungainly hands. Literacy is, from the start, carefully conditioned. Tom's relationship to white language is infan-tile. He approaches literacy as a big simple child, but unlike a child he will never master language. He never learns to write, but even when he gains an elementary ability to read Stowe only allows him to read the Bible. Indeed Tom at his Bible with Eva, and Tom being taught to write by Eva, and Tom sweating over his Bible in his cabin on Legree's plantation, became iconic images in the cheap illustrated versions [**4.37**]. Tom does not read the Bible as Nat Turner read it, for revolutionary inspiration, nor as Nat's distant fic-tional relation, the hero of Stowe's next novel, Dred, was to memorise it in order to prophecy doom. Tom's attempts to read exist within a vista of hopelessness clearly defined by Aunt Chloe: 'How easy white folks all's does things!'[90]

Tom's autodidactic antics are in fact typical and should be seen against a backdrop of songbooks, ballads and prints which treated black attempts to gain literacy as comic. One of the earliest black dialect publications in England, *The History of Jim Crow*, contains a scene where Jim, or 'Double-smut', as he is known, is sent to a 'nigger school' where 'an old negro schoolmaster … professed to teach the free negro children Anglo-American niggerisms'. The teacher 'Septimus Yambobannum' combines the role of teacher and preacher and speaks in an absurd dialect: 'Massa Conkoo, wats you call dat farst letter, wat look for all de world like your two legs stretch't across a gutter, ah?'[91] The formal address by the ignorant black on such subjects as language, politics, fashion and religion were, by this date, part of the general repertoire of the 'nigger minstrels' and constitute a standard ingredient in the social print satires and illustrated 'Nigger Songsters' of the 1830s and 1840s. The broadside *A Black Lecture on*

"I WISH I COULD HELP YOU, TOM!"

Eva.—"O Uncle Tom! what funny things you *are* making, there!"
Tom.—"I'm trying to write to my poor old woman, Miss Eva, and my little chil'en; but, somehow, I'm feared I shan't make it out."—Page 200.

[4.37] Anon., 'Oh Uncle Tom! What funny things you *are* making there' (wood-engraving, 1852). From *Uncle Tom's Cabin* (Clarke and Co.)

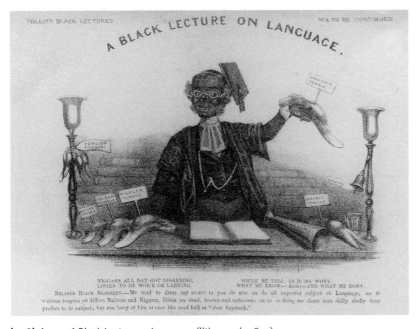

[4.38] Anon., *A Black Lecture on Language* (lithograph, 1827)

Language [**4.38**] shows the black man trying to mimic white institutional language and behaviour. Henri Louis Gates, who includes the broadside within the argument of *The Signifying Monkey*, states 'Dialect signified both "black difference" and that the figure of the black in literature existed primarily as object, not subject; and even sympathetic characterisations of the black, such as Uncle Remus, by Joel Chandler Harris, were far more related to a racist textual tradition that stemmed from minstrelsy, the plantation novel, and vaudeville than to representations of spoken language'.[92] This summary bears directly on the popular adaptation of *Uncle Tom's Cabin*, where several other factors might also be stressed: firstly the early date by which this white fiction of black idiom had been implanted in literature and the entertainment industry; secondly the fact that this was a transatlantic phenomenon; thirdly the scale and consistency of this linguistic negation of black idiom; fourthly the cruel ingenuity of a construct whereby black idiom never had to be taken seriously, because whites had their own version of black language from which the 'real thing' could not be disentangled by a white reading/viewing public; and fifthly the extent to which blacks contributed to the white perception of the black faux-idiom by performing it professionally or socially in front of white people.[93]

The key to the humour in this broadside, and in the representations of Uncle Tom learning to read, lies in the forced union of two worlds. While the conjunction of black and white worlds could be radical, frightening and frame a satire on white inadequacy, these prints demand that the union is either silly or pathetic. The black is presented as hopelessly out of his depth but simultaneously quite contented with his lot. The lithographic imagery compounds these effects.

In *A Black Lecture on Language* a black head is substituted for the 'type' of the wizened, bald, bespectacled, learned white professor. But the head that stares blankly out of the spectacles is horrifying. With a grin like that of a shrunken head, the face is wizened, gap-toothed and desiccated, as if severed from its trunk. The academic cravat forms a tight white horizontal block at the neck, as if a bandage is marking the point of severance. Swamped in academic garb, the black pretender to academic status strikes a rhetorical pose as he extends a physical version of one of the 'tongues' he discusses to the audience. With a hideous complacency this caricature meticulously observes the outward forms of a white professor's performance – the black man's mis-placement in the role is all the humour. Tom learning to read at the hands of white children became the accepted popular envisioning of the slave fighting for literacy.

Tom represents a hard-won and passive literacy within the popular manifestations of the book. The extent to which he provided a model of safe learning, a vision of the containment of learning and of scripture within a programmatics of disempowerment, comes out powerfully in one of the Southern pro-slavery adaptations of Stowe's novel. The beautifully produced little hand-coloured volume *Little Eva, the Flower of the South*

EVA, TEACHING THE ALPHABET.

Here you see, is little Eva teaching the little colored boys and girls the alphabet. See how pleased they are, for they all love Eva, and would do anything to please her ; and Eva takes a great deal of pleasure in teaching them and making them happy. She is teaching them the letters one by one, which she marks on the black-board.

There sat Tom, on a little mossy seat in the court . . . and Eva, gaily laughing, was hanging a wreath of roses round his neck.

[4.39] 'Eva Teaching the Alphabet' (wood-engraving, c. 1855). From *Little Eva the Flower of the South*

[4.40] George Cruikshank, 'There sat Tom' (wood-engraving, 1852). From *Uncle Tom's Cabin* (Cassell)

happily embraced Eva's instructional function with Tom, and developed it into scenes of mass slave education [4.39]. Eva is, after all, everything the South desired of its belles, and a positive advertisement for the benign authoritarianism and Christianity of the slave system. Eva doesn't need to impose her power on the black slave – she is an icon to be worshipped – and the slave personality delights in projecting its powerlessness upon her. The text informs us that the only motive behind the black children's desire to gain literacy lies in their desire to please Eva. Her radical position as illegal educator, breaking the prescriptions on slave literacy which were laid out in the slave codes, is subsumed into a fantasy of black naiveté. Literacy is merely liturgy among Eva's worshippers. With this sort of instructress the docility of the student was assumed and assured.

'A dainty foot and a well made satin slipper': what did the English want most – cannibals or missionaries?

The impact of *Uncle Tom's Cabin* on the popular art market was emphatic. John Ruskin singled out the prints showing Eva garlanding Tom as a crowning example of the debasement and lasciviousness of Victorian popular art, and the packaging of these qualities within a missionary disguise.

189

In *Modern Painters* he talked, with a slightly unhealthy zealousness, of 'the great change by which art became again capable of ministering delicately to the lower passions as it had in the worst days of Rome', and as a prime example of this 'subtle treachery' he pointed to 'the commonest lithograph of some utterly popular subject – for instance the teaching of Uncle Tom by Eva', and asked to what extent 'the sentiment which is supposed to be excited by the exhibition of Christianity in youth is complicated by that which depends upon Eva's having a dainty foot and a well made satin slipper'.[94]

For Ruskin the popular enthusiasm for *Uncle Tom's Cabin* was based in a vicarious and sexually charged emotionalism directed at the image of a small white girl cuddling with a big black man [**4.40**]. This scene was charming, thrilling, peculiar and sentimental, and above all completely divorced from Victorian domestic life and sexuality. Tom's de-sexualisation is paradoxically determined by the readiness with which the illustrators of the day flung him and Eva together. He had become a harmless fiction, the ideal Christian house-slave, probably the only type of black male which Victorian society could imagine in physical contact with virginal white girlhood. Indeed it has been argued that the figure of Tom operates, in relation to Eva, primarily not according to masculine but feminine characteristics, and that Tom is constructed as an ideal Victorian heroine. It is, however, finally the intrusion of Christianity, and explicitly of evangelising Christianity, in Eva's relationship with Tom which, as Ruskin points out, overwrites questions of gender and sexuality. One of the most spectacular examples to combine sentimental evangelicalism, the feminisation of Tom, and nineteenth-century sublime landscape painting is the large 1853 oil painting entitled *Uncle Tom and Little Eva* by the black American artist Robert Duncanson.[95]

The unproblematic racism endemic in the Victorian popular press by the middle of the nineteenth century was of a vast scale and crudity. While the popular codes attached to the interpretation of Africans and blackness that had developed during the seventeenth and, more significantly, eighteenth centuries, still underpinned popular culture, racist attitudes towards blacks changed dramatically in the three decades following the emancipation act of 1833. In the 1850s general assumptions of black inferiority led *Punch* and the popular comic journals to promulgate an unproblematic devolved neo-Knoxianism in the specific comparison of blacks with the lower primates.[96] At exactly the time when *Uncle Tom's Cabin* appeared, Thackeray, observing American blacks, indignantly refuted the famous abolition aphorism 'Am I not a man and a brother' with Victorian solid good sense: 'they are not my men and brethren, these strange people with retreating foreheads and great obtruding lips and foreheads … Sambo is not my man and brother'.[97] Popular assumptions still included the notion that blacks were cannibalistic by instinct. The seediest of the Victorian sex-crime journals, *The Illustrated Police News*, reported a case concerning a black woman from Kingston, Jamaica, who had 'killed and eaten no fewer than twenty six children' [**4.41**]. The article continues: 'is Obeahism dead in Jamaica? … a careful search through the parliamentary blue books would reveal many extraordinary cases in which evidence was given of the monstrous orgies of Obeah, at which a calabash filled with rum and human brains was a standing dish.' The primitive woodcut which accompanied the article presented an elegant white man in stylised planter costume entering a rough cabin. A bestial black woman with her back to him sinks her teeth into the white leg of a baby which has been jaggedly severed at the upper thigh.[98]

[**4.41**] Anon., 'Obeah' (wood-engraving, *c.* 1860). From the *Illustrated Police News*

The violent extremity of this misrepresentation is generated by a sinister source, missionary zeal. The identification of blackness with heathenism and the ways of the devil was still general. The belief that blacks could only successfully interact with whites after conversion to Christianity permeated Victorian views on race and the future of black-white relations in Africa and the former colonies. English Baptist missionaries gave a special emphasis to the position of the emancipated Christianised slave who dedicated his or her life to missionary work in the heathen African homeland. English response to *Uncle Tom's Cabin* reflected this in many ways, of which the conflation of abolition and Christian missionary ambition was the most important.[99]

It was in the context of the established and indeed strengthening links of abolitionism with missionary activity that *Uncle Tom's Cabin* became a classic instructional text. In the illustrated children's versions it became almost a new missionary bible, but the original novel certainly encouraged such a reading – in many ways the book increasingly becomes a missionary tract. It was the imaginative sympathy which English society enjoyed with this theme which led to its emphasis in the imagery the book generated. Both Tom and Eva, or to give her full name Evangeline, are missionaries attempting to convert the heathen blacks, and also the whites whose faith has been corrupted by slavery. George and Eliza Harris and Topsy all end the novel as missionaries in Africa. The majority of children's editions of *Uncle Tom's Cabin* concentrate on Eva and Tom or on Eva's relationship with Topsy and read like, and are illustrated like, missionary tracts.[100]

The section of *Uncle Tom's Cabin* most widely reproduced as a children's book is that dealing with Topsy, and Topsy's story is that of a heathen black brought within the missionary fold through Christian love. The last glimpse of Topsy presents her significantly, not as a free American citizen, but as a black missionary returning to what is termed her own country:

> At the age of womanhood she was, by her own request, baptised, and became a member of the Christian Church ... and [showed] so much intelligence, activity and zeal, and desire to do good in the world, that she was at last recommended and approved as a missionary to one of the missions in Africa; and we have heard that the same activity and ingenuity which when a child made her so multiform and restless in her development is now employed in a safer and wholesome manner, in teaching the children of her own country.[101]

Evangeline's evangelism has certainly paid dividends and Topsy is now designated safe or at least 'safer'. Topsy is fulfilling a fantasy central to the English missionary impulse, and her action would have rejoiced the heart of a Baptist missionary such as William Knibb who described his joy at the 'return' of an emancipated Jamaican as a missionary to Africa: 'a beloved brother, one of the despised, traduced, black Christians, an African by birth, has left this island ... has worked his passage to Africa, and ... is now on the spot from whence he was stolen as a boy, telling his fellow-countrymen the name of Jesus'.[102] Stowe meticulously sets Topsy up for this fate. From the beginning she is not merely an abused infant slave but specifically a heathen African: 'her woolly hair was braided in sundry little tails which stuck out in every direction. The expression of her face was an odd mixture of shrewdness and cunning over which was oddly drawn, like a kind of veil, an expression of the utmost solemnity. Altogether there was something odd and goblin like about her appearance; something as miss Ophelia afterwards said "so heathenish" as to inspire the good lady with utter dismay.' The illustrated book editions elaborated upon this description, and the stage persona of Topsy in the Tom plays took the exaggeration easily into the realms of minstrelsy. Yet Stowe provided ample ammunition for such developments.

To St Clare Topsy is a 'rather funny specimen in the Jim Crow line' and her appeal to American and English audiences lay partly in her strange African-based powers of entertainment. She is 'a sooty gnome from the land of diablerie' and her performances are essentially African: 'the thing struck up in a clear shrill voice an odd negro melody, to which she kept time with her feet spinning round and round, clapping her hands together, in a wild fantastic sort of time, and producing in her throat all those odd guttural sounds which distinguish the native music of her race'. Topsy was found in America but for St Clare she is purely an African heathen. Ophelia and Eva are missionaries who must convert Topsy. St Clare puts the case succinctly: 'That's you Christians all over! you'll get up a society and get some poor missionary to spend all his days among just such heathen. But let me see one of you that would take one into your house with you, and take the labour of their conversion on yourselves.'[103] Topsy's first bath, first dress and first haircut turn her into a mission child; they are specifically christianising: 'When arrayed at last in a suit of decent and whole clothing, her hair cropped short to her head, Miss Ophelia with some satisfaction said she looked more Christian like than she did.' The inner change, however, can only be worked by the Christ-like Eva, and Eva's victory over Topsy is the victory of the Christian Saxon world over the whole 'dark continent':

> There stood the two children, representatives of the two extremes of society. The fair high bred child, with her golden head, her deep eyes, her spiritual noble brow, and prince-like movements; and her black, keen, subtle, cringing yet acute neighbour. They stood the representatives of their races. The Saxon born of ages of cultivation, civilisation and command, education, physical and moral eminence; the Afric born of ages of oppression, submission, ignorance, toil and vice.[104]

Hundreds of interpretations of this scene followed in different contexts within the visual arts. George Thompson's Topsy remained one of the most reproduced prototypes within the graphic arts. Appearing first as an intense and frizzled heathen [**4.42**], she reappears before Eva transformed in every detail [**4.43**]. The arms that clutched each other protectively and neurotically are now held out, crossed at the wrist, as if bound by invisible cords. The darting spirals of hair are shorn into a tight missionary crop. The pursed lips are opened to reveal a row of pearly teeth, and framed by lips parted in a smile of adoration. The bulging terrified eyes are now bent in a charmed gaze upon the white girl. Eva, slightly taller, in strict profile, mouth closed, stares through her little convert.

The climactic scene occurs in the chapter entitled 'The Little Evangelist', where Eva shows Topsy what Christian love is. Readers would have been familiar with the character Evangelist, from the opening pages of Bunyan's *Pilgrim's Progress*, where Evangelist shows Christian the road to salvation. Yet Stowe makes no bones about the fact that in Little Eva's evangelical work we are being shown the missionary conquest of Africa in prophetic miniature. St Clare answers Ophelia's claim that she has given up on Topsy with the argument: 'Why if your Gospel is not strong enough to save one heathen child that you can have here at home all to yourself, what's the use of sending one or two poor missionaries off with it among thousands of just such? I suppose this child is a

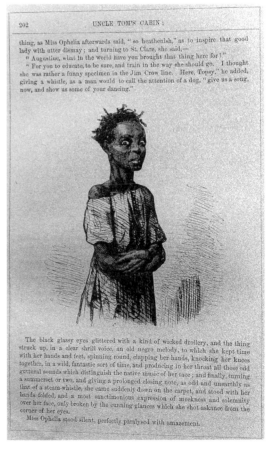

[**4.42**] George Thomas, 'Topsy' (wood-engraving, 1853). From *Uncle Tom's Cabin* (Cooke and Milford)

fair sample of what thousands of your heathen are.'[105] The relation between the heathen and the missionary evangelical is one that sets the dark against the light, black against white, good against evil, supremacy against submission, and it is spelt out with unmistakable exactitude in the ensuing scene:

> The round keen eyes of the black child were overcast with tears; large bright drops rolled heavily down, one by one and fell on the little white hand. Yes in that moment a ray of real belief, a ray of heavenly love penetrated the darkness of her heathen soul. She laid her head down between her knees, and wept and sobbed, while the beautiful child bending over her looked like the picture of some bright angel.[106]

[4.43] George Thompson, 'Topsy's Conversion' (wood-engraving, 1853). From *Uncle Tom's Cabin* (Cooke and Milford)

This scene, with the single exception of Eva garlanding Tom, was the most widely illustrated in all editions of *Uncle Tom's Cabin* and even enjoyed the final apotheosis of popular acclaim in being produced as a Staffordshire figurine.

Topsy's mass appeal to nineteenth-century Victorian parents came out of the way she effortlessly adapted to the two primary English responses to blacks, one religious, one comic. Stowe's evangelical sentiments were music to English ears, articulating the entire rationale for missionary, political and economic colonisation of Africa – namely the enlightenment of the black heathen by the Christian Saxon. White English children had long been encouraged to pity the poor little black Africans and were encouraged to bring them to the love of Jesus. And children's editions of *Uncle Tom's Cabin* most commonly end with the prescription 'Topsy Never Forgot Eva, and that it was from her she first knew the love of Jesus for the poor blacks'.[107]

While Topsy's anarchic energy was thus safely absorbed by her final conversion to the standards and behavioural patterns of Eva, her frolics and tricks were themselves absorbed into a tradition of 'nigger' entertainment.[108] Topsy was an ideal focus for children's publications. Her naughtiness, her comic blackness, her constant desire to perform, caught up and enforced well-established English stereotypes about blacks. Several of the children's editions play up Topsy as a sassy and naughty 'nigger minstrel'. The undated *Topsy's Frolics or Always in Mischief* showed Topsy dressing up as a lady or prancing behind a teacher's back [4.44]. This version took Topsy so far in the direction of entertainer as almost to drown the evangelical drive of the original. In this version Topsy is not entrusted the missionary calling and Eva's conversion is limited to the domestic sphere: 'As the years flew by, Topsy never forgot the dying kiss of Eva … she grew up into a useful and trusted servant of the family, and she always remembered with horror the days of her wicked childhood, when everyone dreaded the result of "Topsy's Frolics".'[109]

The 'real' Uncle Tom and multiple fantasy

It is difficult to calibrate the extent to which *Uncle Tom's Cabin* was corrupted to provide England and America with representations which coincided both with existing Victorian stereotypes of blacks and with the images of blacks which developed around the missionary drive into Africa during the 1850s and 1860s.

To return to Henry James's statement that *Uncle Tom's Cabin* was the ultimate example of 'the ease with which representation is taken up and carried further, even violently to the furthest', consider the example of Josiah Henson. His writings, behaviour and person were fused, in the British popular imagination, with the fictional character of Uncle Tom. Tom can be both low-rent evangelist and ex-slave as public curiosity, but beyond this Henson fulfilled the intense public desire to see Tom rise in flesh and blood from the page, to have the 'state of vision' become corporeal.

Henson, an escaped slave, whose biography overlapped with that of Uncle Tom in several particulars, corresponded with Stowe during the composition of *Uncle Tom's Cabin*. He also featured in her *Key to Uncle*

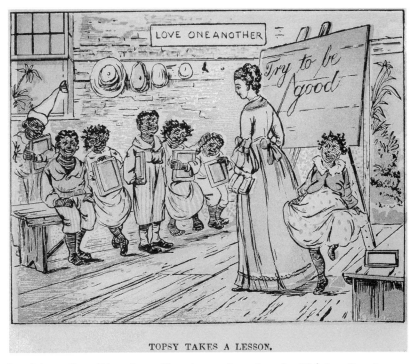

[4.44] Anon., 'Topsy Takes a Lesson' (wood-engraving, coloured *c.* 1860). From *Topsy's Frolics or Always in Mischief*

Tom's Cabin, a *post facto* attempt to provide a historical source for every character and event in the novel.[110] Josiah Henson appeared in several English publications in 1853 and provided the focus for a large article and a plate in Cassell's *Uncle Tom's Cabin Almanac*. During the succeeding twenty years Henson made a career out of the claim that he was the original Uncle Tom and when he came to England for the last time he presented himself, and was presented by his escort and biographer John Lobb, *as* 'Uncle Tom'. Lobb had brought out *Uncle Tom's Story of his Life* in 1876 and claimed that sales had reached 70,000 in six months. A children's version was brought out, *The Young People's Illustrated Edition of Uncle Tom's Story of his Life*, which attempted to allow Henson to capitalise on the continuing popularity of children's adaptations of Stowe's classic.[111] Henson's preface ends with a prayer which demonstrates the extent to which Uncle Tom had made himself a good member of the British Empire: 'God bless our gracious Queen and long may she reign. God bless all the Royal Family. God Bless all your Churches, Ministers and Preachers and Teachers and all your Day Schools and Sunday Schools.'[112] Henson was paraded around the country as the living embodiment of the good Christian ex-slave, the show reaching its climax with Uncle Tom's meeting with the Queen. The event caused a sensation, led to a mini-revival of Stowe's text, and was enthusiastically reported in the leading national dailies:

> There is something almost romantic in the meeting, in Royalty's own home, of the Queen of England with this humble and now aged Uncle Tom, whose only distinction arises from his sufferings, and the great and patient sweet philosophy, and great-hearted piety with which he bore the harshness of stern oppressors. We can picture the negro patriarch now in his eighty eighth year passing up the corridor and into the Oak Room, where her Majesty surrounded by lords and ladies in waiting, and officers of state, took him kindly by the hand ... the scene would be well worth immortalising on the canvas of some great historic painter.[113]

Desperate for, but lacking, a memorial canvas which would monumentalise the encounter, the author provides a creative record of the meeting in the form of verses in the Spenserian stanza concluding, 'He who a legal chattel erst had been / In friendly converse stands with England's gracious Queen'. The book constantly attempts to reconstitute fiction as fact:

> It greatly adds to our interest in Eva to learn from Mr. Henson that such a child is not the creation of Mrs. Stowe's fancy, but did really live, and was actually rescued from drowning by Mr Henson (Uncle Tom). Topsy, too, whose real name was Dinah, was no imaginary character 'she was clear witted, as sharp and cunning as a fox but she purposely acted as a fool or idiot in order to take advantage of her mistress ...'.[114]

Who finally played the fool is hard to judge, but the English reading public puts in a strong claim. The memory of slavery becomes represented within the factualised fictions of *Uncle Tom's Cabin*. Reassuringly unreal, each character must then be located in a historical past.

A state of vision realised: Tom contra the Duke of Wellington

The desire for imaginative submersion in the most sentimental characters and events of *Uncle Tom's Cabin* motivates the popular English images generated by the novel. In the end, however, these were not always enough, even Josiah Henson was not enough. Tom had to be resurrected as historical protagonist. The complicated issue of how the English mind should or could respond to slavery is short-circuited by the Tomist personification. Uncle Tom saturates a good many of the popular spin-offs generated by the novel and some of this material is very odd. An astonishing example of identification with Uncle Tom as a living person is a pamphlet, preached originally as a sermon and then brought out under the ambitious title *Wellington and Uncle Tom or the Hero of this World Contrasted with the Hero in Jesus Christ*.[115] The advertisement apologises for 'assuming the veritableness of Uncle Tom' but continues 'Wellington and Uncle Tom are ... convenient illustrations for the present time' representing 'two distinct principles of life and conduct'. This enthusiastic anti-military tract tells us that 'The soldiers work is coarse, brutal, disgusting, horrifying; and requires a coarse, hard, mechanical self willed genius to do the work. Uncle Tom is far too refined for this sort of work. He has a body able enough but his soul is of too high an order.'[116] He has gained an un-Wellingtonian victory over the English nation: 'Already the silent hearts of millions commend Uncle Tom in a way that Wellington never was and never can be commended. The admiration of the coarse triumphs of the soldier is very shallow and very cold ... [Tom's] great soul could make cunning little baskets out of cherry stones – could cut faces on hickory nuts, and odd jumping figures out of elder pith, to please children. Patiently with his sunny face, and his sunnier heart, labouring and chiselling to amuse children! He is a downright Angel of the first water!'[117] Maybe soap opera and the empathetic projections upon which it thrives were born within the imaginative parameters of Uncle Tomism. The 'World's Columbia Exhibition' featured as one of its central attractions 'Tom's Original Cabin', although the structure was destroyed shortly after the end of the show.[118]

On his return to Canada Henson's celebrity as the original Uncle Tom continued to cling to him in the free slave community which he was instrumental in founding in Dresden, Ontario. His death did not separate him from the powerful association with his fictional alter ego, and his house, carefully preserved to this day, and the centrepiece of a black studies centre, bizarrely carries the name 'Uncle Tom's Cabin'. Stowe's eponymous cabin has been transplanted from Kentucky into rural southern Canada. Henson himself lives on as a wax model seated in an armchair, his wife, a great deal slimmer than Aunt Chloe yet no less devoted to her husband, dutifully

[4.45] 'Uncle Tom's Cabin', interior with model figures,
Uncle Tom's Cabin Museum, Ontario

standing by his shoulder [**4.45**]. Whether those who visit look on his effigy as the venerable father Henson or the resurrected Uncle Tom is a moot point, and causes his direct descendents who run the Uncle Tom's Cabin Trust great unease. Surely, however, the cabin would not have been preserved, and the wax model would not be displayed, were it not for Henson's alignment with Stowe's hero.

Native resources and Tomistic confusions

It is generally held that America had not developed a significant tradition of print satire of its own by the middle of the nineteenth century.[119] While this is largely true of the stylistic and formal operations of the satiric print, there did exist certain quintessentially American themes and narrative incidents that fed into the ideological sub-strata of abolition print propaganda. Abolition propaganda had thrown up fiction of remarkable popularity and power – slave narratives were not only best-selling texts but had a transformative impact on the iconography and semiotic operations of book illustration and print satire.[120] The illustrated editions of *Uncle Tom's Cabin* had provided an iconographic vocabulary of great satiric potential. The popular translation of *Uncle Tom's Cabin* within North American print satire demonstrates both the strength of the evolving American market and its ability to transform European models. It also suggests differences in the race agendas underlying the book's popular absorption in America and England.

    Strong's Dime Caricatures. – No. 3 South Carolina Topsey [*sic*] *in a Fix* is a good place to start when looking at the problems Stowe's characters pose for the graphic artists who would appropriate them [**4.46**].[121] The print involves the iconographic reinvention of two of Stowe's characters, and one of the most famous comic scenes in *Uncle Tom's Cabin*, in the context of an anti-secessionist and pro-abolition Northern satire. Topsy is reinvented as the state of South Carolina, threatening secession; Columbia, holding the damaged flag of the United States, is represented by the stiff New England spinster, Miss Ophelia. In other words the free states are shown as a childless white Northern female, and the slave state is represented as a dangerous type of infant slave. The depiction of Topsy has a precise source and is developed out of one of the most influential sets of English illustrations to the novel. George Thomas's interpretation of Topsy in the deluxe Cooke and Milford illustrated edition, printed in London in 1853, rapidly became a standard [**4.42**]. He drew her as she is first presented to Miss Ophelia: 'she came

[4.46] Anon., *Strong's Dime Caricatures. – No. 3 South Carolina Topsey* [*sic*] *in a Fix*
(wood-engraving, 1861)

suddenly down on the carpet, and stood with her hands folded, and a most sanctimonious expression of meekness and solemnity over her face, only broken by the cunning glances which she shot askance from the corner of her eyes' and this image is the source for Strong's representation of South Carolina [**4.47**]. South Carolina's secessionist position is presented in terms of the comic and dishonest antics of a black slave child.[122] The description of the feigned seriousness comes directly after the presentation of her as an embodiment of heathen otherness, a 'wicked ... thing'.[123] Yet the satiric agenda is, finally, confused. A Southern slaveholding state is being attacked for an assault on the Union while the humour for the attack depends upon the idea that blacks – and especially black, uneducated and parentless infant slaves – are of their essence funny and bad.

The catechising of Topsy, where Miss Ophelia attempts to extract information concerning the girl's origins, only to be brought

[4.47] Anon., *Strong's Dime Caricatures. – No. 3 South Carolina Topsey* [*sic*] *in a Fix*, detail (wood-engraving, 1861)

up short by a series of denials of origin, was one of the most frequently reproduced sections of dialogue from the original novel. In this print it is reinvented in truncated form as a monologue spoken by Topsy: 'Never had no father, no mother nor nothing! I was raised by speculators! I's mighty wicked, any how! "What makes me ack so!" Dun no missis – I 'spects caus i's so wicked!' This works well, and has an ideological coherence lacking in the rest of the satire. Topsy's ignorance of her origins and moral degeneracy are re-inscribed upon the slave states that were responsible for moulding her. Topsy as hopeless, helpless, truthless and Godless orphan is made a precise metaphor for slave government.

The message is not, however, quite this simple. The comparison of the errant state with such a figure as Topsy is supposed to be degrading, but has confusing implications for the free North's relation to the slaves themselves. Ophelia/Columbia, having accused Topsy of the 'wicked work' of 'picking stars out of this sacred flag', in other words seceding, continues: 'What would your old forefathers say, do you think? I'll hand you over to the new overseer, Uncle Abe. He'll fix you.' The whole point of catechising Topsy in Stowe's novel is to prove the arbitrariness of her origins, bred up on a slave farm by speculators. The sudden imposition of a genealogy for South Carolina Topsy going back to the pilgrim fathers confines the satire. The confusion is expanded by the appeal of Ophelia/Columbia to a higher authority figure, a male one, in the form of Abraham Lincoln as a slave overseer, who will whip Topsy. The idea of an overseer whipping a defenceless slave orphan is, despite the attempted comic context, hardly an attractive one. Further uncertainty is generated by the male slave in the background who shouts, 'Hand us over to Abe, eh! I'ze off'. The black slave is supposed to be another symbolic representation of South Carolina, this time as a lazy and disobedient black male, but this leaves the slave population of South Carolina in more of a fix than Topsy. If they are synonymous with idleness, dishonesty and insubordination why would the North go to war for them in the first place? The print shows the difficulties of importing the race stereotypes of Stowe's fiction, and their simplification via book illustration, into the political print. In the end, if the satire works then it demands the unproblematic assumption that black slaves are utterly degraded, and that their depredation provides a comic resource with which to attack the slave states.

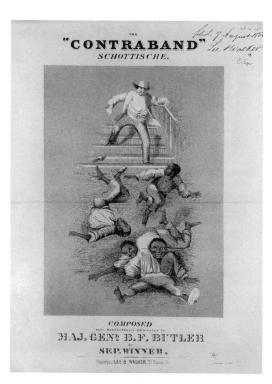

[4.48] Anon., *The Contraband Schottishe*
(stone lithograph, 1853)

There is a similarly unclear use of the illustrative resources thrown up by *Uncle Tom's Cabin* in a print entitled *The Contraband Schottishe* [**4.48**]. Originally the cover to a satiric popular song, this print attacks the Union General Benjamin F. Butler's notorious announcement that captured fugitive slaves were to be considered 'contraband of war'. The statement implied the assumption of slaveholding values on the part of the North, slave property merely changing hands, not status, in the course of the war. While the cover sets out to attack the position, showing a white male, decked out in stereotypical planter costume, pursuing a group of tumbling black youths in comic attitudes, it doesn't provide the blacks with the kind of ennobling presence which would suggest that they have a right to proper human status. They are simply a group of capering Jim Crow buffoons. In fact the design is again lifted directly from George Thompson's 1853 illustrations to *Uncle Tom's Cabin*, and is a precise lithographic copy of Thompson's wood-engraving illustrating the manner in which the slave boys on the Shelby property bait the slave-trader Haley after one of his new purchases has escaped [**4.49**]: 'When at last Haley appeared, booted and spurred, he was

[**4.49**] Anon., 'Haley Confounded' (wood-engraving, 1853). From *Uncle Tom's Cabin* (Cooke and Milford)

saluted with the bad tidings on every hand. The young imps on the veranda were not disappointed in their hope of hearing him "swar", which he did with a fluency and fervency which delighted them all amazingly, as they ducked and dodged hither and thither to be out of the reach of his riding-whip; and all whooping off together, they tumbled in a pile of immeasurable giggle, on the withered turf under the veranda, where they kicked up their heels and shouted to their full satisfaction.' Again it is pertinent to question, bearing the source in mind, the sort of taste which this satire leaves in the mouth. The image of the fugitive slave which is presented is of ineffective, irresponsible youth, incapable of grasping the terrible nature of its political situation.

The repercussions of Stowe's novel on American graphic satire were not restricted to the North. This discussion of the popular imaging of *Uncle Tom's Cabin* concludes with the most brilliant pro-slavery print satire to come out of America. *Uncle Tom's Cabin* illicited a barrage of furious responses from the South. Innumerable replies to, refutations of,

A. DREAM
Caused by the perusal of Mrs. H. Beecher Stowe's popular work Uncle Tom's Cabin.

[4.50] C. R. Milne, *A Dream Caused by a perusal of Mrs. H. Beecher Stowe's popular work Uncle Tom's Cabin* (lithograph, 1853)

and even re-writings of, the novel were brought out. Not much of this work carried imagery, and when it did it was for the most part unremarkable, converting blacks, including Tom, into types of the plantation 'darkey', or celebrating Eva as a wonder of Southern virtue.[124] Yet there are ambitious exceptions to the banality of Southern response. One work stands out in terms of its ingenious absorption of the tradition of European print satire: *A DREAM Caused by a perusal of Mrs. H. Beecher Stowe's popular work Uncle Tom's Cabin*, published in 1853, the work of C. R. Milne of Louisville Kentucky [4.50]. The work is a very exact parody of Jaques Callot's etched masterpiece, the second version of *The Temptation of St Anthony*, which he published at the very end of his career in 1635 [4.51].[125]

Milne's work maintains every narrative incident and almost every figure from Callot's original. There are only three substantial differences between the two prints. Firstly the design is reversed, a natural result of the fact that Milne's copy would have been made the 'right' way round straight onto the lithographic stone. The design would then have been reversed when printed. Secondly Milne has cut out all of the architectural background to Callot's print, and greatly reduced the heavy crosshatching

which fills the entire sky with flames and smoke. Thirdly Milne has introduced three figures in contemporary dress. Callot's St Anthony, bottom
left in the original, has been replaced by Mrs Stowe, bottom right in *A
Dream*, and the naked figure of Vanity, who sits on top of the skull in the
carcass procession in the left middle-ground of *St Anthony*, the right
middle ground of *A Dream*.[126] Milne's third figure, a grinning black man,
standing centre, holding a flag carrying the Union Jack and a slogan
'Women of England to the Rescue', is his own invention, and constitutes
the only major addition to the figure composition of the original. In his
overall treatment of Callot, Milne demonstrates an impressive fluency with
the medium of lithography. He is not hampered by converting the clean
lines of Callot's etching into the more fluid and tonal qualities of crayon
and chalk drawing on stone.

While this print is an impressive technical achievement, it is nevertheless a puzzling work, which in its narrative and allegorical ambition, and
in its unabashed Eurocentrism and high-art origins, stands alone in
nineteenth-century American popular print satire. Why should a lithogra-
pher in the Southern states of America in 1853 have decided to attack *Uncle
Tom's Cabin* and its author through a copy, with slight variations, of one of

[4.51] Jacques Callot, *The Temptation of St Anthony*, second version (etching, 1635)

the most haunting, ambiguous, complicated and bizarre religious prints to come out of seventeenth-century Europe? How would the print have been interpreted by an audience, unfamiliar with the source and its Catholic iconographic conventions?

Callot's print certainly has some qualities which would have made it generally attractive. It has a satiric edge, and although it is an interpretation of a religious theme which had been tackled by the leading painters and printmakers of northern Europe (Schongauer, Bosch, Brueghel had all produced renowned interpretations of St Anthony's temptation), it uses this as a base from which to launch an attack on the abuses and luxury of the Medici court theatricals. The basis of Callot's satire lay in the way he drew on early-seventeenth-century theatrical representations of hell.[127] Callot's use of a shallow pictorial space, which Milne even accentuates, and his employment of pyrotechnical aspects of stage renditions of damnation, have a dramatic and vulgar appeal which had great potential for mid-nineteenth-century America. Of all the versions of the Temptation of St Anthony this one had the greatest elements of showmanship. Given the extent to which Stowe's book had taken off as a theatrical phenomenon in England and America by 1853, Callot's print suggested a way of constructing a counter-propaganda statement that drew on an alternative theatrical tradition of European religious satire.[128]

Be this as it may, one is still faced with the question: why would Milne wish to portray Mrs Stowe as St Anthony? The answer is, he didn't. In substituting Mrs Stowe for St Anthony Milne transformed the entire narrative base of the print. Stowe, clutching her book, does not appear as a saint resisting temptation, but as a fallen woman going to hell. With the disappearance of the saint the landscape changes. Milne is not describing a saint's horrified vision of damnation, but a pro-slavery fantasy of revenge on Harriet Beecher Stowe. She has brought mass desolation and destruction upon the land through her damnable publication, and as a result she belongs to the devil. Stowe, far from resisting the temptations of the flesh, and the terror of satanic torment, is shown being punished for having given in to earthly pride – she is being dragged down to hell as a result of writing the book which she flourishes. Milne has changed the figures surrounding Callot's St Anthony. Callot's figure is assaulted by four devils, one of whom drags him off in chains, and a voluptuous young nude woman runs off to the right. Milne has got rid of the woman, and reduced the devils to the front two figures who cling to the saint's garments. The chains have gone. Perhaps most significantly, where St Anthony stood beneath the stone arch of a ruined church, Mrs Stowe stands at the entrance to a cave mouth, a traditional motif for hell, Satan being believed to live underground.[129]

Milne then has economically translated Callot's print from a Temptation of St Anthony to a Damnation of Mrs Stowe. His largest addition, the grinning black Quaker, transforms Callot's narrative into a

racist satire of great power. In the original the central Devil/Monster
(arguably a representation of Lucifer) which hangs above the other figures is chained and vomits out demons and monsters.[130] Milne maintains
the chains, but while his figure still vomits demons, the grinning black
Quaker now stands directly below the devil's mouth. In order to isolate
the Devil and Quaker, Milne punches a clean space behind the two figures which makes them stand out together harshly in the foreground.
The grinning black man represents the damnable phenomenon of the liberated black. Many free and escaped blacks adopted the Quaker religion
as a result of the fact that Quakers were the first considerable religious
minority to ban slaveholding in any form among their members. They
were also committed to helping fugitives and to the active resettlement of
blacks in the Northern free states and Canada. Quakers are shown as key
figures in the underground railroad, and within the plot of *Uncle Tom's
Cabin* they help George and Eliza Harris to escape. The chained figure of
Lucifer which hovers above the Quaker is a metaphor for black slaves,
and in presenting the portly-free-black-Quaker as the vomit of this monster Milne argues against emancipation. The black slaves may be
metaphorically constituted as a monster with destructive potential, but at
least the monster is chained and under control. Conversely, while free
blacks look civilised, they are an uncontrolled spawn of the devil, even
more terrifying than slaves. The print argues that blacks, slave or free, are
equivalent to devils, and that in arguing for their liberation Mrs Stowe has
become their victim – she has loosed a storm of black evil which she
cannot control and which is destroying her. The contaminating evil of
her book is further emphasised by the Quaker's placard. In calling on the
women of England to defend Mrs Stowe, reference is made to the colossal
success of *Uncle Tom's Cabin* in Britain, where it elicited emotional
response, and many eulogies in poetry and prose from literary women,
including George Eliot.

In this context Milne's substitution of a clothed miniature second portrait of Mrs Stowe for the nude figure of Vanity is very clever. Stowe's position as moral crusader for freedom is challenged. She is presented as
having written the book out of selfish vanity, and her irresponsibility has
loosed powers of destruction and bloodshed which are beyond control. In
the light of Lincoln's fabled comment on first meeting Stowe, just after the
Civil War – 'So you're the little lady who caused this big War' – Milne's
interpretation of the destructive potential of the book might be seen to have
a certain prophetic accuracy. Stowe's book, in terms of the iconographic
inheritance it generated, might be seen as the battleground for an even
bigger war – the war over the racist construction of the black.

Notes

1 Philip D. Curtin, *The Image of Africa: British Ideas and Action 1780–1850* (Madison, Wisconsin University Press, 1964), pp. 255-7, 332-3, 394-9, 411-17; Seymour Drescher, 'The Ending of the Slave Trade and the Evolution of European Scientific Racism', in Joseph E. Inikori and Stanley Engerman (eds), *The Atlantic Slave Trade: Effects on Economies, Societies and Peoples in Africa and the Americas* (Durham and London, Duke University Press, 1992), pp. 365-9 .

2 For anti-slavery racial attitudes in Victorian thought see Douglas A. Lorimer, *Colour, Class and the Victorians: English Attitudes to the Negro in the Mid-Nineteenth Century* (Leicester, Leicester University Press, 1978), pp. 33-7, 51-6, 72-4, 98-100. R. J. M Blackett, *Building an Anti-Slavery Wall: Black Americans in the Atlantic Abolitionist Movement, 1830–1860* (Ithaca and London, Cornell University Press, 1983), pp. 42-3, 52-7, 83-117. For Victorian popular representations of racial type see Mary Cowling, *The Artist as Anthropologist: The Representation of Type and Character in Victorian Art* (Cambridge, Cambridge University Press, 1989), pp. 55-65. For 'black-face' minstrelsy shows in transatlantic culture see Eric Lott, 'Love and Theft: The Racial Unconscious of Blackface Minstrelsy', *Representations*, 39:2 (1992) 22–49; Hans Nathan, *Dan Emmett and the Rise of Early Negro Minstrelsy* (Norman, University of Oklahoma Press, 1962). For the conjunction of race and gender stereotypes in Victorian visual representation see Sander L. Gilman, '"I'm Down on Whores": Race and Gender in Victorian London', in David Theo Goldberg (ed.), *Anatomy of Racism* (Minneapolis and London, University of Minnesota Press, 1990), pp. 146–70. For *Uncle Tom's Cabin* within American nineteenth-century literary and popular paradigms of racism see Leonard Cassuto, *The Inhuman Race: The Racial Grotesque in American Literature and Culture* (New York, Columbia University Press, 1997); James R. Ryan, *Picturing Empire: Photography and the Visualisation of the British Empire* (London, Reaktion, 1997), pp. 146–60; Jan Nederveen Pieterse, *White on Black: Images of Africa and Blacks in Western Popular Culture* (New Haven, Yale University Press, 1992), pp. 152–66; Albert Boime, *The Art of Exclusion: Representing Blacks in the Nineteenth Century* (Thames and Hudson, London, 1990), pp. 99–103.

3 The most comprehensive overview of European cultural constructions of Africans in the 1830–50 period is still Curtin, *Image*. For abolition and racism see Drescher, 'The Ending of the Slave Trade', pp. 361–96.

4 For the relation of anti–slavery and missionary society literatures to the sentimental characterisations of black-face minstrelsy see Lorimer, *Colour*, pp. 70–3, 126–30, and for Uncle Tom and paradigms of popular anti–slavery propaganda pp. 83–6. For media attacks on black abolitionists see Blackett, *Anti-Slavery Wall*, pp. 155–61; C. Peter Ripley (ed.), *The Black Abolitionist Papers*, 5 vols (Chapel Hill and London, University of North Carolina Press, 1985–92), 1, pp. 73–4, 252–41, 568–9.

5 For the longevity and poplar influence of extreme eighteenth-century racist theory see Curtin, *Image*, pp. 46–7, 240–3, 253–7; Anthony J. Barker, *The African Link: British Attitudes to the Negro in the Era of the African Slave Trade 1550–1807* (London, Frank Cass, 1978), pp. 157–94.

6 Lorimer, *Colour*, pp. 69–91, 128–30; Pieterse, *White on Black*, pp. 132–5.

7 For the development of the 'Minstrel Man' out of the more complicated figure of Harlequin see Henry Louis Gates Jnr., *Figures in Black: Words, Signs and the Racial Self* (New York and London, Oxford University Press, 1987), pp. 51–4. For the appropriation and corruption of black English within the context of parodic oratory and graphic satire see Henry Louis Gates Jnr., *The Signifying Monkey* (New York and Oxford, Oxford University Press, 1989), pp. 90–103. For the difficulties this tradition imposes on black and white authors using black vernaculars see Tommy L. Lott, 'Black Vernacular Representation and Cultural Malpractice', in David Theo Goldberg (ed.), *Multiculturalism: A Critical Reader* (Oxford, Blackwell, 1994), pp. 231–58. For the literary construction of Africans in Europe see Anthony Gerrard Barthelemy, *Black Face,*

Maligned Race: The Representation of Blacks in English Drama from Shakespeare to Southerne (Baton Rouge and London, Louisiana State University Press, 1987).

8 The article was published anonymously; attribution to Charles Briggs was made by Margaret A. Brown. See Elizabeth Ammons (ed.), *Critical Essays on Uncle Tom's Cabin* (Boston, G. K. Hall, 1980), p. 35 fn.

9 Ammons, *Critical Essays*, pp. 35–42.

10 Ammons, *Critical Essays*, p. 36.

11 Ammons, *Critical Essays*, p. 38.

12 The two most detailed accounts of the adaptation of *Uncle Tom's Cabin* in America, England and France are Harry Birdoff, *The World's Greatest Hit* (New York, S. F. Vanni, 1947), pp. 144–65, and Thomas F. Gosset, *Uncle Tom's Cabin and American Culture* (Dallas, Southern Methodist University Press, 1985) pp. 164–260. See also Audrey A. Fisch, 'Exhibiting Uncle Tom', *Nineteenth Century Contexts*, 17:2 (1993) 145–58.

13 *A Redemção folha Abolicionista Commercial e Noticiosa*, 1–68 (1887–88).

14 The most popular of the humane society editions were: *Black Beauty; The 'Uncle Tom's Cabin' of the Horse* (Philadelphia, Wannamaker, n.d.); *Black Beauty: his grooms and companions, by A Sewell. The 'Uncle Tom's Cabin' of the Horse* (American edn, Boston, American Humane Society, 1891); *Black Beauty, His Grooms and Companions; the 'Uncle Tom's Cabin' of the Horse. With material by George T. Agall, President of American Humane Education Society* (Boston, Lathrop, 1894); *Black Beauty, His Grooms and Companions, 'The Uncle Tom's Cabin' of the Horse. By Anna Sewell* (New York, J. Hovendon & Co., 1894).

15 See Marcus Wood, '"All Right !": The Narrative of Henry "Box" Brown as a Test Case for the Racial Prescription of Rhetoric and Semiotics', *Proceedings of the American Antiquarian Society*, 107:1 (1997) 97–102. See also *The Slave's Friend*, 1:4 (1832) 1–6; 1:8 (1832) 10–11; 3:10 (1833) 1.

16 There is no comprehensive bibliography of the editions of *Uncle Tom's Cabin* or of the ephemera it generated. The most authoritative bibliography of American editions of the main text is *A Bibliography of American Literature*, 9 vols (New Haven and London, Yale University Press, 1955–91), 8, pp. 73–82, 116–17. For dramatic adaptations see Alardyce Nicholl, *A History of English Drama 1660–1900*, 6 vols (Cambridge, Cambridge University Press, 1923–59) 5, pp. 335, 368, 419, 552, 636, 761, 762; J. P. Wearing (ed.), *The London Stage 1890–99: A Calendar of Plays and Players*, 2 vols (Metuchen, Scarecrow Press, 1976) 1, pp. 123, 262–3; 2, 640. For some English and American children's editions see Joyce Nakamura (ed.), *Children's Authors and Illustrators* (Detroit, Gale Research, 1987), p. 693. Staffordshire figurines of the major characters brought out in the 1850s are listed in P. D. Gordon Pugh, *Staffordshire Portrait Figures and Allied Subjects of the Victorian Era* (London, Barrie and Jenkins, 1970), pp. 30, 238–9. The board game *Justice* is reproduced in Blair Whitton, *Paper Toys of the World* (Cumberland, Maryland, 1986), p. 12. For mass merchandising see Birdoff, *Greatest Hit*, pp. 144–6.

17 For church settings see Bodleian Music Library, 57 e 31, *Uncle Tom* (London, 1878). This piece is described as a 'Church Service … the audience are requested not to manifest applause'. The most distorting of the dramatic adaptations are referred to in Birdoff, *Greatest Hit*, pp. 147–65. For the appeal of the novel as a conversion narrative see Jane Tomkins, *Sensational Designs: The Cultural Work of American Fiction 1790–1860* (Oxford, Oxford University Press, 1985), pp. 127–32. For English and American song sheets see Bodleian, Harding 'Uncle Tom Box', 268.

18 Henry James, *A Small Boy and Others* (London, Macmillan, 1913), pp. 167–8.

19 Val Prinsep, quoted in Oswald Doughty, *A Victorian Romantic: Dante Gabriel Rossetti* (London, Oxford University Press, 1960), p. 249.

20 Harriet Beecher Stowe [adapted by George Aitken], *Uncle Tom's Cabin, or Life Among the Lowly, a domestic drama in Six Acts. Dramatised by George L. Aiken* (New York, Samuel French, 1853), p. 47.

21 Dante Gabriel Rossetti, *The Works of Dante Gabriel Rossetti*, ed. W. M. Rossetti (London, 1911), p. 271.

22 Quoted Rossetti, *Works*, p. 675 fn. Gates, *Signifying Monkey*, p. 103 discusses the parody as an example of white 'signifyin(g)' which uses black dialect.

23 Rossetti *Works*, pp. 674–5, fn.

24 Rossetti, *Works*, p. 675.

25 For pro-slavery use of Carlyle see George Fitzhugh, *Cannibals All! or Slaves Without Masters*, ed. C. Vann Woodward (Cambridge Mass., Belknap Press, 1960), pp. 10–12, 66–7, 254–5. For abolition response to Carlyle see John Greenleaf Whittier, 'Thomas Carlyle on the Slave Question', in *Literary Recreations – Miscellanies*, reprinted Jules Paul Seigel (ed), *Thomas Carlyle: The Critical Heritage* (London and New York, Routledge, 1995), pp. 311–17. For a range of other reviews pp. 318–74.

26 Quoted in Hugh Honour, *The Image of the Black in Western Art from the American Revolution to World War I* (Cambridge Mass., Harvard University Press, 1989), 4:2, p. 159.

27 W. M. Rossetti (ed.), *Rossetti Papers* (London, 1903), p. 175.

28 Doughty, *Victorian Romantic*, pp. 227, 228.

29 Quoted in Doughty, *Victorian Romantic*, p. 237.

30 For Cassell and Cruikshank see Robert L. Patten, *George Cruikshank's Life, Times and Art*, 2 vols (Cambridge, Lutterworth, 1992, 1996), 2, pp. 321–4, 383.

31 Patricia Anderson, *The Printed Image and the Formation of Popular Culture* (Oxford, Oxford University Press, 1991), pp. 50–128.

32 Anderson, *Printed Image*, pp. 50–84, 138–57. For the early nineteenth century see Marcus Wood, *Radical Satire and Print Culture 1790–1822* (Oxford, Clarendon Press, 1994), pp. 58–95, 155–90. Mary Dorothy George, *Catalogue of the Political and Personal Satires: Preserved in the Department of Prints and Drawings in the British Museum* (London, British Museum, 1935–54) [hereafter BM followed by catalogue number]. For the growth of nineteenth-century colour printing see Ronald Vere Tooley, *English Books with Coloured Plates, 1790–1860* (London, Dawson, 1954). For a vivid contemporary account of nineteenth-century burgeoning print culture see Anthony Trollop, *The Way We Live Now*, 2 vols (London, Chapman and Hall, 1875).

33 The best overview of the transmission of American texts in the English nineteenth-century publishing market is still Simon Knowell-Smith, *International Copyright Law and the Publisher in the Reign of Queen Victoria* (Oxford, Oxford University Press, 1968).

34 David Dabydeen, *Hogarth's Blacks* (Manchester, Manchester University Press, 1987) is the only monograph to consider blacks in English graphic art of the mid to late eighteenth century. No equivalent work has been done on English print satire 1790–1820. Cruikshank's later work on *Uncle Tom's Cabin* is mentioned in Honour, *Image of the Black*, 4:1, pp. 199, 201, 203, 209, and figs 125, 131. For the biographical background to some of the prints treating race see Patten, *George Cruikshank's Life*, 1, pp. 98, 195 8, 258.

35 For the complicated codes governing the representation of blacks within English culture at this period see Barker, *The African Link*, pp. 77–179.

36 For the association of the black servant with prostitution and with inappropriate sexual behaviour see Sander Gilman, 'Black Bodies, White Bodies: Toward an Iconography of Female Sexuality in Late Nineteenth-Century Art, Medicine, and Literature', in Henry Louis Gates Jnr. (ed.), *Race, Writing and Difference* (Chicago, University of Chicago Press, 1986), pp. 223–63; Honour, *Image of the Black*, 4:2, p. 22. For the sexual representation of the black in England at this time see Barker, *The African Link*, pp. 121–7, 172–3.

37 James Gillray, BM, 8074, *Anti-sacharites or John Bull and his brother leaving off the Use of Sugar*. For the political context of this print see Draper Hill, *The Satirical Etchings of James Gillray* (New York, Dover, 1976), pp. 25–6.

38 James Gillray, BM, 7848, *Barbarities in the West Indies*.

39 The case is reported in *Parliamentary History*, 29 (18 April 1791) 289. For the print as a parody of abolitionist argument see Ronald Paulson, *Representations of Revolution* (New Haven, Yale University Press, 1987), pp. 204–5.

40 James Gillray, BM, 8793, *Philanthropic Consolations on the Loss of the Slave Bill*. For the political context for this print see Draper Hill, *Fashionable Contrasts* (London, Phaidon, 1966), p. 146.

41 The clearest articulation of this argument by an English radical in the 1790s is to be found in John Thelwall's journal *The Tribune*, 2 (1795) 149–69.

42 For the background to Newton see David Alexander, *Richard Newton and English Caricature in the 1790s* (Manchester, Manchester University Press, 1998), pp. 7–56, and for *A Nice Bit*, p. 131, and plate 43. For Rowlandson's racially based sex prints see BM, 10925, 11961; John Hayes, *Rowlandson* (London, Phaidon, 1972), p. 181.

43 See Alexander, *Newton*, pp. 38, 49 and plate 36.

44 For the earliest Western identification of blacks with the devil see Jean Devisse, *The Image of the Black in Western Art* (Lausanne, Menil Foundation, 1979), 2:1, pp. 70–80. For the later development of these associations see Jean Devisse and Michel Mollat, *The Image of the Black in Western Art* (Lausanne, Menil Foundation, 1979), 2:2, pp. 59–78, 229–32.

45 Edmund Burke, *The Speeches and Writings of Edmund Burke*, 9 vols (Oxford, Clarendon Press, 1991–97), 9, pp. 147–8, 156, 245–6, 272–5.

46 See Gilman, 'Black Bodies', pp. 232–4. For a German adaptation see Stuart Hall, 'The Spectacle of the Other', in Stuart Hall (ed.), *Representation: Cultural Representations and Signifying Practices* (London, Sage Publications, 1997), pp. 268–9.

47 Alexander, *Newton*, pp. 134–5 and plate 52.

48 See Alexander, *Newton*, p. 116 and plate 3. For a detailed analysis of the print in the context of erotic flagellation see pp. 261–2 below.

49 Isaac Cruikshank, BM, 8079, *The Abolition of the Slave Trade*.

50 For blacks in England in the eighteenth and nineteenth centuries see James Walvin, 'Black Caricature: The Roots of Racialism', in *Black and White: The Negro in English Society 1555–1945* (London, Allen Lane, 1973), pp. 159–76; James Walvin, *Slavery and British Society 1776–1846* (London, Macmillan, 1982); Gretchen Gerzina, *Black England: Life Before Emancipation* (London, John Murray, 1995); Peter Fryer, *Staying Power: The History of Black People in Britain* (London, Pluto, 1984) pp. 1–236; Dabydeen, *Hogarth's Blacks*, pp. 17–40; Honour, *Image of the Black*, 4:1, pp. 11–128; 4:2, pp. 7–24. For images of black servants in the eighteenth century see Pieterse, *White on Black*, pp. 124–7.

51 George Cruikshank, etching, handbill, *I was barn in St. Kitts*. (c. 1800). Formerly in the 'George Cruikshank Collection', Victoria and Albert Museum, currently lost.

52 See Patten, *George Cruikshank's Life*, 1, pp. 209–20.

53 For a comprehensive historical overview of the popular reception of the milestones of scientific racism see H. F. Augstein (ed.), *Race: The Origins of an Idea, 1760–1850* (Bristol, Thoemmes Press, 1996). For blacks and pugilism see An Amateur (pseud.) *An Impartial Account of the Battle Between Crib and Molineaux* (London, 1810); Pierce Egan, *Boxiana Sketches of Ancient and Modern Pugilism* (London, 1812), pp. 360–70; Anon. *Lives and Battles of Famous Black Pugilists from Molineaux to Jackson* (New York, Richard Fox, 1890).

54 [Frederick Marryat del.] George Cruikshank sculpt., BM, 13043, *Puzzled Which to Choose!! or the King of Timbuktu Offering one of his Daughters*.

55 For Victorian physiognomic and phrenological theory in relation to race see Ivan Hannaford, *Race: the History of an Idea in the West* (Baltimore, Johns Hopkins University Press, 1996), pp. 235–77; Cowling, *Artist as Anthropologist*, pp. 54–63; Honour, *Image of the Black*, 4:2, pp. 12–22; William Stanton, *The Leopard's Spots: Scientific Attitudes Towards Race in America 1815–59* (London and Chicago, University of Chicago Press, 1960), pp. 35–9. For the Marryat Cruikshank collaboration see Patten, *George Cruikshank's Life*, 1, p. 195.

56 George Cruikshank, *The Comic Almanack, 2nd Series, 1844–53* (London, 1853), frontispiece.

57 George Cruikshank, BM, 12749, *The Court at Brighton à la Chinese!!* For the source see James Gillray, BM, 8121, *The Reception of the Diplomatique and his Sweet at the Court of Pekin*.

58 For a detailed discussion of the cultural ramifications of Saatje see Sander Gilman, 'Black Bodies', pp. 232–40. See also Pieterse, *White on Black*, pp. 180–1. For Saatje, Cuvier and French racism see William B. Cohn, *The French Encounter with Africans: White Response to Blacks 1530–1880* (Bloomington and London, University of Indiana Press, 1980), pp. 210–62.

59 See Richard D. Altick, *The Shows of London* (Cambridge Mass., Belknap Press, 1978), pp. 270–2.

60 George Cruikshank, BM, 13249, *The New Union Club*.

61 See George notes to BM, 13249, and Patten, *George Cruikshank's Life*, 1, p. 196.

62 Patten, *George Cruikshank's Life*, 1, p. 196: 'While it seems to a modern sensibility utterly racist … no one is spared. Blacks and whites are equally subject to hideous distortion.'

63 For the graphic tropes developed to degrade the Irish see Perry L. Curtis Jnr., *Apes and Angels: The Irishman in Victorian Caricature* (Newton Abbot, David and Charles, 1971), pp. 29–94; Perry L. Curtis Jnr., *Anglo Saxons and Celts: a Study of Anti-Irish Prejudice in Victorian England* (Connecticut, Conference of English Studies University of Bridgeport, 1968), pp. 17–36. For the transference of the graphic tropes of scientific racism from black to white in the context of anti-radical state satire see Diana Donald, *The Age of Caricature: Satirical Prints in the Reign of George III* (New Haven and London, Yale University Press, 1996), pp. 180–3. For graphic alignments in caricature between Irish, Jews and Blacks see Pieterse, *White on Black*, pp. 213–15.

64 For revolutionary violence and the generation of propaganda within the English graphic arts see M. Phillips, 'Blake and the Terror', *The Library*, 16:4 (1994).

65 For enlightenment fascination with the piebald negro see Barbara Maria Stafford, '"Peculiar Marks": Lavater and the Countenance of Blemished Thought', *Art Journal*, 46:3 (1987) 185–92.

66 Seal of the Society for the Abolition of the Slave Trade, 'Am I not a man and a brother?', reproduced in Thomas Clarkson, *The History of the Rise, Progress, and Accomplishment of the Abolition of the African Slave-Trade by the British Parliament*, 2 vols (London, 1808) 1, p. 450.

67 George Cruikshank, 'Peterloo Medal', *A Slap at Slop* (London, 1820), p. 1. For the political context to this print see Wood, *Radical Satire*, pp. 210–14.

68 Howard Temperley, *British Anti-Slavery 1833–1870* (London, Longman, 1972), pp. 19–42, 93–168; Drescher, 'The Ending of the Slave Trade', 388–93.

69 See George Cruikshank, *Slavery in the West Indies* (London, 1830), p. 1.

70 Cruikshank, *Comic Almanack*, p. 179.

71 Cruikshank, *Comic Almanack*, plate opposite p. 179.

72 For Victorian scientific racism see Christine Bolt, *Victorian Attitudes to Race* (London, Routledge and Keegan Paul, 1971), pp. 1–29. For equations between Irish and other colonial categories, see Robert J. C. Young, *Colonial Desire: Hybridity in Theory, Culture and Race* (London and New York, Routledge, 1995), pp. 68–98; Augstein, *Race*, pp. 240–60; Donald, *Age of Caricature*, pp. 180–3. For Cruikshank's anti-Irish caricature in its most brutal form see his plates illustrating William Hamilton Maxwell, *History of the Irish Rebellion* (London, 1845).

73 Cruikshank, *Comic Almanack*, plate opposite p. 104.

74 See Pieterse, *White on Black*, pp. 59–63.

75 In 1853 Cassell brought out *Autographs for Freedom. By Mrs. Harriet Beecher Stowe, and Thirty-five other eminent Writers*, a pirated reprint of an American title brought out by the 'Rochester Ladies Anti-Slavery Society'. The preface to the American edition stated that the profits 'will be devoted to the dissemination of light and truth on the

subject of slavery throughout the country'. The English preface made no such claims, but is devoted to puffing the literary reputations of the American contributors for an English audience.

76 George Cruikshank Collection, Victoria and Albert Museum, Box I 95, items 9880 A–Z, 9881 A–T.

77 The best accounts of the development of this theory and its widespread nineteenth-century application to racist theory is John S. Haller Jnr., *Outcasts from Evolution: Scientific Attitudes to Racial Inferiority* (Urbana and London, University of Illinois Press, 1971); see also Pieterse, *White on Black*, pp. 46–9.

78 George Cruikshank, wood-engraving, *A Slap at Slop*, p. 4.

79 See Patten, *George Cruikshank's Life*, 2, pp. 257–60. For Victorian images of female suicide see Brian Maidment, *Reading Popular Prints 1790–1870* (Manchester, Manchester University Press, 1996), pp. 138–67. For Herman Melville's relationship with the image see Robert K. Wallace, *Melville and Turner: Spheres of Love and Fright* (Athens and London, University of Georgia Press, 1992), pp. 372–3.

80 Harriet Beecher Stowe, *Uncle Tom's Cabin*, ed. Elizabeth Ammons (New York, Norton, [1852] 1994), p. 113.

81 See Kynaston McShane (ed.), *Andy Warhol: A Retrospective* (New York, Museum of Modern Art, 1989), plate 266.

82 Jessy Torrey, *A Portraiture of Domestic Slavery in the United States* (Philadelphia, 1817), p. 43.

83 *Uncle Tom's Cabin* (London, Clarke and Beeton, 1853), front and back endpapers.

84 Clarke and Beeton advertised as a companion to *Uncle Tom's Cabin*: '*THE WHITE SLAVE* The people's illustrated edn. Uniform with *Uncle Tom's Cabin*' and more enticingly '*THE WHITE SLAVE* the railway edn. Illustrated with eight engravings with Important Notes from the American and other authorities illustrative of the awful system of slavery. Neatly bound in ornamental boards, price 1s. Be careful to ask for Cooke's edition with notes.'

85 Harriet Beecher Stowe, *Uncle Tom's Cabin, or, Life Among the Lowly, by H.B.S. Illustrated edition Complete in one volume* (London, Sampson Low, 1853).

86 For the argument that Stowe based her portrait of Prue on an account in *American Slavery As It Is* see Bruce E. Kirkham, *The Building of Uncle Tom's Cabin* (Knoxville, University of Tennessee Press, 1977), pp. 101–3.

87 Krafft-Ebbing and Freud cited in Karen Halttunen, 'Humanitarianism and the Pornography of Pain in Anglo-American Culture', *American Historical Review*, 100:2 (1995) 331–2. See also Sigmund Freud, '"A Child is Being Beaten": A Contribution to the Study of the Origin of Sexual Perversions', in *Sigmund Freud, Collected Papers*, ed. Ernest Jones, trans. Joan Riviere, 5 vols (London, Hogarth Press, 1950), 2, p. 173.

88 James Baldwin, 'Everybody's Protest Novel', *Partisan Review*, 16 (1949) 578–85.

89 Stowe, *Uncle Tom's Cabin*, ed. Ammons (1994), p. 18.

90 Karen C. Chambers Dalton, '"The Alphabet is an Abolitionist": Literary and African Americans in the Emancipation Era', *Massachusetts Review*, 32:4 (1992) 545–73.

91 Anon., *The Origin of Jim Crow* (London, 1837), p. 17.

92 Gates, *Signifying Monkey*, p. 176.

93 For the early impact of Virginia Minstrels on English audiences see Nathan, *Dan Emmett*, pp. 135–43. Nathan provides the best historical overview of the development of black idiom within minstrelsy. For the ways the iconography of minstrelsy feeds into later cultural representations of blacks see Pieterse, *White on Black*, pp. 132–48. For the transatlantic dialogue of this imagery see Phillip Lapsansky, 'Graphic Discord: Abolitionist and Anti-abolitionist Images', in Jean Fagin Yellin and John C. Van Horne (eds), *The Abolitionist Sisterhood: Women's Political Culture in Ante-bellum America* (Ithaca, Cornell University Press, in collaboration with the Library Company of Philadelphia, 1994), pp. 220–1.

94 John Ruskin, *The Library Edition of the Works of John Ruskin*, ed. E. T. Cook and A. Wedderburn, 39 vols (London, George Allen, 1903–12), 5, pp. 96–7.

95 For Tom and feminisation see Elizabeth Ammons, 'Stowe's Dream of the Mother Saviour: *Uncle Tom's Cabin* and American Women Writers before the 1920s', in Eric J. Sundquist (ed.), *New Essays on Uncle Tom's Cabin* (Cambridge, Cambridge University Press, 1986), pp. 161–79. For Duncanson see Sharon F. Patton, *African American Art* (Oxford and New York, Oxford University Press, 1998), pp. 74–5.

96 For the symbolic and literary European inheritance see Linda Van Norden, *The Black Feet of the Peacock: The Color-Concept 'Black' From the Greeks Through the Renaissance*, ed. and compiled John Pollock (New York and London, University Press of America, 1985); Peter Mark, *Africans in European Eyes: The Portrayal of Black Africans in Fourteenth and Fifteenth Century Europe* (New York, Maxwell School, Syracuse University, 1974). For the major shifts in racist attitudes towards blacks in England from 1830 to 1860 see Catherine Hall, *White, Male and Middle Class: Explorations in Feminism and History* (Cambridge, Polity Press, 1988), pp. 208–9, 275; Catherine Hall, 'Imperial Man: Edward Eyre in Australasia and the West Indies 1833–66', in Bill Schwarz (ed.), *The Expansion of England: Race, Ethnicity and Cultural History* (London and New York, Routledge, 1996), pp. 130–71. Nancy Stepan, *The Idea of Race in Science: Great Britain 1800–1960* (London, Macmillan, 1982), pp. 1–46. Patrick Brantlinger, *Rule of Darkness: British Literature and Imperialism 1830–1914* (Ithaca and London, Cornell University Press, 1988); Victor Kiernan, *The Lords of Human Kind: Black Men, Yellow Men, and White Men in an Age of Empire* (London, Weidenfield and Nicholson, 1969), pp. 203–55. For racist-Darwinism see Lemuel A. Johnson, *The Devil, the Gargoyle, and the Buffoon: The Negro as Metaphor in Western Literature* (Port Washington, Kennitkat Press, 1969), pp. 57–9. For an overview of the operations of racism in the iconography of European popular culture during this period see Pieterse, *White on Black*, pp. 64–74, and pp. 57–63 for racist content in abolition iconography in the first half of the nineteenth century and its influence on the reception of *Uncle Tom's Cabin*.

97 Thackeray quoted and discussed in Honour, *Image of the Black*, 4:1, p. 204. For endemic racism in the Victorian literary establishment see Pieterse, *White on Black*, pp. 60–1. For an anatomisation of the popular Western vocabulary of racist myth see Roland Barthes, 'African Grammar', in Golberg (ed.), *Anatomy of Racism*, pp. 130–4.

98 For a clever reading of Gericault's 'Raft of the Medusa' in terms of black cannibalism see Garry Wills, 'The Dark Legacy of the Enlightenment', *New York Review of Books*, 36:5 (1989) 11. For cannibalistic tropes in eighteenth- and nineteenth-century popular fictions see H. L. Malchow, *Gothic Images of Race in Nineteenth-Century Britain* (Stanford, Stanford University Press, 1996), pp. 41–124; Kiernen, *Lords of Human Kind*, pp. 224, 258. For the continuation of these tropes see Frantz Fanon, *Black Face, White Masks*, trans. Charles Lam Markmann (London, Pluto, 1986), pp. 113–16; Roland Barthes, 'Bichon and the Blacks', in Goldberg (ed.), *Anatomy of Racism*, pp. 127–30; for Obeah and cannibalism see Leonard de Vries (ed.), *'Orrible Murder: Victorian Crime and Passion Selections from the Illustrated Police News* (London, Macdonald, 1971), p. 103.

99 For the extent of the abolition/missionary semiotic conflation pre-dating *Uncle Tom's Cabin*, see Catherine Hall, *White, Male and Middle Class*, pp. 207–54; Lorimer, *Colour*, pp. 70–2. For the publishing context for nineteenth-century missionary activity see Leslie Howsam, *Cheap Bibles: Nineteenth-Century Publishing and the British and Foreign Bible Society* (Cambridge, Cambridge University Press, 1991). For racism and mid-nineteenth-century missionary activity see Curtin, *Image*, pp. 419–28. For the popular iconography of whites and blacks in the context of missionary expansion and African colonisation see Pieterse, *White on Black*, pp. 64–96.

100 Theodore R. Hovet, *The Master Narrative: Harriet Beecher Stowe's Subversive Story of Master and Slave in Uncle Tom's Cabin and Dred* (New York, University Press of America, 1989), pp. 36–41 provides an ingenious defence of the 'missionary' conclusion to *Uncle Tom's Cabin* in terms of an overriding 'master narrative' which places Tom's death and George's return to Africa in typological correspondence via a universalising

historiographic framework of great complexity. In this reading Stowe's theologico-
historical perspective constructs the Christian emergence of Africa as giving form to
'humanity's proper "home", its "native land"'. This is absurdly over-elaborate. Hovet's
assertion that it is inadvisable to read the conclusion of Stowe's novel in the contexts of
re-colonisation and missionary expansion into Africa is badly weakened by the fact that
he does not allude to Topsy, or the Topsy–Eva relationship.

101 Stowe, *Uncle Tom's Cabin*, ed. Ammons (1994), p. 377.
102 Quoted Hall, *White, Male and Middle Class*, p. 220. For the explosion in the recruit-
     ment of single women to the African missions see Modupe Labode, 'From Heathen
     Kraal to Christian Home: Anglican Mission Education and African Christian Girls
     1850–1900', in Fiona Bowie, Deborah Kirkwood and Shirley Ardener (eds), *Women
     and Missions: Past and Present Anthropological and Historical Perceptions*
     (Providence and Oxford, Berg, 1993), pp. 126–42.
103 Stowe, *Uncle Tom's Cabin*, ed. Ammons (1994), p. 208.
104 Stowe, *Uncle Tom's Cabin*, ed. Ammons (1994), p. 213.
105 Stowe, *Uncle Tom's Cabin*, ed. Ammons (1994), p. 244.
106 Stowe, *Uncle Tom's Cabin*, ed. Ammons (1994), p. 245.
107 *My New Toy Book* (*c.* 1860), p. 10. The only known copy of this volume is uncatalogued,
     in the Opie Collection, Bodleian Library, University of Oxford.
108 For the extent to which Topsy represents an anarchic other within Stowe's text which
     cannot be controlled see Sarah Smith Duckworth, 'Stowe's Construction of an African
     Persona and the Creation of White Identity for a New World Order', in Lowance
     Westbrook and De Prospo (eds), *The Stowe Debate* (Amherst, University of
     Massachusetts Press, 1994), pp. 223–5.
109 *Topsy's Frolics or Always in Mischief* (*c.* 1855), uncatalogued material in Opie Collection,
     Bodleian Library, Oxford. For the centrality of missionary and colonial myths to racism
     in English children's books see Dorothy Kuya, 'Racism in Children's Books in Britain',
     in Roy Preiswerk (ed.), *The Slant of the Pen: Racism in Children's Books* (Geneva, World
     Council of Churches, 1980), pp. 26–45, and Isabelle Suhl, 'Doctor Dolittle – The Great
     White Father', in Judith Stinton (ed.), *Racism and Sexism in Children's Books* (London,
     Writers and Readers Publishing Co-operative, 1979), pp. 19–27.
110 For a summary of Henson's relation to Uncle Tom and Stowe's relation to him see
     Gosset, *Uncle Tom's Cabin*, pp. 107–10; Kirkham, *The Making*, pp. 88–93.
111 John Lobb [Josiah Henson], *The Young People's Illustrated Edition of 'Uncle Tom's'
     Story of his Life from 1789–1877* (London, Christian Age Office, 1877), pp. 7–13. Josiah
     Henson, *'Uncle Tom's Story of his Life' an Autobiography of the Rev. Josiah Henson*
     (London, 1877), p. 11 states that the book 'has been translated into the French, Italian,
     Dutch, Swedish, Welsh and other languages. The English edition is now in its 80'th
     thousand.'
112 Lobb, *Young People's Edition*, p. 16. For a detailed account of the meeting with Victoria
     see Birdoff, *World's Greatest Hit*, pp. 238–40.
113 Lobb, *Young People's Edition*, p. 141. For the effect of the audience with Victoria on the
     reading public see Birdoff, *World's Greatest Hit*, pp. 238–40.
114 Lobb, *Young People's Edition*, p. 55.
115 *Wellington and Uncle Tom: or the Hero of this World Contrasted with the Hero in Jesus
     Christ* (London, Simkin Marshall and Co., 1853).
116 *Wellington*, p. 13.
117 *Wellington*, pp. 17, 19.
118 Birdoff, *World's Greatest Hit*, p. 329.
119 See pp. 276–80 below.
120 Marcus Wood, 'Seeing is Believing or Finding "Truth" in Slave Narrative: The
     Narrative of Henry Bibb as Perfect Mis-representation', *Slavery and Abolition*, 18:3
     (1997) 174–211.
121 Bernard F. Reilly (ed.), *American Political Prints 1766–1876: A Catalog of the
     Collections in the Library of Congress*, (Boston, G.K. Hall, 1991), 1861–11.

122 Harriet Beecher Stowe, *Uncle Tom's Cabin ... with above* 150 *Illustrations by George Thomas* (London, Nathaniel Cook, 1853), p. 202.

123 Stowe, *Uncle Tom's Cabin* (1853), p. 207.

124 The most comprehensive survey of Southern responses to *Uncle Tom's Cabin*, and of anti-Tom literature generally, is in Gosset, *Uncle Tom's Cabin*, pp. 185–238.

125 Reilly (ed.), *American Political Prints*, 1853–61. The print is reproduced in Cassuto, *Inhuman Race*, p. 148, where, oddly, it is related not to Callot but to Bosch.

126 There is much scholarly debate around the symbolic identification of this figure in Callot's print. It now seems most probable that she does represent Vanity, or pride. See H. Diane Russell, *Jacques Callot: Prints and Related Drawings* (Washington, National Gallery of Art, 1985), pp. 156–60, 176–7.

127 For a detailed account of the different stage sets which influenced Callot see Russell, *Jaques Callot*, pp. 156, 159.

128 For immediate and vast number of stage adaptations of *Uncle Tom's Cabin* see Gosset, *Uncle Tom's Cabin*, pp. 260–84, 367–88. Henry James, *A Small Boy*, p. 168 stated that: 'Uncle Tom, instead of making even one of the cheap short cuts through the medium in which books breathe, even as fishes in water, went gaily round about it altogether, as if a fish, a wonderful leaping fish, had simply flown through the air. This feat accomplished the surprising creature could naturally fly anywhere, and one of the first things it did was thus to flutter down on every stage, literally without exception, in America and Europe.'

129 He describes himself as a subterranean figure in Job I: 7–8: 'Whence comest thou, "From walking up and down in the earth and going to and fro in it."'

130 For the Lucifer identification see Russell, *Jacques Callot*, p. 156.

Representing pain and describing torture: slavery, punishment and martyrology

5

l'homme-famine, l'homme insulté, l'homme-torture on pouvait à n'importe quel moment le saisir le rouer de coups, le tuer – parfaitement le tueur – sans avoir de compte à rendre à personne sans avoir d'excuses à présenter à personne [the starvation-man, the insult-man, the torture-man, one could grab him at any time, beat him up, kill him – yes, kill him too – without having to account to anyone, without having to apologise to anyone] (Aimé Césaire, *Cahier d'un retour au pay naturel*)

And he could not forget Father Beron with his monotonous phrase, 'Will you confess now?' reaching him in an awful iteration and lucidity of meaning through the delirious incoherence of unbearable pain. He could not forget. But that was not the worst. Had he met Father Beron in the street after all these years Dr. Monygham was sure he would have quailed before him. This contingency was not to be feared now. Father Beron was dead; but the sickening certitude prevented Dr. Monygham from looking anybody in the face. Dr. Monygham had become, in a manner, *the slave of a ghost*. (Joseph Conrad, *Nostromo*, my emphasis)

Slavery and the language of torture

Slave societies were founded upon a legally encoded property relation: the slave was property, the free owner was not. The enforcement of this relation, as with any human system of absolute power, relied ultimately upon fear. To instil fear and obedience in the powerless requires the systematic application of torture. I am using 'torture' here in a sense usually, but inappropriately, reserved for this century. Many contemporary theorists of torture see an important division between twentieth-century motives for using torture and those of earlier periods: 'The technology of torture in the twentieth century is in part the result of a new anthropology, and its attendant technology. It is not primarily the victim's information, but the victim, that torture needs to win – or reduce to powerlessness.'[1] This assertion is historically rather innocent, for the association of torture with a state of powerlessness (indeed with an articulation of the absence of power in the victim of torture which grows out of the destruction of personality) had been articulated specifically in the context of slavery in the mid-eighteenth century. In the most influential legal disquisition upon the morally abhorrent status of torture to be produced in the West in the last two centuries,

215

Cesare Beccaria made the startling assertion that the complete inadequacy of torture as a means of extracting truth was well known to 'Roman legislators, among whom one does not encounter the use of torture, except with slaves who were denied any personality'.[2] While not as absolute as Beccaria's verdict on Rome, the slave's ethical positioning with regard to torture within plantation slavery systems in the Americas during the eighteenth and nineteenth centuries also defies the chronology of recent torture theory. The treatment of many Southern slaves suggests a full development of the so-called 'new anthropology' of torture. If the slave body was property, the slave personality was not, and the majority of torture inflicted on slaves grew out of the desire to break down the personality of the subject/victim, to generate and then enforce a consciousness of disempowerment and anti-personality. The slave power was consequently an unending network of torture. Psychological methods of abuse permeated day-to-day existence. The anatomisation of the psychological minutiae of domestic oppression within the experience of one woman emerges with a unique clarity in Harriet Jacobs's *Incidents in the Life of a Slave Girl*. Slave 'families' were exposed to the capricious or organised intervention of the owner, or any deputed agent, at any time. Nothing was private: sexual relations and 'marriage', children and childrearing, education, food and the rituals of eating, labour, leisure, everything could be watched and controlled.[3]

The visible evidence of torture was not, however, manifested within the complicated psychological pressures which grew out of perpetual surveillance but via acts, frequently ritualised acts, of physical abuse. These rapidly became an emotional factotum for Western anti-slavery audiences. The representation of slave torture in the art and literature of the West focused around a fairly consistent set of signs and rituals. The following work considers some of the ways in which artists in England and America drew, engraved, sculpted and painted the slave body as a site for the infliction of physical pain. The slave emerges predominantly as an object afflicted, not as a subject capable of describing his or her affliction. The pain of slaves, when translated into imagery and visual narrative, is most commonly related to, and imparted through, a series of objects. These objects are not unique to slavery, but familiar to Western experience: shackles, chains, collars, stocks, brands, gallows, cages, bits, bridles, thumbscrews, fires and whips. These things have existed as the tools of torture for centuries: they have been used, and have been represented within European culture, in the context of punishment. Some of them, such as the scold's bridle, or branks, relate primarily to the punishment or torture of women.[4]

There are judicial and religious contexts for the aesthetic presentation of these objects. In the area of criminology the show trial and the public punishment of criminals generated mass literatures featuring torture and execution.[5] Relevant points of intersection between Western criminology

and the representation of slave abuse are discussed below, but the first
point to make is that the pictures of the infliction of torture upon criminals
within the West cannot easily be equated with the representation of the torture of slaves within the plantation systems of the Americas. Slaves were
denied recourse to the law and they consequently existed in an uneasy
relationship to, indeed frequently outside, Western theories and philoso-
phies of punishment.[6]

When considering religious models for the depiction of pain and torture the black slave inhabits another complicated space. The Passion of
Christ and the martyrdom of the saints lie at the textual and iconic heart of
Christian art, and inform the most influential visual paradigms that the
West possesses for the aesthetic rendering of extreme and ritualised violence.[7] The ordeals which Christ was forced to undergo were specifically
designed to degrade him, and the form of death administered, crucifixion,
was predominantly reserved for Roman slaves. Indeed crucifixion only
ceased to be regarded as a slave punishment when Constantine, following
his conversion to Christianity, legally substituted hanging as the preferred
method of slave execution because he found the association of Christ with
slave too shameful.[8]

Constantine was not the only influential figure to find the comparison
difficult. Christ's whipping provided the site for the most frequent examination of the effects of flagellation within Western visual aesthetics – a
whole iconography of whipping lay open to abolitionists if they wanted to
use it. The fact that the visual codes provided by this inheritance were little
drawn upon in eighteenth- and nineteenth-century depictions of slave
punishment relates to the demonising of the black within the iconography
of Western culture. Blacks occupied an unstable space within Western
iconography from the late twelfth century onwards, but the association of
the colour black with Satan and Anti-Christ led to the early identification
of black Africans with devils, demons and the administration of hellish
punishments. Although some contexts did exist for the positive construction of black Africans, they were more frequently represented in paintings,
sculptures, illuminated manuscripts and stained glass windows showing
the mocking and flagellation of Christ. Giotto's ghastly representation of
the black torturer in his mural of the Mocking of Christ in the Scrovegni
Chapel in Padua [**plate 7**] is the most remarkable example within a tradition
which extends back to the late twelfth century. Giotto's black stands back
from the ring of whites who encircle Christ. He is a figure who, in his psychological complexity and formal elegance, breaks from the dehumanised
figurations of black torturers in earlier Christian art. This man knows what
he is doing, and possesses a poise and control in the administration of violence which separates him from the emotional extravagance, or even self-
indulgence, of the whites surrounding Christ. His impassiveness is
terrifying in its ambiguity – only the extended fingers of his left hand,
reaching out into space, indicate a sense of tension. This image is unique

[5.1] Anon., 'Our Peculiar Domestic Institutions' (wood-engraving, 1840). From *The Anti-Slavery Almanac*

in Western art in the subtlety with which it sets out the black in relation to the conventions of Christian martyrology.[9]

Yet the majority of imagery involving blacks and torture thrown up by Western abolition movements shows the black not as aggressor but as victim, and there are many interpretative traps to evade in reading these images. The viewer must always remain alert to the possibility that the suffering of the slave may emerge as an incidental ingredient in the general rhetoric of accusation directed at the controlling white populations of slave societies. An extreme articulation of the dangers of such an approach is the wood-engraving 'Our Peculiar Domestic Institutions' from the *New York Anti-Slavery Almanac of 1840* [5.1]. It might be argued that such a plate attempts to provide a wider social context for the consideration of the physical abuse of slaves in the Southern states, by presenting a panorama of violent and immoral behaviour considered normal in plantation societies. The imagery could also be seen to grow out of a Hogarthian didactic tradition which attempts to explain ultimate social abuses by setting lesser forms of cruelty against greater, the purest narrative paradigm for such social satire being Hogarth's *Four Stages of Cruelty*.[10] Yet where does the slave stand in relation to the violence inflicted by white men on white men, and by white men on animals? This plate with its frantic panoply of extreme ritualised violence throws together fighting cocks, duellists, bound slaves having cats dragged down their backs, whipped black slave children, lynched whites and random shootings. A melodramatic fantasy emerges in which the South is a maelstrom of barbarism, in which only the fashionable costume of white males

218

suggests that there is a civilisation in which to locate this theatre of cruelty. The black emerges not as a carefully articulated subject of violence but as one of the objects describing the effects of violence. Which is to say the black subject is comprehensively disempowered through the lazy force of generalisation.

The objects and rituals of slave torture are consequently narratively and iconographically 'familiar' territory within Western visual representation. Yet, as we shall see, because of the strange status of the black slave body in the West, this fact does not necessarily facilitate, and in many ways problematises, the depiction of atrocity upon the body of slaves.

The voices of artefacts

There sat on one of the tables inside the Quirinale Palace, a simple modern device, looking something like a microphone, with electrodes dangling from it. The catalogue acknowledged that critics had objected to the inclusion of the instrument in the exhibit. It was not an antique, it lacked the patina of age, the artisinal quality of the other items in the exhibit … this instrument composed of the only too familiar elements of modern technology defamiliarised the devices on exhibit; removing them from the universe of the museum, it identified them with the calculated infliction of human agony. (Page duBois, *Torture and Truth*)

When you cut your finger bandage the knife. (Joseph Beuys)

Wittgenstein asks whether we ought not to be able to speak of the stone that causes hurt as having 'pain patches' on it? (Elaine Scarry, *The Body in Pain*)

To represent slave torture is to make it a comparative experience, its display an artistic, and often an institutional, challenge. To claim the right to describe the experience of the tortured slave is to proclaim access to this experience. The procedure usually involves either the attempt to aestheticise, or the attempt to institutionalise, a memory which lies outside the obvious resources of Western aesthetics.

When suffering was, and is, remembered through the implements which were used by the torturers, or through representations of these implements, it needs to be asked to what extent this constitutes a useful resource for thinking about slavery. The Holocaust indicates how problematic objects can be as memory tools.[11] In his work on Holocaust memorials James Young warns of the power of artefacts to mislead. Meditating on the items now displayed at Majdanek, and in the two display blocks at Auschwitz, Young articulates the gap between the effect which these objects have on viewers and the cause which led to their accumulation: 'What precisely does the sight of concentration camp artefacts awaken in viewers? Historical knowledge? A sense of evidence? Revulsion, grief, pity, fear … what does our knowledge of these objects – a bent spoon, children's shoes, crusty old striped uniforms – have to do with our knowledge of historical events?'[12] The artefacts which were applied and attached to

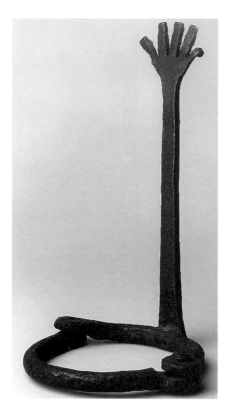

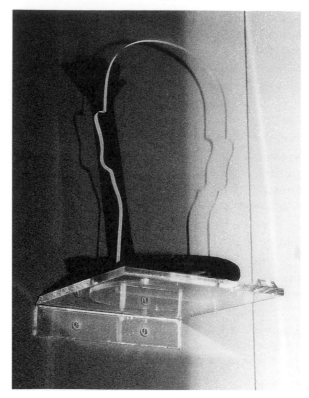

[5.2] Anon., punishment collar (cast iron, eighteenth century)

[5.3] Anon., punishment collar, displayed with perspex cut-out representation of slave head (cast iron, eighteenth century, glass and perspex twentieth century)

the bodies of slaves, and which were then preserved either in museums or in printed representations in books, are not a gateway to knowledge of the events which produced them, or a substitute for the experience of anyone, white or black, involved in the processes of their use.

The slave collar as floating signifier

Inside a glass case in the Transatlantic Slavery Gallery in Liverpool is a beautiful wrought iron punishment collar [**5.2**]. The simple hand-forged semi-circles of the collar form a soft heavy round, and leaping up from this, vertically, is a tapering arm at full stretch, culminating in a fully extended hand. This object could be a bozzetto for a monument. Cast in bronze 18 feet high and placed outside a public building, it might constitute a sculptural celebration of the indominatability of the human spirit. There would be an eternal circle cut through by a vertical line shooting heavenwards and crowned with the maker's hand. In the museum catalogue the object is photographed alone, beautifully lit. In the museum it is displayed with a transparent perspex cut-out of the outline of a human head and neck placed through it [**5.3**]. There is a similar colourless cut-out placed within a neighbouring slave collar. Are these approximations of the human form – without colour, without sex, without character – supposed to get us closer to thinking our way into the collar?[13] The vertical steel rod was beaten out and welded onto the collar to enforce a position of submissive discomfort. Why the hand was placed there will not be known – maybe it was meant to mock the tortured victim in its gesture of freedom. Then again it could be a literalisation of the function of the collar, the hand reaching out to clutch at undergrowth. This collar is beautiful in form and disgusting in function.

Another problematic depiction of the slave collar occurs within the first heavily illustrated American slave narrative, the *Narrative of the Adventures and Escape of Moses Roper*. The first engraving was utterly changed from the 1837 first edition to the 1838 second edition. In the first edition there is a three-quarter page line-drawing of a slave punishment collar, the neck yoke seen from above, the bells and cross struts seen from the side [5.4]. The design is framed by the following text:[14]

> Another mode of punishment which this man adopted was that of using iron horns, with bells, attached to the back of the slave's neck. The following is the instrument of torture … [plate intervenes] This instrument he used to prevent the Negroes running away, being a very ponderous machine, seven feet in height, and the cross pieces being two feet four and six feet in length. This custom is generally adopted among the slave-holders in South Carolina, and some other slave states.[15]

In the second edition this diagrammatic style is rejected for a very different approach [5.5]. This time the same text frames an image of a black woman, drawn small and featureless, her face 'blacked' out. Her legs and arms, drawn without shading, are solid areas of black. She wears a smart white shift, with hemmed neckline, gathered in at the waist with a belt, and a small cotton cap is perched on the top of her

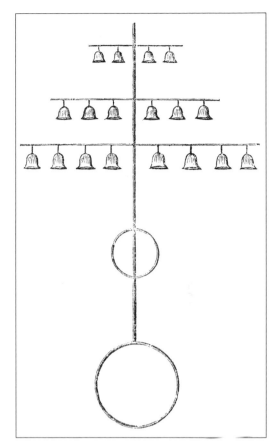

[5.4] Anon., 'Another Mode of Punishment' (wood-engraving, 1837). From *Narrative of the Adventures and Escape of Moses Roper*

A WOMAN WITH IRON HORNS AND BELLS ON, TO KEEP HER FROM RUNNING AWAY.

[5.5] Anon., 'A woman with iron horns and bells on' (wood-engraving, 1838). From *Narrative of the Adventures and Escape of Moses Roper*

head. Rising at a shallow angle in a black line from behind the white cap is a long thin pole narrowing to its tip and angled in exact accordance with the inclination of her head and neck. It supports three bars crossing at right angles and increasing in length towards the base. Hanging from each bar is a series of minute equilateral triangles, four on the first bar, six on the second, eight on the third. The effect is very different from the scientific precision of the earlier design. The collar has been put on, and now, in its delicacy and fragility, it is much more difficult to 'read' and looks like some marvellous toy, or flamboyant head-dress. The image is explained by a caption in heavy capitals: 'A WOMAN WITH IRON HORNS AND BELLS ON, TO KEEP HER FROM RUNNING AWAY'; the accompanying text is otherwise unaltered.

These very different images show how relative, not to say uncontrollable, an affair the representation of objects can be.[16] The punishment collars in slavery museums, and the engravings in Roper's *Narrative,* relate strangely to what I believe to be the first representation within Western art of a slave collar on an African body. It occurs as part of the heraldic paraphernalia on the arms of Sir John Hawkins, pirate and first significant English slaver [**5.6**]. As a result of his first two slave-trading voyages, 'arms were granted to him: sable, on a point wavy a lion passant or; in chief three bezants: and for a crest, a demi-Moor proper in chains'.[17] In other words black slaves populated his coat of arms, and this is not in itself remarkable. The 'black-Moor' had been a standard element within European heraldic vocabularies from the late thirteenth century, and carried a wide series of associations both positive and negative.[18] The Hawkins arms incorporated the black as a figure enslaved and tortured. An enormous armoured helmet surmounts Hawkins's shield and carries as its crest a naked African, depicted from the waist up, his arms in shackles. The bottom quarter of the shield shows three Africans wearing punishment collars. They are painted identically and sit comfortably among the other brilliantly coloured and repeated symbols – lions, anchors, oak leaves and cannon balls. Slave punishment emblazoned in the emblematic sign systems of heraldry is thereafter locked within the cultural bibles of British aristocratic genealogy.

When and how instruments of torture, or the representation of instruments of torture, come alive for an audience, and what, if anything, an audience should have to do with them, are unstable questions. Cultural perspectives inflect the way the objects of torture

[**5.6**] Arms of Sir John Hawkins (line drawing in ink, *c.* 1888). From Mary W. S. Hawkins, *Plymouth Armada Heroes: The Hawkins Family*

ARMS OF SIR JOHN HAWKINS.

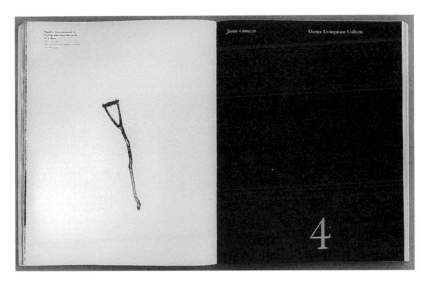

[5.7] Wooden slave yoke, Livingstone Collection. Reproduced in *David Livingstone and the Victorian Encounter with Africa*

are seen. The metal slave punishment collar shifted its iconographic status from one of cold-blooded celebration in Hawkins's day to one of humanitarian outrage in Thomas Clarkson's.[19] Yet not all slave collars carried the same cultural associations. The wooden slave yoke, used to attach a line of slave's in a coffle, was constructed negatively in the West as a symbol of the African overland slave trade. While the carefully forged European iron collars carry one set of associations, the rustic and cumbersome African wooden yokes operate in a very different semiotic arena. The particular association of the wooden yoke with the slave trade on the African mainland remains consistent from the multiple reproductions of slave yokes in Clarkson's 1791 *Letters on the Slave Trade* to its mid-nineteenth-century construction in missionary publications. Central to this tradition was David Livingstone's personal collection of the paraphernalia of African slavery. The 1996 'David Livingstone and the Victorian Encounter with Africa' exhibition at the National Portrait Gallery included a yoke bearing the caption 'Wooden yoke removed by Livingstone from the neck of a slave' [5.7]. In the lavish catalogue the yoke floats, isolated on a white page, while opposite on a completely black page the title of the fourth chapter reads, in thin white letters, 'Doctor Livingstone Collects'. The value of this yoke was, and continues to be, as an object which the heathen hand of an African put round another African neck and which the Christian hand of Livingstone then removed. Livingstone's preservation of this object and its subsequent display relate to a primitive consciousness-raising technique whereby European philanthropy literally objectified the memory of slavery. Once the object of torture has gained such primacy the slave body is no longer necessary in order to remember, or to pretend to remember, slavery.[20]

[5.8] Alexander Anderson, *Injured Humanity* (wood-engraving and letterpress, broadside, 1805)

Looking through the mask of suffering

In 1797 Alexander Anderson made a number of wood-engravings for the spectacular abolition broadside *Injured Humanity* [5.8]. These included four images of slave punishment masks which had been adapted from an earlier English abolition broadside. The mask is identical in appearance to the branks or scold's bridle used on English and Scottish women up until

224

the eighteenth century. A fine example is still on display among Sir Walter Scott's collection of antiquarian curiosities in his Abbotsford residence. Anderson explores what happens when an object of torture is applied to a human, but again it is important to think about what he is asking of the viewer and of the slave.

The iron mask and gag, placed upon runaways and slaves who tried to commit suicide by eating dirt, is described impassively: 'A front and profile view of an African's head, with the mouth-piece … [there] is a flat iron which goes into the mouth, and so effectually keeps down the tongue, that nothing can be swallowed, not even the saliva, a passage for which is made through holes in the mouth plate … An enlarged view of the mouth piece which when long worn becomes so heated as frequently to bring off the skin along with it.' Anderson's designs describing the iron mask [**5.9** and **5.10**] are powerful because he refuses to stop at the depiction of the object in isolation but forces the viewer to confront what happens when it is put upon a human. The mask is initially set out as a piece of uncontaminated hardware, alongside shackles and spurs, and in formal terms possesses a certain serpentine beauty – it could be an antique battle helmet. The mask is then reproduced twice in full face and profile, these portraits of the victim having a forensic air which prefigures the police mug shot [5.9]. The mask is put into action, placed on a slave head, the pure white of the metal matched by the pure whites of the tortured staring eyes. In co-opting and then partially obliterating the standard poses of Western portraiture, Anderson creates an image of mute agony, the tongue and face imprisoned, the only features left free to articulate trauma

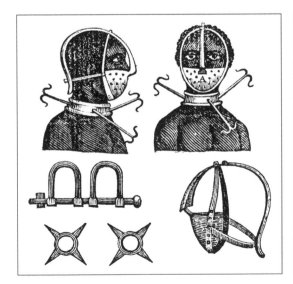

[5.9] Alexander Anderson, *Injured Humanity*, (wood-engraving and letterpress, broadside, 1805), detail 'Enlarged view'

Mouth-piece to prevent his eating—with Boots and Spurs round his legs, and half a hundred weight chained to his body to prevent his absconding.

[5.10] Alexander Anderson, *Injured Humanity*, (wood-engraving and letterpress, broadside, 1805), detail 'Mouth piece'

are the eyes, enclosed within the black face, which is itself formally framed by the perfect geometrical forms of the mask. Adding to the power of this image is its androgyny: the fragments of face, the chest cropped at bust length, could belong to either sex. This enforced androgyny is doubly significant in view of the fact that the slave mask was one of the many punishment devices devised in the West for the punishment of women and then re-adapted for use on both sexes in the colonial slave plantations.[21]

Anderson then extends the visual dialogue yet again, taking the mask up for a fourth time. Half way up the left column of the broadside there is a vignette of a slave hoeing a sugar field while wearing the mask, weights and spurs [5.10]. Here the style is softer and there is more contextualising detail, a hut, another slave, a landscape. The text introduces a note of descriptive irony: the slave is 'accoutred' in the full regalia of torture itemised on the opposite page. The object is subsumed into the day-to-day social activity of slavery, perhaps more poignant in view of the fact that Anderson was probably drawing on his personal observation while in the Caribbean.[22]

In their refusal to let the object of torture erase the slave body, Anderson's images anticipate the way in which the icon was to be adapted by a radical black consciousness in late-nineteenth-century Brazil, and subsequently absorbed nationally into Afro-Brazilian culture. The image of the dirt-eating mask remains the defining feature of the Afro-Brazilian Goddess Anastasia [5.11].[23] Anastasia, slave and martyr, is a Candomblé deity from Rio. She was said to have died wearing a dirt-eating mask, because she refused her master's attempts to rape her. She speaks to us through her eyes, the mouth shut down in the terrible contraption, its clean silver lines running over the skin of her face and head. There is a permanent shrine to her in the small covered garden of the great black church, the Church of our Lady of the Rosary for the Black People, in Salvador Bahia [5.12]. The priests do not allow her in the main body of the church, but she exists comfortably in the small tropical garden, resting up, behind bars, in series of photographs and statues, which are set out alongside a series of other icons from a variety of cultural sources, including fresh flowers, changed daily, candles, money, and Amazon Indian fertility sculptures. The whole installation forms a

[5.11] Anastasia (painted plaster cast, Bahia, c. 1990)

[5.12] Shrine to Anastasia, Church of the Rosary of Our Lady of the Black People, Salvador, Bahia

[5.13] Shrine to Anastasia, Church of the Rosary of Our Lady of the Black People, Salvador, Bahia

typically Bahian blend of eclecticism and narrative precision, and calls to mind Toni Morrison's assertion that the fragmenting experiences of slavery provided African-Americans with an essentially postmodern consciousness well before Western intellectuals developed their cultural theory.[24] The arrangement culminates in a small niche in which an oil painting of St Christopher, a plaster statue of the deposed Christ and the Virgin, another plaster bust of Anastasia, and fresh flowers are placed together [**5.13**]. For the Brazilians who worship her she is not in competition with Christ or his mother, but part of them, and the suffering eyes which stare out from behind the metal mask simply affirm that the memory of slave torture is as much a part of black religious consciousness in Brazil as is the torture of Christ. This statue announces that the atrocity committed against slaves is capable of a mythologisation which avoids descriptive generalisation and, perhaps more importantly, anthropological re-colonisation within a purely African context. The dirt-eating mask moulded in plaster on Anastasia's face, placed in a shrine at the back of a Christian church, and worshipped, is not the same as the dirt-eating masks placed empty on the shelves of slavery museums. It is the human suffering which the torture produces which is finally both Anderson's and the anonymous Brazilian sculptor's subject.[25]

Models for understanding European representations of slave punishment: where is the slave's body in Foucault's archaeology of torture?

> Little makes sense. Little can be pinned down. Only the Indian in the stocks, being watched. And we are watching the watchers so that with our explanation we can pin them down and then pin down the real meaning of terror, putting it in the stocks of explanation. Yet in watching in this way we are made blind to the way that terror makes mockery of sense making, how it requires sense in order to mock it, and how in that mockery it heightens both sense and sensation. (Michael Taussig, *Colonialism, Shamanism and the Wild Man*)

In 1787 Thomas Clarkson bought a series of objects from Liverpool shops which were standard equipment on a slaver, and these were engraved in a design which became a virtual inventory for the displays in subsequent slavery museums [**5.14**].[26] Yet every one of these objects, including even the *speculum oris* used to force feed slaves, relate to familiar histories of suffering which lie within established European medical and penal environments. There has been a shift from a legal to an economic context for their application, but it is difficult to say where such semiotic contamination leaves the viewer of Clarkson's book, or the visitor standing within a clean new slavery gallery. The basic question here concerns the place which slave suffering has come to occupy within the shifting systematics of power which encode the display of ritual violence in the West. No one has provided more challenging structures for approaching this area than Michel Foucault.[27]

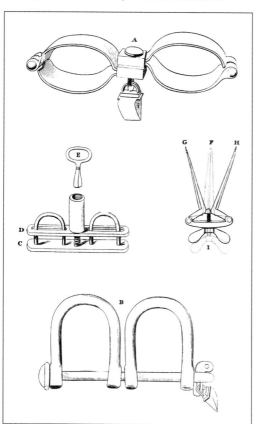

[**5.14**] Anon., 'Items used in the slave trade' (copper engraving, 1808). From Thomas Clarkson, *The History of the Rise, Progress, and Accomplishment of the Abolition of the African Slave-Trade by the British Parliament*

Discipline and Punish invented a new intellectual environment for the analysis of ritualised violence. Before looking at explicit examples of the visualisation of slave atrocity, I want to think about how the Foucaultian theory of violence and power does, or does not, apply to black people enslaved by Europeans during the eighteenth and nineteenth centuries. *Discipline and Punish* could be read as a treatise on the problematics of the description of torture, and yet within the terms of his analysis the relation of race to the language and semiotics of violence is a great silence. Foucault speaks for the victim of European eighteenth- and nineteenth-century

PAIN AND
TORTURE

surveillance techniques, yet how do his intellectual models relate to the way power and violence have been applied to white and to black in colonial societies?

The famous opening of *Discipline and Punish* articulates Foucault's central thesis through the quotation of two sets of texts. The first is a series of accounts of the execution of Damiens, the French Regicide, in 1757. The second is Leon Faucher's rules 'for the House of Young Prisoners in Paris' in 1837. Foucault sees the two approaches to punishment as defining the essential distance between the 'penal styles' of an old world and a modern world. The book's overall argument was summed up in an interview in 1975: [Question]: 'You determine one moment as being central in the history of repression: the transition from the inflicting of penalties to the imposition of surveillance.' [Foucault]: 'That's correct – the moment where it became understood that it was more efficient and profitable in terms of the economy of power to place people under surveillance than to subject them to some exemplary penalty.'[28]

The period 1770–1810 is seen as pivotal in Foucault's analysis. It is at this point that the modern penal codes appear, and the old-style rituals of death and dismemberment, with the public execution at its heart, disappear. Foucault says that 'By the end of the eighteenth and beginning of the nineteenth century, the gloomy festival of punishment was dying out, though here and there it flickered momentarily into life.'[29] Yet what of the colonial cultures, stretching from the Caribbean, and running across the Northern states of America and down through Brazil, Colombia and the majority of South America? In these slave societies millions of transported Africans lived under legal codes and societal structures established by white Europeans, in which physical torture, Foucault's 'gloomy festival of punishment', far from dying out, was flourishing. Yet there is a paradox, for ritualised violence flourished alongside the establishment of the kind of logical, abstract behavioural codes that, in Foucault's post-Enlightenment world, necessarily displaced the spectacle of physical punishment.[30]

So what does it mean that this moment should exist in the late eighteenth century for European societies' treatment of white criminals and not exist at all for the treatment of black African slaves in the colonial areas of the Americas and the Caribbean? These societies were, of course, composed of Europeans and their descendants, who exercised power over Africans and their descendants. Foucault talks of efficiency and profit within an economy of power, but what should be remembered is that within colonial structures in Africa and the Americas it is frequently not an economy simply of power, but of terror.[31] Yet it is precisely within the silences of Foucault's analysis that a context emerges for the analysis of the punishment of the slave body within slave societies. In the end Foucault enables us to question some of the limits within the languages which the West has adopted to describe colonial outrages.[32]

Against Foucault's two defining texts, a chronicle of torture and a timetable, I will set some other texts and pictures, which dissolve the chronology which Foucault sets up for central Europe. The kind of large-scale institutions controlling and timetabling human behaviour which Foucault sees as typifying late-eighteenth-century post-Enlightenment and utilitarian arrangements of Western societies, are already in place within the economies of the slave plantations from the seventeenth century. With the establishment of large-scale sugar production on the plantations of Brazil and French San Domingo in the mid-eighteenth century, and the setting up of elaborate slave codes to order and control the lives and punishment of slaves, the elements of surveillance set out as central to Foucault's eighteenth-century reforms are already in place.[33] But when Foucault states that the late eighteenth century was a time when 'in Europe and the United States, the entire economy of punishment was redistributed', the treatment of the slave populations is not acknowledged. The slave codes, and the operations of large plantations, combined logic and efficiency with barbaric violence, and a display of power which was focused upon the public torture of the body of the slave. Both the slave trade and plantation slavery seem, at every point, to confound the central division, the division between ritualised torture and ritualised surveillance, which lies at the intellectual heart of *Discipline and Punish*. The public spectacle of torture, and the private discipline of the Panopticon, are fused in the private worlds of violence which characterised plantation societies.[34]

John Stedman and William Blake torturing men

> The distinguishing feature of the Negros' contempt for humanity is not so much their contempt for death as their lack of respect for life … They give no thought to the preservation of life or to death itself. The great courage of the negroes, reinforced by their great physical strength, must also be ascribed to this lack of respect for life. (Georg Wilhelm Friedrich Hegel, *Lectures on the Philosophy of World History*, Appendix c, a, Africa)

Written in 1790, published in 1796, and copiously illustrated with engravings by several artists including William Blake, Captain John Stedman's *Narrative of a Five Years' Expedition Against the Revolted Negroes of Surinam* gives multiple accounts of the ritualised executions of slaves, repeating the details of public execution that, according to Foucault, had disappeared from the Western practice of legal punishment. Blake and Stedman come at the description of ritualised atrocity from very different directions. The collision of engraving and printed words are educative.

Perhaps the most notorious depiction of atrocity in Stedman's book is Blake's engraving of 'A Negro hung alive by the Ribs to a Gallows', which has already been looked at as a representation of the middle passage [2.17]. It can also be looked at as a work which humanises the tortured slave in a most un-Hegelian manner. The clean fine outline of the dark exquisitely engraved form hangs in blank space. The face is inverted, foreshortened and carries an expression of bemused concentration. Like a contortionist the victim holds his impossible, broken-backed position, frozen in the laborious web of the graver's labour, as if for applause. The only physical contact with the rest of the design, the only point at which the engraved lines describing the body meet with those describing an object outside the body, is in the hook, which leads the eye, via a series of bridges – the rigid verticals, horizontals and diagonals of the gallows and chain – back down to earth. Consequently the hook, looped through the exposed rib, operates as the central focus, the compositional *hook*, the narrative trauma point, of the picture, the point where the human form and the object of torture meet. Elaine Scarry has noted the ways in which Western literature, from Homer, through medieval mysticism, to modernism, monumentalises the object which causes pain. Scarry states 'the point here is not just that pain can be apprehended in the image of the weapon (or wound) but that it almost cannot be apprehended without it'.[35] Blake expresses compassion, high seriousness, and calmness in the face of an absolute pain. He strikes a balance between victim and the object that causes pain. Stedman's narrator, however, reports a story he has heard in a way that places him close to the fantasy of complete insensitivity which underlies Hegel's view of the African:[36]

> I saw a black man suspended alive from a gallows by the ribs, between which, with a knife, was first made an incision, and then clinched an iron hook with a chain, in this manner he kept alive three days, hanging with his head and feet downwards, and catching with his tongue the drops of water (it being the rainy season) that were flowing down his bloated breast. Notwithstanding this he never complained, and even upbraided a negro for crying while he was flogged below the gallows, by calling out, 'You man? *da cay fassy?* Are you a man? you behave like a boy.' Shortly after which he was knocked on the head by the commiserating sentry, who stood over him, with the butt end of his musket. ... Another negro (said he) I have seen quartered alive; who, after four strong horses were fastened to his legs and arms, and after having had iron sprigs driven home underneath every one of his nails on hands and feet, without a motion, he first asked a dram, and then bid them pull away, without a groan; but what afforded us the greatest entertainment, (continued he) were the fellow's jokes, by desiring the executioner to drink before him, in case there should chance to be poison in the glass, and bidding him take care of his horses, lest any of them should happen strike backwards. As for old men being broken upon the rack, and young women roasted alive chained to stakes, there can be nothing more common in this colony.[37]

Within Stedman's text the torture victim is not unique, but one detail in a landscape of horror. The account opens factually with the crisp description of how the hook is inserted, but the prose does not simply establish a distance from the victims but works hard to place them beyond the pale of Western descriptive codes for human suffering. The black humour and unbelievable stoicism with which the black slaves meet their deaths is not ultimately related to tropes of heroism, but expresses an inability to suffer which is inhuman.

This insensitivity separates the descriptions of rituals of violence with which Foucault chooses to open *Discipline and Punish* from the ritualised deaths of the blacks which are scattered throughout the pages of Stedman's *Narrative*. Blake's elevation of the negro on the gallows to martyrological status is counteracted by a text which tries to create the emotional susceptibilities of the torture victim as eccentric. Stedman's set piece descriptions of the torture of black men present the victims as dropping into a nihilistic buffoonery. The European regicide and New World slave are prescribed different behavioural codes. The details of death in Stedman's account are notably similar to those in Foucault's accounts of the death of Damiens, even down to the inability of the horses to pull the body apart during the quartering. But where Damiens is reported to behave with a grave quietude, and to answer each new stage of torture with blessings upon his torturers and prayers to God for his forgiveness, the tortured black slave plays the fool. Stedman provides a set of comedic, or perhaps more accurately pantomimic, codes for reading the behaviour of the blacks, in ways which disqualify them from the European application of judicial procedures of violence. These figures, who exist outside white legal and moral codes, and who relate only to white legal property codes, cannot be shown to feel. In this sense they are systematically cut off from participation in their own trauma, or rather their trauma is brutally restricted. The Greek '*trauma*' or wound originally related specifically to a wound inflicted on the body. In its later usage, particularly in twentieth-century medical and psychiatric literature, the word has been vastly expanded to take in a wound inflicted not upon the body but upon the mind. This mental wounding, if one agrees with the insights of a post-Freudian trauma theorist such as Cathy Caruth, cannot simply be healed: 'trauma is not locatable in the simple violent or original event in an individual's past, but rather in the way that its very unassimilated nature, the way it was precisely *not known* in the first instance – returns to haunt the survivor later on'. [38] Yet for Stedman's slaves the move from bodily wound to mental wound is not admitted – it is short-circuited by buffoonery.

Stedman's blacks relate to a tradition of gallows humour – the triumph over the power of the state through a staged courageousness that laughs at death – but they relate to this tradition only to negate it through a hyperbolic insensateness. Stedman's blacks define an absolute zero, an inability to suffer, a blindness to suffering, that places the black outside pain. The black male victim in Stedman's writing is an involved parody of the controlled violence of European torture. In one of Stedman's accounts the black man's black humour is ingeniously combined with cannibalism, or rather a charge that the victim's executioners are losing an opportunity in not being cannibalistic:

Neptune … was sentenced *to be broken alive upon the rack*, without the ben-
efit of the *coup de grace* or mercy-stroke. Informed of the dreadful sentence,
he composedly laid himself down on his back on a strong cross, on which,
with arms and legs expanded, he was fastened by ropes: the executioner, also
a black man, having now with a hatchet chopped off his left hand, next took
up a heavy iron bar, with which, by repeated blows, he broke his bones to
shivers, till the marrow blood, and splinters flew about the field; but the prisoner never uttered a groan nor a sigh. The ropes being next unlashed, I imagined him dead, and felt happy; till the magistrates stirring to depart, he
writhed himself from the cross and when he fell on the grass, damned them
all, as a set of barbarous rascals; at the same time removing his right hand by
the help of his teeth, he rested his head on part of the timber, and asked the
by-standers for a pipe of tobacco, which was infamously answered by kicking
and spitting on him; till I, with some American seamen, thought proper to
prevent it. He then begged that his head might be chopped off; but to no purpose. At last, seeing no end to his misery, he declared, 'that though he had
deserved death, he had not expected to die so many deaths, however, (said
he) you Christians have missed your aim at last, and I now care not, were I to
remain thus one month longer'. After which he sung two extempore songs
(with a clear voice) the subjects of which, were, to bid adieu to his dying
friends, and to acquaint his deceased relations that in a very little time he
should be with them, to enjoy their company for ever in a better place. This
done he calmly entered into conversation with some gentlemen concerning
his trial; relating every particular with uncommon tranquillity – 'But' said he
abruptly, 'by the sun it must be eight o'clock, and by any longer discourse I
should be sorry to be the cause of your losing your breakfast.' Then casting
his eyes on a Jew, whose name was *De Vries* 'A-propos, sir,' said he, 'won't you
please to pay me the ten shillings you owe me?' – 'For what to do?' – 'To buy
meat and drink, to be sure – don't you perceive I am to be kept alive?' Which
speech, on seeing the Jew stare like a fool, this mangled wretch accompanied
with a loud and hearty laugh. Next, observing the soldier that stood sentinel
over him biting occasionally on a piece of dry bread, he asked him 'how it
came to pass, that he, a *white* man, should have no meat to eat along with it?'
'Because I am not so rich,' answered the soldier – 'Then I will make you a present, sir,' said the negro; 'first, pick my hand that was chopped off clean to the
bone, next begin to devour my body, til you are glutted; when you will have
both bread and meat, as best becomes you'. [39]

The suffering appears to operate within a vacuum, moral, physical and
descriptive – there is no end to it, but unlike the rituals described by
Foucault, and characterising at least officially the penal codes directed at
whites, there is no point to it either. If the victim is without the capacity to
respond to pain stimuli then there is properly no beginning to the torture
either, for torture strictly only begins with the victim's sufferings. Yet it is
the black himself who points up the very arbitrariness of the elaborate
ritual of dismemberment, his two jokes centring upon a peculiar
metaphorics which play Western economics off against cannibalism.
Neptune wants the debt owed him by the Jew, that he might eat; he wants

to eat because he is being killed so slowly that he is kept alive. The soldier who supervises his death wants money to buy food, so logically the soldier should eat the parts of him that have been cut off. The only figure who laughs at these jokes is the victim and this laughter retroactively mocks the Foucaultian analysis of eighteenth-century punishment. Neptune's behaviour can, of course, be written off as simply incredible. If Elaine Scarry's statement that 'intense pain is world destroying' is true, then what world do Neptune's antics inhabit?[40]

When Blake interpreted Neptune's death he challenged the opposing nihilisms of both Stedman and Scarry [5.15]. In Blake's representation of the scene he has chosen the moment just after the hand has been severed, and just before the delicate shin in the foreground is shattered. Neptune gazes out along the foreground over his severed hand. The empowerment of the gaze, the empowerment of surveillance, is usurped by the victim, and in Blake's interpretation there is no suggestion that this dignified man has chosen to deny his humanity through a display of insane hilarity. He does not register, in Hegel's phrase, 'contempt for humanity', especially his own, nor has his suffering driven him into a territory beyond human communication. Yet while Blake's interpretations of male slave torture appear to move the victims away from disempowering aspects of Stedman's accounts, and in particular to snuff out the elements of black humour, the torture of women emerges as more problematic.[41]

John Stedman and William Blake whipping women

Stedman's descriptions of the torture of male slaves possess a troubled relationship with the consciousness of the black subject, but there is no such tension when he presents the torture of women. Stedman was to provide one whipping scenario in particular which was eagerly developed into pornography in the popular adaptations of his work:

> The first object that attracted my compassion during a visit to a neighbouring estate, was a beautiful Samboe girl of about eighteen, tied up by both arms to a tree, as naked as she came into the world, and lacerated in such a shocking manner by the whips of two negro-drivers, that she was from her neck to her ankles literally dyed over with blood. It was after she had received two hundred lashes that I perceived her, with her head hanging downwards, a most affecting spectacle. When, turning to the overseer, I implored that she might be immediately unbound, since she had undergone the whole of so severe a punishment; but the short answer which I obtained was, that to prevent all strangers from interfering with his government, he had made an unalterable rule, in that case, always to double the punishment, which he instantaneously began to put in execution: I endeavoured to stop him, but in vain, he declaring the delay should not alter his determination, but make him take vengeance with double interest. Thus I had no other remedy but to run to my boat, and leave the detestable monster, like a beast of prey, to enjoy his bloody feast, till he was glutted ... Upon investigating the cause of this matchless barbarity, I was credibly informed, that her only crime consisted in firmly

refusing to submit to the loathsome embraces of her detestable executioner. Prompted by his jealously and revenge, he called this the punishment of dis-obedience, and she was thus flead alive.[42]

The central concern of this writing is the creation of a persona for the nar-rator. He wants to emerge as a man of sentiment, and is writing at the height of the age of sensibility. Stedman also locates himself within a post-Burkeian aesthetics whereby the witnessing of torture is sublime. 'Whatever is fitted in any sort to excite the ideas of pain … is a source of the *sublime*; that is, it is productive of the strongest emotion which the mind is capable of feeling.'[43]

[5.15] William Blake, 'Death of Neptune' (copper engraving, 1796). From John Stedman, *Narrative of a Five Years' Expedition Against the Revolted Negroes of Surinam*

The Execution of Breaking on the Rack.

The woman exists as an object to be enjoyed – even in her agony she is put on display both for Stedman's 'perception' and his audience's. She is introduced first as an 'object', then immediately after as 'a beautiful Samboe girl of about eighteen'. Once her sex, age and beauty (by Western standards) have been established, she is then displayed before us 'tied up … as naked as she came into the world'. In her bondage she is not merely naked, but as naked as a new born baby. The phrase implies innocence ultimately recalling Job's 'naked came I out of my mother's womb', but also contrasts her distance, as a beautiful eighteen-year-old, from the de-sexualised nudity of the new-born. Unlike Stedman's tortured male slaves, this woman has no voice, no presence outside her ruined physical beauty; at no point does she speak. She is pure spectacle: 'I perceived her, with her head hanging downwards, a most affecting spectacle'. Stedman earlier wrote, in his manuscript version of the *Narrative,* 'a most miserable spectacle', but the allusion to her emotional state was replaced, in the published version, with his own reaction. She is punished for refusing rape, yet Stedman's compassion is centred on her desirability. Her relation to slave punishment and to torture is defined by her sexuality.[44] The extent to which Stedman has created an erotic fantasy centred in his own sensibility comes out in the original journal entry which provided the raw material for the worked-up versions: 'This morning I saw a sight of horror. A poor half starved mulatto woman, for having spoke thoughtlessly, was between two whips, lashed stark naked, till no skin was almost left on her thighs and legs, up until above the haunches. Before the execution she was fettered, both her feet together that she could hardly stir.' This is no sambo beauty but a malnourished mulatto, punished not for refusing sexual advances, but for verbal insubordination. The effects of the whipping are described with a factual discompassion, and a vocabulary more normally associated with the farm yard.[45]

The extent to which Blake creates an image at odds with Stedman's prose is difficult to determine [**5.16**]. It is less easy to read the effect of his interpretation of the whipping of the sambo girl in terms of the way it challenges the sexually charged and emotionally cannibalistic gaze of the narrator. The scene lacks the monumental clarity of the descriptions of male torture – there is a fanciful element which blurs the violence. The tiny twig to which the woman is tied, the balletic delicacy of her posture, with one toe touching the ground, and the fact that her back, the site of violence, is completely hidden from the viewer, are elements which camouflage the description of atrocity. In the end it is the confusion of suffering with desirability which problematises the image. Staring front on at an almost naked and physically magnificent young woman, who is pushed right up against the viewer, it is hard not to become compromised. Blake seems to be inviting us to enjoy the sexual frisson elicited by such suffering beauty. With her left knee and thigh raised, wearing a totally improbable (and in Stedman's text explicitly non-existent) modesty veil, which has been provocatively torn into revealing shreds by the whip, it is hard to know

what to think – maybe that is Blake's point. Blake's image teeters on the
verge of pornography in order to confront us with our own corruptibility.[46]

The knife edge balance of his design comes out if it is set against the
lurid frontispiece to the sixpenny pamphlet *Curious Adventures of Captain
Stedman*. This twenty-eight page condensation of Stedman's two folios
contains very few long quotations from the original and only a single plate.
The longest quotation is the full account of the whipping of the sambo girl,
while the plate is a long, folding, hand-coloured etching and aquatint illustrating the account [**5.17**].

[**5.16**] William Blake, 'Whipping of a Samboe Girl' (copper engraving 1796). From John
Stedman, *Narrative of a Five Years' Expedition Against the Revolted Negroes of Surinam*

Flagellation of a Female Samboe Slave.

[5.17] [Isaac Robert Cruikshank], 'Whipping of a Samboe Girl' (hand-coloured etching and aquatint, *c.* 1810). Frontispiece to *Curious Adventures of Captain Stedman*

The time and setting are very different from those chosen by Blake. Blake's turf has been replaced by a spectacular jungle clearing, complete with flying parrots. The overseers and stereotypical planter have been moved up into the foreground and have recommenced the punishment which in Blake's design is still the subject of argument. Meanwhile a spectacularly uniformed and shifty-looking Stedman slopes off in disgust to his boat. Yet the crucial changes which make the work pornographic relate to the colouration and positioning of the figures. Blake's 'samboe girl' is definitely black and is allowed some space, and the four male participants in the scene have been removed, and in terms of scale reduced in importance. In the later print the young woman has been turned completely white. We are allowed to see that she has been whipped not only on her back but on her buttocks and her thighs. She is hedged about by staring clothed white, and semi-clothed black, males. The juxtaposition of the clothed and the naked is a pictorial gesture at the centre of the eroticisation of nudity.[47] Every man is staring at another man, while the woman is staring at nothing, so that the viewer's voyeurism goes unchallenged. This design invites us to enjoy, not to think. It does not represent torture, or even Stedman's fantasy of compassion, but the peculiar desire to interpret the abuse of a young woman as essentially erotic.

Blake treats Stedman's sambo girl with dignity, and manages to leave her at least half alone, but she was soon to be taken up and simultaneously strangely deserted in other graphic contexts. Pushed to the front of Blake's design, in the enormous composite aquatint plates which were made to decorate *L'Amérique Décrite par le Docteur Jules Ferrario* she is comprehensively marginalised.[48] One of the large plates [**5.18**] combines three of Blake's single-page designs from the original edition of Stedman's

Narrative. The sambo girl hangs forgotten in the background, her posture reversed, while the two black overseers move off with their whips. She is a very distant relation of Blake's young woman, unregarded by the text or by the set of participants who make up the other narrative vignettes. If the sambo girl ever existed outside Stedman's desire to gaze upon her, then this wonderfully crafted detail in a gorgeous French aquatint is a peculiar testimony to what she endured.

Slavery and utilitarian punishment: ironic equalities

The hands-off surveillance methods of the utilitarian age, so keenly prioritised by Foucault, did not centrally inflect the popular iconography of slave punishment in the West. There are, however, spectacular examples where the technologies developed for punishing Western offenders within the new penal institutions cross-fertilised with the colonies. In Jamaica, for example, the abolition of slavery in 1833 required the removal of the more extreme and ritualised punishments sanctioned by the slave codes. Yet the apprentice system which directly followed emancipation opened the door for the importation of new mechanised methods of punishment, the most notorious being the treadmill.

[5.18] [William Blake] plagiarisms of plates to Stedman, *Narrative* (hand-coloured etching and aquatint, 1799). From *L' Amérique Décrite par le Docteur Jules Ferrario. II Parte Amérique Meridionale*

By 1835 anxieties over the abuses of the apprentice system were becoming widespread and the London Anti-Slavery Society began formal investigation. In the summer and autumn of 1837 the Society's central committee began a mass publishing campaign. Central to this effort was the narrative of a black ex-slave now an apprentice in Jamaica, the *Narrative of Events since the 1st of August, 1834 By James Williams*. The pamphlet was reproduced with a plate showing conditions in a Jamaican house of correction for apprentices, and the image had enormous impact on a popular audience [**5.19**].[49] It was executed in the conventional style for illustrated Victorian periodicals of the period, a busy ancedotal wood-engraving. The landscape format is dominated by the enormous slatted cylinder of the treadmill, the line of prisoners strapped by the wrists to a pole, and performing their appalling parody of dance. Arranged around the treadmill in a semi-circle are a series of narrative vignettes, all of which in their intimacy exist in a tense relation to the monumental 'efficiency' of the treadmill.

The treadmill has been transported from the 'mother' country, for it originated not in the plantations but was a recent development in English penal theory. Invented in England by William Cubitt in 1818, twenty years later it was a standard feature in most English prisons. It solved the problem of how to punish prisoners and keep them active while confined. It consti-tutes a perfect example of what Primo Levi has termed *useless violence*, in

[**5.19**] Anon., 'Scene from a Jamaica House of Correction' (engraving, 1834). From James Williams, *Narrative of Events*

AN INTERIOR VIEW OF A JAMAICA HOUSE OF CORRECTION.

that the energy extorted from the prisoner was, in most instances, completely unproductive – the prisoner's nicknamed time on the treadmill as 'grinding the wind'.[50] This plate then is far from being only a description of the persecution of the black apprentice; it implies the levelling function of the new technologies of penal discipline. On the treadmill black and white discover equality, a bitter racial union. Social reform in England and English abolition propaganda, in its final mass publicity manifestation, are uneasily and ironically conjoined. Foucault's systematics of punishment is finally exported to the colonies as a direct result of slave emancipation.

Black and white martyrological paradigms for the projection of the violated slave

The abolition martyr complex

Who best / Can suffer, best can do (John Milton, *Paradise Regained*)

I am the man, I suffer'd, I was there.
The disdain and calmness of martyrs,
The mother of old, condemn'd for a witch, burnt with dry wood,
her children gazing on,
The hounded slave that flags in the race, leans by the fence, blowing,
cover'd with sweat,
The twinges that sting like needles his legs and neck,
 the murderous buckshot and the bullets,
All these I feel or am.
I am the hounded slave, I wince at the bite of the dogs,
Hell and despair are upon me, crack and again crack the marksmen,
I clutch the rail of the fence my gore dribs, thinn'd with the ooze of my skin,
I fall on the weed and the stones,
The riders spur their unwilling horses, haul close,
Taunt my dizzy ears and beat me violently over the head with whip-stocks.
Agonies are one of my changes of garments.

(Walt Whitman, *Leaves of Grass*)

The visual presentation of the tortured slave body within Western aesthetic and polemical tradition is intimately linked to Christian martyrdom. Within abolition literatures the slave body was forced to stand in a peculiar, and frequently eccentric, relation to the martyrological paradigms which had been developed with lasting elaborateness from the fifteenth to the eighteenth centuries. For English and American abolition the basic influences were not primarily visual but textual. The crucial texts which set out the conventions for the presentation of righteous suffering within both English and American societies were *The New Testament, The Book of Martyrs* and *The Pilgrim's Progress*. John Foxe and John Bunyan celebrated the ideal of 'suffering for truth's sake'. Christ is of course the ultimate model for the heroic martyr who privileges endurance and fortitude

241

over martial activity.[51] American nineteenth-century abolition took this concept to extremes and developed an obsessive and complex martyrological tradition. It worked initially around comparisons with the pilgrim fathers, but with the anti-slavery activities of the Quakers in early colonial America it soon developed its own historiography and mythology. The literature of abolition martyrology then flourished between 1830 and 1860 into a very exotic creature, and generated its own pictorial conventions. Yet the place of the slave within this tradition is difficult to define, and forms the primary focus for the following discussion.

The achievement of martyr status assumes a volitional element: martyrs may be victims but they have chosen to die. The Western post-Renaissance martyrological inheritance cannot easily be applied to describe the experience of slaves who suffered torture or abuse. Few slaves (Stowe's Uncle Tom is the spectacular fictional exception) were given the opportunity to decide to suffer 'for truth's sake'. Real slaves suffered because an individual with power over them decided that they would, whether there was a reason for it or not. In terms of placating audience expectations, and in terms of conforming with Western aesthetic norms, white abolition martyrs presented a more accessible and readily translatable focus for the exploration of violence through imagery than did the slave body.[52]

The mythology of white abolition martyrdom was significantly developed in North America and begins with the Quakers, although the American tradition relates very closely to an English tradition of religious and radical martyrology.[53] Benjamin Lay, John Woolman and Benjamin Lundy all, in different ways, assumed martyrological status.[54] William Lloyd Garrison, a disciple of Lundy's, learned from the Quaker inheritance and brought commercial acumen and an awareness of the theatrical potential of the show trial to the creation of a personal narrative of persecution during his libel trial of 1829. Garrison continued to create a martyrological cult around himself and his cause: 'Glory to them, who die in this great cause! / *Mobs – Judges* – can inflict no brand of shame, / Or shape of death, to shroud them from applause!'[55] In 1837 Western abolition gained its first martyr to actually die for the cause in the form of Elijah Lovejoy, gunned down by a besieging pro-slavery mob in Alton, Illinois. The abolition press on both sides of the Atlantic met the event with a barrage of popular woodcuts and a unified chorus: 'The blood of martyrdom has begun to flow'; 'A martyr to the fury of a free people murdering in defence of slavery'. Lovejoy's mother was reported to have greeted the death with a fanatical stoicism: "'Tis well! I would rather my son had fallen a martyr to his cause, than that he proved recreant to his principles.'[56] Lovejoy's death fanned an obsession with martyrdom within the American movement which only approached satiety with the extraordinary publicity surrounding the Harper's ferry raid and final execution of John Brown on the eve of the Civil War.[57]

Given the religious grounding of the majority of abolitionist thought and rhetoric, the martyrological bias of so much abolition imagery is not surprising. Christian narrative in the West aspires to martyrdom and desires suffering. The last stages of Christ's corporeal existence are a representation of brutalised innocence: imprisonment, loss of all personal liberties, mocking, degradation, flagellation, betrayal, disempowerment, extreme physical abuse leading to a self-doubt which verges on madness, followed by death by torture. The experiences of Christ are experiences at the heart of slavery and of the abolitionist mythology of slavery. Yet for white abolitionists the slave posed a problem. The abused and tortured body of the slave was closer to Christ's experience than were the bodies of free abolitionists. Ultimate suffering at the hands of the wicked implicitly raises the slave victim above the white audience either inflicting or contemplating the suffering. Consequently the representation of slave suffering within Western iconography can be found to exhibit a degree of envy. To put it another way, abolition rhetoric can be seen to articulate a series of competitive counter-thrusts which attempt to reduce, even to erase, the superiority of the slave's suffering. The rhetorical constructions of Elijah Lovejoy, Prudence Crandall, Jonathan Walker and most spectacularly John Brown do not merely compete with, but are designed to o'er vault, the suffering of the slave. In the imagery that follows I begin by examining some of the extraordinary forms which white anxiety about its displacement from black suffering could take. I then move on to look at attempts by African-Americans to subvert Christological and martyrological narratives of Western culture, focusing on representations of Crispus Attucks and Moses Roper. I conclude with work by Xavier Chagas which demands that we go beyond the conventional symbolic and narratological confines of Western martyrology.

A martyr to the bottle: Alexander Anderson envying pain

> People can be envious of just about anything, so it seems. (Michael Taussig, *Shamanism, Colonialism and the Wild Man*)

A vignette adorns the frontispiece of Heman Humphrey's treatise *Parallel Between Intemperance and the Slave Trade* [**5.20**]. The print was made in 1828 by the greatest and most prolific American wood-engraver, Alexander Anderson, and it fuses English temperance and abolition propaganda. This hybrid is a good place to begin uncovering white envy at black suffering. Anderson's frontispiece to Humphrey's *Parallel* conjoins two famous images from English graphic culture.[58]

The intoxicated skeletal figure of a white man at the bottom left of the print is adapted directly from what is arguably the most powerful temperance print ever made, Hogarth's *Gin Lane* [**5.21**]. This senseless and wrecked white man, dressed in rags, has been cut out from Hogarth's print and set up facing the manacled, fully alert and praying figure of a black

[5.20] Alexander Anderson, *Parallel Between Intemperance and the Slave Trade* (wood-engraving, 1828)

slave. The slave has been precisely reproduced from the ubiquitous seal of the British Society for the Abolition of the Slave Trade (2.5).

Anderson's union of white and black fuses the iconography of the two most powerful reform movements in America in the late 1820s – abolition and temperance. Poor white 'enslavement' to alcohol is presented not merely as equivalent to, but as worse than, the plight of the slave shipped from Africa to the Americas.

[5.21] William Hogarth, *Gin Lane*, detail (copper-engraving, 1751)

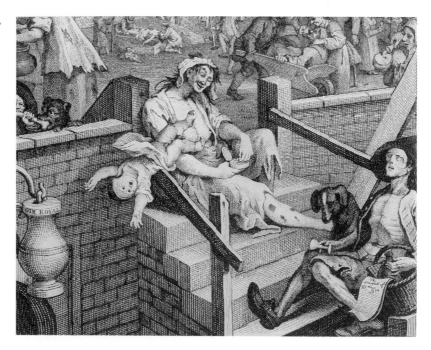

The suffering of the slave is requisitioned; it is a commodity which can not only be compared with, but outreached by, a domestic product. The rhetorical base of the pamphlet is not so much comparative as competitive:

> Glance your eye once more at the poor African captive – trace his bloody footsteps to the ship – let your sympathies all cluster round the sufferer in the middle passage, so proverbial for its horrors – follow him thence to the plantation, and thence through years of toil and pain to his refuge in the grave. Then look at the self immolated victim of intemperance – hobbling – ulcerated – bloated – cadaverous – fleshless – every nerve, and muscle and sensitive organ of his body quivering in the deadly grasp of some merciless disease, occasioned by swallowing the fiery element. Follow him to through the middle passage from health and freedom and happiness to all the habitual woes of habitual intoxication.[59]

The inherited ideology of English abolition literature, concentrating on the description of the hideous conditions of the middle passage, an idea now 'proverbial for its horrors', is set off against the effects of excessive drinking within free white American society. This substitution of white drunk for black slave is carried out at a number of metaphorical levels – drinking itself becomes a 'middle passage' for the drinker. The privileging of the white drunkard over the black slave in terms of the intensity of his suffering, the central theme of the text, is carried out in its most simple and complete form in the title woodcut. The drunk lolls on a doorstep, while a few feet beyond him, in the street, the slave kneels in supplication and prayer. Where the white man is clothed the slave is virtually naked, where the slave is chained the white man is not, but these physical manifestations of freedom are set off against the comparative mental states of the two men: the white is oblivious, mentally absent, the black mentally active.

In the original abolition design the slave articulates the accusatory question 'Am I not a man and a brother?' Here he is given a very different sentiment. He seems to be delivering a prayer of thanks which sets the original events of his capture against the continuing suffering of the alcoholic. The slave announces: 'Drag me bound and bleeding, if you will, from my blazing habitation – but – O bind me not to a rack, where I can neither live nor die under the torture' (title caption). The slave is delivering an astonishing prayer of thanksgiving, articulating the argument that, bad though it is to be a slave, its better than being a 'free' drunk. The logic is extraordinary: the white drunk, who occupies the lowest position in free society, and whose mental and intellectual senses are presented as diseased and numbed, is capable of a degree of suffering which outweighs that of the black slave. It is not, however, any drunkard who is allowed to occupy the key iconic space of the black male slave, but a certain Hogarthian male drunkard.[60] Hogarth's notorious print of the disastrous effects of gin drinking on the poor revolves around one ghastly central image which in narrative and compositional terms dominates the print. At its centre is a bloated inebriated woman, who while leaning to take snuff allows her child to slide over a stair rail, off into space, and certain destruction on the stone steps below. For Anderson, comparative interracial suffering is an all-male affair.

Outright competition and brand loyalties: Walker's hand and the bodies of slaves

In 1844 Jonathan Walker was prosecuted for attempting to run slaves from Florida to freedom in the Bahamas. Walker's punishment and subsequent celebrity as an abolitionist martyr in the North present a fascinating test case for seeing the different ways in which the torture of the bodies of free white and slave black were constructed in Western visual culture.

Between his capture at Key West and his eventual public punishment before the courthouse in Escambia County, West Florida, Walker went through a series of experiences which were read as parodying essential experiences within the history of Atlantic slavery. Bound in chains, he was flung in the filthy hold of a steam boat and made a six-day voyage to Pensacola, a miniature version of the middle passage. Awaiting bail there for several months, he was kept in a cell, secured by an ankle shackle to which a log had been tied, this being a time-honoured device for punishing and restraining runaway slaves and animals. When finally brought to trial, three punishments were ordered: a fine, an hour in the pillory and the branding of SS for 'Slave Stealer' below the thumb of this right hand. Walker's hand became the most infamous hand and the most visible brand in the history of American slavery. The white hand of Walker became a fragmentary monument to the cause of abolition and the suffering of the slave. The image floated, disembodied, in periodicals, children's books, and above the broadside sheets upon which Whittier's extraordinary ballad, 'The Branded Hand', was printed [**5.22**]. The living hand itself was displayed to huge crowds across the Northern states. Walker became a fixture on the lecture circuit and produced a series of lavishly illustrated texts, including a children's book, describing his experiences. In the space of a few minutes you could see the hand, shake it, and take away a representation of it.[61]

Yet despite the striking parallels between Walker's ordeals and the violence experienced by slaves, the abolition publicity surrounding his narrative draws exclusively upon traditions of Western martyrology and political dissent to ennoble him. Walker may have suffered for the slave but he is accreted to white traditions of religious and secular martyrology. The relationship of the white martyr to the slave, and of the slave to the white martyr, are difficult to focus. The branding of Walker's body has a very different significance from the branding of a slave body.

The branding of the initials of the owner, the imprinting of a sign system on an African body, relates to, but differed from, the extant forms of branding within white European and American societies. In the sixteenth

THE BRANDED HAND.

Walker resided in Florida with his family from 1836 until 1841. He then removed to Massachusetts because he would not bring up his children among the poisonous influences of slavery. While in Florida, the colored people whom he employed were treated as equals in his family, much to the chagrin of the slaveholders of that region. In 1844 he returned to Pensacola in his own vessel. When leaving, seven of the slaves who had in former years been in his employ, and were members of the church with which he communed, begged to go with him. He consented. When out fourteen days, a Southern sloop fell in with and seized them. Prostrated by sickness, he was confined in a dungeon, chained on a damp floor without table, bed or chair. He was in the pillory for an hour, pelted with rotten eggs, branded S. S.—slave stealer—in the palm of his right hand, by Ebenezer Dorr, United States Marshal, fined $150, and imprisoned eleven months.

THE BRANDED HAND.

BY JOHN G. WHITTIER.

Welcome home again, brave seaman ! with thy thoughtful brow and gray,
And the old heroic spirit of our earlier, better day—
With that front of calm endurance, on whose steady nerve, in vain
Pressed the iron of the prison, smote the fiery shafts of pain !

[5.22] Anon., *The Branded Hand* (wood-engraving, broadside, *c.* 1845)

and seventeenth centuries there are many examples, in both Europe and the American colonies, of statutes requiring the branding of runaway white servants with V for vagabond or R for rogue.[62] In such cases the motive for the branding was twofold: firstly punitive and secondly as a measure to facilitate future identification. The registration of individual ownership through a gesture which dehumanised the victim played no part in the process.[63]

Branding was familiar in European and American culture as part of the rituals of public punishment. The inscription of the crime on the body was a common practice especially for political crimes. In England in 1637

William Prynne was branded on the cheeks with the letters SL, for Seditious Libeller, and further sentenced to have what remained of his ears, mutilated from a previous Star Chamber conviction, cut off. Prynne transmogrified the branding, producing a pamphlet in which he claimed the letters stood for 'Stigmata Laudis'.[64] A host of religious dissenters and political radicals followed, yet the ritual acts of burning and mutilation which they underwent were celebrated as badges of honour by the victims and their supporters. In the end the State's public disciplining of religious and political dissenters became a liability, owing to the fact that it provided a platform for martyrological celebration which was dangerous.[65] In an age developing a mass communications technology where illustrated texts could be developed quickly, Walker's white hand was a much bigger danger. Photographic reproduction was spectacularly deployed to recreate the hand as a type of holy abolition relic [**5.23**]. In a cleverly conceived daguerreotype, Walker's hand, starkly lit from above, floated, fingers extended, thumb elevated, scarred palm naked and displayed against a black background. The nudity of the hand is accentuated by the glimpse of a crisp white cuff which promises to attach the extremity to an invisible wrist. The hand is both a severed fragment and a monument to suffering, a hand to pity and a hand to shake, but finally the hand of the martyr showing its wound.

The Christological associations of Walker's hand were taken to bizarre extremes by Whittier. His illustrated ballad 'The Branded Hand',

[**5.23**] Anon., *Walker's Branded Hand* (photogravure, *c.* 1845)

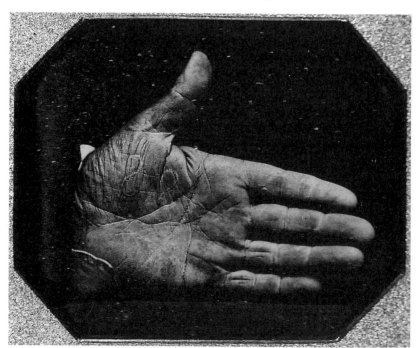

mass-produced and circulated in broadside form, encased Walker's hand within the paradigms of European martyrology. Whittier strangely conflates the passive martyr with the actively heroic soldier of Christ. Walker's endurance of branding is compared with the chivalric sacrifices of the Crusaders, ordeals which, ironically, first brought white Europeans into extensive intimate contact with black Africans. Whittier then goes on to enact a Prynne-like transformation of the branded letters from sign of criminality to triumphant testimony of faith, here the faith of abolition, and SS signifies not 'slave stealer' but 'salvation to the slave':

> Why that brand is highest honour! – than its traces never yet
> Upon old armorial hatchments was a prouder blazon set;
> And thy unborn generations as they crowd our rocky stand,
> Shall tell with pride the story of their father's BRANDED HAND!
>
> As the templar, home was welcomed, bearing back from Syrian wars
> The scars of Arab lances, and of Paynim scimetars,
> The pallor of the prison and the shackles crimson span,
> So we meet thee, so we greet thee, truest friend of God and man!
>
> [...]
>
> Then lift that manly right hand, bold ploughman of the wave!
> Its branded palm shall prophecy, 'SALVATION TO THE SLAVE!'

Photographs and woodcuts of the martyr's hand literally reached out to a mass audience across the free Northern states.[66]

Yet the valorisation of Walker's branding exists apart from the business-like procedures which were practised on the slaves, and which are matter of factly set down in abolition pamphlets.[67] It is significant that there was no fetishisation of the branded slave body within the extant imagery of English or American abolition. When it came to recording the barbarity of slave branding this was done through indirect textual procedures. The letters of branding were extracted from the body of the text of runaway slave advertisements and then reprinted in an abolition publication. Branding irons, as objects, were preserved and exhibited, and still hold a central position among the gruesome memorabilia of slave museums across the world. The disembodied tool, the torture weapon, that is also a stamp of ownership and a piece of type, sits idle within museum displays. Yet if white abolitionists did not celebrate the branded body of the slave, and if Western institutions devoted to the memory of slavery decline to do this, there is evidence that slaves sometimes took the matter into their own hands. In Brazil slaves were branded, not simply for identification but in punishment for running away, and could achieve their own martyrological subversion of branding. The recaptured runaways from the Quilombos of Minas Gerais proudly displayed their brand of F to other slaves as a badge of heroic resistance. The result of this was that slave-owners abandoned branding and replaced it with the simple expedient of cutting the Achilles tendon of one foot.[68]

African-American mimetic secular martyrology: the vanishing and reappearance of Crispus Attucks

Western martyrological codes emerge, in this chapter, as saturating the representation of the slave in abolition art and literature. Yet within martyrology there appear to be blind-spots in white cultural memory. Certain narrative and symbolic routes seem closed to the white abolitionist which African-American abolitionists in the free North insisted upon re-opening. One such blind-spot appears to be the creation of black hero-martyrs within the memory of the War of Independence. In this context a spectacular example of black cultural re-emergence is the commemorative festival held at Fanueil Hall, Boston, on 5 March, 1858. This took the form of an elaborate set of activities organised by African-American artists and intellectuals in an event which had a double focus. It had been organised firstly to celebrate the heroic death of Crispus Attucks, ex-slave and first black martyr of the War of Independence, who fell in the Boston Massacre of 5 March 1770, and secondly to vilify the notorious ruling of Chief Justice Taney, over the Dred Scott freedom suit, on 5 March 1857, a watershed which had denied legal and constitutional rights to escaped slaves.[69] The festival, and the multiple imagery it generated, are a resounding demonstration of the sophistication with which the African-American community in Boston was able creatively to transform the martyrological mythologisations which had been developed around American memory and narrativisation of the War of Independence. This ceremony in fact built on a long-standing performative tradition in which African-Americans had created their own historical agendas for formal celebration.[70]

There was an unbroken history of African-American freedom festivals in the Northern free states, which focused upon dates which had special resonance for those of slave descent in the Americas. From the late eighteenth century there had been a number of festivals organised around various dates which suggested an alternative to 4 July. These included 1 January, a date commemorating Toussaint l'Ouverture's declaration of the independent state of Hayti, and the outlawing of the American Atlantic slave trade; 5 July, because of the passage of 1799 and 1817 gradual abolition legislation; and 1 August, because it commemorated British Emancipation in the Caribbean colonies.[71] Yet in choosing the date of the Boston Massacre the organisers of the 5 March festivities were doing something new. They were reviving an event which had been run annually in Boston from 1770 to 1783 by whites, to celebrate the early heroes of American independence, and they were using it not merely to celebrate a forgotten black ex-slave called Crispus Attucks, but to make a political point about an abused contemporary black slave called Dred Scott. Attucks's excision from the official white history of the war was to be seen in parallel with the continuation of slavery and the ideological hypocrisy which underlay it, elements of American political life crystallised by the Dred Scott ruling.

The elaborate events which occurred on 5 March at Faneuil Hall in Boston brought together many of the most able African-American personalities campaigning against slavery in the free North. Although eminent white abolitionists, including William Lloyd Garrison and Theodore Parker, were present, they were very much a minority and the event was dominated by African-Americans. Among those involved were the multi-talented John S. Rock, the veteran radical abolitionist lecturer Charles Lenox Raimond and the renowned female abolitionist and poet Frances Ellen Watkins Harper. The many musical offerings in the festival included a performance by the Attucks Glee Club, which contained among its members two artists, William Simpson and Edward Bannister, who were probably also involved in the visual aspects of the festival which included eye-catching illustrated broadsides and *tableaux vivantes*.[72]

The festival as a whole engaged with the visual inheritance of slavery at a number of levels. It was a multi-media carnival in which song, poetry, oratory, broadside, graphic art, academic oil painting, museum display and theatricals were combined to question America's past and present in terms of how it remembered and mis-remembered, how it saw and refused to see, slavery. William Cooper Nell, who seems to have been the organisational genius behind much of the festival, had assembled a historical exhibition of 'Emblems Relics – Engravings – Documents … of Revolutionary and other Historic association'.[73] Again this carried out a radical interrogation of the inheritance of the Revolutionary War in terms of what it meant for African-Americans. In what can be considered the first African-American historical museum of slavery, Nell interspersed memorabilia of the War of Independence with items specifically recalling the cultural inheritance of slavery. These included an undated fragment in Arabic written by a slave in North Carolina, the indenture papers of Samson Negro, and two bills of sale, one for a negro boy and a horse from 1760, and one for 'Five Black Men' for April 1770, the month after Attucks's death.[74] This radical gesture uses the fetishisation of historical objects within museum culture to problematise the memorial agendas used to recall the War of Independence. The equally ingenious representations of Attucks's death within the festival publicity should be read within this overall ideological interrogation of the place of the slave in the early cultural memory of America.

The events held at Faneuil Hall in Boston were advertised by hand-bills and broadsides, many of which were illustrated, and there were also illustrated pamphlets. These publications carried eye-catching wood-engravings representing the Boston Massacre. The images constitute a fascinating example of popular African-American art re-establishing the iconic presence of a black man and ex-slave within a space reserved by the art of the Academy for its white male heroes. Attucks reappears in a set of

FANEUIL HALL
COMMEMORATIVE
FESTIVAL,
March 5th, 1858.

PROTEST
AGAINST THE
DRED SCOTT
"DECISION."

"BOSTON MASSACRE. MARCH 5th, 1770."

[5.24] Anon., *Boston Massacre ...
Protest Against Dred Scott Decision*
(wood-engraving, 1858)

MARTYRDOM
—OF—
CRISPUS ATTUCKS!
MARCH 5th, 1770,

"The day which History selects as

the dawn of the American Revolution!"

THE 92nd ANNIVERSARY WILL BE COMMEMORATED

On Wednesday Evening, March 5, 1862,
—AT—
ALLSTON HALL,

BY A SERIES OF EXERCISES, CONSISTING OF

TABLEAUX—Historical, Mythological, Classical, Humorous and Domestic:

To be represented by a Select Volunteer Company of Young Ladies and Gentlemen, Masters & Misses.

The whole interspersed with appropriate Music, and the Vocalising of Operatic gems, by the

Boston Quartette Club.

MISS H. C. WHITEHURST, Soprano. | MR. GEO. L. RUFFIN, Tenore.
MISS ANNA WHITEHURST, Alto. | MR. JOHN A. GRIMES, Basso.

PROGRAMME.

Remarks, . by . WILLIAM C. NELL.

TABLEAU 1. The Scene in State Street,
March 5th, 1770.

" . . . On the evening of March 5th, there was an outbreak in King street, now State st.,
headed by Crispus Attucks, which resulted in his own death and that of several of his
comrads, at the hands of the British soldiery. . . . After the event, they had a funeral,
and the citizens of Boston marched six abreast through the streets, . . . to the Middle
Burying-Ground, now overlooked by the Athenæum, and over their remains erected a
stone, and on it carved this inscription :—

' Long as in Freedom's cause the wise contend, | While to the world the lettered stone shall tell
Dear to your country, shall your fame extend ; | How Caldwell, Attucks, Gray, and Maverick fell !'"
—*Rev. J. M. Manning.*

[5.25] Anon., *Martyrdom of Crispus Attucks*
(wood-engraving, 1862)

prints parodying famous history paintings and political graphics seventy years after his initial erasure.

The 1858 Attucks commemoration gave rise to an annual celebration in succeeding years. The same woodblock was used for the front pages of the 1858 [**5.24**] and 1862 [**5.25**] programmes for the commemorative ceremony of the Boston Massacre. The wood-engraving consists of a reworking of the central section of the most influential and sensational political print in the history of the American graphic tradition: Paul Revere's *The Bloody Massacre*. The print was engraved and published by Revere within three weeks of the Boston Massacre of 5 March 1770 [**5.26**] and is a shocking indictment of British imperial brutality and the machinery of mass state execution. Revere's print deserved its immediate classic status and was reproduced in several contexts in the next few months in England and America.[75] The receding profiles of a row of executioners with rifles levelled at their victims was a device which was to be taken up in two of the greatest nineteenth-century masterpieces painted to

[**5.26**] Paul Revere, *The Bloody Massacre perpetrated in King Street Boston March 5th 1770* (copper engraving, 1770)

describe the atrocity of military execution, Goya's *The 3rd of May: Execution of the Insurgents* [**5.27**] and Manet's *Execution of Maximillian*. It is even possible that Goya may have been directly influenced by the American print.[76]

The first major blood-letting by the British military in the abused American colonies produced one of the most successful artistic responses to atrocity. Yet Crispus Attucks, present in name, is absent in body. Every version of the print carried the venerable litany of the first five martyrs of the Revolution including Attucks, yet despite the fact he was popularly believed to be the first to fall, in every print version no black man is represented in the design.[77] Attucks was to have to wait eighty-eight years for his resurrection within a reworded version of Revere's print [5.24]. In the little wood-engravings on the cover of the Boston pamphlets the composition remains fundamentally unaltered, but the leading figure who falls has a black face and clearly represents Attucks. The accompanying texts suck Attucks further and further towards the centre of white martyrological mythologisation. While the 1858 headline runs 'BOSTON MASSACRE, March 5th, 1770 … PROTEST AGAINST THE DRED SCOTT DECISION', and carries a full account of Attucks on its second page, the 1862 version has moved Attucks, quite literally, on to the centre of the stage [5.25]. Below the headline 'MARTYRDOM OF CRISPUS ATTUCKS' is the detailed programme which centres around a series of 'Tableaux – Historical, Mythological, Classical, Humorous and Domestic'. The first of these consists of 'The Scene in State Street, March 5th 1770 … On the

[5.27] Francisco Goya, *The 3rd of May: Execution of the Insurgents* (oil on canvas, 1814)

NINETIETH ANNIVERSARY OF THE BOSTON MASSACRE,

MARCH 5, 1770.

The day which
History has
selected as the
dawn of the
American Revo-
lution.

COMMEMORATIVE
MEETING,
AT THE
MEIONAON,
ON
Monday Ev'g.
MARCH 5th,
1860.

*Extracts from the Speech of Rev. J. M. MANNING, of the Old South Church, at the Meeting
in aid of John Brown, Martyr of Harpers Ferry, in Tremont Temple, November 25th, 1859.*

[**5.28**] Anon., *Ninetieth Anniversary of the Boston Massacre* (wood-engraving, 1860)

evening of March 5th there was an outbreak in King street, now State st.,
headed by Crispus Attucks, which resulted in his own death and that of
several of his comrades, at the hands of the British soldiery …'. Given the
title woodcut, and the fact that Revere's print was the classic representation of the event, it appears that Attucks's death, in the opening ceremony,
would have taken the form of a full costume historical tableaux mimicking
'The Bloody Massacre'.[78]

Yet the processes of Attucks's rebirth within this print did not stop
here. Having started on the process of heroic transformation in 1858, subsequent festivals produced abolition graphics which appropriated grander
models and turned to Academic history painting. The print which headed
an 1860 handbill commemorating the 'NINETIETH ANNIVERSARY
OF THE BOSTON MASSACRE' saw Attucks oust General Wolfe
[**5.28**].[79] This wood-engraving, which occupies the top third of the sheet,
uses Revere's representation of the British troops, but has wholly altered
the composition of the fallen American citizens. In this rendition Attucks
reclines into the arms of a white comrade; the figure group of which he forms
the central focus is modelled on Benjamin West's notorious *Death of
General Wolf* [**5.29**]. West's painting, popularly disseminated in England,
France and America through the mass sales of the engraving by William
Woollett, created an enduring imperial icon presiding over the British
expulsion of the French presence from Canada. West's bold move in combining a highly theatricalised and academic composition with a minutely
observed representation of contemporary clothing and local colour has
been taken a stage further by the abolition press.[80] This little image fuses the
compositional elements from a famous engraving and a hugely influential

[5.29] William Woollett, after Benjamin West, *Death of General Wolf*
(copper engraving, 1776)

history painting within the conventions of pamphlet wood-engraving. Yet
the narrative status of Attucks is ambiguous: does he overwrite Wolfe, or
does Wolfe subsume him? There is also the question of who produced the
print. Was the festival still as dominated by African-American input in 1860
as in the original festival of 1858? While it is possible to read this image as an
act of cultural subversion in which a white colonial hero is erased and his
place is taken by a black ex-slave, it is equally possible to see the print as
semiotically imprisoned. In such a reading the culture of abolition, whether
black or white, emerges as capable of envisioning black martyrdom only
when it is wrapped within the trappings of an Academic painting which celebrates a crowning moment of British imperial conquest. It is also
intriguing that the exotic Mohawk Indian, who dominates the foreground
of West's painting, has been erased and replaced by nobody.[81]

A secular passion: Moses Roper and Christological subversion

While nineteenth-century white abolitionists might envy the martyrological status of the very images of black suffering they had created, it was also
possible for black slave authors to appropriate and develop the iconography of Christ's Passion. The *Narrative of the Adventures and Escape of
Moses Roper* provides a challenging example of the process. A description
of his torture for running away is accompanied by an image entitled 'A
COTTON SCREW' [5.30]. This image might be located within several
European graphic traditions. The pillar-like structure of the machine,
mounting in vertical steps to a crowning decorative device, makes it appear
like a design for a monument. It relates to Dürer's comic woodcut designs

for civic monuments and beyond this to the generations of parodic variants that followed in European and American print satire.[82] Then again the image is strangely reminiscent of the elaborate rotary machines used for 'treating' the insane and beautifully illustrated in the engravings to Joseph Guilane's *Traité sur l'Aliénation Mentale et sur les Hospices des Aliéns*.[83] Indeed this visual analogue suggests disturbing comparisons between Western systems for categorising slaves and the insane. Both groups existed beyond the pale of conventional protective judicial codes in terms of the experimentation that might be performed upon them by doctors or owners. This grey area resurfaces when Toni Morrison examines the fusion of punishment codes and scientific experiment in the episodes focusing on the character of 'Schoolteacher' in *Beloved*. But Roper's design gains its power, not only from its ironic relationship to these earlier graphic traditions, but because of its presence as fact. It is a monument not

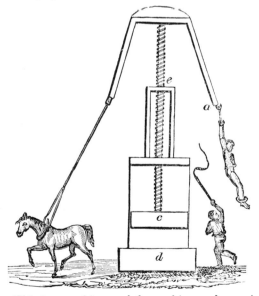

ESCAPE FROM SLAVERY. 39

top of the water. It was as much as they could do to hold me by the chain, the current being very strong. They then took me home, flogged me, put extra irons on my neck and feet, and put me under the driver, with more work than ever I had before. He did not flog me so severely as before, but continued it every day. Among the instruments of torture employed, I here describe one:—

This is a machine used for packing and pressing cotton. By it he hung me up by the hands at letter *a*, a horse moving round the screw *e*, and carrying

[5.30] Anon., 'Cotton screw' (wood-engraving, 1838). From *Narrative of the Adventures and Escape of Moses Roper*

only to Roper's suffering but to the sadistic ingenuity of his master – a tribute to Gooch's ludic imagination.

The design addresses the iconography of the runaway. The black figure running with the whip is evolved out of the icon of the runaway slave in advertisements. Here, however, he runs in a circle, brandishing what the abolitionists had made the emblem of slave-power tyranny, the whip.[84] He runs, but according to the logic of the design, he runs in circles. As a slave himself he follows the circumference of a circle drawn in the air by the suspended body of Roper above him. The whipper's 'freedom' to run in a circle counterbalances the complete physical bondage of Roper, tied by the hands, hooked up by the wrists, with iron bars on his feet. In the mechanical rigour of the process lies the terror of the design: both figures move at the same speed in the same circle, according to the prescribed motion of a machine, which was built to perform an entirely different industrial function.

It is the sense of opportunistic arbitrariness about the process that shocks, the idea that it takes creative insight to be able to convert the packing machine into an ideal instrument of suffering, while at the same time not intruding on its practical function of squeezing cotton bales into their allocated space. No energy or time is wasted, apart from the effort of the slave with the whip. There is a tension as well between the frozen but bound form of Roper, and the horse, which propels the machine which tortures him.

The question of how to combine, within a single graphic image, the economics of slavery and the description of human suffering, was not easily answered. Roper's illustration is one of the most powerful solutions ever conceived. The plate works closely with the prose:

> They then took me home, flogged me, put extra irons on my neck and feet, and put me under the driver, with more work than I ever had before. He did not flog me so severely as before, but continued it every day. Among the instruments of torture employed, I here describe one:- [plate intervenes] This is a machine used for packing and pressing cotton. By it he hung me up by the hands at letter *a*, a horse moving round the screw *e*, and carrying it up or down, and pressing the block *c*, into the box *d*, into which the cotton is put. At this time he hung me up for a quarter of an hour. I was carried up about ten feet from the ground, when Mr. Gooch asked me if I was tired. He then let me rest for five minutes, then carried me round again, after which, he let me down and put me into box *d*, and shut me down in it for about ten minutes. After this torture, I stayed with him several months and did my work very well. It was about the beginning of 1832, when he took off my irons, and being in dread of him, he having threatened me with more punishment, I attempted again to escape from him. At this time, I got into North Carolina: but a reward having been offered for me, a Mr. Robinson caught me, and chained me to a chair, upon which he sat up with me all night, and next day proceeded home with me. This was Saturday. Mr. Gooch had gone to church, several miles from his house. When he came back the first thing he

did was to pour some tar on my head, then rubbed it all over my face, took a
torch, with pitch on, and set it on fire; he put it out before it did me very great
injury, but the pain which I endured was most excruciating, nearly all of my
hair having been burnt off. On Monday, he put irons on me again, weighing
nearly fifty pounds. He threatened me again on the Sunday with another flogging; and on the Monday morning, before day-break, I got away again with
my irons on.[85]

The model for the action is Christ's Passion and the Resurrection. Gooch
puts Roper through a bizarre enactment of Christ's mocking, flagellation,
crucifixion, entombment and apotheosis. Roper is captured, abused,
flogged (by a black man), hung up by the hands, taken down, placed in a
tomb like box, from which he arises and escapes.[86] Using modern technology Gooch has invented a dramatic and practical machinery for the
enactment of a grotesque parody of Christological martyrdom.
Rhetorically Roper could not have made this comparison himself before a
white audience. For a fully blown presentation of the slave as sentimental
Christ substitute audiences had to wait until 1852 and Stowe's depiction of
the death of Uncle Tom. Roper introduces his martyrdom through the
unfamiliar rhetoric of a prose of scientific detachment and a diagram
showing the operation of a machine. These tactics should not, however,
blind the reader to the narrative and mythological undertow.[87]

   The horror of the description is immediately emphasised by the dis-
missive quality of the sentence that follows: 'After this torture I stayed with
him several months and did my work very well.' The torture worked; for a
while it broke Roper's resistance and terrified him into co-operation.
Roper, so often accused by analysts of the slave narrative of a grim and
exacting humourlessness, cannot surely have written 'very well' without a
smile.[88]

   There is a terrible and mesmeric exhaustion about such writing. The
experience of the cotton screw, which is so cleanly amplified in the
graphic representation, is swallowed up in this account. It is simply one
small element in an ongoing and seemingly unending cycle of flight, recapture and punishment. Roper casually tells us that this is 'one' of the
'instruments of torture employed'. As a narrator he is spoiled for choice,
but why he chooses this particular example, and what the other horrors
were he might have chosen to describe, we shall never know. The text has
an appalling openness in this regard. It seems to suggest vistas of suffering which the reader cannot even begin to grasp, and which the narrator cannot begin to tell.

   If the cotton screw has an importance above the other tortures
described, it is simply that in its cyclical nature it embodies the tedious repetition of Roper's experience of bondage. The victim may go on turning
round and round, describing the same perfect circles, as long as the
machine operates, and the machine is in this sense a metaphor for slavery
itself. The cotton screw diagram gives us a metaphor for the runaway as a

martyr to his own failure. Roper succeeds in transforming the impotence of the running figure in the runaway slave advertisement into tragedy.

Whipping and flagellation: Christological, bestial and pornographic paradigms

Within the iconography of punishment in the West whipping, or flagellation, holds an unstable position. The most prominent victims of whipping are Christ and Christian martyrs, prisoners, soldiers, sailors, women, children, domestic animals and slaves. The codes for describing these subjects vary enormously and went through considerable evolution.[89] Elaborate connections between beating and social hierarchies were established in the ancient world, and they continued into plantation societies. T. J. Widerman's fine summary statement relating to whipping in the ancient world – 'beating is not random, it establishes a social hierarchy of husband over wife, parent (or teachers) over children, free person over slaves, slaves themselves were human enough to beat animals' – also has a precise application to the operations of whipping in New World plantation societies.[90]

There is, however, a crucial distinction between the whipping of slaves and that of other humans throughout history. From Greek society onwards flogging and whipping were the standard and pre-eminent forms of punishment for minor and major offences by slaves. Demosthenes points out the reason with brutal clarity, stating that the primary difference in legal terms between the administration of punishment to a slave and a freeman is that the former is punished in his body, the latter in his property. The distinction is perhaps a bogus one in that the slave's only property was his body, and consequently this was the only area in which she/he could be punished. Through Greek and Roman slave systems, on into the middle ages, where under several legal codes flogging could be administered only to slaves, and was considered too degrading for freemen, and on into the colonial slave systems, whipping remained the central and most common form of slave punishment.[91] Yet the status of whipping within the plantation societies of the Americas is further complicated by a number of other factors. One is the fact that whipping was not restricted to punishment, but functioned also within a grey area of agrarian animal labour which incorporated the slave body. Slaves were probably most commonly whipped not in the context of formal punishment at the whipping post, but casually, to make them work harder, or move faster, as horses and oxen were whipped.

Perhaps even more troubling for audiences today is the manner in which whipping has been semiotically contaminated by pornography. The association of flagellation with sexual arousal only became widespread in Western cultures by the middle of the eighteenth century. The late eighteenth century, the decades that saw British involvement in the slave trade peak, and simultaneously saw abolition take off as an international movement, was also the period when sexual flagellation became a mania in

Europe. By the middle of the nineteenth century European sadistic pornography was a big publishing field in which whipping was a central discourse, and was denominated 'the English vice'. America soon developed its own pornographic literatures of flagellation, which inevitably involved the question of slavery. The paradigms developed in these literatures fed and feed into contemporary American and European bondage pornography.[92] The extent to which this newly developed context of whipping inflected abolition work is difficult to determine. Richard Newton's *A Forcible Appeal for the Abolition of the Slave Trade*, of April 1792, can be used as a test case [**5.31**]. The print falls into halves, one of them more erotically charged than the other. On the left the flagellation includes a lot of factual detail, and is an all-male affair. A short stocky black overseer, with an expression of extreme grimness, beats a naked male, who is tied to a tree with weights suspended from his feet. The thongs of the whip carry small lead weights. The sufferer's bared buttocks are exposed, his face turned away from the viewer, his arms spread out as if in crucifixion. The right half of the print appears to invite voyeurism and erotic enjoyment on the part of the viewer. Here a half-naked black woman, with breasts exposed, is beaten by a large black overseer. She turns out towards the audience, her mouth open, her eyes rolled in anguish, tears rolling down her cheeks. A young white woman exorbitantly decked out in fashionable costume, presumably the victim's dissatisfied mistress, looks on smiling towards the whipper whose face is not caricatured and carries an expression of detached concentration. It is genuinely difficult to know how to read the sexual elements of this work. Newton was sixteen when he made the print,

[**5.31**] Richard Newton, *Forcible Appeal for the Abolition of the Slave Trade* (hand-coloured etching, 1792)

and his employer, the print publisher William Holland, was definitely involved in the new market for flagellatory publications. Newton produced pornographic work for Holland which exploited the crudest European stereotypes concerning black female sexuality. This print was probably intended as an atrocity piece for the abolition market, but its messages are genuinely confused. Even the beating of the black male may be sexually charged, given a compositional arrangement where the young white woman is the only person, including the viewer, in a position to look on the victim's genitals.[93]

That a pornographic impulse could dominate the presentation of male slave flagellation is spectacularly demonstrated in the large 1849 academy oil painting by Marcel Verdier, *Punishment of the Four Stakes in the Colonies* [**5.32**]. This clearly crosses the line between propaganda and pornography. One basic function of the pornographic impulse is voyeurism. Here we watch an elaborately dressed planter family, as they watch a beautiful, naked black man, about to receive the first lash upon his naked back, or buttocks. Staked out, spreadeagled, his genitalia are hidden from us, but the infant girl sitting upon her mother's knee is so positioned, and her glance so directed, as to be able to stare between the victim's legs. Verdier's work demonstrates the extent to which the recently eroticised Western interest in slave whipping complicates traditional Christological and martyrological treatments of flagellation.[94]

This volatile interpretational environment meant that for the ex-slave narrator whipping constituted an iconographic problem. The description

[**5.32**] Marcel Verdier, *The Punishment of the Four Stakes in the Colonies* (oil on canvas, 1843)

of whipping is central to many slave narratives, and those of Douglass, Roper and Bibb exhibit a rhetorical variety and achieve a psychological complexity which defines an essential difference between slave descriptions of whipping and those of Northern abolitionists. This is a subject which merits detailed study. In the area of visual representation, however, it is far more difficult to find examples of slaves having described their reaction to whipping. Spectacular examples do, however, exist which demonstrate how slaves could imaginatively colonise and expand extant white aesthetics to explore the effects and implications of flagellation specifically within slave systems.

Whipping as sculpture: the flagellated Christ a suitable subject for a slave

An example recently struck me in Brazil. In Salvador, Bahia, the capital of colonial Brazil, in the mid-eighteenth century, the sculptor Francisco Xavier Chagas carved a set of figures describing the Passion of Christ for the Church of the Venerable Third Order of the Carmelites. Only two figures from the complete cycle survived a fire in the church later in the century. The flagellated Christ now within the sacristy of the neighbouring Carmelite Convent is one of them [**5.33**].

Carved in hardwood, gessoed and then polychromed, the work stands, in terms of art historical classification, as high Luso-Brazilian Baroque. Chagas sculpted a wide variety of sacred works for many churches in Bahia at this period. He produced a polychromed virgin and child, which now stands at the high altar in this same Carmelite church, a statue which is serene, opulent and plump [**5.34**]. His flagellated Christ is very different. This is not, however, merely because of its subject. The way pain is described in this sculpture is specific in terms of the presence of the conventions of late-eighteenth-century Luso-Brazilian sculpture. These conventions might, in turn, be read by relating them to other currents in European seventeenth-century art and thought. The carving was made for a Carmelite church, in other words for a Portuguese branch of the Order which sprang back to life in seventeenth-century Spain inspired by the mystical writings of St John of the Cross and St Theresa. St Theresa provided the subject for the notoriously sexual representation of mystical experience, Bernini's *Rapture of St Theresa*, and Chagas would not have been able to stretch and bend his Christ so far without the example of Italian seventeenth-century Mannerism, translated through the religious Baroque sculpture of early-eighteenth-century colonial Brazil.

But to decipher this sculpture by applying the codes of European mystical revival, or of Portuguese aesthetic tradition, although quite possible, might not be enough, or even appropriate.[95] There is another presence, difficult to acknowledge, a set of secret memories, which provide another interpretative route into this work. Chagas, the sculptor, was a black slave, popularly nicknamed 'O Cabra', meaning the bandit or the

[5.33] Francisco Xavier Chagas, *Flagellated Christ* (sculpture in polychromed wood, *c.* 1750). Convent of the Venerable Third Order of the Carmelites, Salvador, Bahia

[5.34] Francisco Xavier Chagas, *Virgin and Child* (sculpture in polychromed wood, *c.* 1750). Convent of the Venerable Third Order of the Carmelites, Salvador, Bahia

nigger or the goat. This man described Christ's humiliation primarily in the terms of what a whipping could do to a human. The sculpture questions its own formal beauty by presenting Christ as so distorted and numbed by his suffering as to have lost his human presence. In doing so the work breaks a European code, crosses a line, goes beyond the pale, in terms of its rendition of pain. Previous representations of the flagellation showed the stark effects of pain, but these are necessarily counterbalanced by a series of formal moves emphasising fortitude and majesty in the midst of degradation. The flagellated Christ which now stands in the niche originally occupied by Chagas's sculpture exudes strength, controlled elegance, above all, perhaps, a sense of disappointment with his tormentors. There are few treatments of the crucifixion which break the invisible artistic contracts requiring the exhibition of dignity and strength. There are no treatments of the flagellation, apart from that of Chagas, which turn Christ into a dying animal.[96]

Chagas has made a Christ who is so abused as to have passed into a
realm of agonised insensibility where human consciousness has been suspended, driven out, or down through the effects, simply, of physical shock.
This thing is not a God suffering for man, but a human beaten beyond
humanity. The central trauma point in this image is its back [**5.35**]. The
back, texturally and colouristically, has become a thing apart, a landscape
of pain – it has come apart, it appears to have a life of its own, a sense of its
own, built out of the infliction of pain, rather than out of the endurance of
it. The back is both disgusting and beautiful, the drops of blood which
glisten upon the surface consisting of hundreds of rubies set into the gesso.
The back is a sculpture within a sculpture, as if the perfect skin of a man,
finished by the sculptor, were then worked upon by the torturer, his chisel
a whip, his material flesh. This beaten thing should be in a trauma ward,
not a church, and indeed it is presented today in a glass case at the end of
the sumptuous Baroque sacristy of the Convent. Chagas's work is separated from the touch and the gaze by reassuring reflections and a hard
transparent wall; it is as if it had to be put in some kind of aesthetic inten-
sive care unit, or protective tank.

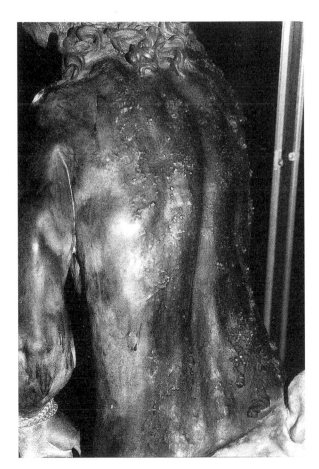

[**5.35**] Francisco
Xavier Chagas,
Flagellated Christ,
detail of back (sculp-
ture in polychromed
wood, *c.* 1750).
Convent of the
Venerable Third Order
of the Carmelites,
Salvador, Bahia

Originally standing in a niche with its back to the wall, the sculpture would have hidden from the view that terrible site of violence. Now that this back is out in the open I want to ask what it means. Is it a beautiful landscape, or a great ugly wound, how can it be loved, does it have an artistic familiar, does its memory live on?

It has at least one familiar, which is to be found, again, when a great black artist remembers slavery, and remembers whipping, and again uncovers the back. The effects of Sethe's terrible whipping, at the hands of a teenaged white boy, in Tony Morrison's *Beloved*, share with Chagas's work an ability to create a beautiful but terrible monument out of this suffering. Such a monument can only grow by fully acknowledging the deformity which the torture produces on the victim's body; with this recognition comes transmogrification. Seth explains to her friend Paul D, years after the event, that she was whipped:

> 'Those boys found out I told on em. Schoolteacher made one open up my back and when it closed it made a tree. It grows there still.'
> 'They used cowhide on you?' …
> Behind her, bending down, his body an arc of kindness, he held her breasts in the palms of his hands. He rubbed his cheek on her back and learned that way her sorrow, the roots of it, its wide trunk and intricate branches. Raising his fingers to the hooks of her dress, he knew without seeing them or hearing any sign that tears were coming fast. And when the top of her dress was around her hips and he saw the sculpture her back had become, like the decorative work of an ironsmith too passionate for display, he could think but not say, 'Aw, Lord, girl'. And he would tolerate no peace until he had touched every ridge and leaf of it with his mouth, none of which Sethe could feel because her back skin had been dead for years.[97]

Only moments later when Sethe has made love to this man she has not seen for years the transforming beauty of his gaze and touch has gone and he can see only a matter of fact: 'and the wrought iron maze he had explored in the kitchen like a gold miner pawing through pay dirt was in fact a revolting clump of scars. Not a tree, as she said. Maybe it was shaped like one, but nothing like any tree he knew, because trees were inviting things you could trust and be near.'[98]

Paul D's loss of vision calls to mind a familiar image. The 'revolting lump of scars', as a fact, is frozen in a notorious early photogravure, and has been reprinted in numerous books on slavery [**5.36**].[99] This figure, contorted, posing in accordance with the instructions of an unseen photographer, almost perversely provides an echo of Morrison's concept of display. Yet what the work of Morrison and Chagas end up by telling us is that the mere factual recording of the scars is only a partial record of 'the results of being whipped'. The results can be terrible, uncontrollable, even paradoxically wonderful. Forensic documentation is at best a limited form of testimony – the body as evidence, as object, is in a sense no-body at all.

This is not to say that Morrison or Chagas avoid the facts; what they do is to take the idea of what the 'results' of torture might be beyond documentation. For both of them, nothing can make it better, nothing can take away the dehumanising experience of torture, or the scars. The feeling will never come back, and the sufferer will always be turned away from the site of suffering, but this site generates feeling. The healing and the trauma lie in the feeling the site produces in others. The site, which is also the memorial of the suffering, has a power which must be allowed to speak out of its terrible muteness. The art of the torturer has created something beyond his or her control – 'the decorative work of an ironsmith too passionate for display' has, and can, and will be displayed. The photograph displays the results of torture precisely in the way they were achieved by the torturer. Chagas and Morrison refuse the banality of this factual inheritance, and through their art inject beauty into the description of the torture process.

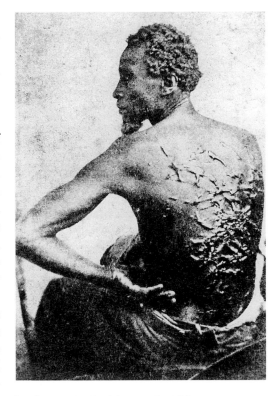

[5.36] Anon., *Gordon* (photograph, 1863)

[5.37] Anon., 'Gordon' (wood-engraving, 1863). From *Harper's Weekly*

GORDON AS HE ENTERED OUR LINES.　　GORDON UNDER MEDICAL INSPECTION.　　GORDON IN HIS UNIFORM AS A U.S. SOLDIER.

Gordon: slave as soldier

But let us return to the documented, the photographic, site of whipping. There are very few photographs of African-American slaves which predate the Civil War, and records of the results of slave torture are even more rare. Early photography does not provide a substantial archive for the revisioning of the plantation societies of the southern states of America.[100] The photogravure of the whipped slave consequently has great value both as a cultural and as an aesthetic artefact, yet what it reveals is a partial truth. Nothing, it might appear, could be more openly displayed than the anonymous figure printed on a piece of board a little smaller than a playing card. This whipped back, so carefully stretched out in an elaborate pose presenting the slave as scientific data, was printed in thousands and passed out to Northern troops as a testimony to the barbarity of the slave power. This figure is a victim of the South, but a patient of the North, cleaned up, sanitised, recorded and displayed. What is significant is the extent to which the processes of display, graphic reproduction and formal interpretation were uncontrollable: the image rapidly spilled out into a variety of publishing arenas. In woodcut form the victim had a name, Gordon, and the image of his whipped back existed as part of a propaganda triptych within the pages of *Harper's Weekly* [**5.37**].[101] Gordon, whether he wanted to or not, holds himself out as an example of what the slave was prepared to do for the North. His whipped back existed at the centre of a narrative of redemption:

A TYPICAL NEGRO

We publish herewith three portraits from photographs by M'Pherson and Oliver, of the negro Gordon, who escaped from his master in Mississippi, and came into our lines at Baton Rouge in March last. One of these portraits represent the man as he entered our lines with clothes torn and covered with mud and dirt from his long race through the swamps and bayous, chased as he had been for days and nights by his master with several neighbours and a pack of blood hounds; another shows him as he underwent the surgical examination previous to being mustered into the service – his back furrowed and scarred with traces of a whipping administered on Christmas day last; and the third represents him in United States uniform, bearing the musket and prepared for duty.[102]

The status of Gordon's whipped back is carefully controlled. The image of his scarring hangs in the central part of a triptych. Yet the triptych parodies its origins within religious iconography. Gordon's status is not one of martyrological elevation but of secular victimhood. Gordon's experience in slavery can be defined only in relation to his present status as a pristinely uniformed private in the United States army, and to his past experience as a starving and ragged runaway. Before he enters the army, and after he has entered it, Gordon's back is hidden by clothing. It is, in fact, only via the process of medical inspection that he may enter the military, and this in turn enables the documentation of his scarring and its public display, through reproduction, to the troops. The photograph provides a sort of forensic Lazarus. The white sheet suggests the cold comfort of the hospital ward, but also a winding sheet. The wood-engraving which has been cut from the photograph also carried a caption 'Gordon Under Medical Inspection'. The medical unit of the Union army has legitimated the record of Gordon's suffering, and resurrected him as a soldier. The presentation of the black body as the afflicted subject within the visual conventions of Christian martyrological iconography was, and is, exceptionally rare. Visual culture would have to wait just over one hundred years for Muhammed Ali to appear on the cover of *Esquire* in the guise of Castagno's St Sebastian in an image which ironically combined the concept of black martyrdom with Ali's refusal to enter the United States armed forces fighting in Vietnam.[103]

Gordon's whipped body is both shown off, and protected by, the United States military, a situation which leads it to play a peculiar semiotic role. The conventional relationship between whipping and the military in Western graphic satire relates to atrocity prints showing the unjustified and brutal military flogging of whites. To take an extreme yet revealing example, the technically ham-fisted yet flamboyant popular satirist C. J. Grant produced a mid-nineteenth-century satire in England focusing on the excesses of military punishment. The print was straightforwardly entitled *The Late Bloody and Brutal Exhibition of Horrid Military Torture, or, Aristocratic Bastards in their Glory* [**5.38**]. The victim's face is frozen in an open-mouthed scream, neck jerked back at an unnatural angle. The cuts of the whip are physically mimicked by the cuts of the engraver's burin. Blood and broken flesh are printed in black striations on the white flesh. The blood then cascades out into space in a shower of black fragments bespattering the whipper. In the frenetic and melodramatic excess of its narrative, this design could not be further removed from the monumental stasis of the figure of Gordon. Where the white man is the pitiful victim of the English military, the black slave can only show his wounds because of the protective compassion of the American army.

Yet Gordon's scars emerge as an unstable phenomenon. Once promiscuously exposed via a photograph, they are then cut into woodblock form. In the cut in *Harper's Weekly* they have become separate objects, like some obscene cartography. The processes of distortion continued as Gordon's scars were transported over the Atlantic, and reappeared in England, on a broadside entitled *Southern Slavery Illustrated* and addressed to the Working Men of Manchester [**5.39**]. Gordon's appearance in England in popular woodcut form involves a final colouristic transformation in which his scars, the signs of his suffering, move from black to white. By this stage Gordon has been turned round in more ways than one, literally reversed in terms of the design, with his scars, hacked out of the wood, appearing like a mass of whipped cream. Photographic realism has been submerged in

[5.38] C. J. Grant, *The Late Bloody and Brutal Exhibition of Horrid Military Torture, or, Aristocratic Bastards in their Glory*, detail (woodcut, *c.* 1835)

[5.39] Anon., *Gordon* (broadside, letterpress and wood-engraving, 1864)

graphic primitivism: the delicacy, the 'truth', of each skein in the terrible web of keloid scarring is travestied in the crude gouging of a broadside woodcut and loses its integrity. There is not much of Gordon's trauma left in this 'faithful copy', which proclaims a fragile link between Gordon and the northern industrial working man. As a representation of the effects of whipping this image stands in aesthetic counterpoint to the sculpture of Chagas.

Experience for innocents: children, slaves, animals and torture

W is the WHIP, which with paddle and chain,
Stocks, thumbscrew and bell, give them terrible pain.

(*The Alphabet of Slavery*)

animals – our fellow brethren in pain, disease, death, suffering and famine, our slaves in the most laborious works, our companions in our amusements, – they may partake in our origin in one common ancestor, we may be all netted together. (Charles Darwin)

The children's books produced in England and America from 1780 to 1865 carried more imagery depicting slavery than any other area of the publishing market. In the second half of the nineteenth century in England children's publishing exploded. By the early nineteenth century children themselves were the focus for a series of new leisure industries. Specialist children's circulating libraries were established in English towns by the first decade of the nineteenth century.[104] The emphasis upon preaching humanity and compassion within juvenile literature, aimed at the new urban bourgeois readership, provided a ripe market for anti-slavery infiltration. Abolitionists preached a doctrine based upon pity for the slave, yet the tensions within texts designed for children, which presented the slaves themselves as wronged and harmless innocents, require careful uncovering. The slave, male and female, was frequently constructed as equivalent in the quality of his/her suffering to both the child and the animal.[105]

Infantilisation and animalisation are powerful tropes for disguising, familiarising and reducing unfamiliar cultures. They are central to the thought and work of pro-slavery and abolition propagandists, and twentieth-century historiographers.[106] They constituted basic weapons within the armoury of the political print satirists of the eighteenth and nineteenth centuries, yet their use was not restricted to such a vulgar context but saturated thought in far more reified intellectual atmospheres. In the late 1820s Hegel saw all Negroes as animals, and specifically domestic animals: 'The negro is an example of animal man in all his savagery and lawlessness … and nothing consonant with humanity is to be found in his character. For this very reason, we cannot properly feel ourselves into his nature, no more than into that of a dog.' Hegel also saw no distinction between the consciousness of Negros, animals and children, all of which were constructed as 'innocent' because they had not become aware of their own being through the development of 'substantial objectivity', a state which allows for an awareness of 'God, the eternal, justice, nature, and all natural things'.[107] Related triangular conflations of child, animal and African slave permeated eighteenth-century thought. They were frequently manifested through the trope of the lamb of God. The point can be made succinctly via two late-eighteenth-century poems. In Blake's 'Holy Thursday' there are multitudes of innocent lamb-children: 'The hum of multitudes was there, but multitudes of lambs, / Thousands of little boys and girls raising their innocent hands.' Harmless lamb/slaves are to be found in Cowper's 'Epigram' innocently conflating the processes of wine and sugar manufacture:

> To purify their wine some people bleed
> A *Lamb* into the barrel, and succeed;
> No Nostrum, Planters say, is half so good
> To make fine sugar, as a Negro's blood.
> Now lambs and negroes both are harmless things,
> And thence, perhaps, this wond'rous Virtue springs,
> 'Tis in the blood of Innocence alone
> Good cause why Planters never try their own.[108]

The slave here loses the martyrological status so central to the way abolitionists constructed themselves and appears instead as sacrificial victim. The suffering innocence of the slave and the suffering innocence of the child equate to an animal innocence.[109] Slave, animal and child are again conjoined in the following account of William Blake raging at the conditions of a child worker in Astley's beast menagerie: 'Blake was standing at one of his windows, which looked into Astley's premises ... and saw a boy hobbling along with a log tied to his foot, such an one as is put on a horse or ass to prevent their straying ... Blake's blood boiled and his indignation surpassed his forbearance. He sallied forth, and demanded in no quiescent terms, that the boy should be loosed and that no Englishman should be subjected to those miseries which he thought inexcusable even towards a slave.'[110] Blake is described looking into a menagerie and sees a white boy who has been treated like one of the exotica in the zoo. The object restraining the boy, a chain and a log, achieves its power to outrage the observer through its association with the restraint of animals and slaves. The outrage is then channelled into an outpouring of nationalistic enthusiasm that is based in race. The treatment of the boy is shocking because despite his infant status he is symbolically 'an Englishman'. With the introduction of this word the boy is separated from his liminal relationship to beast and black and re-established within English civilisation. The comparison finally turns not on similarity but upon the emphasis of imperial difference. In comparing the boy to a slave and an animal Blake is led to announce the fact that the boy can never be equated to either, for he is, like

Blake himself, 'an Englishman'. Blake's nationalism is based in compassionate response, but it is also based in racial distinction, and as such shares a common ground with the mass of pro-slavery literature which would condemn emancipation because the suffering of factory children was equivalent to, or worse than, that of the plantation slave.

The anonymous pro-slavery pamphlet *The Condition of the West India Slave contrasted with that of The Infant Slave in our English Factories* is founded upon this 'logic'. Brought out in England just before emancipation in the British West Indies, it carries a series of caricature plates with commentary which set the sufferings of the white factory child against the riotous degeneracy of the Caribbean black [**5.40**]. The section 'The Whip' carries a plate by George Cruikshank's brother Robert, which shows two 'factory overlookers' beating children, one using a long pole, the other a many-thonged cat. The accompanying text works through elaborate comparison with the whipping of female children, white women and slaves:

THE WHIP

'In order to keep the children awake, and to stimulate their exertions, means are made use of, to which I shall advert,' says Mr. Sadler, 'as a last instance of the degradation to which this system has reduced the manufacturing operatives of this country. Sir, children are beaten with *thongs*, prepared for the purpose! Yes, the females of this country, no matter whether children or grown up, – I hardly know which is the more disgusting outrage, – are beaten upon the face, arms, and bosom, – beaten in your free market of labour, as you term it, like slaves. These are the instruments. – [*Here the honourable member*

[**5.40**] Isaac Robert Cruikshank, 'English Factory Slaves' (etching, *c.* 1830). Plate 3 from *The Condition of the West India Slave contrasted with that of The Infant Slave in our English Factories*

273

exhibited some black, heavy, leathern thongs – one of them fixed in a sort of handle, the smack of which, when struck upon the table, resounded through the house.] – They are quite equal to breaking an arm, but that the bones of the young are, as I have before said, pliant … We speak with execration of the cart whip of the West Indies – but let us see this night an equal feeling rise against the factory-thong of England.'[111]

Much important recent work by race and post-colonial theorists has emphasised the rhetorical conjunction of the European industrial pauper masses with slaves or colonised blacks. Yet this is a very unstable trope within the political, literary and visual discourses of nineteenth-century Europe – the slave and the factory worker do not easily occupy a common rhetorical ground.[112] The coupling frequently operates to stress an absolute difference founded in race(ist) distinction, rather than similarity, and this difference becomes pronounced in the representation of violence. When the beating of English females with whips on the 'face, arms and bosom' is compared to the beating of slaves we are given two different flagellatory codes. The brutalist, male and literally frontal assault on English womanhood and girlhood stands, physically, not only apart from, but on the other side of, the conventions for depicting slave whippings. Slaves are inevitably described, and depicted, as beaten on the back. Then again the final comparison between the 'cart whip' of the West Indies and the 'factory thong' of England suggests two different tools/weapons. The cart whip used to beat horses and oxen is easily adapted to slaves, but the English children are 'beaten with *thongs*, prepared for the purpose'.[113]

While the comparison of cruelty to slaves with cruelty to animals and to children is a standard element within abolition children's literature, the effect these comparisons have upon the status enjoyed by each of the elements is, as the former example suggests, problematic. If the description of the experience of torture is transhistorical and transcultural in these texts, then this comparative omniscience is achieved at a high price. Torture can be seen to equate one living thing with another only through a general blurring and disempowerment – suffering becomes non-specific, transferable, but crucially, quantifiable. Suffering is also once again reduced to the symbolic depiction of the objects which are used to cause it. It doesn't, in the end, matter if you beat or chain up a child, an animal or a black slave, all suffering is brought about through sin, and you use the same whip or chain to sin with. Violence is translated into sin, the victim into a map for the display of sin, and the map is drawn with the object of torture. The slave's experience of violence, when it is submerged in a common pool of suffering innocence, is in danger of being erased by philanthropic enthusiasm. The most complicated body of writing to address the relation between slave suffering, especially that of children, and evangelical concepts of sin, are those of the slave ship captain, and later fashionable London divine, the Rev. John Newton.[114]

One tale from Mary Leatheley's *Large Pictures with Little Stories* plays some bizarre variations on the child/slave/animal conflation, all of which revolve around the image of a master whipping his slave. The story moves rapidly through the destruction of two family units. Sambo is stolen from his African parents and sold into slavery as a twelve-year-old. He 'marries', has a child and is then resold with his family. They are separated. The story concludes with a set of bizarre substitutions which reconstitute the familial order with the black male adult Sambo as the mother, a lamb as the surrogate child, while the role of the father is split between the master and his infant son:

> Poor Sambo's heart was almost broken, and he did not work so steadily as he was expected to do, and this made his master look angrily upon him. There was a little lamb in the house belonging to one of the master's children, who often forgot to feed and attend to it. And Sambo loved the little lamb, for it seemed gentle and innocent, and reminded him of his own little lost baby. So he used to feed it whenever its little master had forgotten it. But one day the cruel Massa came and found him *neglecting his work*, as he said, and cruel was the flogging he gave to the unhappy slave.[115]

Sambo emerges as a curious composite, part child, part pet and part mother. The accompanying coloured etching and aquatint shows the master in top hat and tartan trews poised to strike the kneeling Sambo a backhanded blow with a riding crop, while the lamb unconcernedly drinks [**5.41**]. The scenario of the wronged mother beaten by the Victorian

SAMBO SEVERELY THRASHED FOR THINKING OF A DUMB ANIMAL.

[**5.41**] Anon., 'Sambo and the Lamb' (hand-coloured wood-engraving, c. 1850). From *Large Pictures with Little Stories*

cad would have been familiar to any contemporary readers of the *Illustrated Police News*. Sambo is made to appeal to the conscience of the Victorian child by being presented as wronged and dutiful mother, attacked for attempting to feed her infant. He is not merely emasculated but reinvented as a wet nurse. The maternal and feminised tendencies within the Tomist stereotype are here extended, but the maternal emotion is expended upon an animal. Yet Sambo is simultaneously constructed within what David Brion Davis has argued is the basic paradigm for alienating the slave – comparison with the domesticated animal. In loving the lamb as if it were his own child Sambo becomes a sheep. Beyond this Sambo behaves, within the conventions of the children's book, like a child. This image consequently provides the child with a disempowering set of behavioural analogies for the black male slave.[116]

Mock innocents: violence and the parodic children's book

Children's literature did not merely operate within the dynamic of parent, reader and child audience. Within Europe a tradition existed in which the forms and techniques of children's literature had been transposed to the contexts of political pamphlet literature and print satire. Some of the works produced in the forms of children's nursery rhyme books and primers by English radical artists and publishers in the period 1780–1820 had gained enormous circulation and were translated into other European languages. There was also a resurgence of the sub-genre of the mock-children's book in England in the context of the 1832 Reform Act. American abolitionists saw the potential of presenting their arguments within the structures of children's books, and appear to have adapted the forms used by the most successful English practitioners such as William Hone and John Carpenter. Yet the transposition of the stock scenarios, which worked around slave torture, to the area of children's literature is not rhetorically a straightforward process.[117]

These texts adopt a tone of feigned innocence, and treat atrocity simplistically, reducing the presentation of violence to caricature, symbol and emblem. Several of the most elaborate American political satires based on children's books came out as the Civil War reached its end. This consideration of the representation of slave torture concludes by turning to a satiric print *The House that Jeff Built*, which attempts to encapsulate the history of slave abuse through parodying an illustrated nursery rhyme.[118]

'The House that Jeff Built' and 'The House that Jack Built'

In 1863 David Claypoole Johnston, one of America's most eclectic popular graphic satirists, published *The House that Jeff Built* [**5.42**]. The etching, in twelve sections, is a comprehensive assault on the physical brutality underlying Southern slavery. The nursery rhyme source for the print, 'The House that Jack Built', had peculiar advantages in terms of the narrative and satiric ambition of Johnston's subject. *The House that Jeff Built* is

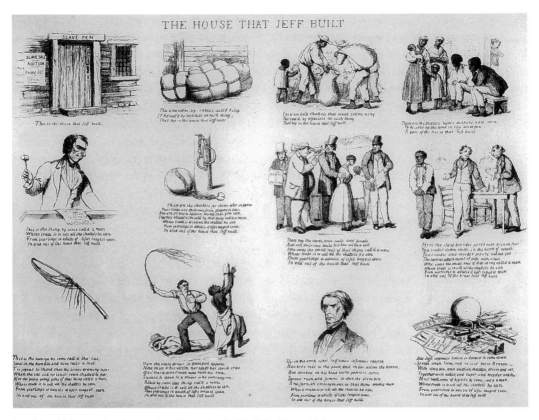

[5.42] David Claypoole Johnston, *The House that Jeff Built* (etching, 1863)

not a specific attack on a single event but an attempt to provide a graphic satiric summary of the origins of the Civil War from the perspective of Jefferson Davis's political agenda. The print attempts a general critique of slavery in the South, it is ambitious, and in narrative and formal terms had to go beyond the narrationally limited resources of the rapidly evolving formulae of the political cartoon. Johnston, in using 'The House that Jack Built', had a model capable of expressing big political ideas and a broad historical narrative. Nursery rhyme parody had been popular in English graphic satire since the 1780s, and 'The House that Jack Built' was the most frequently used rhyme. The ancient nursery rhyme with its mesmeric formulae, rhythmic incremental repetition, and a narrative growth evolving from a series of seemingly ineluctable causal connections, had long been fashionable on both sides of the Atlantic. Johnston's is the latest, and a particularly fine, example in a long line of prints that took up the rhyme in order to attack political abuses.[119]

What I want to think about here is the effectiveness of describing violence against slaves in the language and imagery of children's literature. The greatest English print satire presenting the brutalisation of the labouring poor was produced in the context of the waves of radical agitation that periodically swept England from 1790 to 1820. One option adopted by the satirists to describe atrocity was children's literature. In seeking to speak in the language and literature of children when describing the horrors of the adult world satirists turned to the parodic nursery rhyme. The ancient rhyme 'The House that Jack Built' provided the basis for the most hard-hitting satire to come out of England on the subject of the Peterloo Massacre. William Hone and George Cruikshank's illustrated pamphlet satire *The Political House that Jack Built* caused an international sensation, and it would appear that this passionate outcry against the murder and mutilation of the English poor directly influenced Johnston's passionate outcry against the slave system.

The maturity of Johnston's satire comes out in the subtlety of the verse parody and the variation in satiric technique in the images. The pounding rhythms and sense of inevitable connection between each accumulation and the next are carefully maintained from the original rhyme. The causal relations between the economics of producing and selling cotton by slave labour, and the incidental cruelties required to run such a system, are powerfully brought out. Above all the power inherent in the simplicity of the model is never submerged in too much detail.

As with *The Political House*, Johnston never moves too far from the power of simple pictographic communication. One unadorned symbol or ideogram can have more power in the context of a satiric nursery rhyme than any number of over-worked figure compositions, cluttered up with symbolic baggage. Of the twelve vignettes in the print, five are simply drawn symbols. The first two images follow in the wake of numerous English and American predecessors and depict a building and some sacks, only here the house is not the bank or treasury, but a crude prison door marked 'slave pen', and the 'wealth', bales of cotton.

Once the basic association between cotton and slavery has been set up, the satire introduces figure composition in a series of four vignettes showing scenes of slave life by now stereotypes of popular abolition propaganda – cotton picking, with children working, the slave auction, and three scenes of the buying and selling of slaves, two featuring the public auction of a mother and her children. But these scenes are set against the use of single caricature portraits, and the presentation of objects drawn with diagrammatic clarity. Symbol and caricature interact with the verse inscriptions below.

The verse has a light touch, and unusually for an American print satire handles irony and black humour with delicacy. The method appears simple but is not – the fifth and sixth vignettes are a case in point. The accumulation for the sixth vignette, which simply shows a ball and chain, and a set of ankle shackles hanging on a nail on a post, runs as follows [5.43]:

These are the shackles, for slaves who suppose
Their limbs are their own from fingers to toes,
And are prone to believe say all that you can,
That they shouldn't be sold by that thing call'd a man;

Whose trade is to sell all the chattels he can
From yearlings to adults of life's longest
span;
In and out of the house that Jeff built.

This is clever writing. The key to its success
is the way the apparently unruffled simplicity
of the verse carries an undercurrent of bitter
double meanings. The delicacy of that
second line, elaborating and elongating the
concept of limbs into the details of fingers
and toes, suddenly snaps the reader back to
the image of the shackles which fit around
wrists and ankles, isolating feet and hands,
fingers and toes. The rhyming of 'who suppose' and 'fingers and toes' is possessed of
the kind of colloquial freedom perfectly
suited to doggerel written in nursery rhyme
metre, but its very lightness and absurdity
forces home the bitterness of the message.
The use of the word prone in the next line
occurs in a colloquial clause, 'prone to

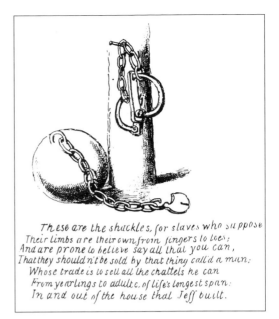

These are the shackles, for slaves who suppose
Their limbs are their own from fingers to toes;
And are prone to believe say all that you can,
That they shouldn't be sold by that thing call'd a man;
Whose trade is to sell all the chattels he can
From yearlings to adults of life's longest span;
In and out of the house that Jeff built.

[5.43] David Claypoole Johnston, *The House that Jeff Built*,
detail (etching, 1863)

believe', but involves a bitter pun – the slaves are not only prone in this
sense, but shackled and defenceless they are physically, literally prone.
The prone-ness of their belief in liberty exists against the precisely con-
trary prone-ness of their physical, shackled being. The reference to the
slave-trader as a 'thing' refers us back to the previous vignette where he
first appeared. The slave-trader's application of a dehumanising vocabulary of farm livestock to the slaves he sells, as in 'chattels' and 'yearlings',
gives a sudden new relevance to his own denomination as a 'thing' – he is a
'thing' in that he is no longer human.

The final line of the rhyme, with its sing-song rhythm, mimetic of the
coming and going of slaves through the market, contrasts starkly with the
pinioned immobility of the first line 'these are the shackles for slaves'. The
commotion of the market-place is set against the cruel stasis of the shackled
victim, and the grimacing auctioneer with hammer poised to descend is set
against the empty shackles on the post, one slave released by sale, another
waiting to move into them. This work is formally clean and ideologically
certain, yet it leaves interpretative spaces for the viewer/reader to fill. This
satire treats a terrible and dark subject with a light economy by feigning the
innocence of a children's book, yet it is also true that the polemic presents
the slave as an emblem of helpless innocence which, both in its formal context and in its characterisation, imposes an infantilised stereotype upon the
slave. In presenting the slave as a figure of child-like simplicity within the
form of a children's book, the work enforces the reduction of slave to infant,
a construction of the black slave which historians and literary critics since

Stanley Elkins have seen as a centrepiece of pro-slavery rhetoric. But the solution to depicting torture itself is still dependent upon objectification. The image of slave whipping caricatures the slave and the master, and in doing so takes away their humanity; only the whip itself is beyond graphic distortion. We are back with the unassailable power of the object, the heart of still life.[120]

Objects that feel and bodies as objects

Almost all of the fear, violence and suffering experienced by slaves during the middle passage, and within the slave systems of the Americas and the Caribbean, went unrecorded and will remain in one sense unknown. Yet the inheritance of this violence is a living thing, which has worked itself out within American and European societies, and it will continue to do so in ways we do not yet, and may never, understand.

Elaine Scarry warns of the perceptual transformation which torture and the world of the torturer can bring about. She explains how the process of physical torture commonly involves 'a mutilation of the domestic which then becomes part of the experience of the tortured'.[121] Within the descriptive armoury of abolition this obscene transformative alchemy of the torturer also seems to hold sway. Any object, every object – bath, chair, bed, sheet, fire, wall, floor, table, spoon – can become a weapon of torture. But beyond this (perhaps finally iconic-soft-option), and within the psychological oppression of slavery systems themselves, lies the terrible truth that all consciousness becomes contaminated with the experience of slavery. Memory itself in its most aesthetically heightened forms can become torture. Toni Morrison's *Beloved* has explained this with an impossible beauty. Even happiness and love change, and when remembered in the context of pain and disempowerment, torture the mind of the enslaved. It is the longevity and the emotional lassitudes of slavery systems in the Americas which finally seal them off from any easy comparison with the Nazi Holocaust. Plantation slavery was rooted in oppression but allowed space for, indeed encouraged, so much happiness and success: the smile of a child, reared to adulthood in a 'loving' environment, but later sold, the words of a lover, maybe a lifetime later beaten to death, can, through the horrible irony of memory, be the most painful experience there is, existing beyond a whipping of one's own body, or the memory of a whipping. It is maybe a shying away from, or an inability to deal with, the universality of this polluting horror (and *this is* the memory of slavery) which finally lies behind the Western obsession with representing the memory of slave torture through objects. The fear of our contamination is also why the history of slavery in England, until recently, boiled down to the history of the abolition of slavery and the celebration of the emancipation moment.

There is no limit to what one could put in a painting or a book about the violence of slavery, and no end to the objects which might be placed in a slavery museum. Yet, in order to recall the atrocities of slavery, acts of visual and cultural containment – perhaps unavoidable simplifications – occur. Within abolition polemic semiotic streamlining could lead to brilliant results. For example, one major problem in the presentation of slave torture relates to the omnipresence of racial codification. If the slave body is black, then it is immediately separated from white experience through racially encoded psychic reflex. How can a white audience get beyond the acculturated sense that they are looking at a skin that appears different from their own, and which consequently must be assumed to respond to pain differently? One powerful solution consists of doing away with the skin completely, and going for what lies beneath it. One little vignette in *The Oasis*, a miniature journal edited by Lydia Maria Child, a propagandist of genius, takes this option to extremes. The slave body is presented as a chained skeleton, picked completely clean [**5.44**]. The slave's humanity is communicated by drawing attention to the universal similitude of human bones – all skeletons are white and they all look the same. The skull stares out grinning at an isolated sugar cane plant, and a miniature planter's mansion sits in the background. The viewer is left to set up their own narrative associations between cane, house, bones and chains. The text below transforms the tentative and subservient words of the abolition seal, 'Am I not a man and a brother', into the confrontational aphorism, 'O man, the blood of thy brother cries from the earth and sea'. The flesh and blood, absent from the bones we look at, are reconfigured within an elemental setting of universal guilt.

The bones that are dead exist half way between body and object; they get beyond race and beyond life at the same time. Perhaps the ultimate

[5.44] Anon., 'O man, the blood of thy brother' (woodcut, 1834). From *The Oasis*

O man, the blood of thy brother cries from the earth and the sea [1]

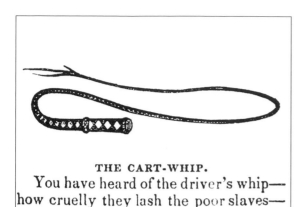

THE CART-WHIP.

You have heard of the driver's whip—
how cruelly they lash the poor slaves—
how many stripes they receive. Each
of the drivers has in his hand, or coiled

THE

SLAVE'S FRIEND.

Vol. II, No. II.   Whole No. 14.

[5.45] Anon., 'The Whip' (wood-engraving, 1833). From *The Slave's Friend*

[5.46] Anon., 'Shackles' (wood-engraving, 1833). From *The Slave's Friend*

gesture of objectification in the representation of torture is to leave out the body completely. This takes us back full circle to the power of objects as signifiers for human agony. Within the pages of *The Slave's Friend*, a miniature children's slavery magazine printed in Boston in the early 1830s, slavery is represented again and again through simple unadorned little woodcuts of the whip, the shackle or the bowie knife [**5.45** and **5.46**]. Again these objects go beyond race; they only have meaning when we imagine them being used, or abused, but are they finally appropriate or dignified symbols of the individual sufferings of slaves? Joseph Conrad defines the encouragement that torture offers to malicious banality: 'The stupidest mind may invent a rankling phrase or brand the innocent with a cruel aspersion. A piece of string and a ramrod; a few muskets in combination with a length of hide rope; or even a simple mallet of heavy hard wood, applied with a swing to human fingers or to the joints of a human body, is enough for the infliction of the most exquisite torture.'[122] This takes us in a terrible direction, and might encourage the thought that, in the end, there may be nothing really worth it that can be created in any form, for any audience, to describe the torture of humankind by humankind. Yet this book rejects that option and argues that the work which directly addresses slavery made by Xavier Chagas, William Blake, Henry Fuseli, William Cowper, the committee that designed the plan of the *Brookes*, J. M. W. Turner, Nat Turner, Henry Bibb, Henry 'Box' Brown, Moses Roper, John Ruskin, Harriet Beecher Stowe and Frederick Douglass, all so different, all so re-memorable, testifies to the human ability to make art which refutes the banality of torture.

Notes

1 Edward Peters, *Torture* (Philadelphia, University of Pennsylvania Press, 1996), p. 164. For an economical repudiation of this position see Page duBois, *Torture and Truth* (London, Routledge, 1991), pp. 147–9, 152. For the legal application of torture in the West, including domestic violence, see Leon S. Sheleff, *Ultimate Penalties: Capital Punishment, Life Imprisonment, Physical Torture* (Columbus, Ohio State University Press, 1987), pp. 285–325. Sheleff's study has implications for the practice of occasional domestic torture within slave systems.

2 Cesare Beccaria, *On Crimes and Punishments*, trans. and intr. Henri Paolucci (Indianapolis, Bobbs-Merrill Educational Publishing, 1977), p. 36.

3 See John W. Blassinghame, *The Slave Community: Plantation Life in the Antebellum South* (New York and London, Oxford University Press, 1972), pp. 77–154; Elizabeth Fox-Genovese, *Within the Plantation Household* (Chapel Hill, Univesity of North Carolina Press, 1988), pp. 37–333; Peter Kolchin, *American Slavery 1619–1877* (London, Penguin, 1995), pp. 93–168; Philip D. Morgan, *Slave Counterpoint: Black Culture in the Eighteenth-Century Chesapeake and Low Country* (Chapel Hill and London, University of North Carolina Press, 1998), pp. 27–420; James Walvin, *Questioning Slavery* (London and New York, Routledge, 1996), pp. 49–72; James Walvin, *A History of British Slavery* (London, Fontana, 1993), pp. 69–214. The most succinct comparative account of the North American slave laws is *A Sketch of the Laws Relating to Slavery in the Several States of the United States of America* (Pennsylvania, 1827), pp. 34–45, 106–19. Robin Blackburn, *The Making of New World Slavery From the Baroque to the Modern 1492–1800* (London, Verso, 1997), pp. 309–63.

4 For the judicial torture of women see E. J. Burford and Sandra Shulman, *Of Bridles and Burnings: The Punishment of Women* (London, Robert Hale, 1992), for whipping pp. 63–80, branks or scold's bridle pp. 49–63, stocks pp. 163–86. For the varieties of scold's bridle see Geoffrey Abbot, *Rack, Rope and Red-Hot Pincers: A History of Torture and its Instruments* (London, Headline, 1993), p. 150, plate 4. For the lurid hold which the objects of 'traditional' forms of Western punishment and torture still exert on the popular imagination see *Hamlyn History of Punishment and Torture* (London, Hamlyn, 1996); Brian Lane *Encyclopaedia of Cruel and Unusual Punishment* (London, Virgin Publishing, 1993). For the 'feminisation' of the New World slave via the introduction of forms of torture and punishment previously reserved for women see Blackburn, *The Making*, pp. 324–5.

5 For popular literatures generated by hangings in England 1770–1865 see V. A. C. Gattrell, *The Hanging Tree: Execution and the English People 1770–1868* (Oxford, Oxford University Press, 1996), pp. 109–96. Gattrell's brilliant study finds no room for discussion of the execution of slaves or free blacks in the English colonies during his period.

6 For the problematic relation of slave abuse to even the most abstract definitions of punishment see Igor Primoratz, 'Punishment as Language', in Antony Duff (ed.), *Punishment* (Dartmouth, International Research Library of Philosophy, 1993), pp. 55–75.

7 For a survey of this material in European high art from the twelfth to early nineteenth century see Lionello Puppi, *Torment in Art: Pain, Violence and Martyrdom* (New York, Rizzoli, 1990). It is significant that this volume finds no place for any images depicting blacks or slaves.

8 See Johan Thorsten Sellin, *Slavery and the Penal System* (New York, Oxford and Amsterdam, Elsevier, 1976), pp. 21, 27–9.

9 For the earliest Western identification of blacks with the execution and torture of saints, the passion of Christ and the flagellation in particular, see Jean Devisse, *The Image of the Black in Western Art* (Lausanne, Menil Foundation, 1979), 2:1, pp. 70–80. For the later development of these associations see Jean Devisse and Michel Mollat, *The Image of the Black in Western Art* (Lausanne, Menil Foundation, 1979), 2:2,

pp. 59–78, 229–32. For an overview of early European constructions of blacks, positive and negative, see Jan Nederveen Pieterse, *White on Black: Images of Africa and Blacks in Western Popular Culture* (New Haven, Yale University Press, 1992), pp. 23–9.

10 For abolition reproductions of *The Four Stages* see pp. 114–15 above.

11 See Geoffrey Hartman, 'Darkness Visible', in Geoffrey Hartman (ed.), *The Shapes of Memory* (Oxford, Blackwell, 1993), pp. 15–22; Shoshana Felman and Dori Laub, *Testimony: Crises of Witnessing in Literature, Psychoanalysis, and History* (New York and London, Routledge, 1992); James E. Young, *The Texture of Memory: Holocaust Memorials and Meaning* (New Haven, Yale University Press, 1993).

12 Young, *Texture of Memory*, p. 132.

13 This convention may well relate to the representation of the interior of the suffering body in medical advertising through the use of a 'chalk drawing, silhouette or stylised outline'. See Elaine Scarry, *Resisting Representation* (New York, Oxford University Press, 1994), p. 28.

14 I am grateful to Philip Lapsansky of the Library Company of Philadelphia for drawing my attention to the illustrational variants between the first and second editions.

15 Moses Roper, *A Narrative of the Adventures and Escape of Moses Roper from American Slavery* (London, 1837), p. 18.

16 For the promiscuity of objects in relation to signification see Roland Barthes, *Image Music Text*, trans. Stephen Heath (London, Fontana, 1977), pp. 32–51.

17 *Dictionary of National Biography,* article 'Hawkins or Hawkyns, Sir John 1532–95'. Philip Gosse, *Sir John Hawkins* (London, John Lane the Bodley Head, 1930), pp. 42–3. Mary W. S. Hawkins, *Plymouth Armada Heroes: The Hawkins Family* (Plymouth, William Brendon and Son, 1888), pp. 65–7.

18 For an overview of incidence of black figures in European heraldry from the thirteenth to sixteenth century see Devisse and Mollat, *Image of the Black*, 2:2, pp. 7–18, 48–55.

19 For the central iconic status of the slave collar in abolition in the 1830s see *Calendar of the Papers of Sir Thomas Fowell Buxton 1786–1845,* vol. 3, Miscellaneous Correspondence, pp. 47–50, letter 30 April 1833, Buxton to W. Lloyd Caldecot.

20 See Jeanne Cannizzo, 'Doctor Livingstone Collects', in *David Livingstone and the Victorian Encounter with Africa* (London, National Portrait Gallery Publications, 1996), pp. 138–68. For an early assault on the African slave yoke see Thomas Clarkson, *Letters on the Slave-Trade and the State of the Natives in those Parts of Africa which are Contiguous to Fort St. Louis and Goree* (London, James Phillips, 1791), pp. 36–7 and plates. For Stanley and anti-slavery public displays see Annie E. Coombes, *Reinventing Africa: Museums, Material Culture and Popular Imagination* (New Haven and London, Yale University Press, 1994), pp. 68–70.

21 Blackburn, *The Making*, pp. 324–5.

22 In March 1799 Anderson travelled to St Vincent in the British West Indies, where he stayed with his uncle. He may have been offered a job on a plantation. See Jane R. Pomeroy, 'Alexander Anderson's Life and Engravings before 1800, with a Checklist of Publications Drawn from His Diary', *Proceedings of the American Antiquarian Society,* 100:1 (1990) 147.

23 There is some debate over the origin of the Anastasian cult. The Goddess became the subject of controversy when her image was included among exhibits in the Museum of Black History in Rio in the 1950s resulting in a mass resurgence of interest in the figure. The Brazilian Catholic Church insisted on her removal. The history is considered in the context of the slave mask exhibits in the National Museums and Galleries Merseyside, Liverpool, Gallery 'Transatlantic Slavery Against Human Dignity', room 4, bill-board display text and photographs.

24 For Morrison's theory see Paul Gilroy, *Small Acts* (London, Serpent's Tail, 1993), pp. 175–82.

25 Transatlantic Slavery Gallery, Liverpool, room 4, display board text: 'Anastasia, said to be an African Princess, was taken to Brazil in the nineteenth century. There she rebelled and died a martyr. This image of her was first shown at the *Museum of Black*

People in Rio, where she became worshipped as a saint. In 1989 the image was removed on the order of the Church who objected to her cult following.'

26 Albert Boime, *The Art of Exclusion: Representing Blacks in the Nineteenth Century* (London, Thames and Hudson, 1990), pp. 69–71.

27 Coombes, *Reinventing Africa*, pp. 6, 78–83 for later-nineteenth-century representation of the slave trade.

28 Michel Foucault, *Power/Knowledge: Selected Interviews and Other Writings 1972–77*, ed. Colin Gordon (New York, Pantheon Books, 1980), p. 38.

29 Michel Foucault, *Discipline and Punish: The Birth of the Prison*, trans. Alan Sheridan (Harmondsworth, Penguin Books, 1979), p. 8.

30 The combination of elaborate rituals of torture with execution persisted in the slave colonies in a manner in which they did not in mainland Britain. Gattrell, *The Hanging Tree*, the most comprehensive survey of execution in eighteenth- and nineteenth-century England, discusses torture only once, pp. 15–16, and that is in connection with Foucault.

31 See Michael Taussig, *Shamanism, Colonialism and the Wild Man: A Study in Terror and Healing* (Chicago, Chicago University Press, 1987), pp. 51–74. Taussig uncovers some of the bizarre rhetorical codes used by the West to translate atrocities perpetrated against Indians during the Putamayo rubber boom into an official discourse. For a passionate assault on the Eurocentric limitations of Foucault's account of the disappearance of torture in the context of the recent histories of Central American post-colonial societies see duBois, *Torture*, pp. 153–7.

32 My simultaneous questioning of, and dependence upon, Foucault's *Discipline and Punish* parallels the approach of Ann Laura Stoler, *Race and the Education of Desire: Foucault's History of Sexuality and the Colonial Order of Things* (Durham and London, Duke University Press, 1995). Stoler reappraises the first volume of Foucault's *History of Sexuality* in the context of post-colonial race theory. The classic post-colonial and deconstructive interrogation of Foucault's intellectual positioning with regard to questions of race, empire and colonialism remains Gayatri Spivak, 'Can the Subaltern Speak', in Cary Nelson and Laurence Grossberg (eds), *Marxism and the Interpretation of Culture* (London, Macmillan, 1988).

33 Eric Williams, *From Columbus to Castro: The History of the Caribbean 1492–1969* (London, Andre Deutsch, 1993), pp. 111–55, 280–92. Michael Craton, *Searching for the Invisible Man: Slaves and Plantation Life in Jamaica* (Cambridge Mass., Harvard University Press, 1978), pp. 1–187.

34 See Stoler, *Race*, pp. 97–8 for the relation of European colonies to the new 'ethics of conduct geared to management' outlined by Foucault .

35 Elaine Scarry, *The Body in Pain* (London and New York, Oxford University Press, 1985), p. 16.

36 G. W. F. Hegel, *The Phenomenology of Spirit*, trans. A. V. Miller (Oxford, Clarendon Press, 1977), pp. 111–17. The renowned articulation of the master-slave dialectic occupies a central position in contemporary Western debates over how to construct in abstract terms the power relations within slavery. Yet this discussion should be set alongside Hegel's view of Africans as articulated in *Lectures on the Philosophy of World History*, trans. H. B. Nisbet (Cambridge, Cambridge University Press, 1975). In the appendix on Africa Hegel asserts that 'substantial objectivity' has not been developed in the consciousness of any negro. The discussion proceeds by denying Africans and their slave descendants a place within the culture in which the master-slave dialectic functions: 'Since human beings are valued so cheaply, it is easily explained why *slavery* is the basic legal relationship in Africa. The only significant relationship between negroes and Europeans has been, and still is, that of slavery.' For a critique of Hegel on race see Henry Louis Gates Jnr., *Figures in Black: Words, Signs and the Racial Self* (New York and Oxford, Oxford University Press, 1987), pp. 19–21.

37 John Gabriel Stedman, *Narrative of a Five Years' Expedition Against the Revolted Negroes of Surinam*, 2 vols (London, 1796), 2, pp. 116–17.

38 Cathy Caruth, *Unclaimed Experience: Trauma, Narrative and History* (Baltimore and London, Johns Hopkins University Press, 1996), p. 4.

39 Stedman, *Narrative*, 2, pp. 307–8.

40 Scarry, *Body in Pain*, p. 29. See her ensuing discussion pp. 29–50.

41 Blake's engravings for Stedman and his relation to slavery are discussed in David Erdman, 'Blake's Vision of Slavery', *Journal of the Warbaurg and Courtauld Institutes* 15 (1952) 242–52; David Erdman, *Blake: Prophet Against Empire* (Princeton, Princeton University Press, 1969), pp. 157, 228–42, 291; Albert Boime, *Art in an Age of Revolution* (Chicago and London, Chicago University Press, 1987), pp. 339–40; Steven Vine, '"That mild beam": Enlightenment and Enslavement in William Blake's *Visions of the Daughters of Albion*', in Betty J. Ring and Carl Plasa (eds), *The Discourse of Slavery* (London, Routledge, 1994), pp. 50–7.

42 Stedman, *Narrative*, 2, pp. 325–6.

43 Edmund Burke, *The Writings and Speeches of Edmund Burke*, ed. Paul Longford, 9 vols (Oxford, Clarendon Press, 1991–97), 1, p. 216.

44 For the manuscript version, John Gabriel Stedman, *Narrative of a Five Years' Expedition Against the Revolted Negroes of Surinam*, ed. and int. Richard Price and Sally Price (Baltimore and London, Johns Hopkins University Press, 1994), p. 264. For the emergence of humanitarian sensibility in the eighteenth century and its relation to pornography and voyeurism see Karen Halttunen, 'Humanitarianism and the Pornography of Pain in Anglo-American Culture', *American Historical Review*, 100:2 (1995) 303–10; Janet Todd, *Sensibility: An Introduction* (London and New York, Methuen, 1986), pp. 10–31, 129–46.

45 John Gabriel Stedman, *The Journal of John Gabriel Stedman Soldier and Author 1744–1797*, ed. Standbury Thompson (London, Mitre Press, 1962), p. 185. For the manner in which increasing hostility to abolition in England inflected Stedman's descriptions of atrocity against slaves, and this scene in particular, in the different versions of the *Narrative* see David Brion Davis, 'The Ends of Slavery', *New York Review of Books*, 36:5 (1989) 30–1.

46 For a recent analysis of this image which sees in it an unproblematic moral outrage, see Boime, *Art of Exclusion*, pp. 49–50.

47 For the eroticisation of nudity in the context of depictions of martyrdom see Richard Leppert, *Art and the Committed Eye: The Cultural Functions of Imagery* (Oxford and Boulder, Westview Press, 1996), pp. 251–6.

48 Jules Ferrario, *L'Amérique Décrite par le Docteur Jules Ferrario. II Parte Amérique Méridionale*, pp. 401–40 constitute a 'Description Générale de Guyane', pp. 393–401 is an introduction 'La Guyane, Française, Hollandaise et Anglaise'. This gives a bibliography of sources which includes 'Voyage à Surinam, et dans l'intérieure de la Guyanne etc. avec des détails sur les indiens de la Guyane [sic] et des Nègres par le Capitaine J. G. Stedman, traduit de l'Anglais par P. F. Henri et.c Paris, 1799 3 vol. in 80'. I am grateful to Philip Lapsansky of the Library Company of Philadelphia for introducing me to the French adaptations of Stedman.

49 Rhodes House, Anti-slavery Archive, *Nineteenth and Twentieth Century Letters, British and Foreign Anti Slavery Society*, C/2 23, Taunton, Richard Ball, 8 Sept. 1837; *Minute Books of the British and Foreign Anti-Slavery Society*, E 2/4, 23 June 1835. *Narrative of Events since the 1st of August, 1834 By James Williams together with the Evidence Taken Under a Commission Appointed by the Colonial Office to Ascertain the Truth of the Narrative* (London, Printed for the Central Emancipation Committee, 1837).

50 For the introduction of the treadmill see Ernest W. Pettifer, *Punishments of Former Days* (Bradford, Clegg & Son, 1939), pp. 168–71. For 'useless violence' see Primo Levi, *The Drowned and the Saved*, trans. Paul Bailey (London, Abacus, 1998), pp. 83–101.

51 The best account of the rhetorical operations of this tradition within English literature is John R. Knott, *Discourses of Martyrdom in English Literature 1563–1694* (Cambridge, Cambridge University Press, 1993), pp. 1–10.

52 For earlier models which might be useful in considering accounts of slave death because they emphasise the constant tension between victimisation and heroism see Knott, *Discourses of Martyrdom*, pp. 150–5.

53 For the transference of Foxeian martyrological paradigms within nonconformist writings at the time of the pilgrim fathers see Gerald R. Cragg, *Puritanism in the Period of the Great Persecution: 1660–1688* (Cambridge, Cambridge University Press, 1957).

54 The rhetorical operations of martyrology within abolition art and literature is a neglected area. Hazel Catherine Wolf, *On Freedom's Altar: The Martyr Complex in the Abolition Movement* (Madison, University of Wisconsin Press, 1952) is the only monograph on the subject but is methodologically crude. There are valuable insights on the intellectual links between early colonial puritan thought and later martyrological models in David Brion Davis, *The Problem of Slavery in the Age of Revolution 1770–1823* (Ithaca, Cornell University Press, 1975), pp. 288–90. For the expansion of the artistic conventions surrounding martyrology into public punishment and torture see Samuel Y. Edgerton Jnr., *Pictures and Punishment: Art and Criminal Prosecution during the Florentine Renaissance* (Ithaca and London, Cornell University Press, 1985).

55 Garrison quoted Wolf, *Freedom's Altar*, p. 24.

56 These examples quoted in Wolf, *Freedom's Altar*, pp. 45–8.

57 For the visual propaganda devoted to John Brown in two decades following his death see Boime, *Art of Exclusion*, pp. 138–43. For the construction of John Brown as martyr see James Claude Malin, *John Brown and the Legend of Fifty-Six* (Philadelphia, American Philosophical Society, 1942), pp. 31–63, 117–70, 247–80. For cults of abolition martyrology 1830–60 see Wolf, *Freedom's Altar*, pp. 50–79. For the linkage of a personal revelation of Christ with consequent persecution in New England enthusiastic sects including Quakers see David S. Lovejoy, *Religious Enthusiasm in the New World: Heresy to Revolution* (Cambridge Mass., Harvard University Press, 1985), pp. 63–85, 120–38, 151–3.

58 For Anderson's work see Pomeroy, 'Alexander Anderson's Life', pp. 137–230; F. M. Burr, *Life and Works of Alexander Anderson, M. D., the First American Wood Engraver* (New York, 1893); Hamilton Sinclair, *Early American Book Illustration and Wood-engravers 1670–1870*, 2 vols (New Jersey, 1968), 2, pp. 82–110.

59 Heman Humphrey, *Parallel Between Intemperance and the Slave Trade* (New York, n.d.), p. 9.

60 For Hogarth's long-standing and widespread popularity in the states see Joan Dolmetsch, 'Prints in Colonial America: Supply and Demand in the Mid-Eighteenth Century', in *Prints in and of America to 1850*, ed. John DeMorse (Charlottesville, University of Virginia Press, 1971), pp. 53–74.

61 The most widely distributed illustrated pamphlet of Walker's experience was *Trial and Imprisonment of Jonathan Walker* (Boston, 1845), also printed in English editions. The story is also included in a children's book: Jonathan Walker, *A Picture of Slavery for Youth* (Boston, J. Walker, n.d.), pp. 20–30. For a fine summary of the legal ramifications of the case see Paul Finkelman, *Slavery in the Courtroom* (Washington, Library of Congress, 1985), pp. 12, 157, 170–5.

62 Winthrop D. Jordan, *White Over Black: American Attitudes Towards the Negro, 1550–1812* (Harmondsworth, Penguin, 1968), pp. 51, 107. For branding of galley slaves and French and Russian public slaves see Orlando Patterson, *Slavery and Social Death: A Comparative Study* (Cambridge, Mass. and London, Harvard University Press, 1982), p. 59.

63 For slave branding in the West as punishment see Sellin, *Slavery*, pp. 38, 40, 43, 44, 49–50, 85, 120, 121, 133.

64 See *Dictionary of National Biography*, article, William Prynne.

65 See Pauline Gregg, *Freeborn John: A Biography of John Lilburne* (London, George Harrap, 1961); Daniel Defoe, 'Hymn to the Pillory', in *Later Stuart Tracts*, ed. George Aitken (London, Archibald Constable, 1903), pp. 205–21; E. P. Thompson, *The Making of the English Working Class* (London, Penguin, 1965), pp. 135–48, 662–3;

Marcus Wood, *Radical Satire and Print Culture 1790–1822* (Oxford, Oxford University Press, 1994), pp. 96–154.

66 Jean Fagan Yellin, *Women and Sisters* (New Haven, Yale University Press, 1989), pp. 129–30.

67 For abolition exploitation of branding see Thomas Clarkson, *Negro Slavery. Argument, That the Colonial Slaves are better off than the British Peasantry* (London, 1824), pp. 1–3; [Theodore Dwight Weld], *American Slavery As It Is* (New York, American Anti-Slavery Society, 1839), pp. 57–94.

68 For penal branding within eighteenth-century English society see Gattrell, *Hanging Tree*, p. 16; for Brazilian slave branding see Patterson, *Slavery*, 59. For patterns of multiple branding in European slave trade see Ronald Segal, *The Black Diaspora* (London, Faber, 1995), p. 31.

69 For the legal applications of the Dred Scott ruling see Paul Finkelman, *An Imperfect Union: Slavery, Federalism and Comity* (Chapel Hill, University of North Carolina Press, 1981), pp. 286–342.

70 The background to the Attucks Festival has been comprehensively uncovered in a superb piece of cultural archaeology by Elizabeth Rauh Bethel, *The Roots of African-American Identity: Memory and History in Free Antebellum Communities* (London, Macmillan, 1997), pp. 1–28, 195–203.

71 Bethel, *The Roots*, pp. 5–7.

72 Bethel, *The Roots*, pp. 7–11.

73 Quoted in Bethel, *The Roots*, p. 7.

74 Bethel, *The Roots*, pp. 17–18.

75 Henry Pelham, *The Fruits of Arbitrary Power or the Bloody Massacre*, copper engraving, 1770. For the historical influence of this print and reproductions of different versions see Wendy Shadwell (comp.), *American Printmaking the First 150 Years* (Washington, Smithsonian Institution Press, 1969), p. 28 and plates 33–7.

76 E. H. Gombrich, *Meditations on a Hobby Horse and Other Essays on the Theory of Art* (Oxford, Phaidon, 1978), pp. 124–5. Gombrich argues that Goya's atrocity paintings and prints of Napoleonic war crimes in Spain may well be influenced by the crude pints of R. K. Porter, produced in England in 1803 as anti-Napoleonic propaganda. None of Porter's prints bears any direct compositional relation to Goya's *3rd of May* which Gombrich reproduces. *The Boston Massacre* anticipates quite closely the essential structure of the figure groups in Goya's great painting. If, as Gombrich suggests, Goya knew the obscure prints of Porter through exposure to the English during the Peninsular war, it is even more likely that Goya saw an English reproduction of the Revere print, which rapidly gained wide circulation and notoriety on both sides of the Atlantic.

77 Boime, *Art of Exclusion*, pp. 28–39 discussing Copley's *Watson and the Shark* in relation to slavery, suggests Watson's posture is based on the corpse in the bottom left corner of Revere's print, and further argues that the body may be that of Attucks, because of his large physical stature. The figure is, however, indisputably a white.

78 American Antiquarian Society, Broadside Collection, item 1858, item 1862.

79 American Antiquarian Society, Broadside Collection, item 1860.

80 The most ambitious recent analysis of the tension between realistic detail and iconic idealisation in West's painting of Wolfe is in Simon Schama, *Dead Certainties (Unwarranted Speculations)* (London, Granta Books in association with Penguin Books, 1991), pp. 21–39. For the history of Woollett's print see Timothy Clayton, *The English Print 1688–1802* (New Haven and London, Mellon Centre and Yale University Press, 1997), pp. 238–40.

81 Boime, *Art of Exclusion*, pp. 34–5; for blacks in related paintings of military deaths based on Copley see Hugh Honour, *The Image of the Black in Western Art from the American Revolution to World War I* (Cambridge Mass., Harvard University Press, 1989) 4:1, pp. 42–5.

82 For mock monuments see Stephen Greenblatt, 'Murdering Peasants: Status Genre and
the Representation of Rebellion', *Representations* 1:1 (1983) 1–8; Wood, *Radical
Satire*, pp. 205–11.

83 For Guilane see Vivian Green, *The Madness of Kings: Personal Trauma and the Fate of
Nations* (New York, St Martin's Press, 1993), p. 4.

84 The iconic status of this image had permeated even to juvenile abolition literature. It is
used as a repeated emblem, for example, in the miniature illustrated periodical *The
Slave's Friend*, 1:4 (1853) 6; 2:2 (1853) 9.

85 Moses Roper, *Narrative*, pp. 52–6.

86 For the association of the black with Christ's flagellation see Devisse and Mollat, *Image
of the Black*, 2:2, pp. 64–7.

87 For a complementary parody of Christian symbolism in the *Narrative of the Life of
Frederick Douglass* see Henri Louis Gates Jnr., 'Binary Oppositions in Chapter One of
Narrative of the Life of Frederick Douglass an American Slave Written by Himself', in
Dexter Fisher and Robert B. Stepto (eds), *African American Literature* (New York,
Modern Language Association of America, 1979), p. 237.

88 The fiercest critique of Roper's *Narrative* in terms of its lack of emotional
engagement is William L. Andrews, *To Tell a Free Story: The First Century of Afro-
American Autobiography, 1760–1865* (Chicago, University of Illinois Press, 1988),
pp. 90–6.

89 For a crude survey of the legal application of whipping to sailors, soldiers, women and
slaves in Europe and the colonies see Abbott, *Rack*, pp. 123–47. For whipping within
English society see Gatrell, *The Hanging Tree*, pp. 337, 507, 578–9. For the whipping
of women see Burford and Schulman, *Of Bridles*, pp. 63–80. For whipping within
German legal codes see Richard J. Evans, *Rituals of Retribution: Capital Punishment
in Germany 1600–1987* (Harmondsworth, Penguin, 1996), pp. 57, 61, 134–6, 180–1.
For the ubiquity of whipping within early colonial American society see Edwin
Powers, *Crime and Punishment in Early Massachusetts: A Documentary History*
(Boston, Beacon Press, 1966), pp. 163–94. For the relation of flogging to erotic flagella-
tion in eighteenth-century British society see Peter Wagner, 'The Discourse on Sex', in
Roy Porter and G. S. Rousseau (eds), *Sexual Underworlds of the Enlightenment*
(Manchester, Manchester University Press, 1987), pp. 50–2.

90 T. E. J. Wiedermann, *Greece and Rome: New Surveys in the Classics no. 19 Slavery*
(Oxford, Published for the Classical Association, Oxford University Press, 1997),
p. 25.

91 See Sellin, *Slavery*, pp. 12–15 for Greeks; pp. 21–2, 26–9 for Romans; pp. 35–9 for
medieval Europe; p. 115 for Russian serfs; pp. 134–8 for American plantation slaves.

92 Wagner, 'Discourse on Sex', p. 51; Steven Marcus, *The Other Victorians: A Study of
Sexuality and Pornography in Mid Nineteenth-Century England* (London, Weidenfeld
and Nicolson, 1966), pp. 72–3, 125–8, 252–65; Haltunnen, 'Pornography of Pain', pp.
315–17; David S. Reynolds, *Beneath the American Renaissance: The Subversive
Imagination in the Age of Emerson and Melville* (New York, Alfred Knopf, 1988), pp.
211–24. For Freud's case studies of sexual fantasies evolved from flagellation within
Uncle Tom's Cabin see pp. 184–5, 211n above. For the historic structures underlying
contemporary American flagellatory pornography see Linda Williams, 'Power,
Pleasure, and Perversion: Sadomasochistic Film Pornography', *Representations*, 27:2
(1989) 37–65. The extent to which contemporary bondage fetishism has evolved out of
the history of slave torture becomes shockingly apparent if the words 'bondage' and
'slavery' are typed into any major search engine on the World Wide Web.

93 For the background to Newton see David Alexander, *Richard Newton and English
Caricature in the 1790s* (Manchester, Manchester University Press, 1998), pp. 7–56,
and for the relation of this print to the flagellation vogue p. 116. For a detailed discussion of Newton's other prints to treat race and slavery see pp. 157–60 above.

94 The painting is discussed in Honour, *Image of the Black*, 4:1, p. 153, as exposing 'the
evils of slavery ... with no apparent motive'.

95 Chagas's work has received minimal attention from scholars. The sculptural context for his work is outlined in Graciela Mann, *The Twelve Prophets of Aleijadinho* (Austin and London, University of Texas Press, 1967).

96 The image may also bear an ironic relation to the Western iconographic convention of including at least one black among Christ's tormentor's, see Devise and Mollat, *Image of the Black*, 2:1, p. 72; 2:2, pp. 64–5, 73–4.

97 Toni Morrison, *Beloved* (London, Picador, 1987), pp. 17–18.

98 Morrison, *Beloved*, p. 21

99 The example taken here is from John Simkin, *Slavery: An Illustrated History of Black Resistance* (Brighton, Spartacus, 1988), p. 18. The photograph is shown, behind an overprinted barred prison door, in Louis Rachames, *The Abolitionists* (New York, Capricorn, 1964), front cover.

100 For the minute number of photographic representations (daguerreotype, ambrotype and tintype) of African-Americans predating 1860 surviving in the United States see [Jackie Napoleon Wilson], *Hidden Witness: African Americans in Early Photography* (J. Paul Getty Museum, 1995). For the context of popular visual satire see Michel Fabre, 'Popular Civil War Propaganda: The Case of Patriotic Covers', *Journal of American Culture*, 3:2 (1980) 223–28.

101 The image is reproduced, but not discussed, in Boime, *Art of Exclusion*, p. 73.

102 *Harper's Weekly*, (4 July 1869) 429.

103 For the operation of temporal narrative elements in nineteenth- and twentieth-century medical advertisement see Scarry, *Resisting Representation*, pp. 23–5 . For Ali as St Sebastian see Philip Thompson and Peter Davenport (eds), *The Dictionary of Visual Language* (London, Bergstrom and Boyle, 1980), p. 202.

104 For publishing background see Wood, *Radical Satire*, pp. 215–57.

105 For slave–animal conflation within Anglo-American humanitarianism see Haltunnen, 'Pornography of Pain', pp. 319–23. For the relation of animals to the development of nineteenth-century humanitarian sentiment see James Turner, *Reckoning with the Beast: Animals, Pain and Humanity in the Victorian Mind* (Baltimore and London, Johns Hopkins University Press, 1980).

106 For animal/slave/child conflations see Leonard Cassuto, *The Inhuman Race: The Racial Grotesque in American Literature and Culture* (New York, Columbia University Press, 1997), pp. 128–34. For comparisons of factory children and animal suffering see Turner, *Reckoning*, pp. 25–37. For William Wilberforce, anti-bull-baiting and slavery see Turner, *Reckoning*, p. 14.

107 Hegel, *Philosophy of World History*, p. 177.

108 William Cowper, *The Poems of William Cowper*, ed. John Baird and Charles Ryskamp, 3 vols (Oxford, Clarendon Press, 1980–95), 3, p. 183.

109 Peter Coveney, *The Image of Childhood: The Individual and Society: A Study of the Theme in English Literature* (London, Penguin Books, 1967), pp. 37–9.

110 Quoted Coveney, *Image*, p. 64.

111 *The Condition of the West India Slave Contrasted with that of the Infant Slave in our English Factories* (London, W. Kidd, *c.* 1835), p. 33.

112 Stoler, *Race*, pp. 123–9 provides the best overview. Catherine Hall, *White, Male and Middle Class: Explorations in Feminism and History* (Cambridge, Polity Press, 1988), pp. 215–50 explores the implications of race in the context of the valorisation of a nineteenth-century Bourgeois domestic norm.

113 Stoler, *Race*, pp. 127–9 emphasises the extreme 'semantic fluidity' of race-class conflation in Victorian writing and culture. She expands the discussion into a critique of Foucault's argument that a 'language of class, *always* emerges out of an earlier discourse of race'.

114 See John Newton, *The Works of the Rev. John Newton, Late Rector of the United Parishes of St. Mary Woolnoth and St. Mary Woolchurch Haw, London. In six volumes* (London, 1808); John Newton, *The Journal of a Slave Trader*, ed. Bernard Martin and Mark Spurrell (London, Epworth Press, 1962).

115 Mary Leatheley, *Large Pictures with Little Stories* (London, Darton, *c.* 1855), pp. 27–8.
116 For Uncle Tom's feminisation see Theodore R. Hovet, *The Master Narrative: Harriet Beecher Stowe's Subversive Story of Master and Slave in Uncle Tom's Cabin and Dred* (New York, University Press of America, 1989), 37–8, and Elizabeth Ammons, 'Heroines in *Uncle Tom's Cabin*', *American Literature*, 69 (1977) 163–71.
117 Wood, *Radical Satire*, pp. 220–63.
118 The most elaborate of these parodies is Iron Gray [Abel Thomas], *The Gospel of Slavery: A Primer of Freedom* (New York, 1864).
119 For the American adaptations of the rhyme see my forthcoming 'The Influence of English Radical Satire on Nineteenth-Century American Print Satire: David Claypoole Johnston's *The House That Jeff Built*, a Case Study', *Harvard Library Bulletin* (2000). The richest print sources are BM, 9044, 11215, 11414; Bernard F. Reilly (ed.), *American Political Prints 1766–1876: A Catalog of the Collections in the Library of Congress* (Boston, G. K. Hall, 1991), 1833–6; 1840–48.
120 For an overview of the centrality of infantilisation to the Sambo stereotype see Cassuto, *Inhuman Race*, pp. 128–31. For the link of Africans, children and animals in European thought see William B. Cohen, *The French Encounter with Africans: White Response to Blacks 1530–1880* (Bloomington and London, University of Indiana Press, 1980), pp. 238–45.
121 Scarry, *Body in Pain*, pp. 40–2.
122 Joseph Conrad, *Collected Edition of the Works of Joseph Conrad: Nostromo* (London, J. M. Dent, 1947), p. 373.

6 Conclusion

'Thus let your streams o'erflow your springs,
'Till eyes and tears be the same things:
And each the other's difference bears;
These weeping eyes, those seeing tears.'
– Tears that see ... Do you believe?
– I don't know, one has to believe.
(Andrew Marvell/Jacques Derrida, Memoirs of the Blind)

'You are saved,' cried Captain Delano, more and more astonished and
pained; 'you are saved: what has cast such a shadow upon you?'
(Herman Melville, *Benito Cereno*)

Cultural configurations of slavery in Bahia and Liverpool

Salvador, Bahia, resonates with the inheritance of slavery; it is visible everywhere, in its people, its food, its buildings, its art and music and even in its
telephone boxes. You can walk for a minute from the Café Quilombo, dedicated to the memory of the rebel slave leader Zumbi, and the great
Quilombo of Palmares, stand outside the preternaturally smooth stone
walls of the Modello market, which during stretches of the eighteenth century was the world's biggest slave market, and make a phone call. To do this
you put your head inside a large striped symbolic representation of the
sound box, a dried hollowed gourd, of a berimbau [**6.1**]. The curved supporting stand forms the bow of the instrument. The phone boxes are built
and painted in the form of the distinctive instrument used to accompany the
slave evolved fighting art of capoeira. This is really the national ballet of
Brazil. Capoeira masters now teach men women and children in most of the
central and northern parts of the country [**6.2**]. From the beaches of Bahia
to the concrete underpasses of Rio and São Paulo the controlled violence
and beautiful rhythms of capoeira flourish, despite the sporadic attempts of
the Brazilian state over the last two centuries to stamp out this manifestation
of black cultural independence.[1] The berimbau has been absorbed across a
broad front of Brazilian music. While for purists the berimbau is at its most
compelling when heard alongside drums accompanying capoeira performers, it has also found its way into the jazz rock improvisation of such
mainstream ensembles as Dori Caymmi. The berimbau is an icon of black
Brazilian culture, and any tourist can buy a badly made brightly painted

miniature berimbau from any number of stalls within the old slave market in Salvador. You don't have to look for the memory of slavery in Bahia – it is engulfing, it is a part of things.[2]

The inheritance of slavery is not so culturally apparent, or so creatively manifested, in Britain. There is no adequate monument or memorial to the slave trade in Britain. There are enormous buildings constructed out of the profits of the slave trade and the sugar plantations. Some of the older decaying waterfront buildings in Liverpool 1, or the Codrington library in All Souls College Oxford, or even by association the Tate Gallery, or the Richard Rogers's Lloyd's Bank building in London, are one very visible bequest of the profits of slavery. They are also indistinguishable from any other large public buildings whether warehouses, museums, Oxford colleges or the headquarters of banks. The pictures gathered within this book raise questions regarding the wider cultural implications of how and why slavery is remembered publicly in the West. Having looked at so much art and propaganda which takes up transatlantic slavery, I would like to think about where the cultures that surround us in the West have got to in terms of the art, the institutions, the objects and the rituals which are used to remember slavery.[3]

The city of Hull remembers slavery through the figure of William Wilberforce, its long-serving and physically fragile MP. Nineteenth-century children's historics of abolition frequently introduced Wilberforce

[6.1] Phone Box, Modello Market, Salvador, Bahia

[6.2] Capoeira, Rio underpass

through the monuments which exist to him in his home town.[4] Rising above the dock gates at Hull the enormous 'Wilberforce Monument' mimics Nelson's column. A statue of Wilberforce stands, swathed in robes, staring out to sea, elevated, remote, erect. Wilberforce House, the self-proclaimed 'World's First Slavery Museum', and the long-term home of the politician, embodies elaborate mythologisations surrounding the abolition of the British slave trade and colonial plantation slavery.[5] At the centre of this museum is the posthumous personality cult focused on a politician who was, among other things, one of William Pitt's close advisers during the white terror in the 1790s. Wilberforce was an inveterate enemy of nascent working-class radicalism and fought the reformers in Parliament tooth and claw; but he professed and exhibited, in the abstract, a deep love for what he termed 'my poor Africans'. As a result, he is a figure who roused contrasting reactions from his contemporaries. William Cobbett, a man whose dislikes were passionate and occasionally irrational, put Wilberforce top of his hate list of hypocrites and political villains. William Hazlitt viewed him with a vast, yet fascinated, disdain. Incontestably repelled by Wilberforce, Hazlitt had great difficulty pinning down wherein his repulsion was located.[6] Hazlitt suggests uncertainty about the definition of what Wilberforce is – like British abolition itself he is a paradox, a moral androgyne, 'He is altogether a *double-entendre*: the very tone of his voice is a *double entendre*'. His morality is suspect. 'His humanity is at the horizon three thousand miles off, – his servility stays at home, at the beck of the minister. He unbinds the chains of Africa, and helps (we trust without meaning it) to rivet those of his own country, and of Europe.'[7] Yet despite the assault of Cobbett, and Hazlitt's quizzical qualifications, Wilberforce was, even before his death at the moment of slave emancipation in the colonies, perceived to be a living saint. To be popularly invented as the figure responsible for the cessation of the slave trade was to be beyond mortal wrong-doing. Hazlitt ironically illustrates the point when he ends his review of Wilberforce in *The Spirit of the Age* with a bitter anecdote. The Whig libertine, politician and dramatist Richard Brinsley Sheridan, picked up blind drunk by the night watch, before being unceremoniously locked up for the night, was asked his name. Sheridan 'made answer – 'I am Mr. Wilberforce!' The guardians of the night conducted him home with all the honours due to Grace and Nature.'[8] For Hazlitt this is 'the best as well as most amusing comment' on Wilberforce's character – he was the incarnation of a national fantasy of erasure. His canonisation gained in momentum during the course of the nineteenth century, and throughout the twentieth, Wilberforce is still surrounded by the 'guardians of the night'. As a sort of semiotic nerve centre for the popular national mythologies surrounding slavery Wilberforce continues to be invaluable.

Wilberforce House possesses many representations of its eponymous ex-owner: statues, portraits, engravings. Perhaps the most peculiar is a life-size wax model of William Wilberforce in his evening gown, reading a book in his study and looking perky, scholarly and content [**6.3**]. Above him in a rich oil painting an emancipated British slave gazes heavenwards, while behind Wilberforce on a shelf stands a porcelain figurine representing the enchained beseeching male slave adapted from the famous seal of the SEAST. Two rooms away, the same building contains an attempt at the recreation, in cross-section, of the slave deck of a slave ship [**6.4**]. Life-sized plaster models lie on their sides stretching their broken fingers out through a wire grill. The fingers are broken because visiting school children kicked them and stamped on them. They were then bandaged and touched up with red paint, by museum staff. The wire grill was set up to protect the slaves from further vandalism. A tape loop circulates a sound track – moans, coughs and retching sounds, and the splashing of water repeating them-selves over and over again. The tape was made by the museum staff. What were they thinking about when they made it, and should they have made it? Are they claiming that the sounds they made are a recreation of, or equiva-lent to, the suffering of Africans shipped as slaves during the 'middle pas-sage'? How do we get close to the memory of slavery?[9]

If the memory of slavery inhabits one location in Britain it is Liverpool. By the early nineteenth century the physical presence of the city itself was configured by Fuseli as a metropolis composed of blood and chains: 'the principal streets of the town may be said to have been marked out by the chains, and the walls of the houses cemented by the blood of Africans!'. This memory lived on. By the middle of the nineteenth century

[**6.3**] Portrait, William Wilberforce

[6.4] Life-sized section of a slave deck, Wilberforce House

the inebriated actor George Frederick Cooke, lambasted by a Liverpool crowd for his sodden incompetence, flung back the reply that 'he was not there to be insulted by a set of wretches, every brick on whose infernal town was cemented by an African's blood!'.[10]

It was as a consequence of Liverpool's domination of the 'Guinea' trade that the Liverpool dock-lands were seen as the fitting site for the second English slavery museum, the 'Transatlantic Slavery' gallery of the Museums and Galleries on Merseyside. As the only serious attempt to provide an appropriate display relating to the British perpetration of the slave trade, this gallery should occupy a central space in our cultural memory, yet does it do what it is supposed to do, and what is it supposed to do anyway? Under the banner announcement 'Transatlantic Slavery Against Human Dignity', the gallery opened in 1992. The display brings into focus continuing problems relating to the visual and linguistic recording of slavery within Western society. 'Dignity' is a wonderfully English verdict on what Atlantic slavery was 'against'. The pursuit of capital has had, and continues to have, an agenda in which the dignity of the exploited is of little if any relevance. It is easy to assume a *post facto* outrage at what slavery was against; it is much more difficult and much more significant to uncover what it was positively for. To answer this question we must blind ourselves to the easy option of an unthinking moral outrage, itself a form of self-blinding. We must see ourselves as still clearly implicated in the question how did Europeans enable themselves to enslave and to kill so many Africans for so long?

The foreword to the catalogue produced to mark the opening of the Liverpool gallery space states that the exhibition 'is meant to bring the slave trade before us without mincing matters', and continues, 'We can come to terms with our past only by accepting it, and in order to be able to accept it we need knowledge of what really happened.'[11] Such sentiments could not be expressed easily about the memory of the Nazi Holocaust, and if they were expressed would fly in the face of the ethically meticulous work of Claude Lanzmann, Kali Tal and a host of artists and intellectuals who have gone a long way to making sure that we continue to understand that the Holocaust is something the West must work very hard never to 'come to terms with'. It is absurd to assume a role of absolute empathy, to think that we have the option to find out 'what really happened'. Surely neither transatlantic slavery nor the Holocaust should be deemed sites for such cultural negotiation: what are the 'terms', and who decides them?

The National Maritime Museum is constructed on several floors of a large warehouse building. In the upper galleries the main display rooms give a narrative survey of ships and shipping in Liverpool from the thirteenth to the twentieth centuries. The first rooms are titled 'Liverpool: the Evolution of the Port 1207 to 1857' and panels tell us that 'this exhibition shows how Liverpool developed from a small fishing village into a major international port'. Within this grand narrative only one small panel mentions the slave trade. This is headed 'Port Trade 1600–1800: Liverpool and the Transatlantic Slave Trade', and the full text runs: 'The first slaving voyage from Liverpool took place in 1700. From the 1730s until its abolition in 1807, the transportation of Africans across the Atlantic was the cornerstone of Liverpool's overseas trade. The full story of the trade over a period of four hundred years is told in the TRANSATLANTIC SLAVERY GALLERY in the basement of the museum.' Slavery is consequently excised from the overall narrative of Liverpool's development and sent down to the basement. The viewer must go through a separate door, down a series of staircases, to a set of underground galleries. Slavery is physically separated, as if it exists in contradistinction to, and down below, indeed out of sight of, the normal growth of the port.

Again, as with Wilberforce House, the centrepiece of the Transatlantic Slavery Gallery contains a mock-up of a section of one of the slave decks of a Guineaman [**6.5**]. The spectator walks into the space past a panel which shows a reproduction of the *Description* of the *Brookes*. The slave deck itself is fitfully lit by spotlights and the bare wood is scrupulously clean. A large cylindrical piece of wood at one end represents a mast, and one section of the ceiling has a mock-up of a grating. The spaces where the slaves would have lain are this time empty, and the sound-track, unlike that at Hull, is the recorded sound of wind and storm at sea. Over this sound actors recite passages from the log book of the notorious Liverpool slave captain, and later

[6.5] Recreation of the slave deck of a slave ship (1995). National Museums and Galleries on Merseyside, Transatlantic Slavery Gallery, Liverpool

evangelical pastor, John Newton, and from the autobiography of the ex-slave Olaudah Equiano. Projectors, black boxes like old-fashioned safes, are the only inhabitants of the spaces where the slaves would have been. These boxes project faint bluish white neo-abstract sequences of black actors rolling over, and sitting against, each other. These sequences of projection go on for about ten or fifteen seconds, then they stop in one section and start in another. The projection boxes, sitting on the edge of the decks, possess a presence which confuses the public. On my last visit to the gallery I overheard a woman say to a friend, 'What are those boxes, they must be where they kept the chains?' It is difficult to know what to think of this display, as it is difficult to know what to make of the venture as a whole. One room away, inside a glass case, is a miniature model of a slave ship with a section cut out to reveal barrels in the hold, little wooden slaves on the slave deck and little wooden sailors carrying whips who walk the decks above [**6.6**]. A miniature sea of glass has a rowing boat with three manacled slaves heading towards the model of the main ship. The whole thing is neat and frozen, 'as idle as a painted ship upon a painted ocean'. If you walk through an arch, past the television broadcasting interviews with contemporary black people from Liverpool and the Caribbean, you come to the emigration exhibit. Here another mock-up of the hold of a ship holds plaster figures representing late-nineteenth-century white, presumably Irish, emigrants on a coffin ship. In this display the sound-track does carry human groans above the sound of the sea, and below decks there are models of white people making the voyage.[12]

Throughout the exhibition tensions exist between the presentation of European and African cultures. The Liverpool we are shown looks foreign because of time, but its foreignness is mediated by the familiarity of historical displays in museums; the Africa we are shown looks foreign because it is foreign. The European side of things is comfortably aged, the artefacts, the figures, the displays call strongly to mind those parts of the National Maritime Museum dealing with the Napoleonic wars. Despite their horrible functions the branding irons and slave collars on display in cases are almost reassuring. Their patina of age, their elegant forms, the clean stands they are placed upon, the neat labels with their dates and matter of fact descriptions place them comfortably within an aesthetics of museum display which can cover any old object from any culture. These objects are sealed off from a contemporary audience, part of an alien past of barbarity and horror, like the axes, racks and whips in the London dungeon. The most effective parts of the exhibition amplify, rather than confirm, the gaps between our present complacency in viewing the past and the forgotten channels into which Liverpool's slave wealth flowed. It is in details such as the painted boards of Liverpool street names, which can be lifted to reveal a narrative of the origins of the wealth of the named individual to lie in slave trafficking, that past and present are forced into violent collision.

The presentation of African cultures is altogether different. The first galleries which the spectator passes through attempt to provide an insight into the African cultures from which the slaves were taken. We are introduced to a model black family (a group of mannequins), who are then to be related to a set of African ancestors (cardboard cut-outs), each with a name, occupation and area of origin attached. Yet in the succeeding spaces the representation of Africa conforms more to the conventions of anthropological and ethnographic exhibits familiar from the displays in institutions, and particularly the Museum of Mankind. The assumption here is that the audience is being brought before something alien and exotic, another style of life, another way of living. There is the peculiar sense that these exhibits are timeless, that they represent not how people in Africa lived at the time of the slave trade, a complicated issue anyway because for

[6.6] (a) Scale model of a slave ship, in cross-section, and (b) detail, National Museums and Galleries on Merseyside, Transatlantic Slavery Gallery, Liverpool

England this is a period spanning at least three hundred years, but how people in Africa have always lived and still live. Geographical, racial, cultural specificities within those coastal areas of the slave coast most heavily affected by the slave trade are swallowed in generalisation.

It is, however, the renditions of the middle passage which are finally most troubling in both Liverpool and Hull. This results from the ways in which they are caught up in certain inappropriate conventions of contemporary museum theory. The mock-ups of the conditions in a slave ship displayed in Hull and Liverpool attempt to concretise, to simulate, the memory of the middle passage. They do this with an emphasis on entertaining the public, on providing an educational experience, which is at the same time intended to be historically authentic. The models and installations have been evolved out a curatorial theory emphasising 'consumer involvement' and 'client participation' and the 'decentring' of both curator and imprisoned object within the 'totalising institution'. Yet, surely, there are subjects and objects which cannot fit within the educational framework of current museum culture. Museum parodies of the experience of the middle passage, which claim to 'put us there', may well do more harm than good. You cannot merchandise, advertise and package the middle passage, and if you do try to do these things where are the limits? The mind boggles at following through the directions in which the 'total immersion' approach to the representation of this mass trauma might lead. Could a privatised company be invited to provide a Disney style, or Spielbergian, 'reliving' of the middle passage for any punter with the money to pay for the ride? In inviting us to think that we are getting a 'total experience', these exhibits simply recast the empathetic yet complacent emotional substitutions with which the West has been mis-remembering and dis-remembering slavery for more than three centuries. The fact that there are many black Liverpudlians who have refused to set foot in the gallery on the grounds that their community was not consulted when the whole institution was planned and built indicates the problematic nature of the venture.[13]

But if these exhibits are not the right way, what is? There are simple and direct gestures of remembrance which attempt to endow the arbitrary sites of disaster with the aura of monuments. On 15 November 1992 members of the National Association of Black Scuba Divers swam to the sea bed, off the coast of Florida, to place an inscribed plaque on the site of the recently discovered wreck of the slave ship Henrietta Marie. The plaque read: 'Henrietta Marie. In memory and recognition of the courage, pain and suffering of enslaved African people. Speak her name and gently touch the souls of our ancestors.' The plaque is reproduced in the web site now devoted to the Henriette Marie.[14] Yet the accompanying text by Dinizulu Gene Tinnie repeats that gesture which strives to re-articulate trauma through empathy with objects. Having stated 'our need to understand the Middle Passage in … human terms rather than as mere diagrams, words and numbers', Tinnie goes on to claim that 'the mute evidence of iron shackles, weaponry, beads and other trade items, pewter ware still with knife marks made by the crew, parts of the ship itself' allow us to 'make tangible contact with an actual ship and with actual people'. My feeling is that the power of these objects emanates precisely from the way they emphasise, with a terrible finality, our inability ever to make such a contact.

Words that change pictures: slavery transformed in Conrad and Coetzee

If the relics of human disaster are limited in their potential to communicate, the same is not always true of art. Visual art can transform how we read words, and words can transform images. These interdependencies can be very powerful in the context of slavery, and I want to end this book by taking two examples. Firstly consider how the middle passage works itself into one of Joseph Conrad's novellas 'Freya of the Seven Isles.' Conrad's writing can change how we look at the slave trade and the memory of slavery, and it can also change how we look at visual art. In this sense Art can rethink history and transform disaster.

The memory of slavery haunts Joseph Conrad's writing. *The Nigger of the Narcissus* is, among other things, a deep exploration of the collective guilt of the slave trade. Conrad is explicit about this: Jimmy, the 'Nigger', is strangely, mortally sick, and his sickness is the sickness of the memory of slavery. The character of Belfast, enormous, gentle, in certain ways innocent, and infatuated with a mysterious love of Jimmy, struggles to articulate his obsession with the dying black man and to break out of an enforced historical amnesia. What Belfast says electrifies the crew: '"The man is dying, I tell ye," repeated Belfast, woe-fully, sitting at Singleton's feet. – "And a black fellow, too," went on the old seaman, "I have seen them die like flies." He stopped, thoughtful, as if trying to recollect gruesome things, details of horrors, hecatombs of niggers. They looked at him fascinated. He was old enough to remember slavers, bloody mutinies.'[15] Jimmy suddenly comes to embody the memory of the slave ship, and of the Atlantic slave trade, and the voyage of the *Narcissus* should be read in the light of this fact. Slavery, its memory, its terrible historical pressures, reaching over continents and centuries, is the central metaphorical concern of much of Conrad's greatest work including *Nostromo*, *Heart of Darkness* and the short stories 'An Outpost of Progress' and 'Gaspar Ruiz'.[16]

Admitting the difficulties which surround the question of how Conrad is to be situated within contemporary debates on race, slavery and empire, I would nevertheless insist that Conrad's art can be read in ways which can instruct the West about how to approach its relation to the memory of slavery. What Conrad writes can give new force to the way we can see pictures of the slave ships. After reading 'Freya' it is not possible to look at the beautiful lines of the last slave-trading brigs the same way again.

This story suggests that the white populations who live after slavery are, in their purest and most intimate demonstrations of love, and their most extreme idealism, powerless to avoid being haunted, and sometimes even destroyed, by the inheritance of slavery. William Faulkner works horrifying but gorgeous variations on this theme in *Absalom Absalom*.

The central male character in Conrad's 'tale' is called Jasper and he is in love with a beautiful Scandinavian woman, Freya. Both of them are young, blond, blue-eyed and white, and they find the focus for their mutual adoration in Jasper's brig the *Bonito*. 'Without her there would have been no future. She was the fortune and the home, and the great free world for them. Who was it that likened a ship to a prison?' The ship possesses a dangerous perfection of form:

> the *Bonito*, brig … Her brasses flashed like gold, her white body-paint had a sheen like a satin robe. The rake of her varnished spars and the big yards, squared to a hair, gave her a sort of martial elegance. She was a beauty. No wonder that in possession of a craft like that and the promise of a girl like Freya, Jasper lived in a state of perpetual elation fit, perhaps, for the seventh heaven, but not exactly safe in a world like ours.[17]

The brig is not 'safe', and after its destruction by the jealous and brutish Heemskirk does end up being the imaginative prison which destroys the two lovers. Its beauty is not innocent, but is anchored in a terrible economic necessity which lies at the heart of the boat's metaphoric function. The *Bonito* was bought from a bankrupt Peruvian:

> The brig herself was then all black and enigmatical, and very dirty; a tarnished gem of the sea, or rather, a neglected work of art. For he must have been an artist, the obscure builder who had put her body together on lovely lines out of the hardest tropical timber fastened with the purest copper. Goodness only knows in what part of the world she was built. Jasper himself had not been able to ascertain much of her history from his sententious, saturnine Peruvian – if the fellow was a Peruvian, and not the devil himself in disguise, as Jasper jocularly pretended to believe. My opinion is that she was old enough to have been one of the last pirates, a slaver.[18]

Perhaps Jasper's joke is not really so funny. The last slavers to sail between Africa and the American, Cuban and South American coasts were some of the most beautiful sailing ships ever made.[19] The reasons were all to do with the rigours of slave-running in a world where it was officially illegal. Some of these pirate slavers sailing in the 1850–80 period were celebrated for their speed and the perfection of their lines; in a straight race slave patrols couldn't get anywhere near them. The 'Celebrated Piratical Slaver l'Antonio', for example, was famous enough to be painted in oils and then circulated in England as a popular engraving [**6.7**]. This craft gives some idea of the terrible beauty of such boats.[20] They were fast, but they had virtually no room at all for slaves, and the scarceness and official illegality of

African slaves at this point made them more valuable than they had ever been. As a result, the conditions for the last slaves smuggled into Havana and Salvador, Bahia, were probably the worst, in terms of space allowance, ever endured.

The unspeakable history of the *Bonito* comes to bear on Jasper and Freya. As the tale develops, the boat exerts a magical hold over Jasper, who is physically obsessed with her. With an unnatural determination he attempts to transform the blackness of this 'dusky gem' into an embodiment of the white of Freya's skin and the gold of her hair:

> she was as sound as on the day she first took the water, sailed like a witch, steered like a little boat, and like some fair women of adventurous life famous in history, seemed to have the secret of perpetual youth; so that there was nothing unnatural in Jasper Allen treating her like a lover. And that treatment restored the lustre of her beauty. He clothed her in many coats of the very best white paint so skilfully, carefully, artistically put on and kept clean by his badgered crew of picked Malays, that no costly enamel such as jewellers use for their work could have looked better and felt smoother to the touch. A narrow gilt moulding defined her elegant sheer as she sat on the water ... I must say I prefer a moulding of deep crimson colour on a white hull.[21]

Yet despite eschewing the colour of blood for gold, the lovers cannot escape the boat's history. The beautiful form is run onto a reef with a deliberate sadism by his rival Heemskirk and Jasper must watch the boat decay. As he watches he sees and feels a buried history restore itself: 'He followed her fine gliding form with eyes growing big with incredulity, wild with horror.'

Heemskirk in leaving the *Bonito* to fall apart on the reef – all that potential speed locked in a perpetual stasis, the perfect white shell, peeling off to reveal blackness, white hope turning to black despair – has, unwittingly, created a monument to the slave trade. Jasper must study this monument until, engulfed by a suicidal despair, he destroys himself:

> Day after day he would traverse the length of the town, follow the coast, and, reaching the point of land opposite that part of the reef on which his brig lay stranded, look steadily across the water at her beloved form, once the home of an exulting hope, and now, in her inclined desolated immobility, towering above the lonely sea-horizon, a symbol of despair.[22]

Conrad's art transforms a boat employed by the slave trade into a site for the memory of this horror, but he works through glorious indirection. The power of this story lies in its message that suffering and guilt are not necessarily educative; they are, most commonly, simply destructive and not understood. Yet out of the destruction art can be made, and Atlantic slavery, whether the West likes it or not, is emerging as a key site for the production of art. This takes me on to my second example.

Blind memory, explicitly in terms of how the West can or cannot remember slavery, is at 'the heart of the story' when J. M. Coetzee comes at the memory of the middle passage from another direction, or indirection, in his novel *Foe*. This seductive and maizey parable-ridden scrutinisation of the place of slavery in *Robinson Crusoe* places the enigma of the slave Friday at its centre. Coetzee's Friday is a black African, woolly haired and splay footed, mute and emasculated, his tongue and genitalia having been cut out at some unknown point by an unknown assailant before the narrative begins. Muteness and blindness are dominant metaphors in Coetzee's rendering of Friday, and the final muteness and blindness are placed within the Western consciousness. Early in *Foe* Friday has been observed, by Coetzee's central narrator, a woman named Susan Barton, floating on a log, out to a mysterious point off Crusoe's island, and then scattering white buds. It is only towards the novel's close, when the fictional Foe speculates upon the motives for Friday's action, that it is revealed that this ceremony might be a commemorative act of mourning for the middle passage:

> you say he was guiding his boat to the place where the ship went down, which we may surmise to have been a slave ship … picture the hundreds of his fellow-slaves – or their skeletons – still chained in the wreck, the gay little fish (that you spoke of) flitting through their eye sockets and the hollow cases that had held their hearts. Picture Friday above, staring down upon them, casting buds and petals that float a brief while, then sink to settle among the bones of the dead.[23]

It is at this point, as he approaches the memory of the slave trade, explicitly shadowed in the image of the still wreck of the ship, the bodies of the slaves, as in Turner's *Slaver*, intermixed with the beauty of marine life, that

Coetzee throws out a challenge to the Western consciousness. His fictional Foe continues to ruminate upon the significance of Friday's private, silent mourning:

> 'In every story there is a silence, some sight concealed, some word unspoken, I believe. Till we have spoken the unspoken we have not come to the heart of the story' … 'I said the heart of the story,' resumed Foe, 'but, I should have said the eye of the story. Friday rows his log of wood across the dark pupil – or the dead socket – of an eye staring up at him from the floor of the sea. He rows across it safe. To us he leaves the task of descending into that eye. Otherwise, like him, we sail across the surface and come ashore none the wiser, and resume our old lives, and sleep without dreaming, like babes.'

Notice how uncannily this is anticipated by the triumphant negations of Aimé Césaire, when, at a climactic moment in the *Notebook of a Return to my Native Land*, he defies the inheritance of slavery by defining the essence of his 'négritude': 'ma négritude n'est pas une taie d'eau morte sur l'oeil mort de la terre' (my negritude is not a blind spot of dead water over the dead eye of the earth).[24] Coetzee sets out the task of the artist, to go into the dark wreck of the slave ship, which with an impossible boldness Coetzee describes himself doing in the short, mysterious final section of *Foe*. Descending through the scattered petals of Friday's offering, Coetzee, as detached and genderless narrational voice, reaches the wreck, passes the bloated drowned body of Susan Barton, and comes finally to the corpse of Friday. Putting his hand in Friday's mouth, he hopes finally to be given the testimony of slavery, to be told 'what really happened':

> His mouth opens. From inside him comes a slow stream, without breath, without interruption. It flows up through his body and out upon me; it passes through the cabin, through the wreck; washing the cliffs and shores of the island, it runs northward and southward to the ends of the earth. Soft and cold, dark and unending, it beats against my eyelids.

What he finds is the same answer that Turner finds, that the final testimony to the middle passage is the cold salt water of the ocean itself, the living tomb of those who died on the middle passage, white and black. And what that water tells us, as it beats on the eyelids, is that the memory of slavery belongs to us all, and requires our acknowledgement, if only we dare to look.

Can there be an art of slavery?

This book concerns the place of aesthetics in the memory of slavery and asserts the primacy of Art as the most effective tributary cultural response. Art can perform what is otherwise impossible: it can represent horror through beauty, it can see beauty in pain, it can force vision beyond the veil of salt tears, it can make the blind see. This achievement might not finally relate to orthodox morality, or a contented liberal ethics, very nicely, if at all. To read Toni Morrison's *Beloved*, or Coetzee's *Foe*, to look upon Turner's *Slaver*, does not allow us 'to come to terms' with the past of slavery – that is quite emphatically what these works do not do. The challenge is to come to understand how art explores guilt, to come and see disaster through the unrelenting gaze of aesthetics, while never generalising about what it is which separates the middle passage and plantation slavery from other cultural and global disasters.

Visual artists think deeply about the links between creativity and blindness. Turner's painting *Regulus* depicted a fanciful classical harbour illuminated by a brilliant sun. This sun is shining straight into the spectator's eyes, just like the sun in the *Slave Ship*, but these eyes are also the eyes of Regulus, the Roman general. Regulus was blinded by the Carthaginians for refusing to turn diplomacy into treachery. His punishment was to be bound facing the midday sun with his eyelids cut off until he went blind. What we see is beautiful, although the beauty destroys and causes agony. Picasso enunciated the links between blindness and insight for the artist, most famously, if somewhat too neatly, in the aphorism 'In the end there is only love. However it may be. And they ought to put out the eyes of painters as they do goldfinches in order that they can sing better.'[25] Of the many approaches to the relation between art, testimony and blindness that of Claude Lanzmann is one of the most powerful. His insistence that he could only make his epic film *Shoah*, which consists of individual testimonies of the Nazi Holocaust, by blinding himself to the 'obscene' question 'Why have the Jews been killed?' is helpful. In Lanzmann's world, speculation is anathema to truth and leads one away from the fact. Lanzmann continues: 'Blindness has to be understood here as the purest mode of looking, of the gaze, the only way not to turn away from a reality which is literally blinding.' The history of the visual interpretation of slavery in the West, and of the readings of these interpretations, is very largely a wholesale process of speculation and of turning 'away from a reality which is literally blinding'.[26] Yet there are different sorts of turning, and different sorts of blindness: the blindness of ignorance, and the blindness that provides, in Yeats's phrase, a 'proper dark' out of which to create. In the conclusion to *Memoirs of the Blind*, Jacques Derrida looks into the blindness of Milton's Samson. What he sees is the ultimate responsibility of the blind artist: 'a terrible punishment becomes the price to pay for a rational mission and a political responsibility. And the blind man *regains*, he guards and regards, retains and recoups, and compensates for what his eyes of flesh have to renounce with a spiritual or inner light – as well as a historical lucidity. For blindness seems to illuminate the 'inward eyes': 'But he, thou blind of sight, / Despised and thought extinguished quite, / With inward eyes illuminated, / His fiery virtue roused From under ashes in to sudden flame.'[27] For some tastes this may be dangerously emotional, oracular, enthusiastic even, in the old sense of the word. Yet for Derrida the artist must go to terrible lengths to achieve this paradox of blind-sight, and in answer to Andrew Marvell's impossible assertion 'Those weeping eyes, those seeing tears', and Derrida's own question 'Tears that see ... Do you believe?', he comes down on the side of impossibility, ending *Memoirs of the Blind* with the beautiful, humble and querulous words 'I don't know, one has to believe'. The 'Blind Memory' which forms the first two words of this book is not easily seen and is not a stable phenomenon: Turner's blindness is not the same thing as Biard's, but it may resemble that of Samson. When we try to look at the inheritance of Atlantic slavery what we are capable of seeing remains to be seen.

Notes

1 For the history of the political persecution of capoeira see Jorge Amado, *Tenda das Milagres* (São Paulo, Livraria Matins Editoria, 1969).

2 The most concentrated resource to represent the cultural impact of slavery on the visual culture of Salvador is the Museu Afro Brasileiro in Salvador. See Norbert Odebrecht, *Museu Afro Brasileiro* (Salvador, Bahia, Meseu Afro-Brasileiro, 1983); see also John Geipel, 'Brazil's African Legacy', *History Today*, 47:8 (1997) 18–24; Roger Bastide, *African Religions of Brazil* (Baltimore, University of Baltimore Press, 1978).

3 The best discussion of the enormous impact of the slave trade on the growth of English banking is Peter Fryer, *Staying Power: The History of Black People in Britain* (London, Pluto, 1984), pp. 44–50. The protean reincarnations of the capital generated by the British slave trade is a subject that deserves a monograph, if not the attention of Stephen Spielberg.

4 The two succeeding plates are taken from the immensely popular Charles D. Michael, *The Slave and his Champions* (London, S. W. Partridge, 1915).

5 Wilberforce House envelopes carry a sticker showing the kneeling slave from the seal of the Society for Affecting the Abolition of the Slave Trade, but the slogan 'The World's First Slavery Museum' has replaced the aphorism 'Am I not a man and a brother?'.

6 See Cobbett's brutal and rhetorically superb assaults on Wilberforce in *The Political Register*, 40:1 (1821) 1–39; 40:3 (1821) 147–86; 47:9 (1823) 513–62; 48:10 (1823) 577–94; 48:11 (1823) 641–94. For Hazlitt on Wilberforce see *The Complete Works of William Hazlitt in Twenty One Volumes*, ed. P. P. Howe (London, J. M. Dent, 1931), 11, pp. 149–51.

7 Hazlitt, *Works*, 11, p. 149; 17, p. 16.

8 Hazlitt, *Works*, 11, p. 150 fn.

9 Full-scale models of slave decks occur in other museums in England and America. See, for example, the Great Blacks in Wax Museum, Baltimore. An advertising brochure states the museum 'has a powerfully moving exhibit of a slave ship which leaves nobody untouched'.

10 The blood metaphor in its application to Bristol and Liverpool is traced in detail in Fryer, *Staying Power*, p. 477, n. 2. Both quotations are taken from Fryer.

11 Peter Moores, 'Foreword', in Anthony Tibbles (ed.), *Transatlantic Slavery, Against Human Dignity* (London, HMSO, 1994), p. 9.

12 For an impassioned and precisely reasoned critique of the Transatlantic Slavery Gallery project within the context of the construction of blacks in British museum cultures see Stephen Small, 'Contextualising the Black Presence in British Museums: Representations, Resources and Response', in Eilean Hooper-Greenhill (ed.), *Cultural Diversity: Developing Museum Audiences in Britain* (London, Leicester University Press, 1997), pp. 50–67. For a detailed discussion of the composition of the

controlling texts for panels and labels within the museum see Helen Coxall, 'Speaking Other Voices', in Hooper-Greenhill (ed.), *Cultural Diversity*, pp. 99–115. Coxall's analysis does not engage with the objects displayed, or the question of 'recreating' experience through installations. See also Nick Merriman and Mima Poovaya-Smith, 'Making Culturally Diverse Histories', in Gaynor Kavanah (ed.), *Making Histories in Museums* (London, Leicester University Press, 1996), pp. 176–88.

13 The most incisive survey of contemporary museum theory and of shifts in museum practice is the heavily Foucaultian work, Eilean Hooper-Greenhill, *Museums and the Shaping of Knowledge* (London, Routledge, 1992), pp. 1–22, 191–215. The vocabulary in parentheses in the preceding paragraph is drawn from this book. For the problematic nature of museum display in the context of postmodernism see Douglas Crimp, *On the Museum's Ruins* (Cambridge Mass. and London, MIT Press, 1996), pp. 2–44.

14 http://www.historical museum.org/exhibits/hm/perspect.htm

15 Joseph Conrad, *Collected Edition of the Works of Joseph Conrad: The Nigger of the Narcissus, Typhoon and Other Stories* (London, J. M. Dent, 1950), pp. 129–30.

16 The short story 'An Outpost of Progress' is in the collection *Tales of Unrest* and constitutes Conrad's most savage assault on the pathology underlying intercontinental slave trading. 'Gaspar Ruiz' is a much neglected short story from *A Set of Six*.

17 Joseph Conrad, 'Freya of the Seven Isles, a story of the shallow waters', in *Collected Edition of the Works of Joseph Conrad: 'Twixt Land and Sea Three Tales* (London, J. M. Dent, 1947), p. 163.

18 Conrad, *'Twixt Land and Sea*, p. 157.

19 See M. K. Stammers '"Guineamen": Some Technical Aspects of Slave Ships', in Tibbles (ed.), *Transatlantic Slavery*, pp. 35–41.

20 Tibbles (ed.), *Transatlantic Slavery*, pp. 80, 165.

21 Conrad, *'Twixt Land and Sea*, pp. 156–7.

22 Conrad, *'Twixt Land and Sea*, p. 229.

23 J. M. Coetzee, *Foe* (London, Penguin, 1987), p. 141.

24 Aimé Césaire, *Notebook of a Return to my Native Land* (Newcastle, Bloodaxe, 1995), p. 114 (my translation).

25 Doré Ashton (ed.), *Picasso on Art: A Selection of Views* (London, Penguin, 1977), p. 78.

26 Lanzmann quoted in 'The Obscenity of Understanding: An Evening with Claude Lanzmann', in Cathy Caruth (ed.) *Trauma: Explorations in Memory* (Baltimore and London, Johns Hopkins University Press, 1995), p. 204.

27 Jacques Derrida, *Memoirs of the Blind*, trans. Pascale-Anne Brault and Michel Nass (Chicago and London, University of Chicago Press, 1993), p. 109.

Bibliography

Manuscripts, prints and drawings

American Antiquarian Society, Worcester, Mass.
   Holdings: BDSDS. Almanacs. Single-sheet political and social print satires.
   American periodicals. Illustrated sheet music.
Andrew Edmunds Gallery, London
   Collection of the prints of Richard Newton.
Bodleian Library, Oxford
Music Library: Illustrated sheet music 57 e 31, *Uncle Tom*.
   Opie Collection, uncatalogued materials: *Topsy's Frolics or Always in Mischief*,
   My New Toy Book.
   Rhodes House Library: Anti-slavery Archive, *Nineteenth and Twentieth
   Century Letters, British and Foreign Anti Slavery Society*, C/2 23 1837. *Minute
   Books of the British and Foreign Anti-Slavery Society*, E 2/4 1835. *Calendar of the
   Papers of Sir Thomas Fowell Buxton 1786–1845*, vol. 3, Miscellaneous
   Correspondence.
Bristol City Archives
   Print Collection: 'Plan of an African Ship's Lower Deck'.
British Library, Manuscript Division
   Abolition Committee Minutes, Add. MSS 21254–56.
British Museum
   Department of Prints and Drawings: Collection of Political and Personal
   Satires: Preserved in the Department of Prints and Drawings in the British
   Museum.
John Rylands Library, Manchester
   Raymond English Anti-Slavery Collection: Boxes 1–20.
Kingston upon Hull, City Museums and Art Galleries
   Wilberforce House Museum Holdings.
Library Company of Philadelphia
   American Broadside Collection. Print Collection. African American Collections:
   Am. 1827, Taylor, 101580.D; Am. 1860 Dra. 72735.0; Am. 1817 Tor 4875.0; Am.
   1837 Roper, 101478.D; Am. 1827 Fer, 5242, F2; Am 1833, Con, 66209.D.
Library of Congress
   American Political Prints 1766–1876 in the Collections in the Library of
   Congress.
Massachusetts Historical Society
   Photographic Collections.
National Maritime Museum, Greenwich
   Manuscript Collections: 'Diary of Lieutenant Francis Meynell'.

National Museums and Art Galleries on Merseyside
  Maritime Museum: Transatlantic Slavery Gallery Holdings.
Newberry Library, Chicago
  Collection of early American type specimen books. American broadside
  collection.
Strong Museum, Albany, New York
  Collection of early American board games: *Justice*.
Victoria and Albert Museum
  Cruikshank bequest: Box I 95, items 9880 A–Z, 9881 A–T.
Yale University Library, Beineke Rare Book Department.
  Illustrated broadside collections.

Primary sources

Aiken, George [Harriet Beecher Stowe], *Uncle Tom's Cabin*, New York, 1852.
Anti-Slavery Bugle.
Anti-Slavery Record.
The Athenaeum.
Autographs for Freedom. By Mrs. Harriet Beecher Stowe, and Thirty-five other eminent Writers, n.d.
Beccaria, Cesare, *On Crimes and Punishments*, trans. Henri Paolucci, Indianapolis, Bobbs-Merrill Educational Publishing, 1977.
Bibb, Henry, *Narrative of the Life and Adventures of Henry Bibb, An American Slave, Written by Himself with an Introduction by Lucius C. Matlack,* New York, 1849.
Bisset, Robert, *The History of the Negro Slave Trade, in its connection with the commerce and prosperity of the West Indies and the Wealth and Power of the British Empire*, 2 vols, London, 1805.
Blackwood's Magazine.
Boston Anti-Slavery Almanac, Boston, 1837.
Boswell, James, *No Abolition of Slavery or the Universal Empire of Love*, London, 1791.
Brown, Henry 'Box', *Narrative of Henry Box Brown, Who Escaped from Slavery Enclosed in a Box 3 Feet Long and 2 Feet Wide*, Boston, 1849.
Brown, Henry 'Box', *Narrative of the Life of Henry Box Brown, Written by Himself*, Manchester, 1851.
Brown, William Wells, *The travels of William Wells Brown: Including Narrative of William Wells Brown; and The American Fugitive in Europe*, Edinburgh, Edinburgh University Press, [1845, 1854] 1991.
Brown, William Wells, *From Fugitive to Free Man: the Autobiographies of William Wells Brown, Narrative of William Wells Brown a Fugitive Slave, My Southern Home,* New York, Mentor, [1848, 1880] 1993.
Burke, Edmund, *The Writings and Speeches of Edmund Burke*, 9 vols, Oxford, Clarendon Press, 1991–97.
Carlyle, Thomas, *Centenary Edition of the Works of Thomas Carlyle in Thirty Volumes*, London, Chapman and Hall, 1896.
Casas, Bartolomé de Las, *A Short Account of the Destruction of the Indies*, Harmondsworth, Penguin, 1993.
Césaire, Aimé, *Notebook of a Return to my Native Land*, Newcastle, Bloodaxe, 1995.

Chapman, Frederik Henric af, *Architechtura Navalis Mercatoria*, Stockholm, 1768.

Charnock, John, *An History of Marine Architecture … from the Earliest Period to the Present*, 3 vols, London, 1800.

Chase, Eugene B., *English Serfdom, American Slavery: or, Ourselves as Others See Us*, Miami, Mnesmosyne Publishing, [1854] 1969.

Clarkson, Thomas, *Letters on the Slave-Trade and the State of the Natives in those Parts of Africa which are Contiguous to Fort St. Louis and Goree*, London, James Phillips, 1791.

Clarkson, Thomas, *The History of the Rise, Progress, and Accomplishment of the Abolition of the African Slave-Trade by the British Parliament*, 2 vols, London, 1808.

Clarkson, Thomas, *Negro Slavery. Argument, That the Colonial Slaves are better off than the British Peasantry*, London, 1824.

Coetzee, J. M., *Foe*, London, Penguin, 1987.

Coleridge, Samuel Taylor, *The Table Talk and Omniana of Samuel Taylor Coleridge*, Oxford, Oxford University Press, 1917.

Coleridge, Samuel Taylor, *Greek Prize Ode on the Slave Trade*, trans. Anthea Morrison, in J. R. Watson (ed.), *An Infinite Complexity*, Edinburgh, Edinburgh University Press, 1985.

The Condition of the West India Slave Contrasted with that of the Infant Slave in our English Factories, London, W. Kidd, *c.* 1835.

Conrad, Joseph, 'Freya of the Seven Isles: a story of the shallow waters', in *Collected Edition of the Works of Joseph Conrad: 'Twixt Land and Sea Three Tales*, London, J. M. Dent, 1947.

Conrad, Joseph, *Collected Edition of the Works of Joseph Conrad: The Nigger of the Narcissus, Typhoon and Other Stories*, London, J. M. Dent, 1950.

Cousin Ann's Stories for Children, Philadelphia, 1849.

Cowper, William, *The Poems of William Cowper*, ed. John Baird and Charles Ryskamp, 3 vols, Oxford, Clarendon Press, 1980–95.

Coxe, Louis Osborne, *The Middle Passage*, Chicago, University of Chicago Press, 1960.

Cross, John, *An Attempt to Establish Physiognomy Upon Scientific Principles*, London, 1817.

Cruikshank, George, and William Hone, *A Slap at Slop*, London, 1820.

Cruikshank, George, *Slavery in the West Indies*, London, 1830.

Cruikshank, George, *The Comic Almanack, 2nd Series, 1844–53*, London, 1853.

Curious Adventures of Captain Stedman, London, *c.* 1810.

Dabydeen, David, *Turner and Other Poems*, London, Cape Poetry, 1994.

Derrida, Jacques, *Margins of Philosophy*, trans. Alan Bass, Brighton, Harvester Wheatsheaf, 1982.

Derrida, Jaques, *Memoirs of the Blind*, trans. Pascale-Anne Brault and Michel Nass, Chicago and London, University of Chicago Press, 1993.

Dickens, Charles, *American Notes*, Oxford, Oxford University Press, [1842] 1987.

Douglass, Frederick, *Narrative of the Life of Frederick Douglass*, London, Penguin, [1845] 1986.

Douglass, Frederick, *My Bondage My Freedom*, Auburn and New York, Miller Orton and Mullington, 1855.

Drake, Richard, *Revelations of a Slave Smuggler: Being the Autobiography of Captain Richard Drake, An African Trader*, New York, 1860.

Dunbar, William, *The Poems of William Dunbar*, ed. James Kinsley, Oxford, Clarendon Press, 1979.

Edwards, Bryan, *History Civil and Commercial, of the British Colonies in the West Indies*, 3 vols, London, 1793.

Ellison, Ralph, *Invisible Man*, London, Gollancz, 1953.

Emerson, Ralph Waldo, *The Collected Works of Ralph Waldo Emerson, Volume II, Essays, First Series*, ed. Alfred R. Fergusson and Jean Fergusson, Cambridge Mass., Belknap Press, 1979.

Equiano, Olaudah, *The Interesting Narrative and Other Writings*, Harmondsworth, Penguin, [1789] 1995.

Fanon, Frantz, *Black Face White Masks*, trans. Charles Lam Markmann, London, Pluto, [1965] 1986.

The Female Disciplinary Manual: A Complete Encyclopaedia of the Correction of the Fair Sex, Wiltshire, Anthony Rowe, 1995.

Fitzhugh, George, *Cannibals All! or Slaves Without Masters*, ed. C. Vann Woodward, Cambridge Mass., Belknap Press, [1856] 1960.

The Flag: The Newspaper of the National Front.

Foucault, Michel, *Discipline and Punish: The Birth of the Prison*, trans. Alan Sheridan, Harmondsworth, Penguin, 1979.

Foucault, Michel, *Power/Knowledge: Selected Interviews and Other Writings 1972–77*, ed. Colin Gordon, New York, Pantheon Books, 1980.

Fraser's Magazine.

Freud, Sigmund, '"A Child is Being Beaten": A Contribution to the Study of the Origin of Sexual Perversions', in *Sigmund Freud, Collected Papers*, ed. Ernest Jones, trans. Joan Riviere, 5 vols, London, Hogarth Press, 1950, 2, 172–201.

Gisborne, Thomas, *Walks in a Forest*, London, 1794.

Glissant, Eduard, *Les Indes*, trans. Dominique O'Neil and Jose Gamarra, Toronto, Editions du Gref, 1992.

Gray, Iron [Abel Thomas], *The Gospel of Slavery: A Primer of Freedom*, New York, 1864.

Harper's Weekly.

Hayden, Robert, *Collected Poems*, New York, Liveright Company, 1985.

Hazlitt, William, *The Complete Works of William Hazlitt in Twenty One Volumes*, ed. P. P. Howe, London, J. M. Dent, 1931.

Hegel, Georg Wilhelm Friedrich, *Lectures on the Philosophy of World History*, trans. H. B. Nisbet, Cambridge, Cambridge University Press, 1975.

Hegel, Georg Wilhelm Friedrich, *The Phenomenology of Spirit*, trans. A. V. Miller, Oxford, Clarendon Press, 1977.

Henson, Josiah, *The Life of Josiah Henson Formerly a Slave Now an Inhabitant of Canada, as Narrated by Himself*, Boston, 1849.

Henson, Josiah, *Truth Stranger than Fiction, Father Henson's Story of his Own Life*, Boston, 1858.

Henson, Josiah, *'Uncle Tom's Story of his Life': an Autobiography of the Rev. Josiah Henson*, London, 1877.

Heyrick, Elizabeth, *Cursory Remarks on the Evil Tendency of Unrestrained Cruelty Particularly on that Practiced in Smithfield Market*, London, Darton and Harvey, 1823.

Jacobs, Harriet, *Incidents in the Life of a Slavegirl*, Cambridge Mass., Harvard University Press, [1861] 1987.

James, Henry, *A Small Boy and Others*, London, Macmillan, 1913.

Johnson, Charles, *Middle Passage*, London, Macmillan, 1990.

Leatheley, Mary, *Large Pictures with Little Stories*, London, Darton, *c.* 1855.

The Legion of Liberty, New York, New York Anti-Slavery Society, 1843.

Levi, Primo, *The Drowned and the Saved*, trans. Raymond Rosenthal, London, Abacus, 1988.

The Liberty Almanac for 1851.

The Liberty Almanac for 1852.

Lindsay, Jimmy, 'Wey you are defend', *Children of Rastafari*, London, GEM Records [RCA], 1980.

Lobb, John, *The Young People's Illustrated Edition of 'Uncle Tom's' Story of his Life from 1789–1877*, London, Christian Age Office, 1877.

Long, Edward, *The History of Jamaica or, General Survey of the Antient and Modern State of that Island*, 3 vols, London, 1774.

Maxwell, William Hamilton, *History of the Irish Rebellion*, London, 1845.

Meredith, George, *The Egoist*, London, Constable, 1897.

Miller, Patrick, *The Elevation, Section, Plan and Views, of a Triple Vessel, and of Wheels with Explanations of the Figures in the Engraving*, Edinburgh, 1787.

Morrison, Toni, *Beloved*, London, Picador, 1987.

Newton, John, *Thoughts Upon the African Slave Trade*, London, 1788.

Newton, John, *The Journal of a Slave Trader*, ed. Bernard Martin and Mark Spurrell, London, Epworth Press, [1750–52] 1962.

New York Anti-Slavery Almanac.

Norris, Robert, *Memoirs of the Reign of Bossa Ahadee, King of Dahomey, An INLAND COUNTRY of GUINEA. To Which are Added the Author's Journey to Abomey, The Capital; and A Short Account of the African Slave Trade*, London, 1789.

Northrup, Solomon, *Twelve Years a Slave, Narrative of Solomon Northrup, A Citizen of New York, Kidnapped in Washington City in 1841, and Rescued in 1853*, Auburn, 1853.

The Origin of Jim Crow, London, 1837.

'Orrible Murder: Victorian Crime and Passion, Selections from the Illustrated Police News, ed. Leonard de Vries, London, Macdonald, 1971.

Papers of Benjamin Franklyn, vol. 4, July 1, 1750, through June 30, 1753, ed. W. Labaree, New Haven, Yale University Press, 1961.

The Political Register.

A Redemção folha Abolicionista Commercial e Noticiosa.

Roper, Moses, *A Narrative of the Adventures and Escape of Moses Roper from American Slavery*, London, 1837.

Rossetti, Dante Gabriel, *The Works of Dante Gabriel Rossetti*, ed. W. M. Rossetti, London, 1911.

Runaway Slave Advertisements: A Documentary History from the 1730s until 1790, ed. Lathan A. Windley, 4 vols, London, Greenwood Press, 1983.

Ruskin, John, *The Library Edition of the Works of John Ruskin*, ed. E. T. Cook and A. Wedderburn, 39 vols, London, George Allen, 1903–12.

Ruskin, John, *The Diaries of John Ruskin*, ed. Joan Evans and John Howard Whitehouse, 3 vols, Oxford, Clarendon Press, 1956–59.

A Sketch of the Laws Relating to Slavery in the Several States of the United States of America, Pennsylvania, 1827.

The Slave's Friend.

Stanfield, James, *Observations on a Guinea Voyage. In a Series of Letters Addressed to The Rev. Thomas Clarkson*, London, 1788.

Stedman, John Gabriel, *Narrative of a Five Years' Expedition Against the Revolted Negroes of Surinam*, 2 vols, London, 1796.

Stedman, John Gabriel, *Voyage à Surinam, et dans l'intérieure de la Guyanne etc. avec des détails sur les indiens de la Guyane [sic] et des Nègres par le Capitaine J. G. Stedman*, Paris, 1799.

Stedman, John Gabriel, *The Journal of John Gabriel Stedman Soldier and Author 1744–1797*, ed. Standbury Thompson, London, Mitre Press, 1962.

Stedman, John Gabriel, *Narrative of a Five Years' Expedition Against the Revolted Negroes of Surinam*, ed. Richard Price and Sally Price, Baltimore and London, Johns Hopkins University Press, [1790] 1994.

Stowe, Harriet Beecher [adapted by George Aitken], *Uncle Tom's Cabin, or Life Among the Lowly, a domestic drama in Six Acts*, New York, Samuel French, 1853.

Stowe, Harriet Beecher, *Uncle Tom's Cabin*, London, Clarke and Beeton, 1853.

Stowe, Harriet Beecher, *Uncle Tom's Cabin, or, Life Among the Lowly, by H.B.S. Illustrated edition Complete in one volume*, London, Sampson Low, 1853.

Stowe, Harriet Beecher, *Key to Uncle Tom's Cabin*, London, 1853.

Stowe, Harriet Beecher, *Dred: a tale of the Great Dismal Swamp* ed. Judy Newman, Halifax, Ryburn, [1853] 1992.

The Substance of the Evidence of Sundry Persons on the Slave Trade Collected in the Course of a Tour Made in the Autumn of the Year 1788, London, James Phillips, 1789.

The Suppressed Book About Slavery, New York, 1857.

Taylor, Isaac, *Scenes in Africa for the Amusement and Instruction of Little Tarry at Home Travellers By the Reverend Isaac Taylor*, New York, 1827.

Torrey, Jessy, *A Portraiture of Domestic Slavery in the United States*, Philadelphia, 1817.

Trollop, Anthony, *The Way We Live Now*, 2 vols, London, Chapman and Hall, 1875.

The Uncle Tom's Cabin Almanack or Abolitionist Memento, London, 1853.

[Weld, Theodore Dwight], *American Slavery As It Is* (New York, American Anti-Slavery Society, 1839).

Wellington and Uncle Tom: or the Hero of this World Contrasted with the Hero in Jesus Christ, London, Simkin Marshall and Co., 1853.

Whitman, Walt, *Leaves of Grass*, New York, Norton, [1881] 1992.

Whittier, John Greenleaf, 'Thomas Carlyle on the Slave Question', in Jules Paul Seigel (ed.), *Thomas Carlyle: The Critical Heritage*, London and New York, Routledge, 1995.

Wilkins, John, *An essay towards a real character, and a philosophical language*, London, 1688.

Williams, James, *Narrative of Events since the Ist of August, 1834 By James Williams together with the Evidence Taken Under a Commission Appointed by the Colonial Office to Ascertain the Truth of the Narrative*, London, 1837.

Secondary sources

Visual arts

Adams, Marion and Lawrence Wroth, *American Woodcuts and Engravings, 1670–1800*, Providence, Associates of the John Carter Brown Library, 1946.

Adhemar, Jean, *Graphic Art of the Eighteenth Century*, London, Thames and Hudson, 1964.

Alexander, David, *Richard Newton and English Caricature in the 1790s*, exhibition catalogue, Manchester, Manchester University Press, 1998.

Amishai-Maisels, Ziva, *Depiction and Interpretation: The Influence of the Holocaust on the Visual Arts*, Oxford, Pergamon, 1993.

Anderson, Patricia, *The Printed Image and the Formation of Popular Culture*, Oxford, Oxford University Press, 1991.

Ashton, Doré (ed.), *Picasso on Art: A Selection of Views*, London, Penguin, 1977.

Athanassogolou-Kallmyer, Nina, 'Gericault's Severed Heads and Limbs: The Politics and Aesthetics of the Scaffold', *Art Bulletin*, 74:4 (1992) 599–618.

Atherton, Herbert, M., *Political Prints in the Age of Hogarth*, Oxford, Oxford University Press, 1974.

Baker, Housten A. Jr., 'Spike Lee and the Commerce of Culture', in Manthia Diawara (ed.), *Black American Cinema*, New York and London, Routledge, 1993.

Barrell, John, *The Political Theory of Painting from Reynolds to Hazlitt*, London, Yale University Press, 1986.

Black, Jeremy, *Maps and Politics*, London, Reaktion Books, 1997.

Boime, Albert, *Art in an Age of Revolution*, Chicago and London, University of Chicago Press, 1987.

Boime, Albert, 'Invisible in the Foreground', review of Honour's *The Image of the Black in Western Art*, *New York Times Book Review*, 2 April 1989.

Boime, Albert, 'Turner's *Slave Ship*: The Victims of Empire', *Turner Studies* 10:1 (1990) 42.

Boime, Albert, *The Art of Exclusion: Representing Blacks in the Nineteenth Century*, London, Thames and Hudson, 1990.

Brett, Guy, *Through Our Own Eyes: Popular Art and Modern History*, London, New Society Publishers, 1987.

Cannizzo, Jeanne, 'Doctor Livingstone Collects', in *David Livingstone and the Victorian Encounter with Africa*, exhibition catalogue, London, National Portrait Gallery Publications, 1996

Cantor, George, *Historic Black Landmarks, A Traveller's Guide*, Detroit, Visible Ink Press, 1991.

Clayton, Timothy, *The English Print 1688–1802*, New Haven and London, Mellon Centre and Yale University Press, 1997.

Cohen, Rena N., *The Black Man in Art*, Minneapolis, Lerner Publications, 1970.

Coombes, Annie, E. *Reinventing Africa: Museums, Material Culture and Popular Imagination*, New Haven and London, Yale University Press, 1994.

Dabydeen, David, *Hogarth's Blacks*, Manchester, Manchester University Press, 1987.

Devisse, Jean, *The Image of the Black in Western Art*, 2:1, Lausanne, Menil Foundation, 1979.

Devisse, Jean, and Michel Mollat, *The Image of the Black in Western Art*, 2:2, Lausanne, Menil Foundation, 1979.

The Dictionary of Visual Language, ed. Philip Thompson and Peter Davenport, London, Bergstrom and Boyle, 1980.

Dodgson, Campbell, *Prints in the Dotted Manner*, London, British Museum, 1937.

Donald, Diana, *The Age of Caricature: Satirical Prints in the Reign of George III*, New Haven and London, Yale University Press, 1996.

Doughty, Oswald, *A Victorian Romantic: Dante Gabriel Rossetti*, London, Oxford University Press, 1960.

Dunlap, William, *History of the Rise and Progress of the Arts of Design in the United States*, 3 vols, New York, Dover, 1969.

Edgerton, Samuel Y. Jnr., *Pictures and Punishment: Art and Criminal Prosecution during the Florentine Renaissance*, Ithaca and London, Cornell University Press, 1985.

Erdman, D. V., 'Blake's Vision of Slavery', *Journal of the Warbaurg and Courtauld Institutes*, 15 (1952) 242–52.

Fabre, Michel, 'Popular Civil War Propaganda: The Case of Patriotic Covers', *Journal of American Culture*, 3:2 (1980) 223–8.

Film and History Special Focus: The Black Image in Film, 25:1–2 (1995).

Friedman, Lester D., *Unspeakable Images: Ethnicity and the American Cinema*, Urbana and Chicago, University of Illinois Press, 1991.

Fuirer, Michele, *Whose Image? Anti-Racist Approaches to Photography and Visual Literacy*, Birmingham, Building Sights, 1989.

Gage, John, *Turner 1775–1851*, exhibition catalogue, London, Tate Gallery, 1974.

Georg Baselitz, Hamburg, Benedikt Taschen, 1990.

George, Mary Dorothy, *Catalogue of the Political and Personal Satires: Preserved in the Department of Prints and Drawings in the British Museum*, London, British Museum, 1935–54.

Gilman, Sander, 'Black Bodies, White Bodies: Toward an Iconography of Female Sexuality in Late Nineteenth-Century Art, Medicine, and Literature', in Henry Louis Gates Jnr. (ed.), *Race, Writing and Difference*, Chicago, University of Chicago Press, 1986.

Golden, Thelma (ed.), *Black Male: Representations of Masculinity in Contemporary American Art*, New York, Whitney Museum of Art, 1994.

Gombrich, E. H., *Meditations on a Hobby Horse and Other Essays on the Theory of Art*, Oxford, Phaidon, 1978.

Hall, Stuart, 'The Spectacle of the Other', in Stuart Hall (ed.), *Cultural Representation and Signifying Practice*, London, Sage Publications, 1997.

Hill, Draper, *Mr. Gillray the Caricaturist*, London, Phaidon, 1965.

Hill, Gillian, *Cartographic Curiosities*, London, British Museum Publications, 1978.

Hogarth, William, *Hogarth's Graphic Works*, ed. Ronald Paulson, Hartford, Yale University Press, 1965.

Honour, Hugh, *The Image of the Black in Western Art from the American Revolution to World War 1*, 4:1, Cambridge Mass., Harvard University Press, 1989.

Honour, Hugh, *The Image of the Black in Western Art From the American Revolution to World War 1*, 4:2, Cambridge Mass., Harvard University Press, 1989.

Hornung Clarence P., and Fridolf Johnson, *220 Years of American Graphic Art*, New York, George Brazillier, 1976.

Klingender, F. D., *Hogarth and English Caricature*, London, Pilot Press, 1944.

Kossoy, Boris, and Maria Luiza Tucci Carneiro, *O Olhar Europeu O Negro na Iconographia Brasileira do Século XIX*, São Paulo, Universidade de São Paulo, 1994.

Leppert, Richard, *Art and the Committed Eye: The Cultural Functions of Imagery*, Oxford and Boulder, Westview Press, 1996.

Maidment, Brian, *Reading Popular Prints 1790–1870*, Manchester, Manchester University Press, 1996.

Mann, Graciela, *The Twelve Prophets of Aleijadinho*, Austin and London, University of Texas Press, 1967.

Moores, Peter, 'Foreword', in Anthony Tibbles (ed.), *Transatlantic Slavery, Against Human Dignity*, London, Her Majesty's Stationary Office, 1994.

Odebrecht, Norbert, *Museu Afro Brasileiro*, museum catalogue, Salvador, Bahia, Museu Afro-Brasileiro, 1983.

Parry, Elwood, *The Image of the Indian and the Black Man in American Art 1590–1900*, New York, G. Brazillier, 1974.

Patten, Robert L., *George Cruikshank's Life, Times and Art*, 2 vols, Cambridge, Lutterworth, 1992 and 1996.

Patton, Sharon F., *African American Art*, Oxford and New York, Oxford University Press, 1998.

Paulson, Ronald, *Art and Revolution*, New Haven, Yale University Press, 1983.

Pieterse, Jan Nederveen, *White on Black: Images of Africa and Blacks in Western Popular Culture*, New Haven, Yale University Press, 1992.

Pomeroy, Jane R., 'Alexander Anderson's Life and Engravings before 1800, with a Checklist of Publications Drawn from His Diary', *Proceedings of the American Antiquarian Society*, 100:1 (1990) 137–230.

Pugh, D. Gordon, *Staffordshire Portrait Figures and Allied Subjects of the Victorian Era*, London, Barrie and Jenkins, 1970.

Puppi, Lionello, *Torment in Art: Pain, Violence and Martyrdom*, New York, Rizzoli, 1990.

Reilly, Bernard F. (ed), *American Political Prints 1766–1876: A Catalog of the Collections in the Library of Congress*, Boston: G. K. Hall, 1991.

Russell, H. Diane, *Jacques Callot: Prints and Related Drawings*, Washington, National Gallery of Art, 1985.

Ryan, James R., *Picturing Empire: Photography and the Visualisation of the British Empire*, London, Reaktion, 1997.

Schiff, Gert (ed.), *Johann Heinrich Fussli 1741–1825 Text und Oeuvrekatalog*, 2 vols, München, Verlag Berichthaus, Zurich, 1973.

Stafford, Barbara Maria, '"Peculiar Marks": Lavater and the Countenance of Blemished Thought', *Art Journal*, 46:3 (1987) 185–92.

Thistlewood, David, *Joseph Beuys: Diverging Critiques*, Liverpool, Liverpool University Press and Tate Gallery Liverpool, 1995.

Tisdall, Caroline, *Joseph Beuys Coyote*, Munich, Schirmer Mosel, 1976.

Tisdall, Caroline, *Joseph Beuys*, London, Thames and Hudson, 1979.

Tooley, Ronald Vere, *English Books with Coloured Plates, 1790–1860*, London, Dawson, 1954.

Turner, J. M. W., *The Paintings of J. M. W. Turner*, ed. Martin Butlin and Evelyn Joll, 2 vols, New Haven and London, Yale University Press, 1984.

Vilaire, Patrick, Michele Oriol and Reginald Cohen, *Images d'Espanola et de Saint-Domingue*, exhibition catalogue, Paris, Henri Deschampes, 1981.

Vogler, Richard A., *Graphic Works of George Cruikshank*, New York, Dover Publications, 1979.

Warhol, Andy, *Andy Warhol: A Retrospective*, exhibition catalogue, New York, Museum of Modern Art, 1989.

Weitenkampf, Frank, *American Graphic Art*, New York, Macmillan, 1970.

Whitton, Blair, *Paper Toys of the World*, Maryland, Cumberland Press, 1986.

Wilson, Jackie Napoleon, *Hidden Witness: African Americans in Early Photography*, exhibition catalogue, Santa Barbara, J. Paul Getty Museum, 1995.

Wilton, Andrew, *The Life and Works of J.M.W Turner*, London, Academy Editions, 1979.

Wolfe, Brian, 'All the World's a Code: Art and Ideology in Nineteenth-Century American Painting', *Art Journal*, 44 (1984) 328–40.

Wood, Marcus, '"All Right!": The Narrative of Henry "Box" Brown as a Test Case for the Racial Prescription of Rhetoric and Semiotics', *Proceedings of the American Antiquarian Society*, 107:1 (1997), 65–104.

Wood, Marcus, 'Imagining the Unspeakable and Speaking the Unimaginable: Visual Interpretation and the Middle Passage', *Lumen*, 16 (1997) 211–45.

Wood, Marcus, 'The Influence of English Radical Satire on Nineteenth-Century American Print Satire: David Claypoole Johnston's *The House That Jeff Built*, a Case Study', *Harvard Library Bulletin*, 2000, forthcoming.

Ziff, Jerrold, 'Turner's "Slave Ship": "What a red rag is to a bull"', *Turner Studies*, 3:4 (1984) 28.

General

Abbott, Geoffrey, *Rack, Rope and Red-Hot Pincers: A History of Torture and its Instruments*, London, Headline, 1993.

Aberbach, David, *Surviving Trauma: Loss, Literature and Psychoanalysis*, New Haven and London, Yale University Press, 1989.

Abzug, Robert, *Passionate Liberator: Theodore Dwight Weld and the Dilemma of Reform*, New York, Oxford University Press, 1980.

African American Poetry Full Text Data Base, Chadwyck Healey Inc., CD Rom, 1994.

The African Slave Trade from the Fifteenth to the Nineteenth Centuries. Reports and Papers of the Meeting of Experts Organised by UNESCO at Port Au Prince, Haiti, 31 January to 4 February 1978, Paris, UNESCO, second impression 1985.

Allen, Theodore W., *The Invention of the White Race, Volume One: Racial Oppression and Social Control*, London, Verso, 1994.

Alloula, Malek, *The Colonial Harem*, Manchester, Manchester University Press, 1987.

Altick, Richard D., *The Shows of London*, Cambridge Mass., Harvard University Press, 1978.

Amateur (pseud.), *An Impartial Account of the Battle Between Crib and Molineaux*, London, 1810.

Ammons, Elizabeth (ed.), *Critical Essays on Uncle Tom's Cabin*, Boston, G. K. Hall, 1980.

Ammons, Elizabeth, 'Stowe's Dream of the Mother Saviour: *Uncle Tom's Cabin* and American Women Writers before the 1920s', in Eric J. Sundquist (ed.), *New Essays on Uncle Tom's Cabin*, Cambridge, Cambridge University Press, 1986.

Anderson, Benedict, *Imaginary Communities: Reflections on the Origin and Spread of Nationalism,* London, Verso, 1983.

Anderson, S. E., *The Black Holocaust for Beginners*, New York, Writers and Readers Publishing, 1995.

Andrews, William L., *To Tell a Free Story: The First Century of Afro-American Autobiography, 1760–1865*, Chicago, University of Illinois Press, 1988.

Anstey, Roger, *The Atlantic Slave Trade and British Abolition 1760–1810*, London, Macmillan, 1975.

Augstein, H. F. (ed.), *Race: The Origins of an Idea, 1760–1850*, Bristol, Thoemmes Press, 1996.

Baldwin, James, 'Everybody's Protest Novel', *Partisan Review*, 16 (1949) 578–85.

Balibar, Etienne, and Immanuel Wallerstein, *Race, Nation, Class: Ambiguous Identities,* London, Verso, 1991.

Barker, Anthony J., *The African Link: British Attitudes to the Negro in the Era of the African Slave Trade 1550–1807*, London, Frank Cass, 1978.

Barker, Francis, and Margaret Iversen (eds), *Colonial Discourse, Postcolonial Theory,* Manchester, Manchester University Press, 1994.

Barthelemy, Anthony Gerrard, *Black Face, Maligned Race: The Representation of Blacks in English Drama from Shakespeare to Southerne*, Baton Rouge and London, Louisiana State University Press, 1987.

Barthes, Roland, *Image Music Text*, trans. Stephen Heath, London, Fontana, 1977.

Barthes, Roland, 'African Grammar' and 'Bichon and the Blacks', in David Theo Golberg (ed.), *Anatomy of Racism,* Minneapolis, University of Minnesota Press, 1990.

Bastide, Roger, *African Religions of Brazil*, Baltimore, University of Baltimore Press, 1978.

Baudrillard, Jean, *America*, trans. Chris Turner, London, Verso, 1987.

Baudrillard, Jean, *The Evil Demon of Images*, Sidney, Power Institute Publications, 1988.

Baum, Joan, *Mind-Forg'd Manacles: Slavery and the Romantic Poets*, North Haven, Conn., Archon Books, 1994.

Bethel, Elizabeth Rauh, *The Roots of African-American Identity: Memory and History in Free Antebellum Communities*, London, Macmillan, 1997.

Billington, Louis and Rosamand, '"Burning Zeal for Righteousnes": Women in the British Anti-Slavery Society, 1820–1860', in Jane Rendall (ed.), *Equal or Different: Women's Politics 1800–1914*, Oxford, Basil Blackwell, 1987.

Birdoff, Harry, *The World's Greatest Hit*, New York, S. F. Vanni, 1947.

Blackburn, Robin, *The Overthrow of Colonial Slavery 1776–1848*, London, Verso, 1990.

Blackburn, Robin, *The Making of New World Slavery From the Baroque to the Modern 1492–1800*, London, Verso, 1997.

Blackett, R. J. M., *Building an Antislavery Wall: Black Americans in the Atlantic Abolitionist Movement, 1830–1860*, Ithaca and London, Cornell University Press, 1983.

Blanchot, Maurice, *The Writing of the Disaster*, trans. Ann Smock, Lincoln and London, University of Nebraska Press, 1995.

Blassinghame, John W., *The Slave Community: Plantation Life in the Antebellum South*, New York and London, Oxford University Press, 1972.

Bloom, Harold, *The Ringers in the Tower: Studies in Romantic Tradition*, Chicago and London, University of Chicago Press, 1971.

Bloom, Harold, *Figures of Capable Imagination*, New York, Seabury Press, 1976.

Bolt, Christine, *Victorian Attitudes to Race*, London, Routledge and Keegan Paul, 1971.

Borer, Alain, *The Essential Joseph Beuys*, London, Thames and Hudson, 1996.

Boyle, Jimmy, *A Sense of Freedom*, London, Pan Books, 1977.

Brantlinger, Patrick, *Rule of Darkness: British Literature and Imperialism 1830–1914*, Ithaca and London, Cornell University Press, 1988.

Brooks, Chris, and Peter Faulkner (eds), *The White Man's Burdens: An Anthology of British Poetry of the Empire*, Exeter, University of Exeter Press, 1996.

Bull, Malcolm, 'Slavery and the Multiple Self', *New Left Review*, 231 (1998) 94–131.

Burford, E. J., and Sandra Shulman, *Of Bridles and Burnings: The Punishment of Women*, London, Robert Hale, 1992.

Burr, Frederick Martin, *Life and Works of Alexander Anderson, M. D., the First American Wood Engraver*, New York, 1893.

Bush, M. L. (ed.), *Serfdom and Slavery: Studies in Legal Bondage*, London, Longman, 1996.

Caruth, Cathy, *Unclaimed Experience: Trauma, Narrative and History*, Baltimore and London, Johns Hopkins University Press, 1996.

Caruth, Cathy (ed.), *Trauma: Explorations in Memory*, Baltimore and London, Johns Hopkins University Press, 1995.

Cassuto, Leonard, *The Inhuman Race: The Racial Grotesque in American Literature and Culture*, New York, Columbia University Press, 1997.

Clifford, Hugh, *The Predicament of Culture: Twentieth-Century Ethnography, Literature, and Art*, Cambridge, Harvard University Press, 1988.

Clifford, James, and Georg E. Marcus (eds), *Writing Culture: The Poetic and Politics of Ethnography*, Berkeley, University of California Press, 1986.

Cohn, Norman, *Noah's Flood: The Genesis Story in Western Thought*, New Haven and London, Yale University Press, 1996.

Cohen, William B., *The French Encounter with Africans: White Response to Blacks 1530–1880*, Bloomington and London, University of Indiana Press, 1980.

Connerton, Paul, *How Societies Remember*, Cambridge, Cambridge University Press, 1989.

Conrad, Robert, *The Destruction of Brazilian Slavery*, Berkeley, University of California Press, 1972.

Coupland, Sir Reginald, *The British Anti-Slavery Movement*, Oxford, Oxford University Press, 1933.

Coveney, Peter, *The Image of Childhood: The Individual and Society: A Study of the Theme in English Literature*, London, Penguin Books, 1967.

Cowling, Mary, *The Artist as Anthropologist: The Representation of Type and Character in Victorian Art*, Cambridge, Cambridge University Press, 1989.

Coxall, Helen, 'Speaking Other Voices', in Eilean Hooper-Greenhill (ed.), *Cultural Diversity: Developing Museum Audiences in Britain*, London, Leicester University Press, 1997.

Cragg, Gerald R., *Puritanism in the Period of the Great Persecution: 1660–1688*, Cambridge, Cambridge University Press, 1957.

Craton, Michael, *Sinews of Empire: A Short History of British Slavery*, London, Temple Smith, 1974.

Craton, Michael, *Searching for the Invisible Man: Slaves and Plantation Life in Jamaica*, Cambridge Mass., Harvard University Press, 1978.

Craton, Michael, James Walvin and David Wright (eds), *Slavery, Abolition and Emancipation*, London, Longman, 1976.

Crimp, Douglas, *On the Museum's Ruins*, Cambridge Mass. and London, MIT Press, 1996.

Curtin, Philip D., *The Image of Africa: British Ideas and Action 1780–1850*, Madison, Wisconsin University Press, 1964

Curtin, Philip D., *The Atlantic Slave Trade, A Census*, Madison, Wisconsin University Press, 1969.

Curtis, Perry L. Jnr., *Apes and Angels: The Irishman in Victorian Caricature*, Newton Abbot, David and Charles, 1971.

Dahl, Edward H. (ed.), 'Responses to J. B. Harley's article, "Deconstructing the Map"', *Cartographica*, 26:3–4 (1989) 89–127.

Dalton, Karen C. Chambers, '"The Alphabet is an Abolitionist:" Literacy and African Americans in the Emancipation Era', *Massachusetts Review*, 32:4 (1992) 545–73

Davis, Charles T., and Henry Louis Gates Jnr. (eds), *The Slave's Narrative*, Oxford and New York, Oxford University Press, 1985.

Davis, David Brion, *The Problem of Slavery in the Age of Revolution 1770–1823*, Ithaca, Cornell University Press, 1975.

Davis, David Brion, *The Emancipation Moment*, Gettysburgh, Gettysburgh College, 1983.

Davis, David Brion, *The Problem of Slavery in Western Culture*, Oxford, Oxford University Press, 1988.

Davis, David Brion, 'The Ends of Slavery', *New York Review of Books*, 36:5 (1989) 30–1.

Diddleton, David, and Derek Edwards (eds), *Collective Remembering*, London, Sage, 1990.

Donald, James, and Ali Rattansi, *'Race' Culture and Difference*, London, Sage, 1992.

Drescher, Seymour, *Econocide: British Slavery in the Era of Abolition*, Pittsburgh, University of Pittsburgh Press, 1977.

Drescher, Seymour, 'The Ending of the Slave Trade and the Evolution of European Scientific Racism', in Joseph E. Inikori and Stanley Engerman (eds), *The Atlantic Slave Trade: Effects on Economies, Societies and Peoples in Africa and the Americas*, Durham and London, Duke University Press, 1992.

Drescher, Seymour, 'Whose Abolition? Popular Pressure and the Ending of the British Slave Trade', *Past and Present*, 142 (1994) 136–66.

Drescher, Seymour, and Stanley L. Engerman (eds), *A Historical Guide to World Slavery*, New York, Oxford University Press, 1998.

duBois, Page, *Torture and Truth*, London and New York, Routledge, 1991.

Duckworth, Sarah Smith, 'Stowe's Construction of an African Persona and the Creation of White Identity for a New World Order', in Lowance Westbrook and De Prospo (eds), *The Stowe Debate*, Amherst, University of Massachusetts Press, 1994.

Duff, Anthony, *Punishment*, Aldershot, Dartmouth, 1993.

Dumond, Dwight Lowell, *Anti-Slavery: The Crusade for Freedom in America*, Ann Arbour, University of Michigan Press, 1961.

Dykes, Eva Beatrice, *The Negro in English Romantic Thought, or a Study in Sympathy for the Oppressed*, Washington, D.C., 1942.

Edwards, Paul, *Black Personalities in the Era of the Slave Trade*, London, Macmillan, 1983.

Egan, Pierce, *Boxiana Sketches of Ancient and Modern Pugilism*, London, 1812.

Elkins, Stanley, *Slavery: A Problem in American Institutional and Intellectual Life*, New York, Grosset and Dunlap, 1963.

Elliott, R. C., *Satire and Magic*, Princeton, Princeton University Press, 1960.

Ellison, Ralph, *Shadow and Act*, New York, Random House, 1953.

Erdman, D. V., *Blake: Prophet Against Empire*, Princeton, Princeton University Press, 1969.

Escobar, A., 'Discourse and Power in Development: Michel Foucault and the Relevance of his Work to the Third World', *Alternatives*, 10 (1984–85) 377–400.

Etlin, Richard A., *The Architechture of Death*, Cambridge Mass., Harvard University Press, 1984.

Evans, Richard J., *Rituals of Retribution: Capital Punishment in Germany 1600–1987*, Harmondsworth, Penguin, 1996.

Felker, Christopher D., *Reinventing Cotton Mather in the American Renaissance*, Boston, Northeastern University Press, 1993.

Felman, Shoshana, and Dori Laub, *Testimony: Crises of Witnessing in Literature, Psychoanalysis, and History*, New York and London, Routledge, 1992.

Ferguson, Moira, *Subject to Others: British Women Writers and Colonial Slavery, 1670–1834*, London, Routledge, 1992.

The Fight Against Racism: A Pictorial History of Asians and Afro-Caribbeans in Britain Book Four, London, Institute of Race Relations, 1986.

Finkelman, Paul, *An Imperfect Union: Slavery, Federation and Comity*, Chapel Hill, University of North Carolina Press, 1981.

Finkelman Paul, *Slavery in the Courtroom*, Washington, Library of Congress, 1985.

Finkelman Paul, *His Soul Goes Marching On: Responses to John Brown and the Harper's Ferry Raid*, Charlottesville, University Press of Virginia, 1995.

Finkelman, Paul, *Dred Scott v Sandford: A Brief History with Documents*, Boston, Bedford Books, 1997.

Fisch, Audrey A., 'Exhibiting Uncle Tom', *Nineteenth Century Contexts*, 17:2 (1993) 145–58.

Fisher, Dexter, and Robert B. Stepto (eds), *African American Literature*, New York, Modern Language Association of America, 1979.

Fladeland, Betty, *Abolitionists and Working-Class Problems in the Age of Industrialisation*, Baton Rouge, Louisiana State University Press, 1984.

Foner, Philip S., *History of Black Americans from the Emergence of the Cotton Kingdom to the Eve of the Compromise of 1850*, 3 vols, Westport and London, Greenwood, 1983.

Ford, Glyn, *Fascist Europe: The Rise of Racism and Xenophobia*, London, Pluto Press, 1992.

Foster, Frances Smith, *Written by Herself: Literary Production by African American Women, 1746–1892*, Bloomington and Indianapolis, Indiana University Press, 1993.

Fox-Genovese, Elizabeth, *Within the Plantation Household*, Chapel Hill, University of North Carolina Press, 1988.

Fraser, Antonia, *A History of Toys*, London, Weidenfield and Nicolson, 1966.

Fredrickson, George M., *The Black Image in the White Mind*, New York, Harper and Row, 1971.

Freyre, Gilberto, *Os Escravo nos Anúncios de Jornais Brasileiros do Século XIX*, São Paulo, Companhia Editoria Nacional, 1979.

Friedlander, Saul (ed.), *Probing the Limits of Representation*, Cambridge, Harvard University Press, 1992.

Frostick, Elizabeth (ed.), *Slavery Living History Fact Pack*, Hull, Hull City Museums and Art Galleries, 1989.

Fryer, Peter, *Staying Power: The History of Black People in Britain*, London, Pluto Press, 1984.

Gara, Larry, 'The Professional Fugitive in the Abolition Movement', *Wisconsin Magazine of History*, 48:2 (1965) 196–204.

Gates, Henri Louis Jnr., 'Binary Oppositions in Chapter One of *Narrative of the Life of Frederick Douglass an American Slave Written by Himself*', in Dexter Fisher and Robert B. Stepto (eds), *African American Literature*, New York, Modern Language Association of America, 1979.

Gates, Henry Louis Jnr., *Figures in Black: Words, Signs and the Racial Self*, New York and London, Oxford University Press, 1987.

Gates, Henry Louis Jnr., *The Signifying Monkey*, New York, Oxford University Press, 1988.

Gates, Henri Louis Jnr., *Loose Canons: Notes on the Culture Wars*, Oxford, Oxford University Press, 1992.

Gattrell, V. A. C., *The Hanging Tree: Execution and the English People 1770–1868*, Oxford, Oxford University Press, 1996.

Geipel, John, 'Brazil's African Legacy', *History Today*, 47:8 (1997) 18–24.

Gerzina, Gretchen, *Black England: Life Before Emancipation*, London, John Murray, 1995.

Gifford, Lord Tony, Walley Brown and Ruth Bundy, *Loosen the Shackles: First Report of the Liverpool 8 Inquiry into Race Relations in Liverpool*, London, Karia Press, 1989.

Gilman, Sander, *Difference and Pathology: Stereotypes of Sexuality, Race and Madness*, Ithaca, Cornell University Press, 1985.

Gilman, Sander, *Sexuality, an Illustrated History: Representing the Sexual in Medicine and Culture from the Middle Ages to the Age of AIDS*, New York; Chichester, Wiley, 1989.

Gilman, Sander, '"I'm Down on Whores": Race and Gender in Victorian London', in David Theo Goldberg (ed.), *Anatomy of Racism*, Minneapolis and London, University of Minnesota Press, 1990.

Gilroy, Paul, *The Black Atlantic: Modernity and Double Consciousness*, London, Verso, 1993.

Gilroy, Paul, *Small Acts,* London, Serpent's Tail, 1993.

Glenn, Myra C., *Campaigns Against Corporal Punishment: Prisoners, Sailors, Women and Children in Antebellum America*, Albany, State University of New York Press, 1984.

Goldberg, David Theo, *Racial Subjects: Writing on Race in America*, New York and London, Routledge, 1997.

Gosset, Thomas F., *Uncle Tom's Cabin and American Culture*, Dallas, Southern Methodist University Press, 1985.

Graham, John, *Lavater's Essays on Physiognomy: A Study in the History of Ideas*, Berne, Peter Lang, 1979.

Green, Vivian, *The Madness of Kings: Personal Trauma and the Fate of Nations*, New York, St Martin's Press, 1993.

Greenblatt, Stephen, 'Murdering Peasants: Status Genre and the Representation of Rebellion', *Representations* 1:1 (1983) 1–29.

Griswold, Charles L., 'The Vietnam Veterans Memorial and the Washington Mall: Philosophical Thoughts on Political Iconography', in Harriet F. Seine and Sally Webster (eds), *Critical Issues in Public Art: Content, Context, and Controversy*, New York, Harper Collins, 1992.

Hall, Catherine, *White, Male and Middle Class: Explorations in Feminism and History* Cambridge, Polity Press, 1988.

Hall, Catherine, 'Imperial Man: Edward Eyre in Australasia and the West Indies 1833–66', in Bill Schwarz (ed.), *The Expansion of England: Race, Ethnicity and Cultural History*, London and New York, Routledge, 1996.

Hall, David, *Worlds of Wonder, Days of Judgement,* Cambridge, Harvard University Press, 1985.

Haller, John S. Jnr., *Outcasts from Evolution: Scientific Attitudes to Racial Inferiority*, Urbana and London, University of Illinois Press, 1971.

Haller, William, 'John Foxe and the Puritan Revolution', in Richard F. Jones (ed.), *The Seventeenth Century: Studies in the History of English Thought and Literature from Bacon to Pope*, Stanford, Stanford University Press, 1965.

Halttunen, Karen, 'Humanitariansm and the Pornography of Pain in Anglo-American Culture', *American Historical Review,* 100:2 (1995) 308–9.

Hamlyn History of Punishment and Torture, London, Hamlyn, 1996.

Hannaford, Ivan, *Race: The History of an Idea in the West*, Baltimore, Johns Hopkins University Press, 1996.

Hanson, Elizabeth, 'Torture and Truth in Renaissance England', *Representations,* 34 (1991) 53–84.

Harley, J. B., 'Deconstructing the Map', *Cartographica*, 26:2 (1989) 1–20.

Harrison, J. F. C., *The Second Coming: Popular Millenarianism 1780–1850*, London, Routledge and Keegan Paul, 1979.

Hartman, Geoffrey, 'Darkness Visible', in Geoffrey Hartman (ed.), *The Shapes of Memory,* Oxford, Blackwell, 1993.

Hawkins, W. S., *Plymouth Armada Heroes: The Hawkins Family,* Plymouth, William Brendon and Son, 1888.

Henderson, Mae G., 'Toni Morrison's *Beloved*: Re-Membering the Body as Historical Text', in Hortense J. Spillers (ed.), *Comparative American Identities: Race, Sex and Nationality in the Modern Text*, London, Routledge, 1991.

Hennesy, James Pope, *Sins of the Fathers: A Study of the Atlantic Slave Traders 1441–1807*, London, Weidenfield and Nicolson, 1967.

Henriques, Louis Fernando, *Children of Caliban: Miscegenation*, London, Secker and Warburg, 1974.

Herbert, Christopher, *Culture and Anomie: Ethnographic Imagination in the Nineteenth Century*, Chicago, Chicago University Press, 1991.

Higginbottom, A. Jnr., *In the Matter of Colour: Race and the American Legal Process in the Colonial Period*, New York, Oxford University Press, 1980.

Hildreth, Margaret Holbrook, *Harriet Beecher Stowe: A Bibliography*, Hamden, Archon, 1976.

Hilton, Tim, *Ruskin: The Early Years*, New Haven and London, Yale University Press, 1985.

hooks bell, *Black Looks: Race and Representation*, Boston, South End Press, 1975.

hooks, bell, *Outlaw Culture: Resisting Representations,* New York and London, Routledge, 1994.

Hooper-Greenhill, Eilean, *Museums and the Shaping of Knowledge*, London, Routledge, 1992.

Horne, Donald, *The Great Museum: The Re-Presentation of History*, London, Pluto, 1984.

Howsam, Leslie, *Cheap Bibles: Nineteenth-Century Publishing and the British and Foreign Bible Society*, Cambridge, Cambridge University Press, 1991.

Hovet, Theodore R., *The Master Narrative: Harriet Beecher Stowe's Subversive Story of Master and Slave in Uncle Tom's Cabin and Dred*, New York, University Press of America, 1989.

Hudson, Larry E. Jnr. (ed.), *Working Toward Freedom: Slave Society and Domestic Economy in the American South*, New York, University of Rochester Press, 1994.

Hyam, Ronald, *Empire and Sexuality: The British Experience,* Manchester, Manchester University Press, 1990.

Inikori, Joseph E., and Stanley Engerman (eds), *The Atlantic Slave Trade: Effects on Economies, Societies and Peoples in Africa and the Americas*, Durham and London, Duke University Press, 1992.

Janowitz, Annie, *England's Ruins: Poetic Purpose and the National Landscape*, Oxford, Basil Blackwell, 1990.

James, C. L. R., *The Future in the Present: Selected Writings,* London, Allison Busby, 1977.

James, C. L. R., *The Black Jacobins*, London, Alison and Busby, [1963] 1989.

Johnson, Lemuel A., *The Devil, the Gargoyle, and the Buffoon: The Negro as Metaphor in Western Literature*, Port Washington, Kennitkat Press, 1969.

Jordan, Winthrop D., *White Over Black: American Attitudes Towards the Negro, 1550–1812*, Harmondsworth, Penguin, 1968.

Karcher, Carolyn, *The First Woman in the Republic: A Cultural Biography of Lydia Maria Child,* Durham and London, Duke University Press, 1994.

Kiernan, Victor, *The Lords of Human Kind: Black Men, Yellow Men, and White Men in an Age of Empire*, London, Weidenfeld and Nicholson, 1969.

Kirkham, Bruce E., *The Building of Uncle Tom's Cabin*, Knoxville, University of Tennessee Press, 1977.

Knapp, Steven, 'Collective Memory and the Actual Past', *Representations*, 26:1 (1989) 123–47.

Knott, John R., *Discourses of Martyrdom in English Literature 1563–1694*, Cambridge, Cambridge University Press, 1993.

Knowell-Smith, Simon, *International Copyright Law and the Publisher in the Reign of Queen Victoria*, Oxford, Oxford University Press, 1968.

Kocks, D., 'L'esthétique des planches de l'*Encyclopédie*', in Peter-Eckhard Knabe and Edgar Mass (eds), *L'Encyclopédie et Diderot*, Koln, DME, coll. 'Kolner Schriften zur Romanischen Kultur 2/Textes et Documents', 1985.

Kolchin, Peter, *American Slavery 1619–1877*, London, Penguin, 1995.

Kuya, Dorothy, 'Racism in Children's Books in Britain', in Roy Preiswerk (ed.), *The Slant of the Pen: Racism in Children's Books*, Geneva, World Council of Churches, 1980.

Labode, Modupe, 'From Heathen Kraal to Christian Home: Anglican Mission Education and African Christian Girls 1850–1900', in Fiona Bowie, Deborah Kirkwood and Shirley Ardener (eds), *Women and Missions: Past and Present Anthropological and Historical Perceptions*, Providence and Oxford, Berg, 1993.

LaCapra, Dominick, *Representing the Holocaust: History, Theory, Trauma*, Ithaca and London, Cornell University Press, 1994.

Lamming George, *In the Castle of My Skin*, London, Michael Joseph, 1953.

Lamming, George, *The Pleasures of Exile*, London, Michael Joseph, 1960.

Lamming George, *Natives of My person*, London, Holt Rinehart and Wintson, 1972 .

Lane, Brian, *Encyclopaedia of Cruel and Unusual Punishment*, London, Virgin Publishing, 1993.

Lapsansky, Phillip, 'Graphic Discord: Abolitionist and Anti-abolitionist Images', in Jean Fagin Yellin and John C. Van Horne (eds), *The Abolitionist Sisterhood: Women's Political Culture in Ante-bellum America*, Ithaca, Cornell University Press, in collaboration with the Library Company of Philadelphia, 1994.

Law, Robin, *The Slave Coast of West Africa 1550–1750: The Impact of the Atlantic Slave Trade on an African Society*, Oxford, Clarendon Press, 1991.

Lewis, Gladys S., *Message, Messenger and Response: Puritan Forms and Cultural Reformation in Harriet Beecher Stowe's Uncle Tom's Cabin*, New York, University Press of America, 1994.

Lindsay, Jack, *J. M. W. Turner, his Life and Work: A Critical Biography*, London, Long Adams and Mackay, 1966.

Lindsay, Jack, *The Sunset Ship: The Poems of J. M. W. Turner*, London, Scorpion Press, 1966.

Lives and Battles of Famous Black Pugilists from Molineaux to Jackson, New York, 1890.

Loades, D. M., *John Foxe and the English Reformation*, London, Scolar, 1997.

Lorimer, Douglas A., *Colour, Class and the Victorians: English Attitudes to the Negro in the Mid-Nineteenth Century*, Leicester, Leicester University Press, 1978.

Lossing, Benson J., *A Memorial of Alexander Anderson, M. D., the First Engraver on Wood in America*, New York, 1872.

Lott, Eric, 'Love and Theft: The Racial Unconscious of Blackface Minstrelsy', *Representations*, 39:2 (1992) 22 49.

Lott, Tommy L., 'Black Vernacular Representation and Cultural Malpractice', in David Theo Goldberg (ed.), *Multi-Culturalism: A Critical Reader*, London, Basil Blackwell, 1994.

Lovejoy, David S., *Religious Enthusiasm in the New World: Heresy to Revolution*, Cambridge Mass., Harvard University Press, 1985.

Lovejoy, Paul E., *Transformations in Slavery: A History of Slavery in Africa*, Cambridge, Cambridge University Press, 1983.

Lowance, Mason I. Jnr., Ellen E. Westbrook and R. C. De Prospo (eds), *The Stowe Debate: Rhetorical Strategies in Uncle Tom's Cabin*, Amherst, University of Massachusetts Press, 1994.

Lumley, Robert (ed.), *The Museum Time Machine: Putting Cultures on Display*, London, Routledge, 1988.

Luttrell, Barbara, *Mirabeau*, Hemel Hempstead, Harvester Wheatsheaf, 1990.

Lyotard, Jean François, *The Post Modern Condition*, Manchester, Manchester University Press, 1984.

McCalman, Iain, 'Anti-Slavery and Ultra-Radicalism in Early Nineteenth-Century England: The Case of Robert Wedderburn', *Slavery and Abolition* 7:2 (1986) 100–17.

McCalman, Iain, *Radical Underworld: Prophets, Revolutionaries and Pornographers in London 1790–1845*, Cambridge, Cambridge University Press, 1988.

McCalman, Iain (ed. and intr), *The Horrors of Slavery and Other Writings by Robert Wedderburn*, Edinburgh, Edinburgh University Press, 1991.

Malchow, H. L., *Gothic Images of Race in Nineteenth-Century Britain*, Stanford, Stanford University Press, 1996.

Malin, James C., *John Brown and the Legend of Fifty Six*, Philadelphia, American Philosophical Society, 1942.

Mama, Amina, *Beyond the Masks: Race, Gender and Subjectivity*, London, Routledge, 1995.

Mansir, Richard A., *A Modeler's Guide to Naval Architecture*, New York, Moonraker, 1983.

Marcus, Steven, *The Other Victorians: A Study of Sexuality and Pornography in Mid Nineteenth-Century England*, London, Weidenfeld and Nicolson, 1966.

Mark, Peter, *Africans in European Eyes: The Portrayal of Black Africans in Fourteenth and Fifteenth Century Europe*, New York, Maxwell School, Syracuse University, 1974.

Merriman, Nick, and Mima Poovaya-Smith, 'Making Culturally Diverse Histories', in Gaynor Kavanah (ed.), *Making Histories in Museums*, London, Leicester University Press, 1996.

Michael, Charles D., *The Slave and his Champions*, London, S. W. Partridge, 1915.

Mirabeau, Gabriel Honoré de Raqueti Compte de, *Mémoires Biographiques, Littéraires et politiques de Mirabeau Écrits par Lui-Même, Par son Père, son oncle et son fils adoptif*, 8 vols, Paris, 1834.

Morgan, Philip D., 'Colonial South Carolina Runaways: Their Significance for Slave Culture', *Slavery and Abolition*, 6:3 (1985) 57–79.

Morgan, Philip D., *Slave Counterpoint: Black Culture in the Eighteenth-Century Chesapeake and Low Country*, Chapel Hill and London, University of North Carolina Press, 1998.

Morrison, Anthea, 'Coleridge's Greek Prize Ode on the Slave Trade', in J. R. Watson (ed.), *An Infinite Complexity: Essays in Romanticism*, Edinburgh, Edinburgh University Press (for the University of Durham), 1983.

Morrison, Toni, *Playing in the Dark*, London, Picador, 1993.

Moses, Wilson Jeremiah, *Black Messiah's and Uncle Toms*, University Park, Pennsylvania State University Press, 1982.

Murray, Timothy, *Drama Trauma: Spectres of Race and Sexuality in Performance, Video, and Art*, London and New York, Routledge, 1997.

Nacimento, Regina Aparecida do Nascimento, and Isabel Fonseca da Cruz, *Encyclopédia Negra Brasileira*, São Paulo, Universidade de São Paulo, 1994.

Nathan, Hans, *Dan Emmett and the Rise of Early Negro Minstrelsy*, Norman, University of Oklahoma Press, 1962.

Nattras, Leonora, *William Cobbett: The Politics of Style*, Cambridge, Cambridge University Press, 1992.

Newberry, Michael, 'Eaten Alive: Slavery and Celebrity in Antebellum America', *English Literary History*, 61:1 (1994) 159–87.

Nicholl, Charles, *The Creature in the Map: Sir Walter Ralegh's Quest for Eldorado*, London, Vintage, 1996.

Norden, Linda Van, *The Black Feet of the Peacock: The Color-Concept 'Black' From the Greeks Through the Renaissance*, ed. and compiled John Pollock, New York and London, University Press of America, 1985.

Oldfield, J. R., *Popular Politics and British Anti-Slavery: The Mobilisation of Public Opinion Against the Slave Trade 1787–1807*, Manchester, Manchester University Press, 1995.

Olds, Bruce, *Raising Holy Hell*, London, Quartet, 1996.

Olney, James, '"I was born". Slave Narratives, their Status as Autobiography and as Literature', in Henry Louis Gates Jnr. and Charles T. Davis (eds), *The Slave Narrative*, New York and London, Oxford University Press, 1985.

Orico, Osvaldo, *O Tigre da Abolição,* Rio de Janeiro, Grafica Olimpica, 1953.

Osgood, Nancy, 'Josiah Walcott, Artist and Associationist', *Old Time New England*, 76:264 (1998) 5–34.

Palmie, Stephan (ed.), *Slave Cultures and the Cultures of Slavery*, Knoxville, University of Tennessee Press, 1995.

Patterson, Orlando, *Slavery and Social Death: A Comparative Study*, Cambridge Mass. and London, Harvard University Press, 1982.

Peters, Edward, *Torture*, Philadelphia, University of Pennsylvania Press, 1996.

Pettifer, Ernest W., *Punishments of Former Days*, Bradford, Clegg & Son, 1939.

Plasa, Carl, and Betty J. Ring (eds), *The Discourse of Slavery: Aphra Behn to Toni Morrison*, London, Routledge, 1994.

Potkay, Adam, *Black Atlantic Writers of the Eighteenth Century: Living the New Exodus in England and the Americas*, London, Macmillan, 1995

Powers, Edwin, *Crime and Punishment in Early Massachusetts: A Documentary History*, Boston, Beacon Press, 1966.

Preble, George Henry, *Our Flag: The Origin and Progress of the Flag of the United States*, New York, 1872.

Price, Richard, *Representations of Slavery: John Gabriel Stedman's 'Minnesota' Manuscripts*, Minnesota, James Ford Bell Lecture, 1989.

Primoratz, Igor, 'Punishment as Language', in Antony Duff (ed.), *Punishment*, Dartmouth, International Research Library of Philosophy, 1993, 55–75.

Quarles, Benjamin, *Black Abolitionists*, New York, Oxford University Press, 1969.

Quinby, Lee, *Freedom: Foucault and the Subject of America*, Boston, North Eastern University Press, 1991.

Raboteau, *Slave Religion*, New York and Oxford, Oxford University Pres, 1978.

Rachames, Louis, *The Abolitionists,* New York, Capricorn Books, 1964.

Rawley, James A., *The Transatlantic Slave Trade*, New York and London, Norton, 1981.

Reynolds, David S., *Beneath the American Renaissance: The Subversive Imagination in the Age of Emerson and Melville*, New York, Alfred Knopf, 1988.

Ricoeur, Paul, *History and Truth*, trans. Charles Kelbley, Evanston, Northwestern University Press, 1965.

Ripley, C. Peter (ed.), *The Black Abolitionist Papers*, 5 vols, Chapel Hill and London, University of North Carolina Press, 1985–92.

Roth, Michael S., *The Ironist's Cage: Memory, Trauma, and the Construction of History*, New York, Columbia University Press, 1995.

Rushdy, Asnaf, '"Rememory": Primal Scenes and Constructions in Toni Morrison's Novels', *Contemporary Literature*, 31 (1990) 300–23.

Said, Edward, *Culture and Imperialism*, London, Vintage, 1994.

'Sam', Genuine 'Dicky' (pseud.), *Liverpool and Slavery*, Liverpool, 1884.

Samuel, Raphael, *Patriotism: The Making and Unmaking of British National Identity*, 3 vols, London, Routledge, 1989.

Sandiford, Keith, *Measuring the Moment: Strategies of Protest in Eighteenth-century Afro-English Writing*, New York, Associated Universities Press, 1988.

Scarry, Elaine, *The Body in Pain*, London and New York, Oxford University Press, 1985.

Scarry, Elaine, *Resisting Representation*, New York, Oxford University Press, 1994.

Schama, Simon, *Dead Certainties (Unwarranted Speculations)*, London, Granta Books (in association with Penguin Books), 1991.

Schwartz, Bill (ed.), *The Expansion of England: Race, Ethnicity and Cultural History*, New York and London, Routledge, 1996.

Segal, Ronald, *The Black Diaspora*, London, Faber, 1995.

Sellin, J. Thorsten, *Slavery and the Penal System,* New York, Oxford and Amsterdam, Elsevier, 1976.

Sheleff, Leon Shaskolsky, *Ultimate Penalties: Capital Punishment, Life Imprisonment, Physical Torture*, Columbus, Ohio State University Press, 1987.

Silver, Rollo G., *The American Printer, 1787–1825*, Charlottesville, University Press of Virginia, 1967.

Simkin, John, *Slavery: An Illustrated History of Black Resistance*, Brighton, Spartacus, 1988.

Slavery: An Introduction to the African Holocaust, Revised Edition with Special Reference to Liverpool 'Capital of the Slave Trade', Liverpool, Black History Resource Working Group, 1997.

Small, Stephen, 'Contextualising the Black Presence in British Museums: Representations, Resources and Response', in Eilean Hooper-Greenhill (ed.), *Cultural Diversity: Developing Museum Audiences in Britain*, London, Leicester University Press, 1977.

Smith, Abbot Emerson, *Colonists in Bondage: White Servitude and Convict Labour in America 1607–1776*, Chapel Hill, University of North Carolina Press, 1947.

Smith, Bernard, *European Vision and the South Pacific 1768–1850*, Oxford, Oxford University Press, 1960.

Smith, Billy G., and Richard Wojtowicz, *Blacks who Stole Themselves: Advertisements for Runaways in the Pennsylvania Gazette, 1728–90*, Philadelphia, University of Pennsylvania Press, 1989.

Smith, John Stores, *Mirabeau: A Life History*, 2 vols, London, 1848.

Spillers, Hortense J. (ed), *Comparative American Identities*, New York and London, Routledge, 1991.

Spivak, Gayatri, 'Can the Subaltern Speak', in Cary Nelson and Lawrence Grossberg (eds), *Marxism and the Interpretation of Culture*, London, Macmillan, 1988.

Stachniewski, John, *The Persecutory Imagination: English Puritanism and the Literature of Religious Despair*, Oxford, Clarendon Press, 1991.

Stammers, M. K., 'Guineamen: Some Technical Aspects of Slave Ships', in Anthony Tibbles (ed.), *Transatlantic Slavery Against Human Dignity*, exhibition catalogue, London, HMSO, 1994.

Stanton, William, *The Leopard's Spots: Scientific Attitudes Toward Race in America 1815–59*, Chicago and London, University of Chicago Press, 1960.

Stepan, Nancy, *The Idea of Race in Science: Great Britain 1800–1960*, London, Macmillan, 1982.

Stepto, Robert B., *From Behind the Veil: A Study of Afro-American Narrative*, Urbana, Chicago and London, University of Illinois Press, 1979.

Stewart, James Brewer, *Holy Warriors: The Abolitionists and American Slavery*, New York, Farrar Strous and Giroux, 1993.

Still, William, *The Underground Railroad: A Record of Facts*, Philadelphia, Porter and Coates, 1872.

Stoler, Ann Laura, *Race and the Education of Desire: Foucault's History of Sexuality and the Colonial Order of Things*, Durham and London, Duke University Press, 1995.

Sturken, Marita, 'The Wall, the Screen, and the Image: The Vietnam Veteran's Memorial', *Representations*, 35:3 (1991) 118–42.

Suhl, Isabelle, 'Doctor Dolittle – The Great White Father', in Judith Stinton (ed.), *Racism and Sexism in Children's Books*, London, Writers and Readers Publishing Cooperative, 1979.

Sulivan, G. L., *Dhow Chasing in Zanzibar Waters and on the Eastern Coast of Africa Narrative of five years' experiences in the suppression of the slave trade*, London, 1875.

Sundquist, Eric J. (ed.), *New Essays on Uncle Tom's Cabin*, Cambridge, Cambridge University Press, 1986.

Sypher, Wylie, *Guinea's Captive Kings: British Anti-Slavery Literature of the xviii'th Century*, Chapel Hill, University of North Carolina Press, 1942.

Tal, Kali, *Worlds of Hurt: Reading the Literatures of Trauma*, Cambridge, Cambridge University Press, 1996.

Taussig, Michael, *Shamanism, Colonialism and the Wild Man: A Study in Terror and Healing*, Chicago, Chicago University Press, 1987.

Taussig, Michael, *The Nervous System*, New York and London, Routledge, 1992.

Temperley, Howard, *British Anti-Slavery 1833–1870*, London, Longman, 1972.

Thomas, Hugh, *The Slave Trade: The History of the Atlantic Slave Trade 1440–1870*, London, Picador, 1998.

Thomas, Isiah, *The History of Printing in America,* ed. Marcus A. McCorison, New York, Imprint Society, 1970.

Thompson, E. P., *The Making of the English Working Class*, London, Penguin, 1965.

Thornton, John, *Africa and Africans in the Making of the Atlantic 1400–1680*, Cambridge and New York, Cambridge University Press, 1998.

Thrower, Norman, *Maps and Civilisation: Cartography in Culture and Society*, Chicago and London, University of Chicago Press, 1996.

Tise, Larry B., *Proslavery: A History of the Defence of Slavery in America, 1701–1840*, Athens and London, University of Georgia Press, 1987.

Todd, Janet, *Sensibility: An Introduction*, London and New York, Methuen, 1986.

Tomkins, Jane, *Sensational Designs: The Cultural Work of American Fiction 1790–1860*, Oxford, Oxford University Press, 1985.

Tooley, R. V., *Maps and Map-Makers*, London, Batsford 1987.

Torgovnik, Marianna, *Gone Primitive: Savage Intellects, Modern Lives*, London and Chicago, Chicago University Press, 1990.

Turner, James, *Reckoning with the Beast: Animals, Pain and Humanity in the Victorian Mind*, Baltimore and London, Johns Hopkins University Press, 1980.

Unsworth, Barry, *Sacred Hunger*, London, Penguin, 1992.

Vaughan, Aldent T., and Virginia Mason, *Shakespeare's Caliban: A Cultural History*, Cambridge, Cambridge University Press, 1991.

Vine, Steven, "'That mild beam': Enlightenment and Enslavement in William Blake's *Visions of the Daughters of Albion*', in Betty J. Ring and Carl Plasa (eds), *The Discourse of Slavery*, London, Routledge, 1994.

Wagner, Peter, 'The Discourse on Sex', in Roy Porter and G. S. Rousseau (eds), *Sexual Underworlds of the Enlightenment*, Manchester, Manchester University Press, 1987.

Walcott Derek, *Omeros*, London, Faber and Faber, 1990.

Walcott, Derek, *The Antilles: Fragments of an Epic Memory*, London, Faber and Faber, 1993.

Wallace, Robert K., *Melville and Turner: Spheres of Love and Fright*, Athens and London, University of Georgia Press, 1992.

Walvin, James, 'Black Caricature: The Roots of Racialism', in *Black and White: The Negro in English Society 1555–1945*, London, Allen Lane, 1973.

Walvin, James, *Slavery and British Society 1776–1846*, London, Macmillan, 1982.

Walvin, James, *Black Ivory: A History of British Slavery*, London, Harper Collins, 1992.

Walvin, James, *Questioning Slavery*, London and New York, Routledge, 1996.

Weber, Samuel, *Mass Mediauras Form Technics Media*, Stanford, Stanford University Press, 1996

White, Shane, and Graham White, 'Slave Clothing and African American Culture', *Past and Present*, 148 (1995) 149–87.

Wiedermann, T. E. J., *Greece and Rome: New Surveys in the Classics no. 19 Slavery*, Oxford, Published for the Classical Association, Oxford University Press, 1997.

Wilberforce, I. R. and S., *Life of William Wilberforce*, 5 vols, London, 1838.

Williams, Eric, *Capitalism and Slavery*, London, André Deutsch, 1944.

Williams, Eric, *From Columbus to Castro: The History of the Caribbean 1492–1969*, London, André Deutsch, 1993.

Williams, Gomer, *History of the Liverpool Privateers and Letter of Marque, with an Account of the Liverpool Slave Trade*, London, 1897.

Williams, Linda, 'Power, Pleasure, and Perversion: Sadomasochistic Film Pornography', *Representations*, 27:2 (1989) 37–65.

Wills, Garry, 'The Dark Legacy of the Enlightenment', *New York Review of Books*, 36:5 (1989) 11–12.

Wolf, Hazel Catherine, *On Freedom's Altar: The Martyr Complex in the Abolition Movement*, Madison, University of Wisconsin Press, 1952.

Wolff, Cynthia Griffin, 'Passing Beyond the Middle Passage: Henry "Box" Brown's Translations of Slavery', *Massachusetts Review*, 37:1 (1996) 23–43.

Wood, Marcus, *Radical Satire and Print Culture 1790–1822*, Oxford, Clarendon Press, 1994.

Wood, Marcus, 'Seeing is Believing or Finding "Truth" in Slave Narrative: The Narrative of Henry Bibb as Perfect Mis-representation', *Slavery and Abolition*, 18:3 (1997) 174–211.

Wooden, Warren W., *John Foxe*, Boston, Twayne, 1983.

Yates, Frances A., 'Foxe as Propagandist', *Encounter*, 27:4 (1966) 78–86.

Yellin, Jean Fagan, *Women and Sisters*, New Haven, Yale University Press, 1989.

Yellin, Jean Fagan, and John C. Van Horne (eds), *The Abolitionist Sisterhood: Women's Political Culture in Ante-bellum America*, Ithaca and London, Cornell University Press, in collaboration with the Library Company of Philadelphia, 1994.

Young, James E., *The Texture of Memory: Holocaust Memorials and Meaning*, New Haven and London, Yale University Press, 1993.

Young, Robert J. C., *White Mythologies: Writing History and the West*, New York and London, Routledge, 1990.

Young, Robert J. C., *Colonial Desire: Hybridity in Theory, Culture and Race*, London and New York, Routledge, 1995.

Index

Note: page references in *italics* refer to illustrations

A Redemção 146
abolition bill (1807) 24
abolition seal 22, *22*, 171–2, 245–6
Abolition Societies, America
    and children's books 114–17,
      191–5, *196*, 271–3, 276–80
    and martyrology 217–18, 251–7,
      258–9
    propaganda 32–3, 79, 84–6, 94–9,
      105–113, 118–34, 199–201,
      243–60, 282
    and recolonisation 121–2
    and temperance 243–6, *244*
    see also Attucks; Child; Garrison;
      Lovejoy; Lundy; Walker
Abolition Societies, England
    British Anti-Slavery Society 106
    British Society for the Abolition of
      the Slave Trade 171, 244
    and children's books 33, 191–5,
      196, 271, 277
    international impact 27–9
    propaganda 21–7, 106–7, 194–8
    and slave trade 15, 123–4
    see also Clarkson; *Description*;
      Newton; *Plan*; Wilberforce
African slavery
    and Atlantic slave trade 10
    and missions 172, 191–4
    in museums 299–300
    in visual arts *6*, 36–8, *38*
Aiken, George *see* Stowe, Harriet
    Beecher
Albanoz 24
Ali, Muhammad 269
American Anti-Slavery Almanac 97,
    98
American Anti-Slavery Society 84
American Museum 32

*American Slavery As It Is, Testimony of
    a Thousand Witnesses* 84, 85
Amishai-Maisels, Ziva 68
Anastasia (Goddess) 226, *227*
Anderson, Alexander 225–6, 243–6
    Injured Humanity 224, *224*, 225
    *Parallel Between Intemperance and
      the Slave Trade* 244
Andrews, William 124
    To tell a Free Story 99
Anelay, Henry 183
Ansdell, Richard: *Hunted Slaves* 95–6,
    96
Anti-Slavery Mass Convention of the
    Abolitionists of New York 106
Anti-Slavery Record 93, 94, 125, *125*
Attucks, Crispus 243, 250–6
Attucks Glee Club 251

Baldwin, James 185
Bannister, Edward 251
Barrett, David 93
Bartolozzi, Francesco 130
Baselitz, Georg 49
Baudrillard, Jean 31
Beccaria, Cesare 216
Behn, Aphra: *Oroonoko* 78
Bentley, E. C. 1
Bento, Antonio 146
Bernini, Gianlorenzo
    Rapture of St Theresa 263
Beuys, Joseph 117
Biard, August 44, 45
    Scene on the African Coast 7, 43, *46*
Bibb, Henry 79, *119*, 263, 282
    *Narrative of the Life and
      Adventures of Henry Bibb* 101,
      117–34, *121*, *123*, *125*, 128–9,
      132

Bibb, Malinda 121, 124, 125, 126,
127
Bibb, Mary Frances 124
Billings, Hammatt 183, *184*, 185
'Spitting on a runaway advertise-
ment' (wood-engraving) *86*
Binny & Ronaldson 89
Bisset, Robert 19
Black Holocaust for Beginners, The
34, *35*
Black Lecture on Language, A 187–8,
187
Blake, William 38, 40, 230–9, 272–3,
282
'Death of Neptune' (copper
engraving) 235
'Holy Thursday' 272
'Negro hung alive by the Ribs to a
Gallows, A' 38–40, *39*
'Whipping of a Samboe Girl' *237*
Blanchot, Maurice 8
Bloom, Mordecai 56
Book of Martyrs, Foxe's 85, 241
Bosch, Hieronymous 204
Boston Anti-Slavery Almanac 84, *121*
Boston Massacre 250, 251, 253
Boswell, James: *No Abolition of
Slavery; or the Universal Empire
of Love* 58
Boyle, Jimmy 117
Brady, Terence: *Fight Against Slavery,
The* 35
Brazilian slavery
in Bahia 292–3
berimbau 292–3
and candomblé 226–7
and capoeira 292
Caymmi, Dori 292
Quilombos 78, 249, 292
and visual arts 226–7, *226, 227*
Zumbi 78, 292
see also Chagas
Briggs, Charles 145
Brissot 27
British Anti-Slavery Society *see*
Abolition Societies, England
British Society for the Abolition of the
Slave Trade *see* Abolition
Societies, England

Brookes (slave ship) 25–9, *28*, 282
Brown, Hablot K. 182
Brown, Henry 'Box' 79–80, 93, 282
Narrative of H.B. Brown 79–80
*Narrative of Henry Box Brown,
Who Escaped from Slavery
Enclosed in a Box 3 feet Long
and 2 Feet Wide* 103–17
*Narrative of the Life of Henry Box
Brown, Written by Himself* 104,
108
Brown, John 242, 243
Brueghel, Peter 204
Landscape with Fall of Icarus 48
Bunyan, John: *Pilgrim's Progress, The*
193, 241
Burdett, P. P. 16, *17*
View of the Custom House, A 17
Burke, Edmund 158–9
'Letter to a noble Lord' 159
'Letters on a Regicide Peace' 159
Butler, General Benjamin 201
Buxton, Sir Thomas Fowell 43

Callot, Jaques 202–5
Temptation of St Anthony, The
202–4, *203*
Camper, Petrus 176–7
Carlyle, Thomas 50
French Revolution 51
'Occasional Discourse on the
Nigger Question' 150
Carpenter, John 276
Cartography and slavery 1–6
Caruth, Cathy 48, 232
Cassell, John 151, 152, 174–5
Uncle Tom's Cabin Almanack 34
'Celebrated Piratical Slaver l'Antonio'
302, *303*
Césaire, Aimé 305
*Notebook of a Return to my native
Land* 305
Chagas, Francisco Xavier 243, 263–7,
271, 282
Flagellated Christ 264, *265*
Virgin and Child 264
Child, Lydia Maria 281
Chin, Julia 92
Clark, Kenneth 42

Clarkson, Revd Thomas 19, 24, 26, 27, 43, 82–3, 223, 228
  'Abolition Map' 1–6, *2–3*
  History of the Rise, Progress, And Accomplishment of the Abolition of the African Slave-Trade by the British Parliament 1, 27, 33, 228
  Letters on the Slave Trade 223
  Negro Slavery 82
Cobbett, William 294
  Bone to Gnaw for the Democrats, A 81
Coetzee, J. M.: *Foe* 304–6
Coleridge, Samuel Taylor 80–2
  'Hint for a New Species of History' 81
Collins, William 38
  'Slave Trade, The' 36
Condition of the West India Slave contrasted with that of The Infant Slave in our English Factories 273, *273*
Conrad, Joseph 282
  'Freya of the Seven Isles' 301–4
  'Gaspar Ruiz' 301
  Heart of Darkness 301
  Nigger of the Narcissus, The 301
  Nostromo 301
  'Outpost of Progress, An' 301
Contraband Schottische, The 200, *201*
Cooke, George Frederick 296
Cousin Ann's Stories for Children 114, *115*
Cowper, William 23, 40, 52, 282
  'Epigram' 272
  'Sweet Meat has Sour Sauce: or, the Slave-Trader in the Dumps' 23
Craft, Ellen 93
Craft, William 93
Crandall, Prudence 243
Cruikshank, George 7, 151–82, 273, 278
  Apotheosis of W. W. 169
  Banquet of the Black Dolls, The 173, *173*
  Country Here is Swarmin with the Most Alarmin Kind o' Varmin 173, *174*

Court at Brighton a la Chinese, The 164, *164*, 165
De Black Dollibus 172, *173*
Drunkard's Children, The 178, *179*
I was barn in St. Kitts 162, *162*
Plantation Scene 172
Political House that Jack Built 278
Probable Effects of Over Female Emigration or importing the fair sex from the Savage Islands in Consequence of Exporting all our own to Australia 163–4, *164*
Puzzled Which to Choose!! or the King of Timbuctoo Offering one of his Daughters 163, *163*
Cruikshank, Isaac 154
  Abolition of the Slave Trade, The 160–1, *160*
Cruikshank, Isaac Robert 273, *273*
  'Whipping of a Samboe Girl' 238
Cruikshank's Comic Almanack 173, *173*
Cubitt, William 240
Curious Adventures of Captain Stedman 237, *238*
Cutty Sark 17
Cymon and Iphigenia 156

Dabydeen, David 153
  Turner 55
Dali and Buñuel
  Un Chien Andalou 179
Damiens, Robert François 229, 232
Davis, David Brion 8, 276
Davis, Jefferon 277
Dawe, George: *Negro Overpowering a Buffalo, a fact which Occurred in America in 1809* 96
Deane, Anthony: *Doctrine of Naval Architecture* 26
Defoe, Daniel: *Robinson Crusoe* 304
'Deluge' (engraving) *54*, 55
de Man, Paul 48
Derrida, Jacques 133–4, 306–7
  Margins of Philosophy, 133–4
  Memoirs of the Blind 306, 307

Description of slave ship *Brookes* 7,
   16–40, *18*, 92, 297
Dickens, Charles
   American Notes 85
   Oliver Twist 181
Dolben's Bill for the Stowage of Slaves
   26
Domeque, Adele 57, 58–9
Douglass, Frederick 79, 111, 112,
   124, 263, 282
   *Narrative of the Life of Frederick
     Douglass* 100–3
Drake, Richard: *Revelations of a Slave
   Smuggler 44*, 45, *46*
Dunbar, William: 'Ane Blake Moir'
   159
Duncanson, Robert 190
Dundas, Henry 157
Dürer, Albrecht 256

Edwards, Bryan 19, 54
   *History Civil and Commercial, of
     the British Colonies in the West
     Indies* 20, 53
Edwin, David 131
Effects of the Fugitive-Slave-Law
   111–12, *111*
Egan, Pierce 162
Eliot, George 205
Elkins, Stanley 280
Emerson, Thomas 94–5
   'Essay on History' 94
Encyclopaedia Britannica 31
Equiano, Olaudah *131*, 298
   Interesting Narrative 131, 131,
     153
Eyre Defence Committee 41

Faucher, Leon 229
Faulkner, William: *Absalom, Absalom*
   302
Felman, Shoshana 11
Fenimore Cooper, James 95
'For Liberia' (woodblock) *121*, 122
Foucault, Michel 228–30, 233, 239
   Discipline and Punish 228–9, 230,
     232
Foxe, John 241
   Actes and Monuments 85

Franklin, Benjamin 87
Freud, Sigmund 185
Fugitive Slave Act (1850) 111
Fugitive Slave Law 106
Fugitive's Song, The 103, *103*
Fuseli, Johan Heinrich, 38, 40, 49,
   282, 295

Garner, Margaret 78
Garrison, William Lloyd 242, 251
Gates, Henri Louis 19, 22, *23*, 188
   Signifying Monkey, The 188
Gatewood, William 122
George, Prince Regent (1816) 164–5
George III 157
Gericault, Theodore, 49–50
   Severed Limbs 49, 50
Gillray, James 153, 154–6, 163, 167–8
   *Anti-sacharites or John Bill and his
     brother leaving off the Use of
     Sugar* 154
   Apotheosis of Hoche, The 168,
     169
   Barbarities in the West Indies 155,
     155
   Cymon and Iphigenia 162
   *Philanthropic Consolations on the
     Loss of the Slave Bill* 155, *156*
   *Promis'd Horrors of a French
     Invasion* 168
   *Reception of the Diplomatique and
     his Sweet at the Court of Pekin*
     164
   Union Club 167, *167*, 169
Gilroy, Paul 43, 99, 100
Giotto 217
Gisborne, Thomas
   'Summer' 52
   Walks in a Forest 52
Gooch, Mr 258–9
Goodall, Reverend W.: 'Companion to
   the Key to *Uncle Tom's Cabin*'
   183
Gordon (slave) *267*, 268–71
Gospel of Slavery, The 97, *98*
Goya, Fransisco 64
   *3rd of May: Execution of the
     Insurgents, The* 63, *254*
   Quinta del Sordo 169

Grant, C. J. 269
    Late Bloody and Brutal Exhibition
        of Horrid Military Torture, or,
        Aristocratic Bastards in their
        Glory, The 269, *270*
Grenville, Lord 165
Grimke, Angelina 84
Grimke, Sarah 84

Harper, Frances Ellen Watkins 251
Harper's Weekly 268, 269
Harris, Joel Chandler 188
Hawkins, Sir John 222
Haydon, Benjamin Robert: *Anti-*
        Slavery Society Convention, The
        61, *61*
Hazlitt, William 15, 16, 60, 294
    Spirit of the Age, The 294
Heath, William 165
    Pair of Broad Bottoms, A 165,
        165
Hegel, G. W. F. 231, 234, 271
Henson, Josiah 195, 196, 197, 198
Herald, The 107
Hildreth, Richard
    Archie More or The White Slave 78,
        101, 183
History of Jim Crow, The 187
HMS *Victory* 17
Hogarth, William 153
    Election Entertainment 166, 167
    Four Stages of Cruelty 114, *114,*
        218
    Gin Lane 243, *244*
Holbein, Hans 130
Holland, William 262
Holocaust, Jewish
    and slave museums 219–20, 306–7
    and slave trade 11–12, 45–6
Homer 64
Hone, William 177, 276, 278
    Political House that Jack Built
        278
Honour, Hugh 153
House that Jack Built 276–80
'Howard and His Squirrel' (wood
        engraving) 115, *115*
Hull 293
    and Slavery Museum 294–6

Humphrey, Heman: *Parallel Between*
        Intemperance and the Slave
        Trade 243
Hutchinson, Jesse, Jnr 102
    Fugitive's Song, The 102, 103

Illustrated Police News, The 190, *191,*
        276

Jacobs, Harriet: *Incidents in the Life of*
        a Slave Girl 216
James, Henry 147, 151, 195
Johnson, Eastman: *Ride of Liberty*
        95
Johnson, Richard M. 92
Johnston, David Claypoole
    House that Jeff Built, The 276–80,
        277, 279
Jordan, Winthrop 80
Justice (card game) 146, *147*

Kali Tal 297
Keats, John: *Ode on a Grecian Urn* 93
Kimber, Captain 161
Kingston Mercantile Advertiser 82
Kircher, Athanasius: *Arca Noe* 30, *54,*
        55
Knibb, William 192
Krafft-Ebbing, Richard von 185

Landseer, Sir Edwin
    Stag at Bay, The 96
Lane, Daniel 132
Lanzmann, Claude 297, 306
Lay, Benjamin 242
Leatheley, Mary: *Large Pictures with*
        Little Stories 275, *275*
Leech, John 182
Legion of Liberty, The 97, *98*, 122,
        123
Lely, Sir Peter 153
Levi, Primo 99–100, 240
Liberator, The 118
Liberty Almanac, The 112, *112*, 113
Lin Maya 46
Lincoln, Abraham 205
Lipscombe, Jane 150
Little Eva, the Flower of the South
        188–9, *189*

Little Scipio: a favourite plaything in the family of Egalité, Duke of Orleans 154, *154*
Liverpool
  slave museum 293, 295–301
  slave trade 16–17, 25
Livingstone, David 223
Lobb, John 196
  Uncle Tom's Story of his Life 196
London Anti-Slavery Society 240
Long, Edward 19
Lovejoy, Elijah 242, 243
Low, Sampson 183
Lundy, Benjamin 242
  Genius of Universal Emancipation, The 37, 38

Macaulay, Lord 24
Manet, Edouard: *Execution of Maximillian* 254
Marley, Bob: *Survival* 34
Marryat, Frederick 163, 165
Marryat, Joseph 166
Martin, John: *Sadak in Search of the Waters of Oblivion* 97
Martin, Peter 125
Marvell, Andrew 307
McKim, James 105
Melville, Herman 42–3
  Moby Dick 43
Meredith, George: *Egoist, The* 49
Meynell, Lieutenant Francis 23, 24, 25, 32
middle passage
  abolitionist constructions of 22–31, 36–8
  and biblical typology 24, 29–32, 54–5, 110
  in twentieth century visual culture 2, 34–6, *35*, *36*, 296–301, *296*, *298*
  see also Blake; *Description*; Fuseli; Gates; Morland; Turner
Milne, C. R. 203, 205
  Dream Caused by a perusal of Mrs. H. Beecher Stowe's popular work Uncle Tom's Cabin, A. 202, *202*
Milton, John 4, 306

Mirabeau, Gabriel Honoré de Raqueti Compte de 27–9
Mirror of Slavery, The 106
Moran, Thomas: *Slave Hunt, The* 97
Morant Bay rebellion (1865) 41
Morland, George 38
  African Hospitality 10, 36
  Execrable Human Traffic, The 10, 36, *37*
Morris, William 150
Morrison, Toni 227, 257, 266–7
  Beloved 68, 78, 100, 257, 266, 280, 306

Narrative of Events since the 1st of August, 1834 By James Williams 240
National Association of Black Scuba Divers 300
National Era, The 144
Negro, Samson 251
Nell, William Cooper 251
New York Anti-Slavery Almanac 84, *218*
New York Anti-Slavery Society 97, 131
New York Gazette 89
Newton, Rev. John 25, 274, 298
  Thoughts Upon the African Slave Trade 23
Newton, Richard 153, 156–7, 261–2
  First Interview, the 159, *159*
  Forcible Appeal for the Abolition of the Slave trade, A 160, 261, *261*
  Full Moon in Eclipse, The 158, 159
  Nice Bit, A 156
  Real San Culotte, A 158, *158*
  Slave Trade, The 157, *157*
Noah in the Ark 111
Noah's Ark 29–30, 54–5, 110–11, *111*
Norris, Robert 19

Oasis, The 154, 281, *281*
'On Receiving the Box' (wood engraving) *112*
Ouverture, Toussaint l' 250

Parker, Theodore 251
Parkhurst, V. S. W. 147

Paton, Sir J. Noel: *Capture of a Slave Ship* 24, *24*
Paulson, Ronald 155
Pennsylvania Society for the Abolition of the Slave Trade 32
Perry, Captain 26
Peterloo Massacre 278
Peterloo Medal 171, *172*
Philips, James 17, 26
Phiz *see* Brown, Hablot K.
Picasso, Pablo 306
    Guernica 63
Pitt, William 156, 157, 294
Plan (Plymouth) 25–6, 32
Plan of an African Ship's Lower deck with Negroes in the proportion of only One to a Ton 17, *20–1*
Pope, Alexander 4
Pope-Hennessy, James: *Sins of the Fathers* 35
pornography
    and abolition 44–5, 189–90
    and children 45, 263, 273–4
    and female slaves 44–5, 57–9, *184*, 226, 236–9
    and male slaves 261–3, *262*
    and pro-slavery sexual fantasy 19, 53–4
    and *Uncle Tom's Cabin* 183–4, 189–90
    see also Blake; Cruikshank; Newton; Stedman; Thackeray
Prynne, William 248
Punch 190
Putnam's Monthly 145

Quakers *2–3*, 22, 204–5, 242

Rabbits, The 161, *162*
racism 148–51, 190–1, 194
    and abolition 4–6, 19–25, 102–3, 156–7, *157*, 268–9, *267*
    and Irish black conflations 167–8
    and miscegenation 169–171, 184–5
    in pro slavery propaganda 10, 19–20, 87–91, 160–1
    scientific 176–7, 190, 212

and sexuality 162, *163*, 190–1, 236–9
and the visual arts 22, 47, 49, 154, *156, 157, 158, 160*, 173–9
Raimond, Charles Lenox 251
Reason, Patrick H. 130
Reform Act (1832) 276
Resurrection of Henry Box Brown at Philadelphia 104, 110–11
Revere, Paul: *Bloody Massacre, The* 253, *253*
Reynolds, Sir Joshua 153
Ripley, Thomas 16
Rochester's Jests 156
Rock, John S. 251
Rooker, E. 16, *17*
Roper, Moses 243, 256–60, 263, 282
    Narrative of the Adventures and Escape of Moses Roper 221, *221*, 256
Rossetti, Dante Gabriel 148–51
    Bride, The 150
Rowlandson, Thomas 153, 154, 156–7
Royal Gazette of Jamaica 82
runaways
    in abolition polemic and art 81–6, 94–99, 102–3
    and advertising 79, 87–91, *88, 90, 91*
    construction in slave narratives 79–80, 100–34
    impact in England 106–8
    in panoramas 106, 107
    and slave power 79, 87–94
    and suicide 98–99, *99*
Ruskin, John 41, 42, 48, 49, 56–63, 64–7, 189, 282
    Modern Painters 41, 56, 57, 58, 59, 60, 190

Sadler, Mr 273
Sancho, Ignatius 131, 153
San Domingo 168–9, 171, 230
Scarry, Elaine 231, 234, 280
Schongauer, Martin 204
Schwarz-Bart, Andre 45
Scott, Dred 250–1
Scott, Sir Walter 225

Sewell, Anna: *Black Beauty* 146
Shakespeare, William 55
    Macbeth 64–7
    Tempest, The 58
Sharp, Granville 24, 122, 123
Shelley, Percy Bysshe: *Ozymandias* 49
Sheridan, Richard Brinsley 294
Shoah 306
Simpson, William 251
Slap at Slop, A 177, *177*
'Slave mother suicide' 181–2, *181*
Slave's Friend, The 97, *98*, 282, *282*
Smith, J. C. A. 106
Smith, John Raphael: *Slave Trade, The* 37
Smith, Samuel 105
Société des Amis des Noirs 27
Society for Effecting the Abolition of the Slave Trade (SEAST) 14, 15, 17, *18*, 22, 27, 32, 36
'Song sung by Mr Brown on being removed from box' 108, *109*
Southern Slavery Illustrated 269, *270*
Springer, Sam 162
Stanfield, James: *Observations on a Guinea Voyage* 15
Stearns, Charles 104, 105, 108
Stedman, Captain John 78, 230–9
    Narrative of a Five Years' Expedition Against the Revolted Negroes of Surinam 38, *39*, 230–2, *235*, 237
Still, William 105, 108
    Underground Railroad, The 78
Stothard, Thomas 54
    'Voyage of the Sable Venus, from Angola to the West Indies, The' 22
Stowe, Harriet Beecher 148, 242, 259, 282
    Dred, A Tale of the Dismal Swamp 78, 101
    Key to Uncle Tom's Cabin 195–6
    Uncle Tom's Cabin 7, 9, 78, 84, 86, 101, 143–205
Strepto, Robert Burns 105
Strong, Jonathan 122, 124

Strong's Dime Caricatures. – No. 3 South Carolina Topsey in a Fix 198, *199*
Stuart, Gilbert 131
Sulivan, Captain G. K.: *Dhow Chasing in Zanzibar Waters* 34, *34*
Suppressed Book About Slavery 127, 128, *128*, *129*

Taney, Chief Justice 250
Taylor, Isaac: *Scenes in Africa for the Amusement and Instruction of Little Tarry at Home Travellers* 33, *33*
Teale, Isaac: 'Sable Venus; an Ode, The' 20, 53
Thackeray, William Makepiece 41, 43–5, 190
Thomas, George 183, 198
Thomas, Hugh: *Slave Trade, The* 35
Thompson, George 193, *193*, *194*, 201
Tinnie, Dinizulu Gene 300
Topsy's Frolics or Always in Mischief 194, *195*
Torrey, Jessey: *Portraiture of Domestic Slavery in the United States, A* 181
torture, of abolitionists 241, 243–9, *244*, *247*, *248*
    see also Lovejoy; Walker
torture, of slaves
    branding 83, 249–50
    breaking on the rack 233–4, *235*
    with cats 217–18
    chains and weights 85, 224–5, *225*, 278–9, *281*, 282
    cotton screw 257, 60, *257*
    with dogs 96–7, *96*, *98*, *128*
    drowning 62–3
    flagellation/whipping 62–3, 85, 86, 184–5, 260–7, 217–18, 236–9, 258–9, 260–71, 275, 277, 282
    hanging with ropes, chains and hooks 38–40, *40*, 85, *98*, 228, 230–2
    middle passage 15–16, 28–9, 245, 295–7
    paddle 125–6, *125*

psychological 68, 101–2, 126, 180–2, 215–16, 219, 232, 266, 280–2
punishment collar 85, 220–3, *220*
punishment mask 224–7, *224, 225, 226, 227*
shooting *111*, 217–18, 251–3
speculum oris 228, *228*
stocks 216
thumbscrews 228, *228*
treadmill 240–1, *240*
yoke, 223–4, *223, 224*
see also Anderson; Bibb; Blake; Brown; Chagas; Foucault; Gordon; Roper
Transatlantic Slavery Gallery, Liverpool 220, 296–9, *297, 298*
Turner, J. M. W. 282, 307
Regulus 306
Slave Ship 40, 306
Slavers Throwing Overboard the Dead and Dying, Typhon Coming On 6, 7, 16, 41–68, *47*, 304, 306
Turner, Nat 67–8, 78, 282
Confessions 67
Twain, Mark 42

Uncle Tom's Cabin
in American graphic art 198–205
and black literacy 187–9
as children's book 194–7
in English graphic art 157–196
and mass entertainment 143–7, 196–8
see also Cruikshank; Henson; James; Rossetti; Stowe
Uncle Tom's Cabin Almanac 176, 196
'United States Slave Trade' *37*, 38
Unsworth, Barry: *Sacred Hunger* 35, *36*

Verdier, Marcel: *Punishment of the Four Stakes in the Colonies, The* 262, *262*
Vietnam Veterans Memorial 46

Walcott, Josiah 106
Walker, Jonathan 243, 246–50
War of Independence 250, 251
Weld, Theodore Dwight 84, 85
Wellington and Uncle Tom or the Hero of this World Contrasted with the Hero in Jesus Christ 197
West, Benjamin: *Death of General Wolf* 255, *256*
Whittier John Greenleaf 246–9
'Branded Hand, The' 246, *247*
Widerman, T. J. 260
Wilberforce, William 24, 28, 43, 52, 155, 156, 161, 166, 171, 293–5
Wilkins, John, Bishop of Chester 30, *30, 31*
Williams, Charles 165
Wilmot, John 156
Wolfe, General James 255–6
Wolverhampton and Staffordshire Gazette 107
Woollett, William: *Death of General Wolf* 256
Woolman, John 242
Wright, Elizur 94, 95
Chronotype 118

Young People's Illustrated Edition of Uncle Tom's Story of his Life 196
Young, James 219

Zoffany, Johan
'Invasion of the Cellars of the Louvre, 10 August 1792' 168
Zong (slave ship) 63